A Guide To Treasure In California
2nd Edition

By Thomas Penfield

Published since 1982 by
Carson Enterprises, New Mexico, USA

New Millennium Edition (2nd Edition)
Leanne Carson Boyd, Editor & Publisher
Waybill To Adventure LLC, Arizona, USA
www.WaybillToAdventure.com

TREASURE GUIDE SERIES

"Buy land, they're not making it anymore."
~Mark Twain

Copyright Notice

Copyright © 2012 Leanne Carson Boyd
All Rights Reserved.

Legal Notice: Reproduction or translation of any part of this work beyond that permitted by section 107 or 108 of the 1976 United States Copyright Act without permission of the copyright owner. Waybill To Adventure LLC, is unlawful. Requests for permission or further information should be addressed to the publisher/primary book author.

The copyright owner of this book and any accompanying materials has used best efforts in preparing this book. The copyright owner makes no representation or warranties with respect to the accuracy, applicability, fitness, or completeness of the contents of this book. The copyright owner shall in no event be held liable to any party for any direct, indirect, punitive, special, incidental, or other consequential damages arising directly or indirectly from any use of this material, which is provided "as is," and without any warranties.

This publication is designed to provide accurate and authoritative information in regard to the subject matter covered. It is sold with the understanding that the copyright owner is not engaged in rendering legal, accounting, or other professional services. If legal advice or other expert assistance is required, the services of a competent professional person should be sought.

This book is a learning product. The information contained in this book is strictly for educational purposes. Therefore, if you wish to apply ideas contained in this book, you are taking full responsibility for your actions.

All trademarks and copyrights discussed here, if any, are property of their respective owners. Waybill To Adventure LLC is not associated with any product or vendor mentioned in this book.

First Printing, 2012

ISBN-13: 978-1479233397

ISBN-10: 1479233390

Printed in the United States of America

Dedication

This book is dedicated to my Dad, Glenn Carson.
Indeed, all the aspects of new adventures started in 2012
for my company, Waybill To Adventure LLC, are dedicated to him.
He has been a mentor and a creative guiding light for many – his children,
his grandkids, and his students... but maybe even more so for the 1000s of his
"partners in grime" – the coinshooters and treasure hunters who know him as the
GRANDDADDY OF TREASURE HUNTING.

Leanne Carson Boyd

He who strives for the pot of gold
at the base of the rainbow finds himself
alone in the gathering dusk after the
rainbow disappears, miles from
home, feeling foolish, having
to walk home in the dark.
~Glenn Carson

Early-Bird Alerts For New Books – Go REGISTER!!
Register For Email Alerts   :::   http://www.1wbta.com/login?action=register

The Treasure Chest

Table Of Contents

Dedication iii
   Early-Bird Alerts For New Books – Go REGISTER!! iv
Table Of Contents v
Frontispiece ix
Introduction: The Importance Of Research 1
   Your Primary Reason For Searching 2
   Many States Do Not Allow Metal Detectors In The State Parks Without Authorized Permission 3
   To Gain Admittance To Any Location, First Obtain The Land Owner's Permission, Then Respect His Rights 3
Tips For How To Approach Research (Including Treasure Hunting!) 4
   Finding Resources, Setting Up A "Plan Of Action," & Practice Makes Perfect! ... 4
Treasure Tales Around The Campfire 5
How To Use This Book 6
The Map Code System In This Book 7
   Time Marches On… Using The Map Code System In 2012 7
   Modern Tools Increase Your Chances Of Success In Treasure Hunting 8
   Illustrated: Treasure! The Internet Makes It Yours For The Taking! 8
Chapter 1: California — Treasure Galore 9
   California's Kaleidoscopic History 9
   Treasure And Artifact And Relic Sites 10
   The California Desert — Words Of Warning 11
   A Dream Of Completeness 11
   California's Mother Lode Country 12
   The "Big Blue River" 12
   Travelers To Mother Lode Country Today See No Sign Of The Big Blue River ... 13
   What Happened To The Big Blue? 14
   The Rest Of The Dead River Story 15
   Illustrated: Who Really Made Money In The Gold Rush? 16
Chapter 2: Begin Your California Research 17
   Your Topic Will Be Tied To An Event 17
   To Get You Started, Check Out These Web Sites 18
   Part 2.1: 1895 Map, Section 1 of 6 20
   Part 2.2: 1895 Map, Section 2 of 6 21
   Part 2.3: 1895 Map, Section 3 of 6 22

Part 2.4: 1895 Map, Section 4 of 6 23
Part 2.5: 1895 Map, Section 5 of 6 24
Part 2.6: 1895 Map, Section 6 of 6 25
Part 2.7: There Are 58 Counties In California 26
Part 2.8: Missing Some Counties? 27
- Glenn County 27
  Glenn County: Of Interest To Treasure Hunters 27
- Kings County 30
  Kings County: Of Interest To Treasure Hunters 30
  Kings County: The Mussel Slough Tragedy 32
A Tiburcio Vasquez Treasure Tale... In Kings County! 33
- Madera County 34
  Madera County: Of Interest To Treasure Hunters 34
  Gold Rush To Ghost Town In Madera County 36
- Sacramento County 37
  Sacramento County: Of Interest To Treasure Hunters 37
  Vigilantes Of California In Sacramento County 39
- Yolo County 40
  Yolo County: Of Interest To Treasure Hunters 40
  The Last Great West, The Pacific Coast States Of America 41
  The Color Of Gold Is RED In Yolo County! 42

Chapter 3: Treasure Sites Of California 43
Chapter 4: Treasure Sites By County 45
Counties A – D 45
Narrowing Down A Tale With USGS Maps 46
- Snowshoe Thompson's Lost Gold-Bearing Quartz Mine 46
  Pinpoint Your Locations In The Tale 47
  Your Best Followup Techniques 49
Counties E – H 57
Counties I – L 63
- The Lost Golden Eagle Mine 78
  An Old Prospector's Bones Near Smith Mountain 79
  Detailing The "Alkali" Jones Story 80
- Secret Gold Mine On Mount Disappointment 103
  And... Big Payoff When Eating Wild Onions For Lunch!? 103
Counties M – P 115
- Lost Gold Vein On The Marin Side Of Golden Gate 116

  Covered Up When The Golden Gate Bridge Was Erected! 116
- Whiteman's Lost Cement Mine In The Burnt Country 122
  Reddish Cement Holding Gold "Like Raisins In A Pudding" 122
  Detailing The Whiteman's Mine In Burnt Country Story 123
- Throwing The Country Into A Frenzy Of Excitement 124
- Mysterious Land & Mine, Mysterious Disappearances 125
- Frenchman Henry Gordier's Buried Gold 137
  Murder, Mayhem & Four Unsavory Characters Hanged 137

Counties Q – S 139
- Pegleg Smith And His Rich Black Nuggets Of Gold 139
  A Field Day With The Lost Pegleg Smith Mine Story! 139
- The Story Of Kokoweef Mountain's Cave Of Gold 146
- A Wash Tub Of Gold Nuggets In The Turtles 159
- San Luis Rey Mission – $10,000,000 In Spanish Gold 161
- The Bucksnorts' Buckskin Bag Of Gold Nuggets 171
- Five Lost Mines Right In The Heart Of San Francisco 177
- Lost Treasure Chest Between Redding & French Gulch 190

Counties T – Z 201
- Davenport's Lost Treasure On The Trinity River 202
- X Really *Does* Mark The Spot In Yuba County! 211

Chapter 5: Metal Detector Sites Of California 213
Illustrated: Metal Detecting For Mines, Finland, WWII 213
Illustrated: The Power Of Magnifying The Advantages 214

Chapter 6: Metal Detector Sites By County 215
Counties A – D 215
- Carson Hill: Richest Diggings In The Entire Mother Lode 218
- Port Costa: The Gold Was In The Grain 221
- Calaveras County – Carson Hill Mine In Melones 222

Counties E – H 223
- The 1848 Mad Race To The California Gold Fields 224

Counties I – L 227
- Imperial County: Kane Spring's Treasure Galleon 228

Counties M – P 235
- Mono County – Bodie "The Wildest" & The Bodie Jail 240

Counties Q – S 247
- San Bernardino: 29Palms, Joshua Tree, Dale Mining 1, 2, And 3! 251

Counties T – Z 261

- Tuolumne County: Rawhide, Table Mtn. & $6,000,000! 262

Afterword: Treasure For A Modern Day Hunter... Your "Ticket To Ride" 265
- The Accumulative History Of This Great Land 265
- Doing Your Duty In Researching Everything 265
- Illustrated: Be Careful What You Water Your Dreams With 266

Acknowledgments 267
- Illustrated: The Valuables Left Behind 268

Bibliography 269

Ghost Towns 271

Save Yer' Eyes! Download Our Catalog! 272

Some Other Helpful & Interesting Books For Any State's Treasure Buffs: Our Catalog For Waybill To Adventure's New Millennium Edition Treasure Library .. 273
- Early-Bird Alerts For New Books – Go REGISTER!! 273
- The NEW Waybill To Adventure Catalog! 273
- Web Site Table Of Contents 273
- Treasure Guide Series 274
- Waybill To Adventure Core Books 275
- Waybill's Historical Maps Series 277
- Waybill's TH'ing & Real-Life Fun Stuff 278
- Principal Gold-Producing Districts – New Millennium Versions @Waybill 278
- Software By Waybill To Adventure 279
- Illustrated: Yreka! 280
- Illustrated: Eureka! 281

Resource: The 1982 Version Of This Book 282

Resource: Related Items Are Available 282

Resource: LOC.GOV, The Library Of Congress – We The People Are Grateful 283
- Usage Herein 283

Parting Words & Sage Advice: Poker Alice 284

About The Publisher/Authors 285

Frontispiece

"Joseph Sharp, with pick axe in hand, 1849 gold miner, of Sharp's Flats," ca.1905
Source: http://content.cdlib.org/ark:/13030/tf7p301079/?query=&brand=calisphere
Courtesy Calisphere, University of California

"This portrait, labeled 'Joseph Sharp of Sharp's Flats,' appears to have been taken just before Mr. Sharp went to work in the California gold fields, most likely in a makeshift photographer's booth at a location where miners purchased provisions, possibly near Sacramento or San Francisco.

"Sharp's Flats does not appear in *Goude's California Gold Camps*.

"All of his gear is new, as he has just been outfitted, and the gun and his rakish pose are distinctly meant to indicate, however comically, that Mr. Sharp is prepared to defend his territory. The fact that 'Sharp's Flats' was named for him probably means that he was about to become an employer of miners, one who mostly managed the operations while Chinese and/or other workers did the rough work. The purpose of this portrait was probably to show family and friends at home that Mr. Sharp was off for the gold fields well equipped and ready."

Source: "Dressed for the Photographer: Ordinary Americans and Fashion, 1840-1900" By Joan L. Severa
Publication Date: March 1997 - p. 121

The Ancient Researcher

Introduction: The Importance Of Research

In compiling a work such as this, an author has to use any source of material that he finds helpful, but since he is human, he is subject to error.

Every precaution has been taken to avoid errors and inaccuracies in this work, but its very nature makes such an accomplishment almost an impossibility.

History does not always agree on dates, or places, nor on the manner in which events occurred.

This volume lays no claim to being all-inclusive; most of the stories related herein have several variations. I have given the most widely accepted and authenticated versions that research and history will allow.

Better Chances Of Locating A Profitable Site

Naturally, the more time spent by an author in research, from as many sources as possible, gives the treasure hunter a better chance of locating a profitable site.

Everyone will not agree with the information given here. The treasure hunter usually accepts the version that appeals to him personally.

Treasure sites are where a lost mine or mines, or buried, sunken, or hidden treasure of any amount has been documented or reported. Not all "lost" treasures are reported. Sometimes a distrustful loner or a criminal buried their savings or ill gotten money and then died or was killed before they could retrieve their cache. For instance, in the southern states, during the Civil War, so much treasure was buried that very little mention of it is made in local histories of the period. It was an accepted fact and the only thing to do during those war years.

Several of the more widely-known treasures listed have been searched for before and will continue to be sought after until some lucky treasure hunter finds them. Because of erosion, earthquakes, forest fires, dam and road building, strip mining, and rivers having changed their courses, some of the legendary treasures are not likely to ever be found, but they will always be there, just to be looked for.

Regardless of how exaggerated a treasure story may sound, there is almost always some basis in fact to it. The lure of treasure (in one form or another) has attracted and fascinated man since before the dawn of recorded history.

Your Primary Reason For Searching

Metal detector sites are those locations where a treasure hunter might find a few coins, but his primary reason for searching is to find relics or artifacts from the past. These could include any number of things, such as tools, weapons, toys, or coins of an historical nature.

Listed are ghost or near-ghost towns. These were communities that came into being because of water transportation, railroads, mining, and timber cutting.

- Some of these early villages disappeared completely or fell into decay when the reason for their existence vanished and the people moved away.
- Several of the locations changed their names or were absorbed by neighboring communities.
- Some of them disappeared because of floods or a river changing its course.

The searcher for one of these former communities should inquire at the county seat of the county in which he intends to search.

Historical societies, old church records (they tell where camp meetings were held years ago), libraries, State Geological reports, senior citizens, State Archives, and census reports are very good sources of information to check when searching for these vanished towns or lost treasure sites.

Also listed are early forts, where the pioneers gathered for protection from the Indians, Indian village sites, river boat landings, taverns, stagecoach stops, War sites, old amusement parks, and ferries. All of these locations are interesting, and any one of them could be profitable to the searcher.

Many States Do Not Allow Metal Detectors In The State Parks Without Authorized Permission

Occasionally, each state will allow a controlled hunt for artifacts, or to prove a definite location of an historical site. The items found are given to the state museums or historical societies. The area for the treasure hunter to search is private land near the parks. Most of the state properties only cover a small part of the original area of a fort, battleground, trading post, or ghost town.

To Gain Admittance To Any Location, First Obtain The Land Owner's Permission, Then Respect His Rights

After searching, leave the property <u>exactly</u> as you found it. If these rules are followed, others can almost always gain access to search interesting and sometimes profitable sites.

If my research in this volume guides someone to a successful treasure, I shall feel rewarded for my efforts. If no treasure is found, it is my wish that they at least had fun in searching.

Remember, research, permission, proper equipment, and patience are the keys to a successful treasure hunt.

Tips For How To Approach Research (Including Treasure Hunting!)

My best example is in the Broomfield chapter of <u>The Guide To Treasure In Colorado, 3rd Edition</u>. View at Amazon: www.1wbta.com/Waybill-To-Adventure-LCB. Simple search engine research will bring you similar results for any town! Focus on historical or genealogical sites... you will have an excellent start.

Finding Resources, Setting Up A "Plan Of Action," & Practice Makes Perfect!

- Broomfield Genealogy Society: www.1wbta.com/Broomfield-Genealogy-Society

- Broomfield Depot Museum: www.1wbta.com/Broomfield-Depot-Museum

- Heritage Quest Online: www.1wbta.com/Heritage-Quest-Online

- Mamie Doud Eisenhower Public Library: www.1wbta.com/M-D-Eisenhower-Library

    - Online Resources (huge, excellent list): www.1wbta.com/M-D-Eisenhower-Resources

- MetaLib: www.1wbta.com/MetaLib
  MetaLib is a federated search engine that searches multiple U.S. Federal government databases, providing direct links to resources available online.

Treasure Tales Around The Campfire

So you want to hear about treasures in California? Well, you've come to the right place. I see some of you've brought fold-down chairs; the rest of you can pull around that old log, or use that food chest there. Glad to see you brought the ladies, or they brought you, whichever.

There's plenty to tell. Things have been lost or hidden on purpose... from the Nevada state line to the Pacific shoreline, stashed from the border into Arizona north to where Oregon begins. There are tales of treasures that, with 3 hops and a jump you're almost in Canada, down to where, if you walk aways, you'll be in Baja California.

This State has all sorts of treasure stories, but I want to remind you that for every such tale you listen to here there are a hundred more that never offended a human ear. Don't ever forget it; folks don't talk about good things they've found, then lost. Nor do most people talk about stashes they've put down. The things they hid were meant to stay hidden, so don't worry about ever running out of treasures still lost and hidden away.

Yes, get settled down comfortable. Pull that end of the log up closer to the fire. I see you found a good stump. One of you pass around the rest of that coffee, if you will, and then be good enough to get another pot going. No use sitting here uncomfortable. Might better put on a jacket, too. It might have been almost hot today, but these evenings cool off fast enough.

You say you're all ready? California Treasures?

...Well, Let's Get On With It!

How To Use This Book

You can almost use this book as a computer tool! Each link given will take you to a Topo map. The Web addresses (URLs) I provide are intuitive titles. Fairly simple, straight-forward words. Watch for the dashes and the capital letters.

I used the best topographic/Topo map service I've found for today, which is TopoQuest, and this book's links are to their maps. It is a free service. You can save maps from there by right-clicking on the map image and saving to your computer.

Keep an eye out for the Kindle version of the book! All the links will be active! The best way to do this is to go to our Web site, and REGISTER! I will be sending out alerts to that list whenever I publish new books or products.

Go →→ http://www.1wbta.com/login?action=register

The Map Code System In This Book

The Map Code at the end of each listing refers to the current edition (at the time of original publication, 1972) of the *Rand McNally Standard* or *Commercial Road Atlas*, and works like this:

- Map Code 12 D-4, for example, indicates that the reader should turn to the map on page 12,
- Follow the left or right index (D)
- To the point where it intersects the top or bottom index (4).
- This point of intersection indicates the point sought.

The highway numbers used herein are also those found in the *Rand McNally Road Atlas*, but it should be pointed out that these assigned numbers are sometimes changed, especially as interstate highway numbers replace state or county numbers. Remember also that portions of highways are frequently relocated, and that new highways come into being from time to time.

Time Marches On… Using The Map Code System In 2012

A map with the coordinates Mr. Penfield used is unavailable. It has been suggested that the County Clerk in each county be contacted as a place to begin your search. The coordinates used on any map can give only an approximate location. Even a pin-point on any map would be a diameter of about 50 miles.

(If Mr. Penfield knew ***exactly*** where any of these treasures were, he would have retrieved one or more of them, and not written about them in a book.)

Modern Tools Increase Your Chances Of Success In Treasure Hunting

I have found that, using any similar older map or atlas, you can do some darned good guessing! You will soon see that my favorite tools are the Internet, an excellent topographic map Web site (I love www.TopoQuest.com), and the exact names of places in this book. It's amazing what that, and a keyword-rich Google search, will reveal!

Illustrated: Treasure! The Internet Makes It Yours For The Taking!

Chapter 1: California — Treasure Galore

Good storytelling group! Gather closer to the campfire and grab a cup of that coffee to chase away the chill. What a beautiful California night on the mountain! Keep your eye on that yellow moon... it looks just like the gold coins so abundant in the legends of this state! Good to see the ladies here, and what a bunch of kids, tonight! Pass around those marshmallows... now, THAT is treasure!

California... Just the word creates pictures in the minds of most people. Today this land might mean sprawling multi-million dollar homes, and the jaunts of our fave celebs. But, singing in the wind of time and memory, California beckons with a sometimes thrilling, throaty voice... and other times with a slight whisper that barely hides a shouted "Eureka!" or a moaning shriek of terror in the midst of despair or atrocity.

For some, the Westward dream was realized here in this colorful place. For many others, the realities of humanity's feral escape across a plain riddled with hidden monsters, became that last trek to death or insanity. The best and the worst of "we, the people," reside in the tales of California.

Yes, the wind brings a long sigh of triumph that many times ended in a soft gurgle, as happenstance and the Devil cut the heart out of a dance that began in jubilee. There is, like with money, no evil in gold. But the lust in a man's heart... that is where evil grows. Gather 'round, good treasure friends, and let's share the tales of California gold.

California's Kaleidoscopic History

It is hard to imagine any state being richer in its number and variety of buried and sunken treasures, lost mines, and artifact and relic sites than California. Each flash of California's kaleidoscopic history has produced its legends of lost treasures and mines, and left its trail of artifact and relic sites. Native Indians, Spanish-

Californians, Mexican-Californians, mission padres, explorers, Yankee traders, gold-seeking Forty-Niners, military expeditions and emigrating settlers all left their mark as they marched across California's stage.

Out of California's mountains and deserts came gold and silver in quantities never before heard of, and the armies of men who dug and panned it moved from strike to strike, leaving behind their camps when they moved on.

Some of these camps have survived and are populous towns today. Many, many others hang on with a mere trickle of their former population, while literally hundreds of others are now only sites, their names forgotten, their remains ground into almost unrecognizable rubbish.

Treasure And Artifact And Relic Sites

While buried treasure and lost sites located within the boundaries of National Parks and Monuments in California are listed herein, it is merely to make the listing as complete as possible, and does not suggest that any searches can be made on such federally-held lands without specific permission of the proper authorities.

On the other hand, artifact and relic sites located within National Parks and Monuments in California are not knowingly listed herein. Whereas it is improbable that one is going to locate a buried treasure or lost mine in the National Parks or Monuments, many artifact and relic sites can easily be found in these areas — but cannot be legally touched.

Within Death Valley National Monument are some of the best preserved and most interesting ghost towns in the United States, as well as many artifact and relic sites whose surfaces have hardly been scraped. But a special regulation applying to Death Valley National Monument specifically states: "Disturbance, destruction, defilement or injury of any ruins, relics, buildings, signs or other property is prohibited."

In spite of the penalty for infraction of these regulations — a $500 fine, six months' imprisonment, or both — several ghost towns in the Monument have been heavily vandalized in the past. This has resulted in renewed vigilance by park rangers to see that such infractions are held to a minimum in the future.

Treasure and artifact and relic sites located within state and county parks and historic sites in California are listed herein because regulations governing searches within such areas are somewhat flexible. Permission to search such sites is frequently granted under specified conditions.

A few treasure and artifact sites listed herein are located on such military installations as the Naval Ordnance Test Station, the Marine Corps Training Center and the Fort Irwin Military Reservation. The reason for this is that the boundaries of these installations are not always permanent, and changing conditions may bring changes in these boundaries, or eliminate them entirely. Until such changes occur, however, these areas are strictly off limits to the public unless specific permission to enter them is secured from the appropriate authorities.

The California Desert — Words Of Warning

A special word of warning is given here to those treasure hunters and lost mine and artifact seekers who are not familiar with California deserts, which cover a vast area of the southeastern section of the state.

Due to difficult and near hazardous trails and roads in many parts of the California deserts, and also because of excessive heat at certain times of the year, as well as the scarcity of water in many locations, it is advisable that those not thoroughly familiar with California desert conditions avoid venturing off the main desert roads alone.

A further word of caution is directed to anyone searching in areas of open shaft mining. In certain sections of the Mother Lode country, hillsides are still pocked with hundreds of open shafts — some descending to amazing depths. When these become covered with broken branches and shrubbery, they can be veritable death traps for the unwary.

A Dream Of Completeness

As in the case of any other works of this nature and scope, the author can dream of completeness — and know it is but a dream. Others will know of lost treasures and lost mines that this writer's many years of research have failed to uncover. And many more years of research would not complete the job.

Nor will all readers agree with the essential details of the lost treasure and lost mine stories related herein. Almost every such story has more than a single version, and different writers see these versions in a different light. This writer has attempted to select the most accepted version of each story, except in the case of a few important stories where more than one version is given.

In the field of artifact and relic sites, the hope of attaining completeness is even more remote, for every foot of soil that man has trod from prehistoric days to this very moment is a potential artifact or relic site. We could but list herein those sites of record, and usually we have tried to select those sites having an association with history.

California's Mother Lode Country

One of the reasons why California is foremost among all states in treasure sites and lost mines is, of course, the vast amount of mining done here since John Marshall's discovery of gold at Coloma, and the great quantities of gold taken from the California earth. There were many mines to become lost and much treasure to bury or hide. Geologists say there is still more gold to be found in California's Mother Lode country. In fact, some geologists state that the true source of the Mother Lode gold has never been found.

The "Big Blue River"

Geologists refer to this source as the "Big Blue River." Only 65 miles of its ancient channel has ever been determined, but miners took from it, gold dust and nuggets at the rate of more than $3,500,000 per mile!

Since most geologists believe the Big Blue River was at least 200 miles long, it figures that there must be at least a billion dollars in gold left to be dug up by future Argonauts somewhere along the western slope of the lofty Sierra Nevadas.

But not even the experts can do any more than guess where the unfound portion of the Big Blue River lies. Some believe it may be underneath present streams, while others reason that it could lie under many, many feet of volcanic rock. But you can be sure that when the Big Blue River is found, there, too, will be found the rest of the fantastic riches of the Mother Lode.

The known portion of the Big Blue starts in the neighborhood of Little Grizzly, California, and disappears 65 miles south-southwest at Forest Hill. It runs almost parallel with the main crest of the Sierras and about 30 miles west of the towering mountain range.

The elevation at Little Grizzly is just under one mile above sea level, while at Forest Hill it is a little less than a half mile. The average fall of the Big Blue River in this area, therefore, was roughly 33 feet to the mile, and when a river falls at that rate it is capable of carrying fantastic quantities of sediment along with it.

Travelers To Mother Lode Country Today See No Sign Of The Big Blue River

… And the Forty-Niners likewise saw none. How, then, was it discovered? The Big Blue flowed generally north and south, and parallel to the main ridges of the Sierras, while many of today's rivers and creeks flow out of the Sierras in an east-west direction — or at right angles to the Sierras. When they came to the ancient bed of the Big Blue, they cut deep canyons through it, also more or less at right angles.

As miners worked up the river and creek beds toward the crest of the Sierras, they would find gold dust and nuggets becoming more and more plentiful until they arrived at a place which was fantastically rich. As this was worked out and they continued up the streams, the gold became less and less abundant until it played out entirely. This was repeated over and over in most of the creeks running west out of the Sierras. The richest strikes would invariably appear about 30 miles west of the crest of the Sierras, and always in a north-south line.

When the gold played out, the miners would return to the spot of their richest finds and poke into the stream banks. Then they tunneled into the ridges between the east-to-west rivers and creeks. This was the ancient bed of the Big Blue, and here was found an amazingly rich gravel of a peculiar blue color, about 5 feet thick and half a mile wide. This was the width of the old stream bed. In tunneling between the ridges separating the streams, miners working northward invariably met miners working southward, and in this manner the entire known bed of the Big Blue River was worked out for a distance of 65 miles.

The streams were from one to six miles apart, and the great vein was from 200 to 1,000 feet below the ridge tops — far too much dirt to remove, hence the tunneling. Several mining camps at the point of rich finds were thus connected by tunnels.

While, as previously stated, this very rich vein of gold-bearing gravel was about 5 feet thick, the whole auriferous deposit varied in depth from 100 to 300 feet. The predominant color of the gravel was bluish-gray, and it was almost exclusively quartz — the mother of gold. At an average thickness of 200 feet and a width of one half of a mile, there were at least 5 billion cubic yards of blue quartz in the bed of the Big Blue's 65 discovered miles.

Where did all of this quartz come from? If you had the answer to that, you would have the secret to what is probably the richest source of gold in the whole world.

The pebbles in the bed of the Big Blue were all well water-worn, and the big boulders were likewise ground smooth and showed no signs of having washed down from the slopes of the Sierras. Rather, they showed evidence of having tumbled along the bed of the Big Blue for miles upon miles, so the ancient stream had to be swift to move such sensational loads of quartz.

What Happened To The Big Blue?

What caused it to dry up? Maybe it did not dry up, as some geologists contend, but merely changed its course. It must have been about the size of the Columbia River — the second largest river in the United States — and it might have been the Columbia, as some geologists believe.

The gradual upheaval of the Sierra Nevadas might have caused the Big Blue to change its course, or perhaps the many other streams coming down from the Sierras flowed into and formed the Big Blue.

Dammed by volcanic action, these streams may have changed individually to a western course instead of turning south into the Big Blue, thus diverting that stream into another stream farther west. This stream could not gain access to the Pacific Ocean because of another mountain range — the Coast Range — and so, another north-south river was formed.

Was it the Sacramento?

Where the Columbia River now turns west at Wallula, Washington, at one time it could have continued south and west to form the Big Blue. This is the theory of some geologists.

At any rate, find the rest of the Big Blue River's ancient bed, and the greatest reservoir of gold in the world will be waiting for you.

It most certainly is in California — or Oregon.

Thomas Penfield
Los Angeles, California
February, 1972

The Rest Of The Dead River Story

reasure tales always begin with another story... the story behind the story, my good treasure buddies. Because we sit here 'round a roaring campfire atop a California mountain, part of what we sense are the rolling eons of time that it took to produce such a vista. The story of the Big Blue is a fascinating one. Hunker down on your log or your campstool, and read more about Big Blue. You owe it to yourself!

Attribution: Rob Lavinsky, iRocks.com – CC-BY-SA-3.0
http://www.irocks.com – Source: http://www.1wbta.com/Crystallized-Gold

This fine sample is not from California! (Use the links above to read about this golden miracle.) But it embodies the excitement of the California Gold Rush, and what a "dead river" might tell us.

Now, back to the Big Blue River topic. You DO owe it to yourself to add this article to your research. Read about "Dead Rivers Of California: Tertiary Channels Rich In Gold Nuggets," here:

http://www.1wbta.com/Dead-Rivers-Of-California

Illustrated: Who Really Made Money In The Gold Rush?

Well, the local banks and the mercantile, of course! Those who supplied the miners were the stable element!

We all gotta eat, and we all need a shovel and pickax!

"Historic American Buildings Survey / Wells Fargo Museum, San Francisco / San Francisco" ca. 1875
Bush Street From Sansome, Looking West - Mercantile Library Building, Historic View,
Bush & Sansome Streets, San Francisco, San Francisco County, CA
Source: http://www.loc.gov/pictures/item/ca0671.photos.016081p/
Courtesy LOC.GOV, Library Of Congress, USA

Chapter 2: Begin Your California Research

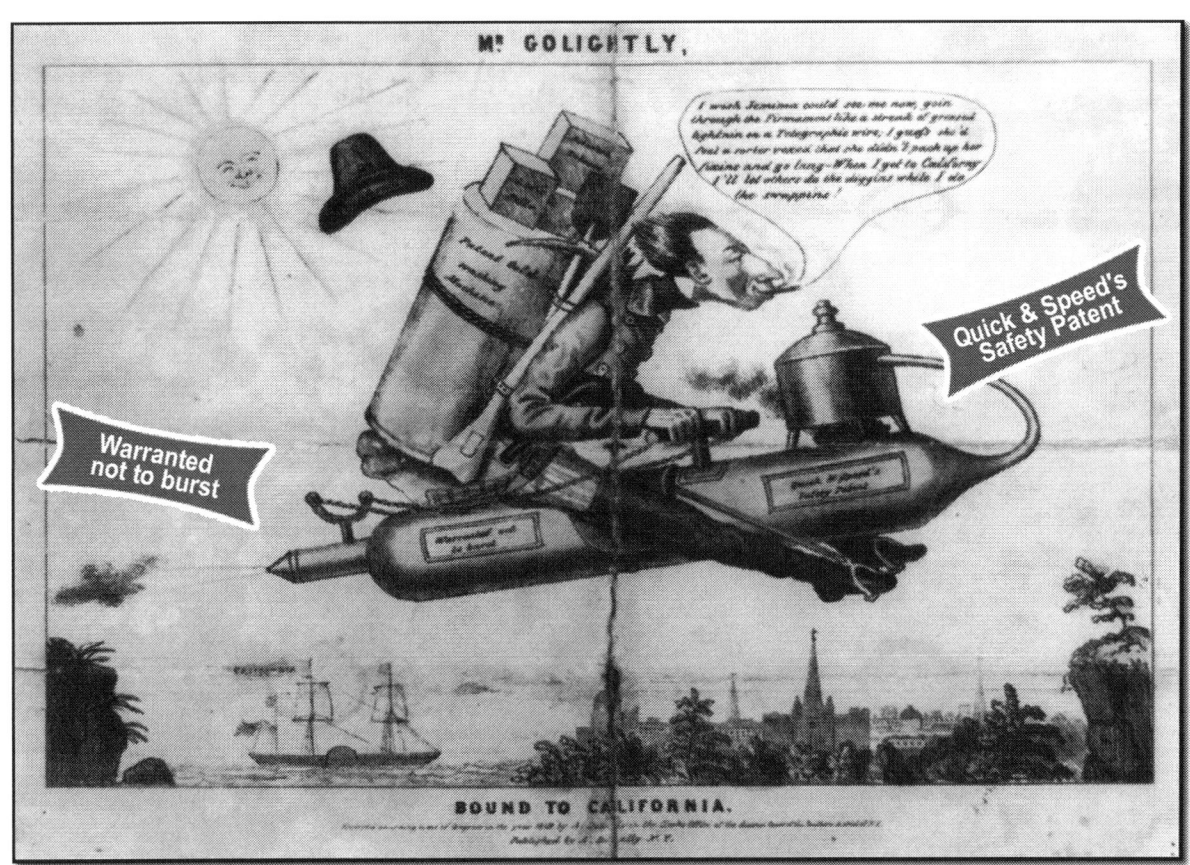

"Mr. Golightly, Bound To California" - c1849, A. Donnely, NY
Caricature of man riding on rocket with items to sell to gold miners.
Sales personnel, Rockets, Gold rushes--California, Cartoons & Caricatures (Commentary)--1840-1850.
"I wish Jemima could see me now, goin' through the Firmament like a streak of greased lightnin'
on a Telegraphic wire; I guess she'd feel a sorter vexed that she didn't pack up her fixins and
go 'long -- When I get to Californy I'll let others do the diggins while I do the swappins!"

Your Topic Will Be Tied To An Event

If you are treasure seeking in the state of California, then you most likely need a hefty dose of research in all-things "Gold Mine." Most treasure tales and leads are, in one form or another, tied to some event of the fabulous Gold Rush.

To Get You Started, Check Out These Web Sites

- The Library of Congress is always a great way to start a research project.
  Web site: www.loc.gov/index.html
  You will find images, writings, tips and techniques. You have access to the librarians, which may well speed up your search in great form.
  Why not start with topics of interest for gold mining in Death Valley?
  Location: http://www.loc.gov/pictures/

- Topoquest – **Web site:** http://www.topoquest.com/places.php

  (The Place Finder: For most map needs, this is an excellent starting point.)

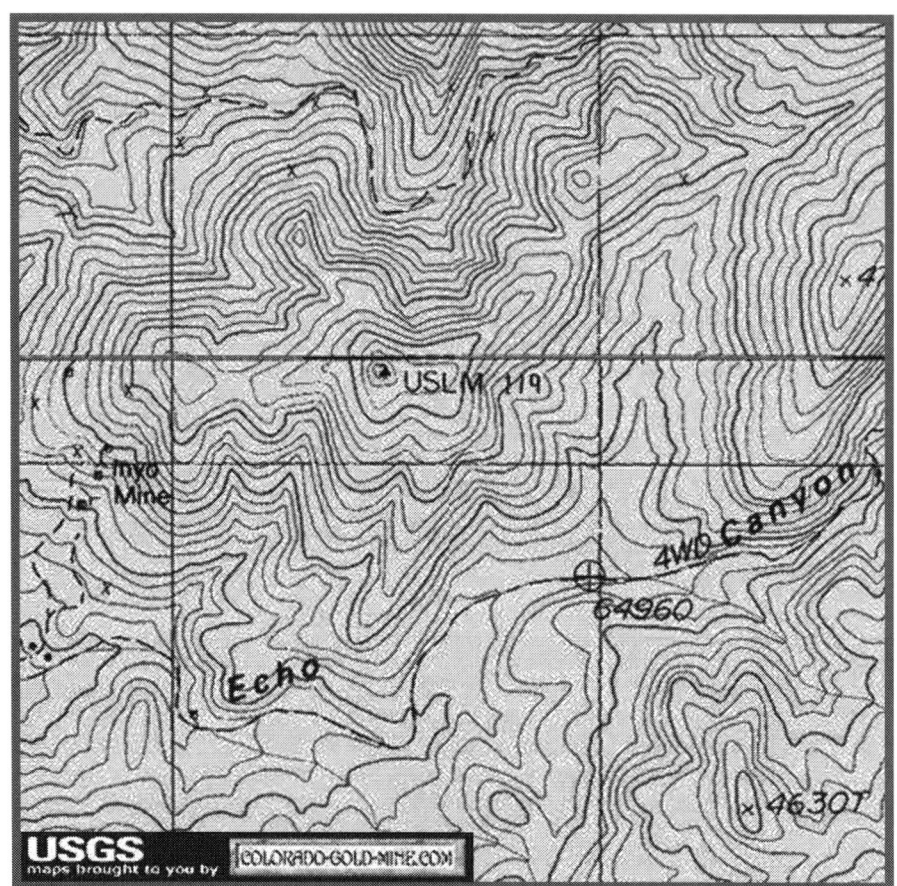

Inyo County, California - Inyo Mine

Map This On A Topo Map: http://www.1wbta.com/Inyo-County-California-Inyo-Mine

- Wikipedia – **Web site:** (English) http://en.wikipedia.org/wiki/Main_Page
  Wikipedia – **Web site:** (Choose language) http://www.wikipedia.org/

  Seriously. You can find so much information here, you will feel pure drunk!

- Access Genealogy — **Web site:** www.accessgenealogy.com/

    Free California Genealogy Data and Links
    Location: www.accessgenealogy.com/california/
    This amazing site for California (and for each USA state) has huge, FREE information in three main categories: "Free California Genealogy Data and Links," "Free RootsWeb Databases," and "Additional Free California Genealogy." It will be well worth your time to research at this site.

- Your major search engines such as Google, Yahoo, and Bing are your best friends. Perhaps you've located a Death Valley mine that captures your interest. The search engines may lead you to Web sites and blogs where others have journeyed where you want to go. You will find journals, maps, or photos that will pin-point your desired gold mine. Perhaps that mine is the Inyo Mine in Inyo County, California. The personalized information in a blog, for instance, will give you an insight on your topic that cannot be found on other strictly informational sites.

INYO MINE & THE FUNERAL MOUNTAINS

Part 2.1: 1895 Map, Section 1 of 6

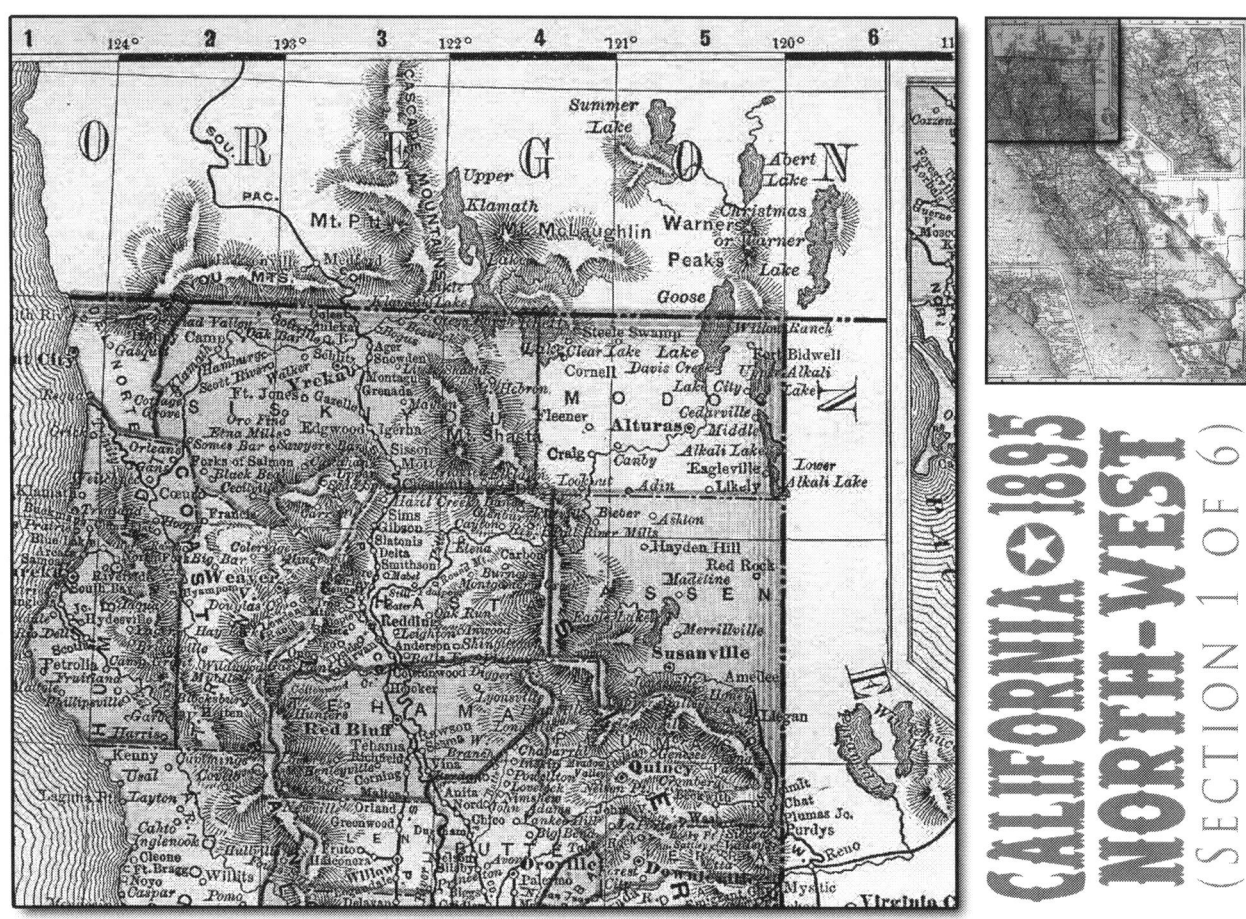

See the big picture... uhh... MAP!
http://www.1wbta.com/California-1895-Atlas-Map

Part 2.2: 1895 Map, Section 2 of 6

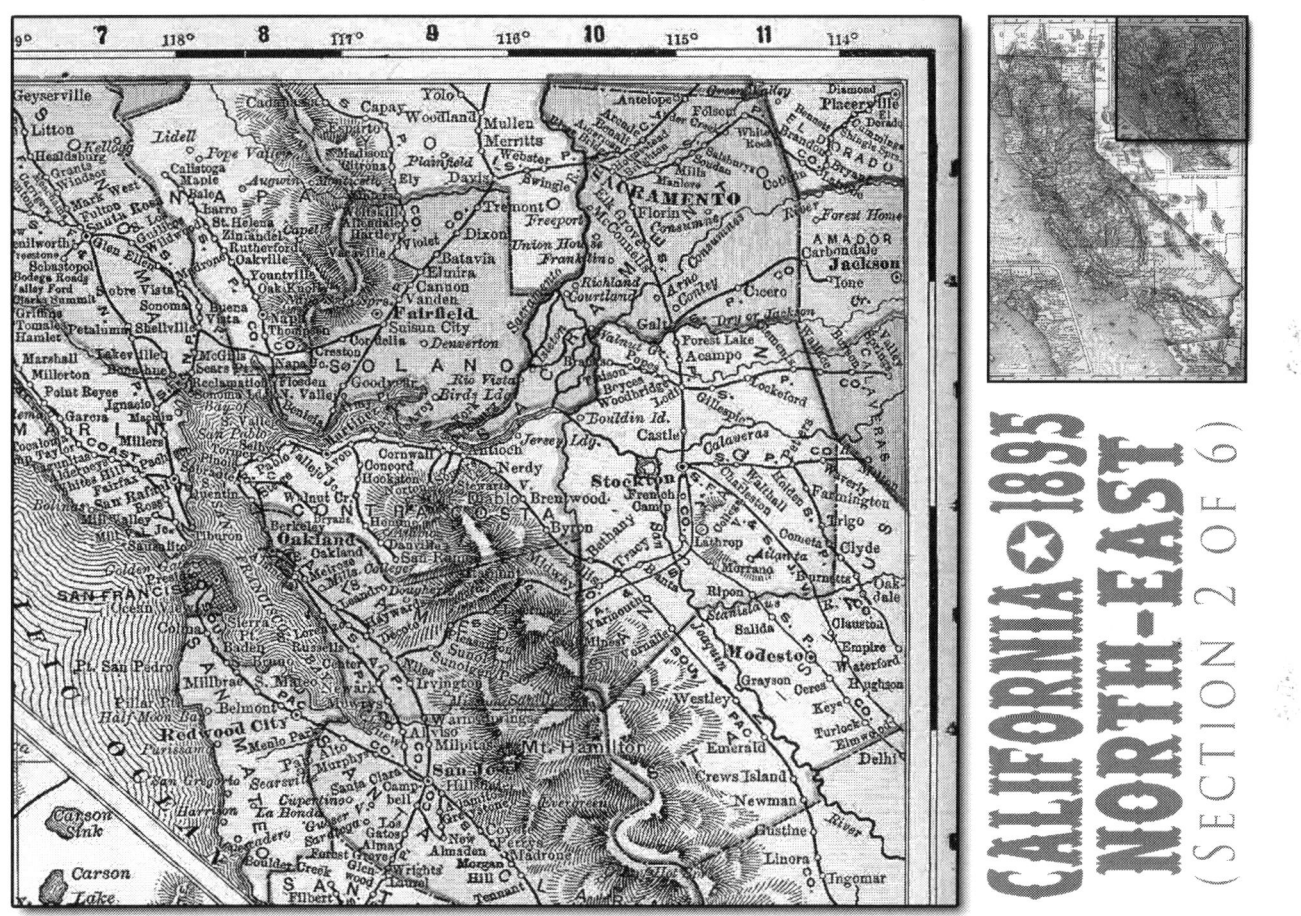

http://www.1wbta.com/California-1895-Atlas-Map

Part 2.3: 1895 Map, Section 3 of 6

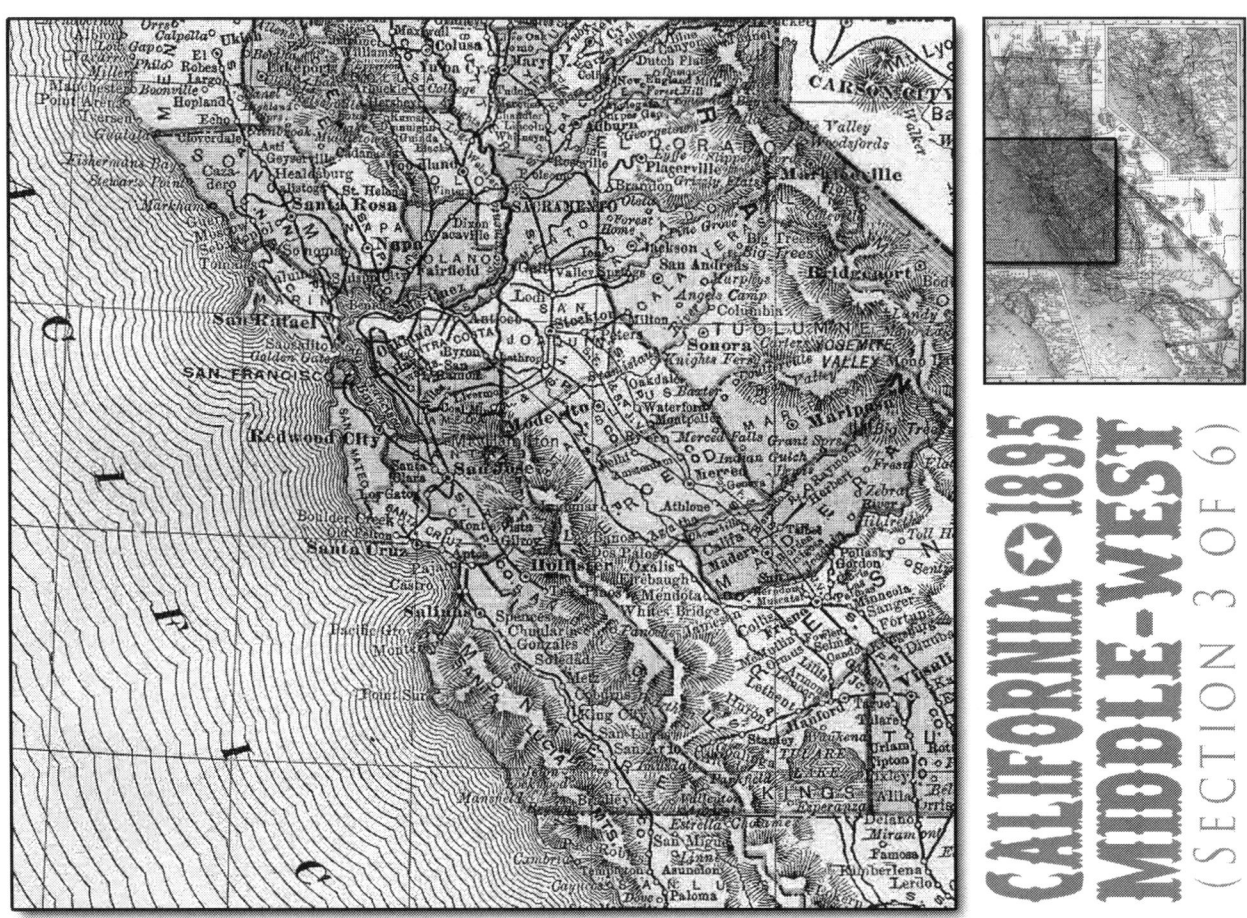

See the big picture... uhh... MAP!
http://www.1wbta.com/California-1895-Atlas-Map

Part 2.4: 1895 Map, Section 4 of 6

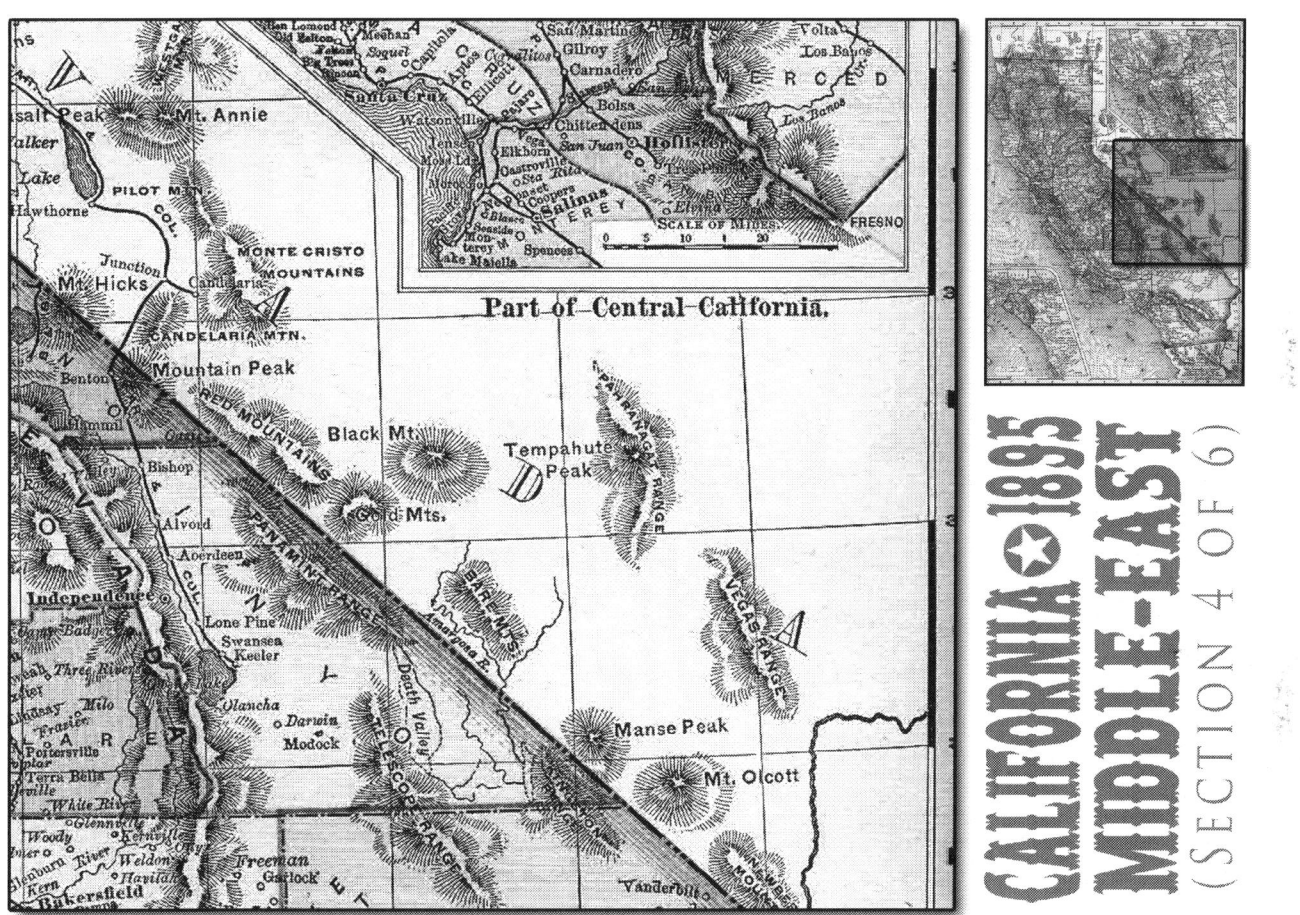

http://www.1wbta.com/California-1895-Atlas-Map

Part 2.5: 1895 Map, Section 5 of 6

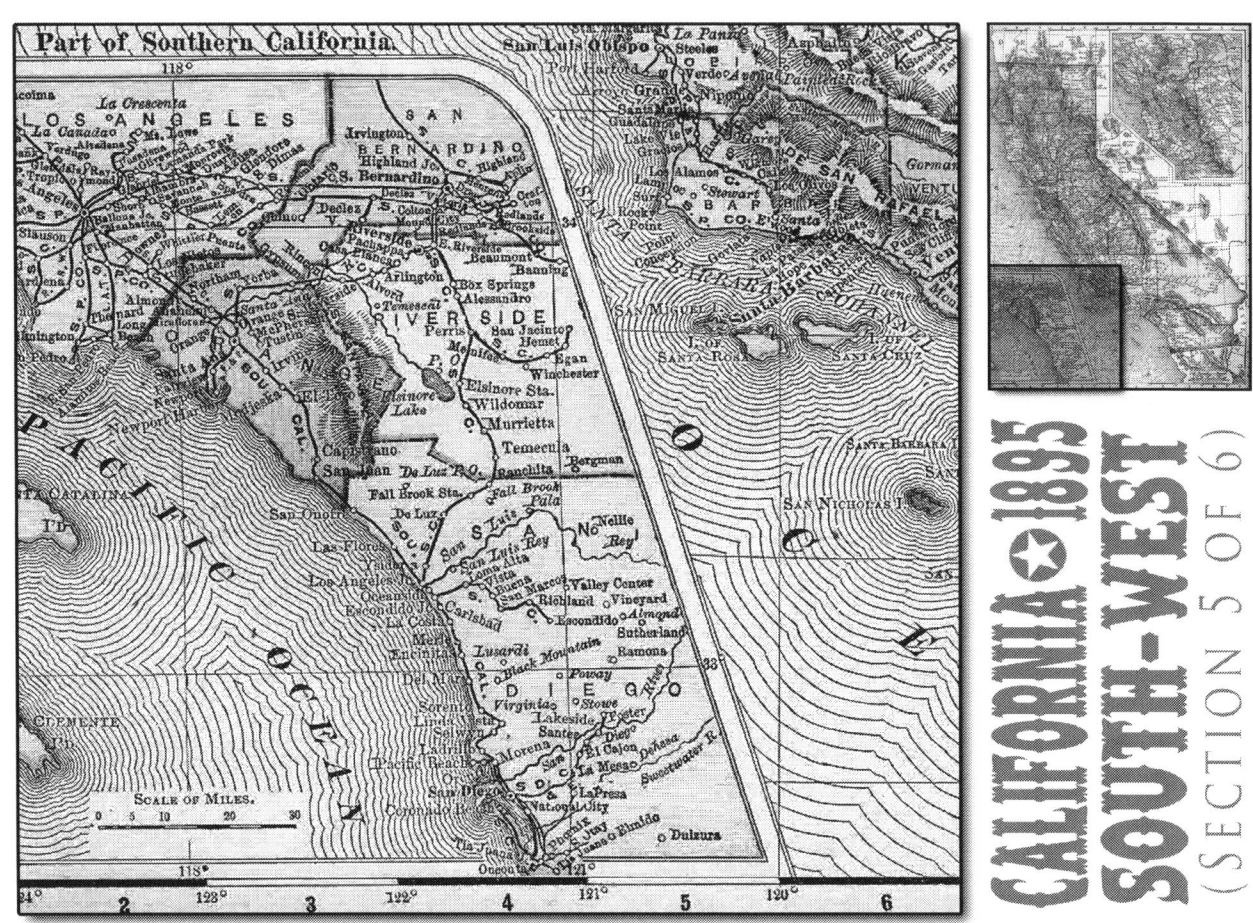

See the big picture... uhh... MAP!
http://www.1wbta.com/California-1895-Atlas-Map

Part 2.6: 1895 Map, Section 6 of 6

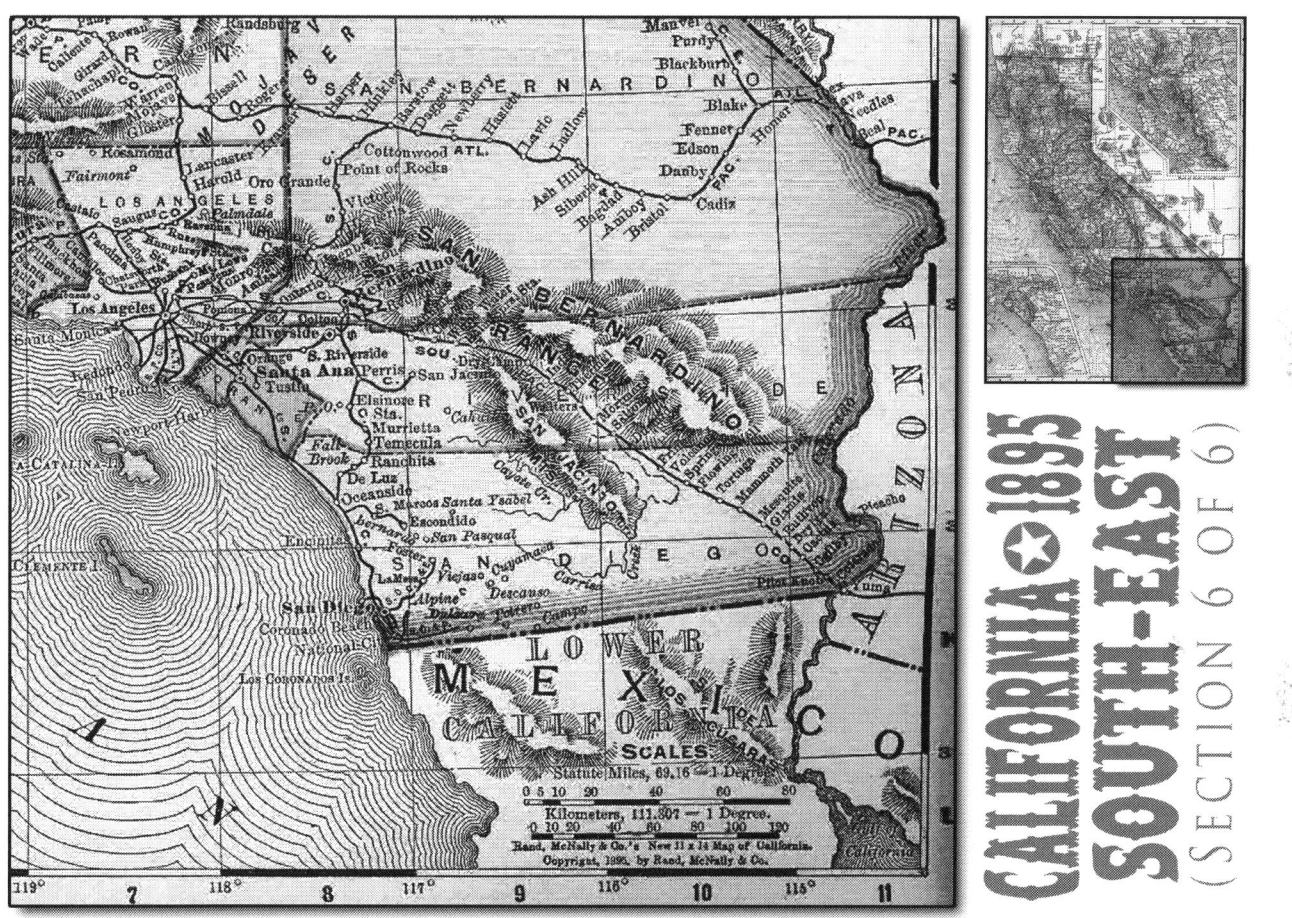

http://www.1wbta.com/California-1895-Atlas-Map

Part 2.7: There Are 58 Counties In California

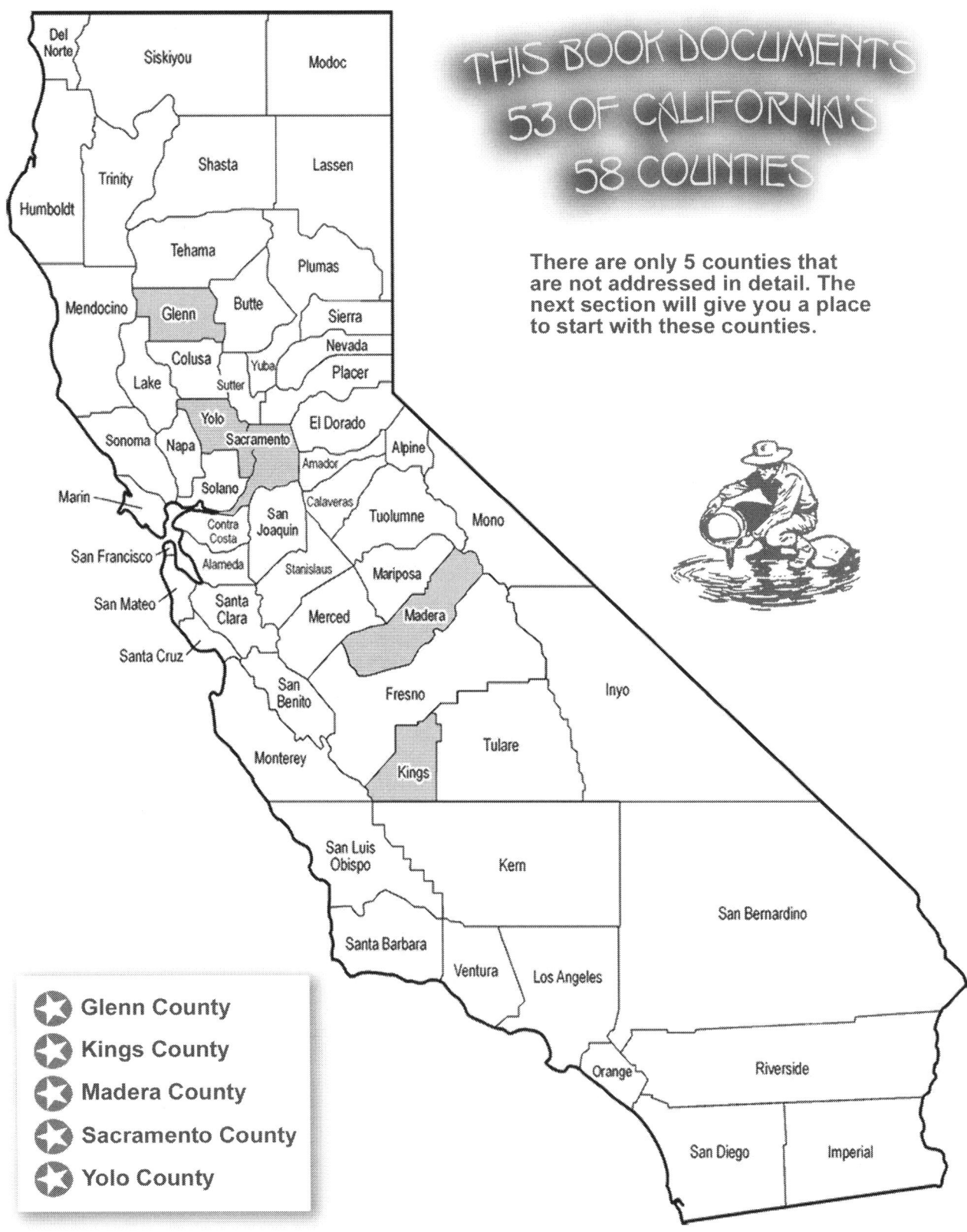

THIS BOOK DOCUMENTS 53 OF CALIFORNIA'S 58 COUNTIES

There are only 5 counties that are not addressed in detail. The next section will give you a place to start with these counties.

- ⭐ Glenn County
- ⭐ Kings County
- ⭐ Madera County
- ⭐ Sacramento County
- ⭐ Yolo County

Part 2.8: Missing Some Counties?

Although every place has its share of hidden treasures, not every county was a player in that state's major events or history. You may find that this book doesn't include those counties in the Treasure or Coinshooting pages.

Here in this sub-chapter, however, you will find some general information and inspiration!

- ## GLENN COUNTY

Glenn County was formed in 1891 from parts of Colusa County. It was named for Dr. Hugh J. Glenn, who was the largest wheat farmer in the state during his lifetime, and a man of great prominence in political and commercial life in California.

Glenn County: Of Interest To Treasure Hunters

Historic Places

- ♦ **National Register of Historic Places listings in Glenn County, California:** http://en.wikipedia.org/wiki/National_Register_of_Historic_Places_listings_in_Glenn_County,_California

- ♦ **Gianella Bridge:** Listed: July 8, 1982; Location: Hamilton City; Oldest highway swing bridge in use in the United States at the time of its removal. Last swung to let river traffic pass in 1972. Replaced with a modern concrete bridge in 1987.

- **US Post Office – Willows Main:** Listed: January 11, 1985; Location: 315 W. Sycamore St., Willows
- **National Register Information System – National Register of Historic Places:** http://nrhp.focus.nps.gov/natreg/docs/All_Data.html

National Protected Areas

- Mendocino National Forest (part)
- Sacramento National Wildlife Refuge (part)
- Sacramento River National Wildlife Refuge (part)

The Last Hurrah

- **CA Tombstone Project/Glenn County:** http://usgwtombstones.org/california/glenn.html
- **Cemeteries:** http://www.cagenweb.com/glenn/glenn.cem.htm

Stone Quarries, Glenn County

Rich in minerals, if not gold:

http://quarriesandbeyond.org/states/ca/quarry_photo/ca-glenn_photos.html

Railroads

California Northern Railroad shortline serves Willows. The main line runs north to Tehama and south to Davis, where the railroad interchanges with the Union Pacific Railroad.

Prior to the line being leased to the California Northern, the route was operated by Southern Pacific and was known as the West Side Line.

- The railroad first reached Willows on December 28, 1879, from Davis.
- In 1882 the extension from Willows to Tehama was completed.
- In 1884 the West Side and Mendocino Railroad constructed a line east from Willows to Fruto.

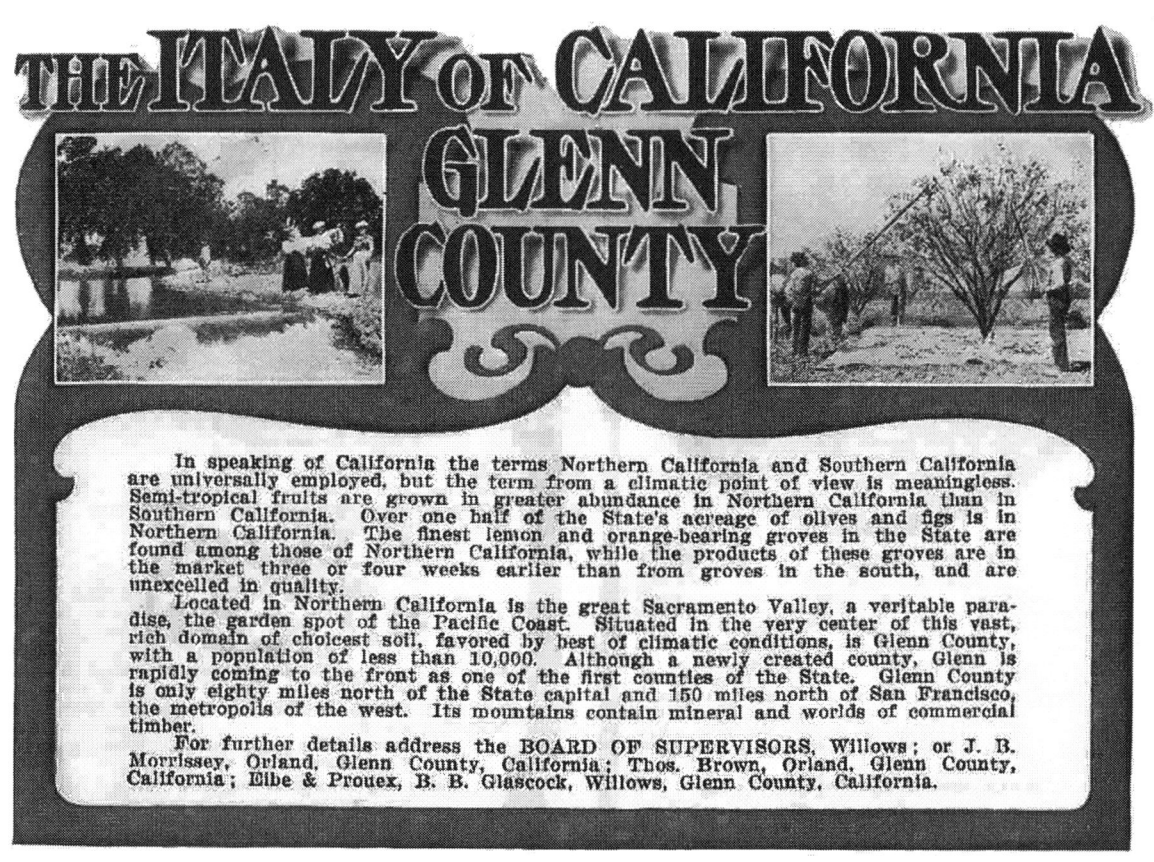

- # KINGS COUNTY

Kings County is located in the Central Valley of California. It is located in a rich agricultural region. Kings County is also home to NAS Lemoore, which is the U.S. Navy's newest and largest master jet air station. The county seat is Hanford.

The area was inhabited for thousands of years by indigenous peoples. It was colonized by Spain, Mexico, and the United States. An 1805 expedition probably led by Spanish Army Lieutenant Gabriel Moraga recorded discovering the river, which they named El Rio de los Santos Reyes (River of the Holy Kings) after the Three Wise Men of the Bible. At the time of the United States conquest in 1848, the new government changed the name to Kings River.

In 1928, oil was discovered in the Kettleman Hills, located in the southwestern part of Kings County. The Kettleman North Dome Oil Field became one of the most productive oil fields in the United States. Source: http://en.wikipedia.org/wiki/Kings_County,_California

Kings County: Of Interest To Treasure Hunters

Historic Places

- ♦ **Historical Overview of Kings County California, by Kings County Library**
  http://www.kingscountylibrary.org/res/hstk2.htm

- **Hanford Carnegie Library**
- **Kings County Courthouse**
- **Kingston**

Kingston, California is gone today but was thriving in 1870
Photo courtesy California Digital Archives
http://www.oac.cdlib.org/search.image.html

- **National Register of Historic Places listings in Kings County, California**
  http://en.wikipedia.org/wiki/National_Register_of_Historic_Places_listings_in_Kings_County,_California
- **El Adobe de los Robles Rancho, built by Daniel Rhoads**
- **The Witt Site**

The Last Hurrah

- **Kings County Cemetery Records, California – Genealogy**
  http://www.interment.net/us/ca/kings.htm
- **The Cemeteries of Kings County**
  http://www.cagenweb.com/kings/cemeteries.htm

Kings County: The Mussel Slough Tragedy

In 1880, a dispute over land titles between settlers and the Southern Pacific Railroad resulted in a bloody gun battle on a farm 5.6 miles northwest of Hanford, where seven men died. This event became known as the Mussel Slough Tragedy.

MAP THIS ON A TOPO MAP – www.1wbta.com/Kings-County-Mussel-Slough-Tragedy

Kings County - Mussel Slough Tragedy

List of involved persons

Marshal's group
- Alonzo W. Poole, U.S. Marshal
- William H. Clark, railroad land grader
- Walter J. Crow, settler (killed)
- Mills Hartt, settler (killed)

Settlers' group
- James N. Patterson, leader of the group
- William Braden
- B. S. Burr
- James Harris (killed)
- Edwin Haymaker (died of pneumonia soon and was considered a victim of the fight)
- John E. Henderson (killed)
- Daniel Kelly (killed)
- Iver Knutson (killed)
- Archibald McGregor (killed)
- W. L. Morton
- Wayman L. Pryor
- John D. Pursell

The "Mussel Slough Five"

www.1wbta.com/Kings-County-Mussel-Slough-Story

A Tiburcio Vasquez Treasure Tale… In Kings County!

The Kingston Lost Loot Of Tiburcio Vasquez

Kings County - In 1873, the small town of Kingston, California was a stopping place on the Overland Stage route between Stockton and Visalia, California. In December of 1873, Tiburcio Vasquez and his outlaw band made a bold raid, robbing the entire village and holding 39 men hostage. When an alarm was raised, the bandits dashed to their horses and began to flee. However, in the ensuing melee, three of the outlaws were shot and killed, and the man carrying the stolen loot was wounded.

Unable to reach a horse, the injured bandit escaped on foot and made his way across the Kings River. Though the outlaw was pursued, neither he nor the loot could be found. Years later, a skeleton was discovered in the area and was thought to have been the injured bandit, but again, the ill-gotten cache remained unrecovered.

By the 1890s, the town of Kingston had totally been abandoned and is completely gone today. The site of the town is now a California Historical Landmark, which can be found in Kingston Park in the city of Hanford.

Source: www.1wbta.com/Kings-County-Kingston-Lost-Loot

"Bear Valley is the hidden treasure of the Sierra." (Alpine County)   ~Lloyd Bridges

- ## MADERA COUNTY

Madera County is located in the Central Valley and the Sierra Nevada north of Fresno County. It comprises the Madera-Chowchilla, CA Metropolitan Statistical Area. The county derives its name from the town of Madera, named when the California Lumber Company built a log flume to carry lumber to the Central Pacific Railroad there in 1876.

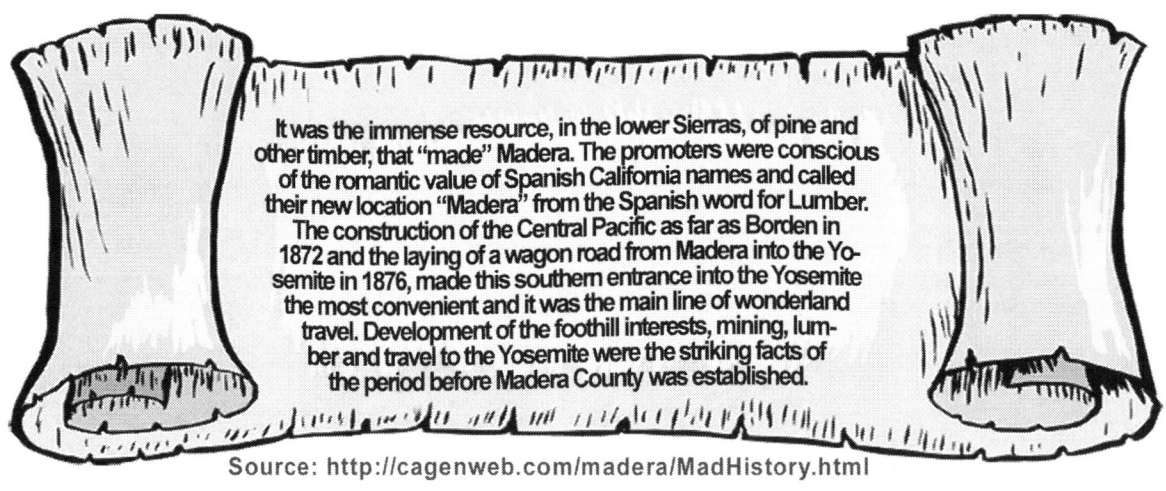

It was the immense resource, in the lower Sierras, of pine and other timber, that "made" Madera. The promoters were conscious of the romantic value of Spanish California names and called their new location "Madera" from the Spanish word for Lumber. The construction of the Central Pacific as far as Borden in 1872 and the laying of a wagon road from Madera into the Yosemite in 1876, made this southern entrance into the Yosemite the most convenient and it was the main line of wonderland travel. Development of the foothill interests, mining, lumber and travel to the Yosemite were the striking facts of the period before Madera County was established.

Source: http://cagenweb.com/madera/MadHistory.html

Madera County: Of Interest To Treasure Hunters

The Gold Rush in 1849 brought a hoard of settlers looking for prosperity. The "Gold Rush" uncovered claims from Ahwahnee through Hildreth (famous for numerous stage coach holdups) and mining towns sprang up with names of Coarsegold (also called Gold Gulch – 8 miles south of Oakhurst on Hwy 41 along Coarse Gold Creek), Grub Gulch, Fine Gold, Cassidy's Bar and Fresno Flats (now Oakhurst). In 1851, tensions between the Indians and miners resulted in the formation of the Mariposa Battalion, which pursued the Indians and eventually discovered Yosemite and Crane Valleys (Bass Lake).

Coarse Gold Gulch PO was opened in 1878, and the name changed to Coarsegold in 1899. Miners from Texas found gold at the place in 1849 and the community that developed there first was known as Texas Flats. In 1874, the area was called Michaels, for Charles Michaels that operated the first business there. Mexican miners called the area Oro Grosso. The current name derives from the California Gold Rush of the mid-19th century, when prospectors discovered coarse lumps of gold in a nearby creek. At one time, several dozen gold mines operated in the area.

Historic Places

- **Starville** – Located 23 miles northeast of Fresno Flats (Oakhurst), Starville PO was opened in 1889 and closed in 1891; the name was from the Star Mine.

- **Zebra** – 10 miles southeast of Raymond. Zebra PO was opened 6 miles northeast of Bates in 1886, closed in 1888, opened in 1890, closed for a few months in 1894, moved 4½ miles southwest in 1901, and closed in 1904 in favor of O'Neals. The name was from the Zebra Mine which had dark and light ore veins.

Gold Panning & Prospecting in Madera County

http://2getgold.com/prospecting/maderacounty.htm

- **Madera County** was never the "Shining Star" of the gold country in prospecting attempts, as the total production has been less than a quarter million ounces to date. There does remain, however, the occasional find that may bring you back for more, as this area didn't receive the flood of attention that many of the areas farther north did.

- **In the Raymond and Knowles area,** a pretty fair amount has been recovered on what is now privately held land. There were intermittent finds at the granite quarry in Raymond. Recovery may still be had throughout the back hills in the grouping of: Raymond, Knowles, Coarsegold, North Fork, and O'Neal's. The creeks in this area have been known to produce, although not too much "coarse gold" in and around here, although the name of Coarsegold may lead you to think so. You might want to try the two larger watercourses through this area, the Chowchilla and Fresno Rivers. There have been a number of smaller lode mining operations in this area over the years. Individual prospecting attempts result some success as well.

♦ **Coarsegold Creek** can still produce pretty well in small stuff.

♦ **Farther north of Coarsegold on HI-41** may produce a little color in the area of Sugar Pine. There was some modest prospecting here at one time near what was a logging camp, saw mill, lumber flume and railroad.

♦ **At the town of Friant** on the San Joaquin River, pretty good recovery was recorded although none recently. During the building of the dam, there was fairly significant production which helped to offset the dams construction costs.

Gold Rush To Ghost Town In Madera County

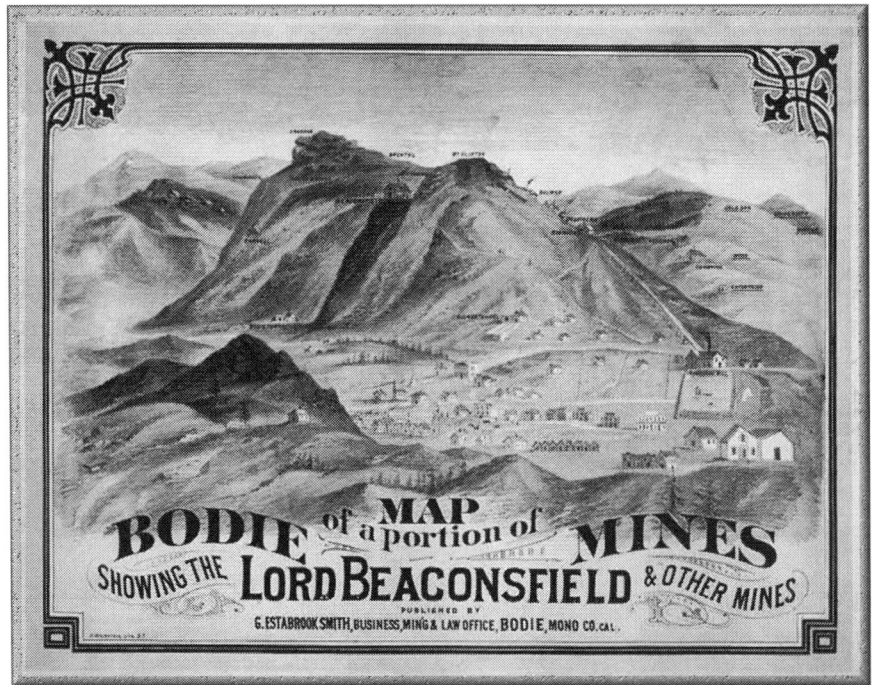

Source: www.1wbta.com/Bodie-Bill-No-AB-California-State-Senate

Bodie became a boom town in 1877 and by 1879 had a population of approximately 10,000 with 2,000 buildings. The town became more known for its wild living than for its big gold resources... numerous saloons and breweries dotted the mile long main street.

By 1882, the town was in the grips of decline - the rich mines were playing out and mining companies were going bankrupt. Two fires, one in 1892 and the other in 1932 ravaged the business district and Bodie faded into a ghost town in the 1940s.

Today, Bodie stands just as time, fire, and the elements have left it - a genuine California gold-mining ghost town.

- ## SACRAMENTO COUNTY

Sacramento County was one of the original counties of California that were created in 1850 at the time of statehood. The county was named after the Sacramento River, which forms its western border. The river was named by Spanish cavalry officer Gabriel Moraga for the Santisimo Sacramento (Most Holy Sacrament).

Sacramento County: Of Interest To Treasure Hunters

Sutter's Fort

When John Sutter arrived in the provincial colonial capital of Monterey in 1839, Governor Juan Bautista Alvarado provided Sutter with the land he asked for and Sutter established New Helvetia, which he controlled

Sutter's Fort in Sacramento, California, 1847
Photo courtesy Library of Congress

absolutely with a private army and relative autonomy from the newly independent Mexican government. The California Gold Rush started when gold was discovered at Sutter's Mill, one of Sutter, Sr.'s assets in the city of Coloma in 1848. The arrival of prospectors in droves ruined Sutter's New Helvetia.

The United States and Mexico initiated the Mexican-American War in 1846 in the wake of the annexation of the Republic of Texas by the United States, which Mexico did not recognize officially. California was annexed by the United States in the 1848 Treaty of Guadalupe Hidalgo, and Sutter's New Helvetia fell under American control.

In January 1848, a flake of gold was detected at the site of Sutter's new mill, and after conducting tests, it was determined the mineral's authenticity. Word leaked about the discovery nearly immediately. When news reached San Francisco, a rush of hopeful prospectors began to move northwards to the Sacramento Valley, and by the middle of the year, so-called "Argonauts" flooded Sutter's holdings in search of gold.

By 1852, Sutter's New Helvetia had collapsed completely, and Sutter's Fort had been abandoned. Sacramento's commerce had become reliant on coins, and the city had outgrown its unstable Gold Rush boomtown status.

With the advent of the railroad and the introduction of refrigeration, wheat prices dropped and fruit became a significant cash crop. As a result, in 1883 onwards, until the start of the 20th century, grain ranches that had previously profited from wheat began to go bankrupt and close. The original owners of the ranches soon died off, and the heirs deeded land to those who were seeking it. This era brought about a land boom.

Today, one plan for the City of Sacramento's future suggests building a massive park in Downtown Sacramento called Gold Rush Park which would rival in size the largest municipal parks in the nation.

Historic Places

- **A Century of California Post Offices, 1848-1954** – Sacramento County - List Created 18 February 1850
  http://www.1wbta.com/Sacramento-Century-Of-California-Post-Offices
- **Old Sacramento** – With 53 historic buildings, Old Sacramento probably has more buildings of historic value in its 28 acres than any area of similar size in the west.

Vigilantes Of California In Sacramento County

Members Of The "Vigilantees" Posse On Horseback
W/Right Hands Raised, Being Sworn In - ca. 1880

Sacramento was the first of the large towns to organize a committee of its citizens for the protection of social order, and its executions became celebrated for the interest displayed in them by the people of the surrounding country.

The first of these was at night on the Plaza, in the light of a great fire and in the presence of a great multitude. The office of hangman was conceded as a post of honor to the most reputable and wealthy citizen of the town.

Two days after, he paid the penalty of this honor by being himself shot by the desperadoes.

Sometimes a single individual became at once judge, jury, and executioner. On the highway from San Francisco to San Jose was found a corpse shot through the body, and to the lower button hole was tied a placard upon which were written, in very legible characters, these significant words:

> "I shot him because he stole my mule"
> John Andrew Anderson, Anderson Rancho Santa Clara Valley

He was not a murderer, but an executor of the law – the unwritten law – against all cattle thieves. If ten men could capture and slay him for the crime, the same right belonged to but one of the party, provided he alone could accomplish it.

Source: http://www.legendsofamerica.com/we-vigilantes.html

- ## YOLO COUNTY

Yolo County was one of the original counties of California, created in 1850 at the time of statehood. The city of Woodland is its county seat, though Davis is its largest city. The eastern part of Yolo County is in the Sacramento metropolitan area.

Yolo County: Of Interest To Treasure Hunters

Ahhh... Treasure Hunting! Keep remembering that treasure is EVERYWHERE! When you least expect it, something will land in your lap and it will slowly dawn on you just how valuable your find is! Old Glass can bring some astounding prices, and there are 1000s of collectors out there! Things like old wine bottles can show up in any hunt... an old farm, a vintage city building... YOUR basement!?

Historic Places

- The California Gold Rushes of 1848 and 1850 brought an increased population in Yolo County. There was some prospecting for gold, but most immigrants realized very early on, that the fortunes to be created in Yolo County were through farming and ranching. The name Yolo is derived from the Patwin Indian word "Yoloy," which means the place of rushes. The complete west bank of the Sacramento River had, at one time, great fields of tule rushes, and the County was plentiful in swamplands, marshes, and sloughs.

- National Register of Historic Places listings in Yolo County, California: R. H. Beamer House at Woodland; Canon School at Brooks; Downtown Woodland Historic District; William B. Gibson House at Woodland; Main Street Historic District at Winters; Nelson Ranch at Woodland; Rumsey Town Hall; Southern Pacific Railroad Station at Davis

- Yolo County CAGenWeb Project (history & genealogy)
  Yolo County, Calif., map 185-? at The Bancroft Library
  Source: http://cagenweb.com/yolo/yolhist.htm

The Last Great West, The Pacific Coast States Of America

Rice Bindery, Fair Ranch, Knights Landing - 1916
Collection: Photographs Related to Rice Growing and Irrigation in California
Contributing Institution: UC Berkeley, Bancroft Library
Courtesy Calisphere, University of California
Source: http://www.1wbta.com/Yolo-Rice-Bindery-Fair-Ranch

"Almost in the center of California, and the great fertile Sacramento Valley – is Yolo County. Our argument has to do primarily and principally with the farmer, the man of family who is seeking a location in the last great West, the Pacific Coast States of America... Yolo is truly a progressive county. It is really an agricultural community without any great city to overtop and dominate its affairs."

> ~ H. S. Maddox, in the chapter on "Yolo County," described the county as follows, circa 1915. (*Sacramento Valley and Foothill Counties of California: An Illustrated Description of all the Counties Embraced in this Richly productive Geographical Subdivision of the Golden State*, compiled and edited by Emmett Phillips and John H. Miller, published under the direction of The Sacramento Valley Exposition, J. A. Filcher, Director-in Chief, January, 1915)
> **Source:** http://cagenweb.com/yolo/yolhist.htm

The Color Of Gold Is RED In Yolo County!

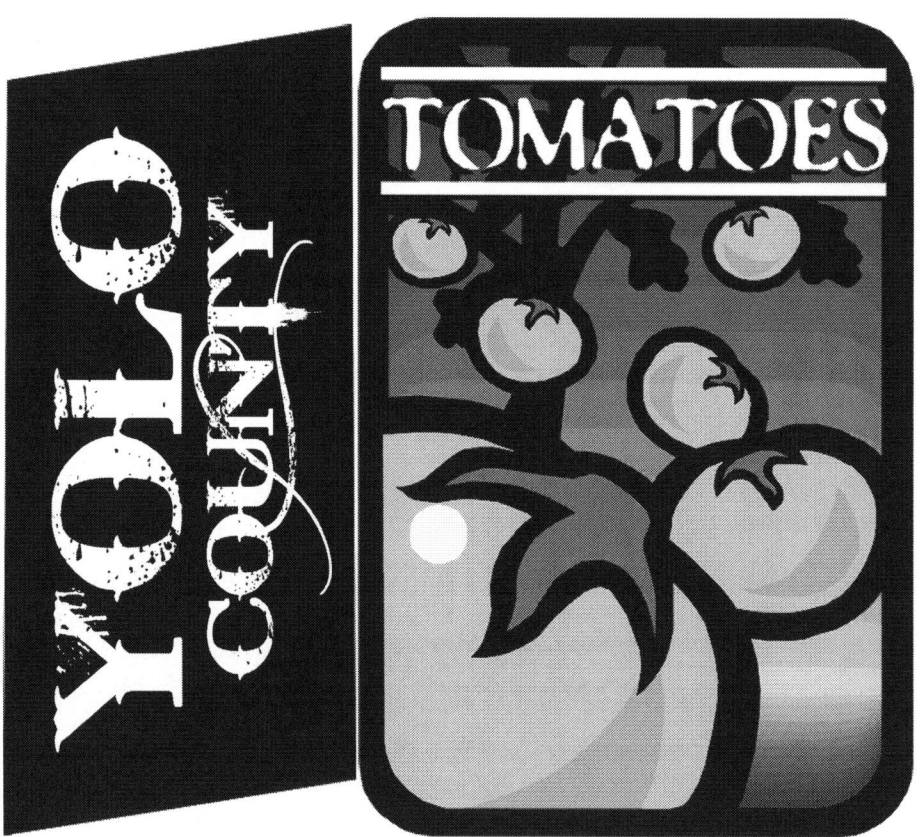

Yolo County remains a relatively rural agricultural region. This is evidenced by the multi-billion dollar California tomato industry, centering around Yolo County, dominating 90% of the canning and processed tomato market in the United States.

Chapter 3: Treasure Sites Of California

An Unidentified Gold Camp, Gold Rush Days In California

The California Gold Rush (1848–1855) began on January 24, 1848, when gold was discovered by James W. Marshall at Sutter's Mill, in Coloma, California. News of the discovery soon spread, resulting in some 300,000 men, women, and children coming to California from the rest of the United States and abroad. The early gold-seekers, called "Forty-niners" (as a reference to 1849) traveled to California by sailing boat and in covered wagons across the continent, often facing substantial hardships on the trip.

At first, the prospectors retrieved the gold from streams and riverbeds using simple techniques, such as panning. More sophisticated methods of gold recovery developed which were later adopted around the world. At its peak, technological advances reached a point where significant financing was required, increasing the proportion of corporate to individual miners. Gold worth billions of today's dollars was recovered, which led to great wealth for a few. However, many returned home with little more than they had started with.

In what has been referred to as the "first world-class gold rush," there was no easy way to get to California; forty-niners faced hardship and often death on the way. At first, most Argonauts, as they were also known, traveled by sea. From the East Coast, a sailing voyage around the tip of South America would take five to eight months, and cover some 18,000 nautical miles. An alternative was to sail to the Atlantic side of the Isthmus of Panama, to take canoes and mules for a week through the jungle, and then on the Pacific side, to wait for a ship sailing for San Francisco. There was also a route across Mexico starting at Veracruz. Many gold-seekers took the overland route across the continental United States, particularly along the California Trail.

Source: www.miningartifacts.org/California-Mines.html

Hupp McMurray Gold Mine - Trinity County

The California gold rush was not merely an American happening--it was a world event. Many mines, especially in the south, were worked by foreigners who came solely for the gold. Chinese, Chileans, Mexicans, Irish, Germans, French, and Turks all sought their fortune in California. Like their American-born counterparts, foreign miners had no intention of staying in California... No part of California would be the same after the gold rush.
Source: www.miningartifacts.org/California-Mines.html

Chapter 4: Treasure Sites By County

Counties A – D

Treasure hunting in California, my friends, always comes back to the BIG ONE... the Gold Rush. But, what stories these are! Tonight, good food, good campfire, and good storytelling friends, I am reminded of what has been said: "Good listeners, like precious gems, are to be treasured." (Walter Anderson)

Now it is onwards, with the core of California stories! "Gold! Gold! Gold from the American River!" (Samuel Brannan, running through the streets of San Francisco when the first gold was found, waving a bottle of gold dust in the air.)

Alameda County — In 1821, two men from South America came to the Rancho de los Tularcitos near Warm Springs in Alameda County. They announced to the ranch's owner, Jose Higuera, that they had $80,000 in gold between them, and that they wished to purchase cattle from the ranch.

As was the Spanish custom of those days, before doing business on this scale, Jose Higuera gave a fiesta which lasted several days. At the height of the festivities, both South Americans became violently ill and soon died.

Higuera concluded the cause of death was cholera, and urged his guests to leave before they contracted it. He then instructed a group of Indians to cart the bodies to a remote section of the vast ranch and bury them. At the last moment, he decided that the gold was also contaminated with cholera and ordered it buried with its owners.

Supposedly this was done, but there is a story that the Indians, not realizing the danger, buried the money separately, but never recovered it. Although there has been considerable digging for the unmarked graves and the money, it is believed that neither has ever been found. ^(Map Code 12 G-4)

Alameda County — Lake Merritt is a 160-acre lake of tidal salt water in the center of Oakland. In 1893, before the unsightly tidal basin was converted into a public recreational area, Adams Point, which juts into the lake, was the scene of a treasure search for loot supposed to have been buried there by two bandits. In a quarrel over the division of the spoils, one of the men killed the other, hid the body in a nearby brick kiln, and buried the money close at hand, intending to recover it at a later date. However, he was almost immediately arrested, tried and sentenced to San Quentin Prison. Before dying in San Quentin, he gave a minister the instructions for locating the treasure, but it is said that the loot was never recovered. ^(Map Code 13 B-10)

Alameda County — Brushy Peak is a remarkable natural formation about 8 miles northeast of Livermore. The front forms a prominent brush-covered eminence which rises high above the surrounding hills. Beyond it lies a beautiful valley in which is located a group of immense rocks and many small caves.

This place is said to have been used as a hideout by Joaquin Murrieta and his gang, and tradition says that they left treasure buried here. This same tradition applies to a dozen or more other places in California associated with Murrieta's name. ^(Map Code 12 G-4)

Alameda County — About 1895, there was a great deal of digging at the base of an oak tree at Second Avenue and East 11th Street in Oakland. The object of the search was a box of gold coins valued then at $80,000, the loot stolen by a bandit and buried shortly before his capture. Because this bandit also died in San Quentin after revealing where the loot was buried, this story is frequently confused with the bandit loot supposedly buried on Adams Point in Lake Merritt (see above). ^(Map Code 13 B-10)

Narrowing Down A Tale With USGS Maps

- ### SNOWSHOE THOMPSON'S LOST GOLD-BEARING QUARTZ MINE

Alpine County — Snowshoe Thompson had a home in Diamond Valley in the northern corner of Alpine County, south of the West Fork of the Carson River, and between Fredericksburg and Woodfords.

For some 20 years, he faithfully carried the mail on homemade snowshoes from Placerville across the Sierras to the little communities of Alpine County, never knowing whether he would be paid for his services or not.

Pinpoint Your Locations In The Tale

Woodfords And The Carson River

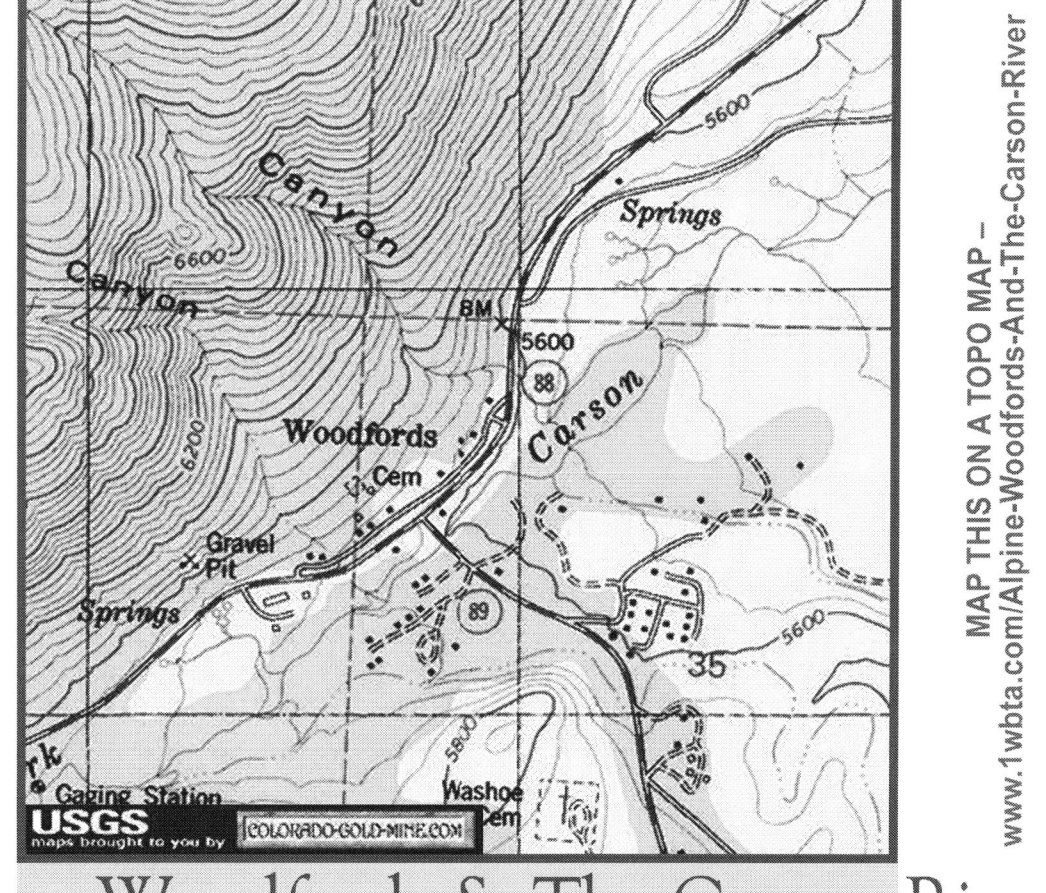

MAP THIS ON A TOPO MAP —
www.1wbta.com/Alpine-Woodfords-And-The-Carson-River

He was acquainted with every foot of the Sierras between his home and Placerville, and from time to time he brought in chunks of quartz richly flecked with gold. He often told his wife that he would work the mine when he was no longer able to carry the mail.

He never told her where his find was located, however, until, on his deathbed, he tried to show her that his mine could be seen from his bedroom window.

Horseshoe Canyon

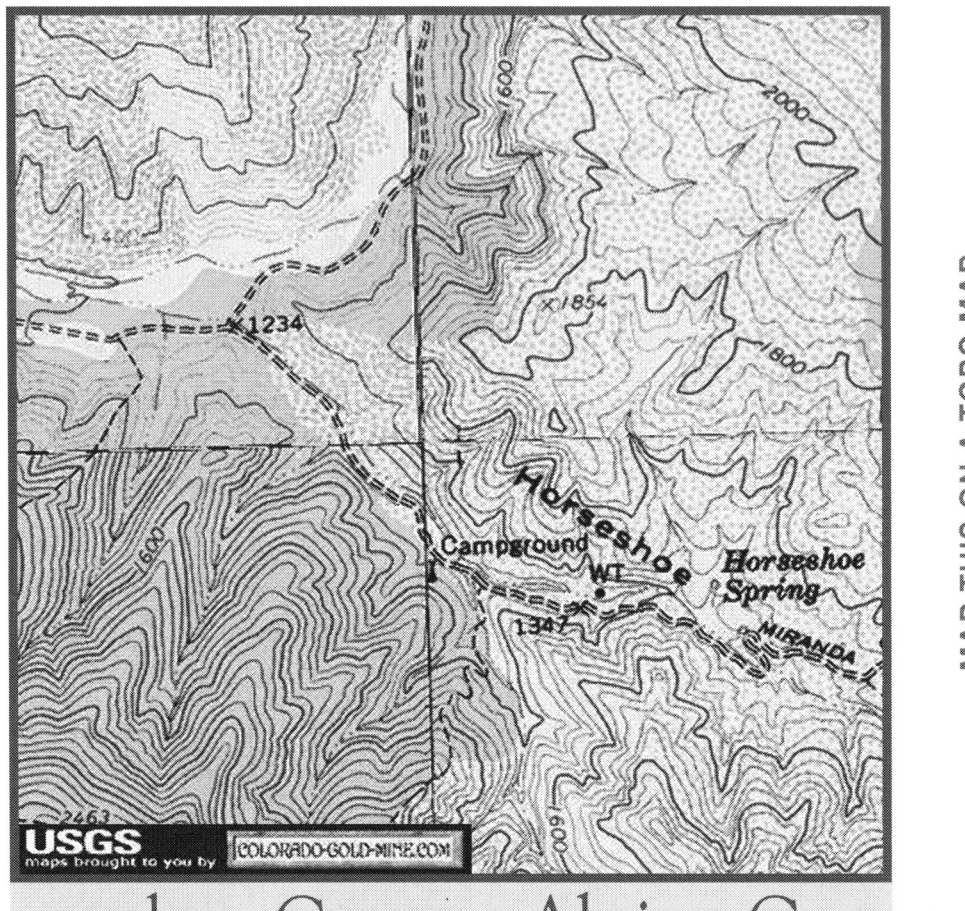

Horseshoe Canyon Alpine County

MAP THIS ON A TOPO MAP —
www.1wbta.com/Horseshoe-Canyon-Alpine-County

After Thompson's death, and because of his great reputation for integrity and honesty, a concentrated effort was made to locate the source of his rich gold-bearing quartz. It was the general opinion then that the mine was located somewhere in the area between Horseshoe Canyon and Hawkins Peak.

More Information: Some online sources show Horseshoe Canyon to be in Mono County, southeast of Alpine County. **Resource:** www.1wbta.com/Horseshoe-Canyon-Mono-County

Hawkins Peak

MAP THIS ON A TOPO MAP — www.1wbta.com/Alpine-Hawkins-Peak

Your Best Followup Techniques

From this small overview in this book, there is much more to be done.

- ♦ Purchase actual USGS Maps! These places may be on only one map, or, according to your key places, it may take more than one.

- ♦ Do some serious research online, to see if you can find other vintage maps, such as for mining locations, post offices, pertinent geological areas.

- ♦ If you are going to actually follow through, then you must GO there. This may take more than one trip. You need to scout things out and familiarize yourself with the layout of the land.

- Visit nearby towns and also the County Clerk's office. They may have a wealth of information not found anywhere else.

- Locate some old-timers if possible. Again, these folks are possible sources of huge information. But, these oldsters are quickly fading into the past... Their children and grandchildren, however, may also be able to remember the tales they've heard all of their lives.

It is quite possible that some geologic disturbance has buried Snowshoe Thompson's find, for it is this writer's opinion that it almost certainly existed and has never been found. **Map Code 13 E-6**

<u>Amador County</u> — Drytown, located on Dry Creek, was far from dry in its heyday. It had 26 saloons, none of which ever closed their doors. The gulches around Drytown were rich in gold and it was commonplace for a miner to take out $100 in a single pan. No one knows quite how one Joe Williams acquired $80,000 in gold coins, but a story has it that he buried that amount near Drytown.

One account of the story states that Williams worked a rich claim in nearby Murderer's Gulch and had its proceeds converted into gold coins, which he placed in small wooden boxes made for him by a carpenter. Each of these boxes of coins was buried in a different place, but never more than four feet away from another.

When begged on his deathbed to tell where his gold was buried, Williams only comment was, "Nobody will find it in a hundred years." Joe Williams has been dead now more than 100 years, and so far as it is known, nobody has found his boxes of gold coins. Of course, if Joe never buried them, nobody's going to find them in a thousand years. **Map Code 12 F-5**

<u>Amador County</u> — Drytown, the oldest town in Amador County, was founded in 1848 when gold was discovered in the area. In its earliest days, two partners worked a secret mine on Rancheria Creek above Drytown. Wishing to make a trip to their homes in Pennsylvania, the partners concealed their mine and left for a prolonged stay. While in the east, one of the partners died and the second suffered a lingering illness.

In the late 1890s, however, the survivor was well enough to return to Drytown and begin a search for the long concealed secret mine. Many old shafts were searched without any success, and the miner finally drifted away. **Map Code 12 F-5**

Amador County — The little town of Volcano, north of Pine Grove (US 88), once boasted a population of 8,000, but can barely muster 125 souls today. With the surrounding area producing more than $90,000,000 in gold, it was one of the richest camps in the Mother Lode. Many good finds were made — and then abandoned by the finders to seek richer ones. When the area began to play out, the earlier abandoned strikes were relocated and worked.

The story is told that an unnamed Mexican made a rich strike on Dry Creek west of Volcano. Hearing of a richer strike some distance away, he covered his strike and moved on to the new Golconda. When this failed to work out, he returned to work his original strike, but could not find it. With slight variations, this story is told of a dozen or more early mining camps in California. **Map Code 12 F-5**

Amador County — Fiddletown was so named because its founders, a group of Missourians, were fond of fiddle music. An early hotel keeper was so ashamed of the name that he persuaded the citizens to change it to Oleta, an Indian name meaning "old home spring." But local pride revived eventually, and today this little town, located 5 miles east of Plymouth (State 49) is known by its original name.

In the 1870s, an old Spanish miner lived in a cabin just north of Fiddletown and prospected a region that was considered to have been worked out years previously. Because the old Spaniard made loans to friends in gold nuggets and gold coins, it was presumed that he was working a secret mine someplace in the area of his cabin.

When the old man died about 1880, his cabin and the grounds around it were thoroughly searched for the secret cache which many thought he maintained. Others scoured the area in the hills around the cabin, seeking the source of his gold nuggets. Neither the cache nor the mine were ever found. **Map Code 12 F-5**

Butte County — In the vicinity of Round Mountain, a few miles from Chico (State 99), lies the ghost town of Cherokee, which produced $24,000,000 worth of gold in 25 years. And in the area of Cherokee, where Mike Maher found a perfect blue diamond in his sluice box in 1866, some 400 ice-clear diamonds have been found.

In 1907, the United States Diamond Mining Company was formed, with stock being sold to local citizens. Two years later, workers took 100 gems out of the soft blue clay. Shortly after this the mine entrance was boarded up and barricaded. So far as it is known no one has entered the shaft since. Stockholders who complained were offered the return of their investments. No one knew for certain who ordered the productive mine closed, but it was speculated that the DeBeers diamond syndicate of Africa had gained control of the California mine and had ordered it closed to prevent competition with its African interests. An occasional diamond is still found around the old camp of Cherokee, but most of the land suspected of containing diamonds is private property and freelance diamond hunters are generally not welcome. Some limited free pickings are offered along the right-of-way of State 99-149 between Chico and Oroville. **Map Code 12 D-4**

Butte County — The town of Oroville (State 70) has had two gold booms, one in the winter of 1849-1850 when gold was first discovered, and again in 1856 when a canal brought water to the dry diggings. With the advent of dredging in 1898, a company offered to move and rebuild the whole town if permitted to wash out the gold-bearing gravel beneath it. The town refused to move. There is a story told of a lone Indian who, in 1884, periodically brought a bag of gold nuggets into Oroville and traded them. The Indian made no secret of the fact that he was working a rich mine, and when his tongue loosened with liquor, he boasted that it was rich enough to make fifty men rich for life. All attempts to follow him failed, and on one of his sprees in Oroville he became sick and died. His mine is still known as the Lost Indian Ledge. **Map Code 12 D-4**

Calaveras County — The ghost camp of San Antone is now located on the ranch of Ray Cuneo, near Murphys. Cuneo's grandfather lived in San Antone when the camp was rich and miners had their pockets full gold. He related that he had weighed $40,000 worth of gold on his store scales for a Negro miner known only as Buster, and had exchanged other gold for $10,000 worth of gold coins. Cuneo claimed that Buster had hidden or buried this hoard near his little cabin on San Antone Creek, or in the hills directly behind it.

Buster was an escaped slave who had come to California before the gold rush. When gold was discovered along San Antone Creek, he staked out a claim and struck it rich. It was believed that Buster's first name was Dan, and that he had been bilked out of a sum of money by a white attorney he had retained to secure his mother's freedom. When asked one time what he was going to do with his hoarded wealth, Buster replied: "Ain't no white man ever gonna find it!"

Buster lived in San Antone 13 years. When he died in 1863, townspeople tore down his cabin and dug beneath the floor, searching for his fortune. Virtually every inch of the area around his cabin was dug up, but so far as it is known,

Buster's gold is still intact just where he placed it. The Cuneo family acquired the entire Camp San Antone townsite when the miners pulled out in the 1860s, and two generations of Cuneos have searched in vain for Buster's gold.
Map Code 13 F-6

Calaveras County — The old Dorrington Hotel, in the Mother Lode hamlet of Dorrington in the northeastern corner of Calaveras County, is said to be haunted with the ghost of Rebecca Dorrington Gardner, wife of John Gardner who built the hotel in the early 1850s.

Rebecca is said to have died of pneumonia contracted when she walked out to the barn one night in a bad storm. Some old-timers insist that Rebecca's urgency to get to the barn that night was to see that the treasure she had buried there was intact, or to add something to the cache. If Rebecca had a treasure cache secreted in the barn, there is no record that it was ever found and the barn has long since disappeared.
Map Code 13 F-6

Calaveras County — There are two or three lost gold ledges reported in the Blue Mountains in the northeastern section of Calaveras County. One prospector who found a ledge that looked promising had no means of breaking off a sample except by prying with the barrel of his gun, which was broken in the process. The sample proved to be rich in gold, but the prospector was never again able to locate the ledge, which is marked by the piece of broken rifle left there. **Map Code 12 F-5**

Calaveras County — An unnamed man who had been working at the settlement of Sheep Ranch, started to walk to Douglas Flat, a nearby camp that had produced in a short time enough gold to make a lot of people rich. Along the way, he stumbled upon a rich ledge of gold, knocked off a few samples, and continued on his way.

Believing he would be returning by the same route and would have no trouble locating the ledge again, he did not bother to mark it. Instead of walking back to Sheep Ranch, however, he was offered a ride in a buggy and accepted. Afterwards, when he tried to locate the ledge, he failed. Finally, he paid an experienced prospector $100 to search for the ledge, but this effort also produced nothing. **Map Code 13 F-6**

Calaveras County — Whiskey Slide, once an important mining camp northeast of San Andreas (State 49), was populated mostly by Mexicans. One unnamed Sonoran miner accumulated $15,000, and like many miners of the time, buried it outside his small cabin for safekeeping. When a bandit attempted to force him to tell where his money was hidden, the miner resisted and was killed in the fight that ensued. An immediate search for the cache failed to produce it, and supposedly the treasure is still there. **Map Code 12 F-5**

Calaveras County — Camp Seco is a mere ghost of the town it was during the gold boom there in the 1860s. One of the miners here was a southerner who brought his personal slave with him, a Negro known only as Jim.

When the master died, he left all of his earthly possessions to the trusted Jim, including his mine and his cabin in one of the gulches emptying into the Mokelumne River. Before the old slave died, he said his master had told him that he had buried several cans of gold in different places around his cabin. Jim stated on his deathbed that he had never found the cans of gold, which are presumably still there. **Map Code 12 F-5**

Calaveras County — While resting on the bank of the Stanislaus River near the little town of Big Trees, a hunter happened to spy a large piece of gold-bearing ore. Upon exploring the area, he was able to trace the ore to the ledge from which it had fallen.

To mark the site, he tied a red handkerchief to the limb of a tree, and continued with his hunt. Shortly before being killed in an accident, he told a friend of the find and made plans to take him in as a partner. So far as it is known, the "Lost Red Handkerchief Mine" has never been found. **Map Code 13 F-6**

Calaveras County — Even before Marshall's discovery of gold at Coloma in 1848, certain tribes of Indians actively engaged in a crude form of mining of the precious metal. After Marshall's find at Sutter's Mill, some Indians became active miners. Around Murphys (State 4), a group of Indians operated a secret gold placer.

The dust and small nuggets taken from this mine were carefully placed in goose and turkey quills and used as a medium of exchange among other tribes. The source of this gold is believed never to have been found after the Indians apparently abandoned it. **Map Code 13 F-6**

Colusa County – On the foggy morning of Feb. 5, 1865, the river steamer Belle left Sacramento for Red Bluff at the head of navigation on the Sacramento River.

Onboard were two express messengers, Robert McCabe, representing Rhodes & Company, and Charles Bowen, acting for Wells Fargo. In the vessel's safe was $100,000, mostly in gold coins. An Adams Express messenger had boasted that he could outpace the steamer ashore, so the messengers aboard the Belle urged the captain to pour on the steam and he obliged. The ship's 40 passengers were having breakfast as the ship was passing the town of Grimes (State 45). Suddenly, an enormous explosion ripped the steamer apart and it went to the bottom immediately with all hands.

So far as it is known, this treasure, probably badly scattered and mud-covered, is still at the bottom of the Sacramento. **Map Code 12 E-4**

<u>Contra Costa County</u> — On Sept. 24, 1856, the California medical pioneer, Dr. John Marsh, was attacked and tortured to death while on the road from his ranch to the town of Martinez.

The only explanation for the murder was that the attacker or attackers were attempting to force Marsh to reveal where his considerable wealth was concealed.

After his murder, no money of consequence was found among his effects. For years, Marsh's son Charles tried to locate his father's wealth on his Rancho Los Medanos, located about 9 miles from Brentwood (State 4). John Marsh's hidden wealth had been valued as high as $435,000, although some insist that it is considerably less.

Inquire in Brentwood for directions to the old Marsh ranch house, known locally as the "Stone House." **Map Code 12 F-4**

<u>Contra Costa County</u> — Mount Diablo, located almost in the center of Contra Costa County, east of Oakland, is a rugged peak of 3,849 feet altitude, rising abruptly from the level plain to dominate the countryside for a great distance in every direction. Since 1851, the positions of all lands in the State of California, excepting the southern part, have been determined from this reference point.

Historians do not agree as to the circumstances in which Mount Diablo received its name, but the Indians had an explanation for it, and it concerned a lost mine.

When the Spanish padres arrived in California, some of the Indians were easily converted to the ways of white men, while others preferred their own ways of life and never accepted Christianity. To those Indians accepting Christianity, the padres often showed a fatherly kindness, and the Indians, in return, frequently brought in little gifts to show their appreciation.

Among the tributes brought to the mission padres of northern California were quantities of gold nuggets. When the priests asked where this gold came from, the Indians pointed to a high mountain, which, according to their legends, had once been an active volcano. The padres determined that this mountain was the one now known as Mount Diablo.

But these padres were more interested in having their neophytes tend the crops and livestock than in collecting gold. Perhaps they also knew how gold could corrupt the minds of men. At any rate, they discouraged the Indians from bringing in more gold, and the obedient Indians made no more trips to Mount Diablo — Devil Mountain. **Map Code 12 G-4**

Contra Costa County – Mount Diablo

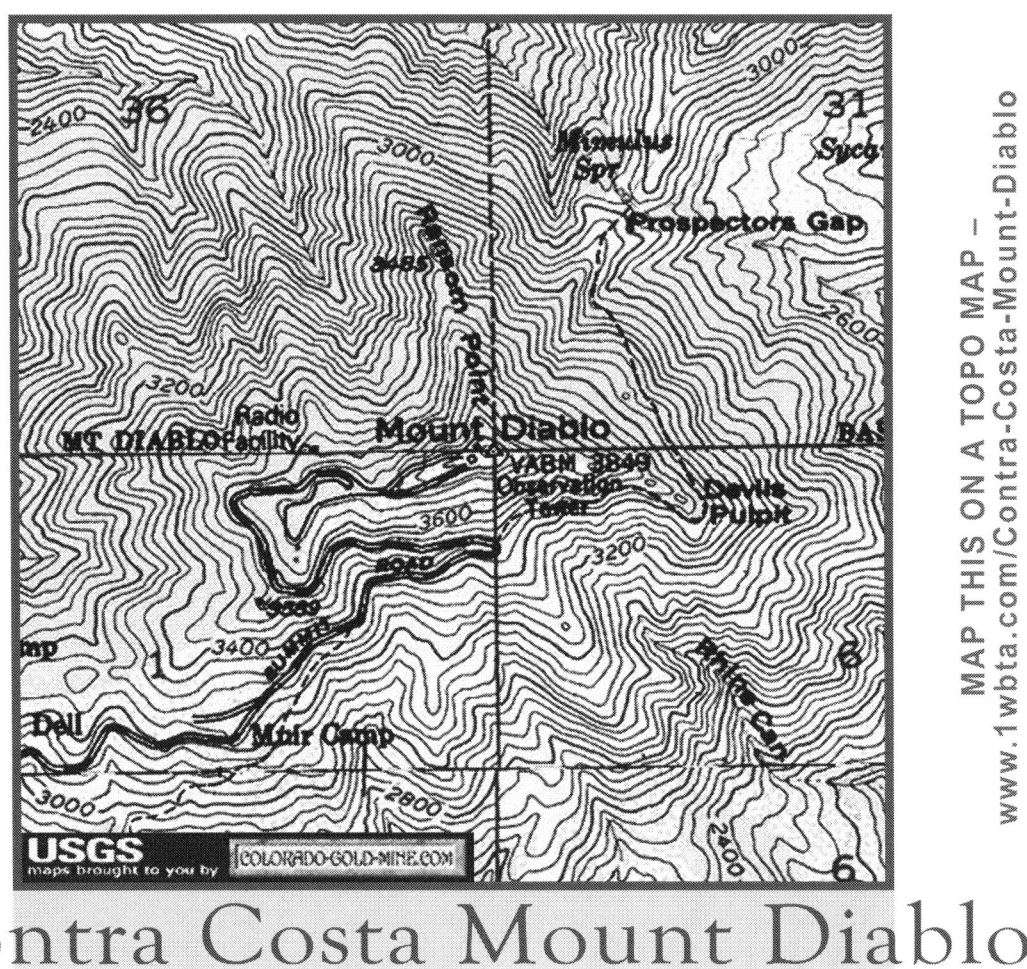

MAP THIS ON A TOPO MAP — www.1wbta.com/Contra-Costa-Mount-Diablo

Counties E – H

ll the children here tonight! Pull up the sleeping bags and keep them warm! In the gentle waves of their dreams, they will still hear our tales. I am reminded of something once told to me... "Free imagination is the inestimable prerogative of youth and it must be cherished and guarded as a treasure." (Felix Bloch) Many young people came to California in the Gold Rush. Many died, but those who survived the hardships were forever changed by being a part of such an incredible, always unfolding story. Yes, your kids are treasures!

❖❖❖

<u>Del Norte County</u> — Perhaps the most publicized sunken treasure on the west coast is that of the Brother Jonathan.

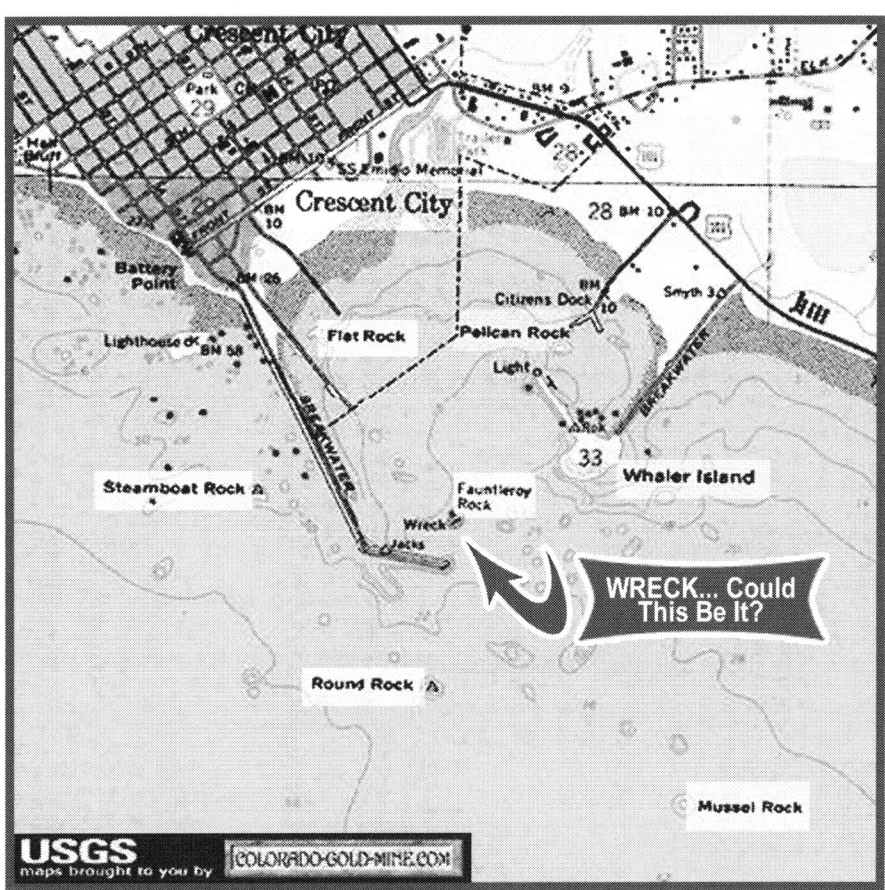

Del Norte Brother Jonathan Shipwreck

MAP THIS ON A TOPO MAP —
www.1wbta.com/Del-Norte-Brother-Jonathan-Shipwreck

A large ship in her day, the side-wheeler Brother Jonathan was loaded with 700 tons of freight (including 300 hogs-heads of whiskey), 192 passengers, 54 crew members, and a reported $800,000 to more than $1,000,000 in gold coin and bullion when she sailed from San Francisco on July 28, 1865, bound for Portland, Oregon, and Victoria, British Columbia. Pushed along by following seas, she covered half the distance in good time.

On July 30, fighting heavy seas and high winds, the captain headed the Brother Jonathan shoreward as she neared Crescent City. Here he was to make a stop for the purpose of placing ashore a chest containing upwards of $200,000 in gold coins for the pay of federal troops in the area. But vicious coastal currents pulled the vessel off course, and a sudden cloudburst darkened the sky. Lurching wildly, the Brother Jonathan scraped her bottom on a submerged rock, opening a gash in her hull below the waterline. Overloaded, the vessel went to the bottom in a reported 12 minutes. All but 19 of the 246 persons aboard perished.

Where does the treasure wreck lie? Almost certainly on one of the rocks of St. George Reef... but, which one? Northwest Seal Rock? Southwest Seal Rock? Whale Rock? East Rock? All of these have been named, but there is no agreement upon which one, and there seems to be no evidence that her hulk has ever been located. One writer of undersea treasure stories has recently written that he is the only person who knows exactly where the wreck of the ill-fated Brother Jonathan lies. **Map Code 12 A-2**

<u>Del Norte County</u> — In the summer of 1850, an unnamed prospector is said to have struck a rich vein of gold in the hills and ravines near the mouth of the Klamath River. He built a small cabin and after each day's work, buried the proceeds of his mine in an underground hiding place in or near his cabin. He is said to have accumulated a considerable sum of gold when Indians suddenly attacked, burned his cabin to the ground, and left the miner for dead.

He regained consciousness, however, and days later made his way into a mining camp where he told his story. Unable to work because of his injuries, friendly miners took up a collection and paid his way back east to regain his strength.

He was never able to travel again, however, and gave relatives directions for locating the remains of the burned cabin and the secret cache. A party of them went west and made a fruitless search. Eventually, they drifted south and founded the town of Crescent City, probably the only town in the United States founded by seekers of a lost mine. The mouth of the Klamath River is at Requa, a small town near Klamath (US 101). **Map Code 12 A-2**

Del Norte County — In the early 1930s, two prospectors worked the area near Willow Creek. They struck a rich ledge of gold and decided that it had enough potential to justify bringing in mining equipment. Marking the scene only in their minds, lest they draw someone else's attention to it, they left for San Francisco. After arrangements were made for equipment to be shipped to them by boat, they returned north, only to discover that they could not find the ledge. After fruitless years of search, they gave up, and the Lost Willow Creek Mine is still lost. **Map Code 12 A-2**

El Dorado County — Garden Valley, a small town on an unnumbered road between Coloma and Georgetown, has both a lost mine and a treasure story. Old miners in the area told of a stranger who came into the camp one night and bedded down beneath an overhanging ledge in the nearby hills. On the following morning, he found the ledge to be rich in gold and immediately took out 37 pounds. On an emergency trip of some nature to Napa Valley, he concealed his find, expecting to return to it, but met with a fatal accident. The ledge is still sought.

The May, 1932 issue of *The Pony Express Courier* (no longer published) reported that a cache of gold was buried near the Garden Valley School during the mining boom in the region. No details were given, but the statement was made that this gold has never been found. **Map Code 12 E-5**

El Dorado County — A half-gallon glass fruit jar filled with $50 gold coins is said to be buried on a farm near State Highway 49 just outside Placerville. It was buried shortly before its unidentified owner was murdered. Many years later, the cache was found by the owner of the land on which it was buried. He reburied the treasure in a different location, and shortly afterwards he, too, was killed by parties seeking the jar of gold coins. It is said that this treasure has never been recovered. **Map Code 12 E-6**

El Dorado County — In its prime, Georgetown (State 193), originally called Growlersburg, was the trading center for 10,000 miners in almost a hundred nearby camps. It is said that one of a group of Oregonians who discovered gold here in 1849 refused to work as a member of the party and prospected on his own, finding a rich ledge which he worked secretly. This mine, lost when its owner died suddenly, is thought to have been located just north of Georgetown. **Map Code 12 E-5**

El Dorado County — Alabama Flat, once a busy mining camp near Placerville (US 50), has now completely disappeared from maps. One of the successful miners here was John Chapman. He frequently boasted that he had a fortune buried near his shack at the edge of the camp. That fortune has been variously estimated by different sources at between $4,000 and $40,000. One morning as Chapman sat in the Alabama Flat House having his breakfast, he was shot and killed by an unknown assailant, presumably over some long-seething feud or fancied grudge. Immediately after Chapman's funeral, the entire camp turned out to search for his buried wealth. So far as it is known, not a cent of it was ever found.
Map Code 12 E-5

El Dorado County — The little town of Lotus, on State 49 between Placerville and Auburn, was once known as Uniontown, and it was in the very heart of the Mother Lode country. One unnamed miner working placers here during the peak of the gold rush took the gold out of a number of rich pockets and had it converted into gold coins.

When he had accumulated $80,000, he told a trusted friend he was going to bury it because there were no banks available, and he wouldn't trust Wells Fargo to transport it to San Francisco for deposit. Shortly afterwards, the miner took sick and died. A search of his effects failed to reveal any gold coins, and it was assumed by many who searched for his treasure at the time, that he had buried it.
Map Code 12 E-5

El Dorado County — Diamond Springs is a hamlet on State 49 about 3 miles southwest of Placerville. In 1864, a miner named Edmund Cooper built a cabin here and lived in it while he worked the diggings. He took out a sizeable fortune before his placer played out. When he left for other diggings, he buried his wealth at the base of an oak tree, not wishing to carry it with him. When he returned two years later, he found that the oak tree had been cut down and that the stump had been covered with the earth removed from a railroad cut. All of his probing failed to reveal the stump, and although he lived to be over a hundred years of age, he never found his buried fortune. **Map Code 12 E-5**

Fresno County — The ledge of clay-like substance was some four feet thick, according to a Hollander named Schippe, and was loaded with gold. It was located high up on the walls of a roaring river which he thought to be the Kings River, but it might have been one of its forks — he wasn't sure. Because of Schippe's reputation as a shiftless no-good, no one believed him until he showed samples of a peculiar clay-like substance filled with chunks of gold. Schippe said he had been following a bear trail through a thicket of undergrowth and live oaks when he stumbled upon the ledge.

Schippe offered to lead a party to the ledge, but before they could leave, he became involved in a quarrel and was killed. It is said that he had previously written to relatives in Holland and gave directions to the clay-like ledge, and that one of them later came to Fresno County and attempted to locate the ledge, which is often called "Schippe's Lost Pipe Clay Mine." **Map Code 14 H-6**

Fresno County — Between Fresno and Centerville (State 180) was a ranch once owned by a man named Byrd, about whom very little is known except that he was supposed to have been very wealthy. When he died suddenly, a friend related that Byrd had confided in him that he had secreted $60,000 on his ranch because he had no faith in banks. The treasure was believed to have been buried at the base of a tree marked by the placing of an oil can between two main branches. In an exchange of ownership, the tree was cut down and the ground was plowed. When a rusty old oil can was turned up by the plow, it touched off a search for the treasure, but it is believed never to have been found. **Map Code 14 H-6**

Fresno County — About 16 miles north of the town of Coalinga (State 198-33) are four massive buttes known as Tres Piedras (Three Rocks), because only three of them are visible from the valley floor. From the summit of these buttes, one can see for miles around in all directions. Located on the old Los Angeles Trail, it was used as a hideout and stronghold by Joaquin Murrieta and his band of outlaws. A great deal of searching has been done for the treasure the Mexican bandit is said to have buried here. **Map Code 14 1-6**

Fresno County — Joaquin Murrieta and Tiburcio Vasquez, two of California's most famous early day bandits, obtained supplies and secured protection from the law at the little Mexican settlement of Las Juntas, located at the confluence of the San Joaquin River and the Fresno Slough. It was a rendezvous for disreputable characters of all types. Vasquez is said to have left buried treasure here, but all accounts are vague as to the type of treasure and approximate site. Vasquez, like Murrieta, reportedly left treasure buried at every one of his many hideouts. **Map Code 14 H-6**

Fresno County — In the area of Horseshoe Bend on the South Fork of the Kings River, near its confluence with the Middle Fork, a man described only as a "Dutchman" once made camp with his dog. When the dog took out after a bear, the Dutchman, fearing for its safety, went after it. Returning along a deer trail, the Dutchman fell and, clawing to regain his feet, uncovered a rich deposit of gold. Gathering samples, he went to Fresno to file a claim. When he found the recorder's office closed for the day, he decided to celebrate his good luck with a little liquor. The next morning his body was found back of a saloon, his samples gone. So far as it is known, the Dutchman's lost mine has never been found. **Map Code 14 H-7**

<u>Humboldt County</u> — Shelter Cove is a hamlet off Point Delgada in the extreme southwestern corner of Humboldt County. Tradition says that a sailing ship carrying a large amount of gold to the mint in San Francisco sailed into Shelter Cove to ride out a furious storm, but ran aground and washed up on the beach. Indians and renegade whites are said to have seized the gold and to have carried it up the cliffs to a small flat where it was buried. As a marker, they placed the ship's bell in a nearby tree.

When they returned to the wrecked vessel, alerted troops had arrived and a fight ensued in which all the Indians and whites, except a few women and children, were killed. Many years later, a party of deer hunters found the ship's bell and carried it away, not knowing that it marked the treasure site. It was some time before they heard the story of the wrecked treasure ship and the bell's relation to it. Although a search was made for the tree in which the bell was found, it could not be located. Presumably, the treasure is still there.
Map Code 12 C-2

Counties I – L

One can't help but wonder how many of the Forty-Niners actually felt after arriving to such chaos! Many a tale concerns the destiny of these travelers. "They were seeking out the treasure of their destiny, without actually wanting to live out their destiny." (Paulo Coelho). All you 'round this fire with such rich stories... What is your destiny?

<u>Imperial County</u> — Kane Springs, on San Felipe Creek to the southwest of the southern tip of the Salton Sea, is the oldest known waterhole on the Colorado Desert.

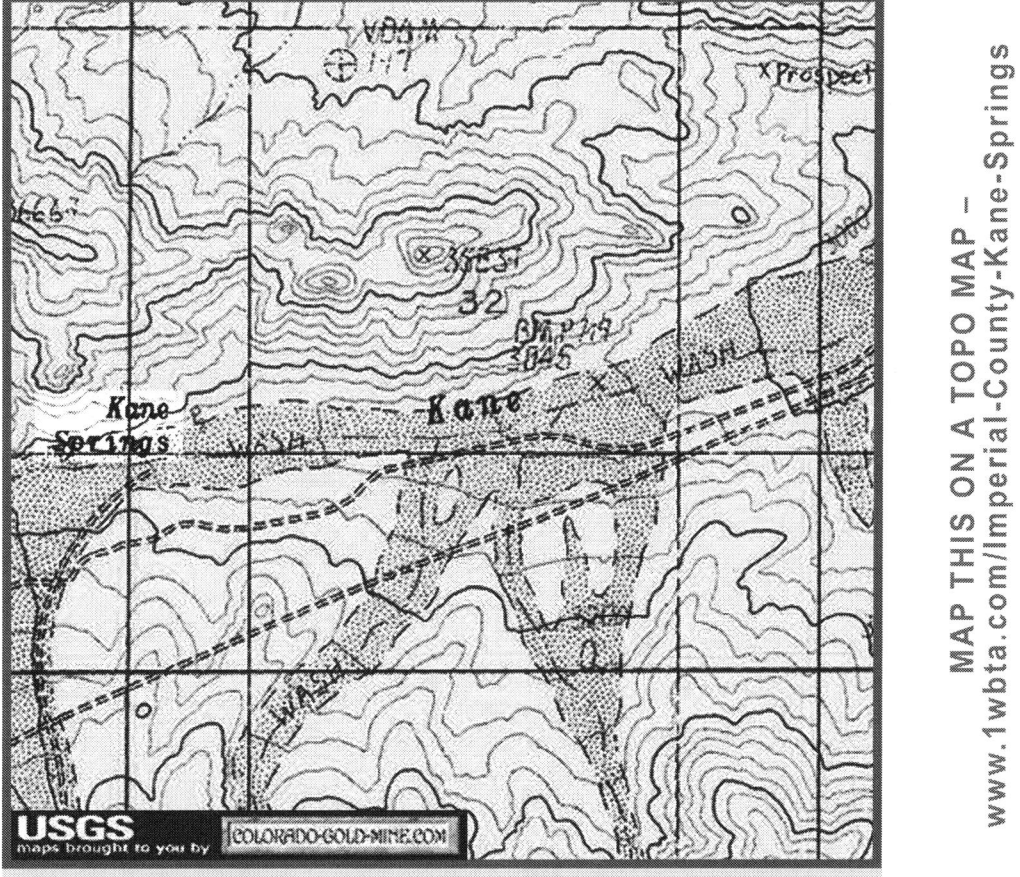

MAP THIS ON A TOPO MAP (See more on Kane Springs on <u>page 228</u>) — www.1wbta.com/Imperial-County-Kane-Springs

It's been a camping place for untold hundreds of years. The Indians of this area have many legends of great ships that came here when the region was the northernmost arm of the prehistoric Gulf of California. The most persistent story is of a Spanish galleon that sailed into the area carrying a fabulous cargo of gold. Unable to navigate out of the region, the vessel and its precious cargo was abandoned.

As the sea dried up over the years, the hulk gradually sank beneath shifting sands. It is claimed that the timbers of this ship have been seen when winds whip away the sands, only to be covered up again. It is even said by some that one man recovered a chest from the old timbers, but others question this.

Whether or not there is the hulk of a Spanish treasure galleon beneath the desert sands of Kane Springs seems to be anybody's guess, but the origin of and survival of the story is one of the greatest mysteries of the Colorado Desert. **Map Code 15 M-11**

<u>Imperial County</u> — Traventine Rock is located just to the west of State 86, and just south of the Riverside-Imperial county line. Although it is on private property, it is open to the public and is a favorite camping spot for dune buggy fans. Vandals and litterbugs have desecrated the area, and if this continues, it will soon be closed to the public.

Traventine Rock may be the site of a fantastic treasure. The story goes like this. In 1750, a band of French and Spanish renegades pushed through this way, loaded with loot stolen from churches in Mexico. Aware that they were being followed by a party of Indians, they sought a place to conceal their treasure before the anticipated attack by the approaching redmen. In the waning hours of the day, they found a cave and in it stored their vast plunder. The delay cost them their lives.

The Indians attacked before a defensive position could be prepared and the Spanish and French were wiped out. In recent years, there was discovered on Traventine Rock, the crudely carved figures of a Papal Cross and the Cross of Lorraine, small but very evident. The late U. S. District Judge Clarence A. Routhe believed this indicated that the Spanish-French treasure was hidden somewhere near there, most likely in a cave that had been carefully sealed up. He pointed out that the longstanding popularity of Traventine Rock as a camping place and landmark, would have more than likely brought the Spanish-French party along this route. Judge Routhe died before he could launch a full scale search for the Traventine Rock Treasure. **Map Code 15 M-11**

<u>Imperial County</u> — San Felipe Creek and Carrizo Wash meet near a desert waterhole called Harper's Well, in the wide angle formed by the junction of State

78 and State 86. In this general area is said to be buried 10 or more cartloads of Spanish gold and jewels. Besieged by Indians in the early morning, a party of Spaniards held off the attackers until the treasure could be unloaded and buried beneath the sand. Finally, the members of the caravan were overcome by the greater number of Indians and all were killed on the spot, or as they attempted to flee. Note the similarity between this story and the one immediately above. Except for differences in minor details, this same story appears at various locations throughout the Southwest, a dozen or more times.
Map Code 15 M-11

<u>Imperial County</u> — In June, 1917, a strange little man half-walked and half-stumbled into the Southern Pacific Railroad station at Ogilby. He was almost crazed with thirst and babbled incoherently, but he clung tenaciously to a bag containing 17 pounds of gold nuggets. The telegrapher took him in and cared for him. When he recovered, he told that he had been leading a pack mule and was headed for the Cargo Muchacho Mountains to prospect.

While making his way through the Algodone Dunes, he had been overtaken by a choking sandstorm. His burro wandered away, taking his supply of food and water. When the storm let up, he headed for the railroad tracks, knowing this would lead him to help. While picking his way through a pass between two high dunes, he had found a place where the sand was completely swept away, revealing the hardpan bed which was covered with gold nuggets. Taking what he could carry, he struggled into Ogilby.

When the stranger was well, he took the train into Los Angeles and sold his gold. Here he became incurably ill. Before he died, he is said to have described the place in detail to his doctor, and further supplied him with a rough map of the area. The owner of the map searched for the gold in 1918, but could find no landmarks to fit the map. The Algodone Dunes are traveled today by dune buggies, but the hills of today are the valleys of tomorrow, constantly shifted by strong winds. They are located to the north of Interstate 8 at Grays Well.
Map Code 15 N-12

<u>Imperial County</u> — Someplace in the Chocolate Mountains, south of the old ghost town of Picacho and east of Picacho Peak, is a ledge of yellowish quartz rich in gold. It was discovered in 1910 or 1911 by an unnamed Dutchman who gave Ed Rochester 50 pounds of the ore for rowing him across the Colorado River. He said that he wanted to get to Quartzsite in order to outfit himself for working the rich

strike, the approximate location of which he gave Rochester. A reputable and well-known prospector, Rochester later determined that the Dutchman arrived in Quartzsite, purchased provisions and an outfit, and left.

He was never seen again and what happened to him is as much a mystery as the location of the yellowish ledge of quartz. Ed Rochester was convinced of the truth of the Dutchman's story and made a long search for the ledge, but failed to find it.
Map Code 15 M-13

Imperial County — Just to the south of the little town of Mt. Signal (State 98), and across the international boundary in Mexico, is Signal Mountain, a prominent landmark jutting up from the flat desert floor. Its name comes from the fact that Indians used the peak as a place to light their signal fires. According to an old Mexican legend, a wealthy Spaniard and his party of servants, fleeing a political upheaval in Mexico about 1810, reached Signal Mountain with 60 horses loaded with treasure and belongings, when they noted that they were being followed by a large party of Indians.

The Spaniard's party hurried their animals north, crossed the border, and selected a place to fight off the expected attack. Finally surrounded in a small arroyo, the Spaniard ordered the treasure unpacked and buried, after which he deliberately killed six of his servants and dumped their bodies on the treasure, believing the superstitious Indians would not molest the treasure, guarded as it was by six dead men.

The massacre was complete, and the bodies of the Spaniard and his party were left to bleach in the desert. Many years later, an early Spanish breastplate was found in the vicinity, and this incident is employed to support the fact of the story. However, many Spaniards passed this way and the breastplate was never proved to be the property of the wealthy Spaniard who buried treasure here.
Map Code 15 N-11

Imperial County — The Lost Dutchman Mine in Arizona is famous as the most-sought-after lost mine in the Southwest, but it is by no means the only mine found and lost by a Dutchman. One day when Charles Knowles was camped in Carrizo Wash in the southwestern part Imperial County, a half-crazed German wandered into his camp carrying four black rocks which Knowles, an experienced prospector, immediately recognized as being rich in gold. The "Dutchman" could not recall where he had picked them up, but thought it was not far from Knowles' camp. Knowles spent years in searching for the source of the black rock.
Map Code 15 N-11

Imperial County — The Cargo Muchacho Mountains consist of a small group of rugged peaks in the extreme southeastern corner of Imperial County. Rich gold mines and placers have been worked in this area since the memory of man. In the region between Imperial Dam and Pebble Mountain, James Sullivan, a bouncer for the Stingaree Saloon in Tumco (now a ghost town), had a fancy vest which an Indian took a liking to, and asked for it as a gift. Sullivan told the old Indian to bring him some gold and he could have the vest. This, the Indian refused to do, but said that he would take Sullivan to where there was plenty of gold.

They finally arrived at what is believed to have been the pile of boulders known as Pebble Mountain, and there was the gold — plenty of gold. Suffering from the heat and thirst, Sullivan became ill and barely made it back to Tumco, where he soon died. The old Indian, fearful that the tribe would punish him for showing the gold, vanished… never to be seen again. Experienced prospectors later searched for the Lost Sullivan Mine, but so far as it is known, it has never been found. **Map Code 15 N-13**

Imperial County — Around 1928, an aged prospector, while camping in Rock Springs Canyon some 30 miles west of Brawley (State 86), found placer gold so rich that he was able to deposit $90,000 in a San Diego bank during a period of three months. In leaving the area of his mine one day with his two burros, the one he was riding slipped and fell, breaking the prospector's hip. He finally managed to mount the surviving burro and made his way to Kane Springs, where he was picked up and taken to Los Angeles and hospitalized.

Realizing he was going to die, the prospector told a friend of his mine and drew a rough map. This map was passed from hand to hand, but none of its owners was able to follow its directions. Presumably, the old prospector's rich placer is still there — and someone has a crude map that won't work. **Map Code 15 N-11**

Imperial County — The Santa Rosa Mountains stretch in a southeast to northwest direction to the west of the upper half of the Salton Sea. The area has been the scene of much prospecting and is the locale of several lost mine stories. Fig Tree John, an old Indian well-known around Palm Springs, knew many tales of gold found by his people, and is the subject of his own lost mine story (see Riverside County).

He once told that the squaws of his tribe picked up large gold nuggets from a placer revealed after a desert cloudburst. Fig Tree John said this placer was located on a hill above Grave Wash, which runs off US 99 in the extreme northwestern corner of Imperial County. Most searchers of this well authenticated placer conclude that it has been covered by nature. **Map Code 15 M-11**

<u>Imperial County</u> — In 1914, a man named Ebner and an unnamed companion were crossing the desert from Picacho, driving pack burros. It was winter and snow was falling. Somewhere before they dropped down into Mammoth Wash, between Niland and Glamis, which would lead them to the Salton Sea, they came to a place which was littered with heavy metal. With the weather worsening, they gathered a few samples and pushed on. The metal proved to be native copper.

Ebner returned to the site in 1920 and determined that several truckloads of the copper could be picked up from the surface deposits alone. Again he left without making any effort to recover the copper. But he returned in 1933, down on his luck after working several years as a lumberjack in the northwest. This time he was determined to raise a stake and get the surface copper ore out.

He met Seward White and a man named Pierce who were prospecting in the Chocolate Mountains. Both men were interested in Ebner's copper find, and the three started out to further survey the site. After several days of fruitless searching for the copper deposit, Ebner confessed he was confused because he had never entered the area from this direction. Eventually they gave up, and White and Pierce never saw Ebner again. Both men were convinced that Ebner had really found a rich deposit of copper ore near the lower end and east of the Salton Sea. **Map Code 15 M-12**

<u>Imperial County</u> — Late in 1780, the Spanish established two mission-pueblos on the California side of the Colorado River above Yuma and a short distance below what is now known as Laguna Dam. These were the missions San Pedro y San Pablo de Bicuner and Purisima Concepcion. Every physical evidence of these missions have disappeared, but the story of their buried gold — probably the earliest lost treasure in California history — is still with us.

The upper mission, San Pedro y San Pablo de Bicuner, was located on one of the richest gold placers in the Southwest — the Potholes Placers — and directly across the river in Arizona was another, the Laguna Placers. From all evidence, it appears that the mission padres used the Yuma Indians (they called themselves Quechans) to gather this gold. Apparently this was forced labor, for the Indians rose in revolt, pillaged and burned the pueblos, and massacred most of the padres and soldiers.

Years later, an old Indian told how his ancestors had worked the gold for the padres, and how the gold became a curse to them. This was why they revolted, the Indian related, and after killing or driving away the padres and soldiers, they gathered up the mission's accumulation of gold and buried it in the pueblo before it was burned.

The earliest recorded search for the gold of Bicuner was made in 1936 by Thomas Russell and Peter Weldon, apparently under the auspices of the alcalde of San Diego and certain Mexican officials. At any rate, when the party returned empty-handed, Russell and Weldon were jailed on the charge that they had found something, but were holding out.

Hundreds have searched for the Bicuner gold, and these searches have contributed to the complete obliteration of the old mission sites. Today they are extremely difficult to locate, and perhaps it would be a waste of time to search for them. Another old Quechan Indian once said that all the accumulated gold was gathered up and thrown into the Colorado River. **Map Code 15 M-13**

Imperial County — In the early 1860s, a special stage was scheduled to carry a shipment of gold coins from El Paso, Texas, to San Diego. It was to carry no passengers — just the driver and the most experienced guard available. The stage eventually reached Yuma where it was to remain for a day. While there, the guard took ill and another could not be secured. Under orders to get the coins through, the driver continued on alone.

Just east of the old Carrizo Stage Station, almost on the Imperial-San Diego county line, a lone bandit held up the stage and made away with the shipment of coins after wounding the driver.

Before the driver died of his wounds, he fired at the fleeing bandit, apparently hitting him, for his body was found two days later, a short distance from the scene of the holdup.

What happened to the gold coins? Some contend that the bandit would have buried or hidden the treasure so that he could recover it in the event he survived his wound. Others are just as certain that the bandit would have been more concerned with his wound than with concealing his loot, that he abandoned it when hit, and that it was shortly afterwards found by a traveler. **Map Code 15 N-11**

Imperial County — In 1920, and for several years thereafter, L. R. Harpending, a Long Beach resident with considerable mining experience, searched for a lost ledge of silver-bearing ore in the western slopes of the Chocolate Mountains, about 10 miles northeast of Glamis, a station on the Southern Pacific Railroad. Harpending had once found the ledge, but was called to a job in Plumas County, where he remained for three years. He finally concluded that a desert cloudburst had washed down tons of debris and sand which had covered the ledge. **Map Code 15 M-12**

Imperial County — Somewhere in the area of Picacho Peak, an unnamed man, traveling from Yuma to Dos Palmas (Riverside County), became ill and stopped for a rest. He was about to resume his journey when he noticed the outcropping of a ledge nearby and saw the glitter of gold in the rock. At the base of the ledge was the accumulation of placer gold that had washed out of it. Removing his vest, he folded it and placed it on the ledge, and then, from his pack, secured a spare muleshoe, which he placed on the vest, together with some loose rocks. Carefully noting the details of the surrounding country, he rode on, intending to return later.

The man's illness persisted, however, and he was eventually admitted to the Sawtelle Veterans Hospital in Los Angeles. Before his death, he gave a crude map of the area to a distant relative, W. H. Smith. Smith searched for the ledge for several years, but without success. **Map Code 15 M-12**

Imperial County — An unnamed prospector worked a rich ledge of gold ore someplace in the northern reaches of the Carrizo Badlands, and close to the Imperial-San Diego county line. The mine is said to have been worked for about eight years before the old miner became very ill. Before he died, he called in a friend and gave him directions for reaching the secret mine, but before the friend could locate it, he dropped dead of a heart attack. Some searches for this mine have been conducted in the area south of the old Carrizo Stage Station on Carrizo Creek. **Map Code 15 N-11**

Imperial County — While three prospectors were repairing their boat along the Colorado River south of Blythe, one of the men prospected through the Palo Verde Mountains and into the Black Hills, where he is said to have discovered a rich deposit of gold in one of the canyons. Taking samples of ore with him, he returned to the boat. Unable to persuade his two partners to return to the Black Hills with him, the three men moved on and none of them ever worked the find.

Years later, an unnamed Frenchman found the same deposit and worked it. When he had accumulated a large amount of ore, he packed it out by mules to the Colorado River, where it was poled to the Gulf of California and transshipped to San Francisco and thence to France. Before sailing with his ore to France, the miner gave directions for reaching his mine to a friend, explaining that the shaft was covered with planks, one of which had a metal ring attached to it.

Because the ring was believed to have been a bull ring — to go through the nose of a bull — this mine became known as the Lost Frenchman Bull Ring Mine. The area in which it is supposedly located is one of the most arid and barren in southern California, and only those with experience in the ways of the desert should enter it. **Map Code 15 M-12**

Imperial County — According to an old Quechan (Yuma) Indian, a mule load of gold was being transported from the placers worked by the Indians at the Mission San Pedro y San Pablo de Bicuner. In a narrow defile near the present Indian shrine on E-Vee-Taw-Ash, the Spanish train was ambushed by revolting Indians. After the massacre of the entire party of Spaniards, the gold was unloaded and dumped into a cave near the entrance to which was a badger hole. It is said that this gold has never been recovered. The shrine of E-Vee-Taw-Ash may be reached by an unnumbered road running north out of Winter-Haven (US 80). **Map Code 15 M-13**

Imperial County — After six months of successful prospecting in the California gold fields, an eastbound party of prospectors traveling in a single wagon was attacked by Indians on the United States side of the border just north of Signal Mountain, Mexico. Anticipating the attack when they saw smoke signals rising on Signal Mountain, the miners hurriedly buried their gold and prepared to defend themselves. But the number of Cocopahs swarming upon them was too great and they were massacred to a man. It is said that the Indians recovered the gold and reburied it a short distance away. The fact that two other very similar incidents took place in this same area leads one to believe that one or more of the stories here do not hold up. **Map Code 15 N-11**

Imperial County — One day, a young Indian squaw staggered into a construction camp on the Southern Pacific Railroad at Salton, on the east shore of the Salton Sea. She said that she was a member of the San Luis Rey tribe from eastern San Diego County, and that she and her man, while traveling afoot to a Cocopah village north of Yuma, had climbed a small hill to get a better view of the country for directions. Here, her man had taken a drink of bad water, became very ill and died. Completely lost, she had wandered until she came to the railroad, and then followed it into Salton.

After she had sufficiently recovered, the squaw displayed a sack of gold ore which she said she and her man had picked up at the base of the "bad water hill." She could give no other description of the area, nor any directions to it. It has been said that the gold ore brought to Salton by the Indian girl was the same as that found by Pegleg Smith, but this is of little consequence when one doesn't even know what direction to take in searching for the Lost Bad Water Mine.
Map Code 15 M-11

<u>Imperial County</u> — On a hot day in 1906, an Indian girl stumbled into the Southern Pacific Railroad station of Glamis. She was lugging a heavy pack and was obviously suffering from thirst. Helped to the water bucket, she drank heavily, and soon became violently ill and died. The contents of her pack proved to be nothing more than a collection of black rocks, which were dumped aside. About a month later, a surveyor happened to pick up one of the rocks, broke it open out of curiosity, and found it rich in gold. An immediate search was made for the black butte from which the ore was presumed to have come. The search for the Lost Black Butte Mine has gone on intermittently for years, but without success. It is said to be located in the Chocolate Mountains to the northwest of Glamis (State 78).
Map Code 15 M-12

<u>Inyo County</u> — The story of the Lost Chicken Bones Mine is a hard one to believe, but it is told and retold and many people do believe it. In the early 1900s, a prospector named Charles Wilson trudged into Johannesburg (US 395) leading six burros loaded with 10 or 12 sacks of ore samples. He took the samples to the Red Dog Custom Mill to be assayed.

With the remark to the assayer that he would give him a half interest in his claim if the ore proved promising, he said he was leaving for Los Angeles and would be back in a week or two. Knowing that this was a familiar dodge to get a free assay, the assayer threw the ore aside.

Weeks later, the assayer's wife cleaned out her husband's office and threw a piece of the ore into the rubbish heap where she had previously tossed some chicken bones. Sometime later, the assayer happened to notice that the chicken bones were covered with globules of pure gold.

He concluded that the bones had acted as a reagent in separating the gold from the ore when the refuse heap was set afire.

Keeping the news to himself, he rushed off to Los Angeles to locate the prospector. He arrived too late. The man had been killed by a streetcar. After a six-month search for the mine, the assayer gave up and revealed the story. He said the prospector had told him that the ore was taken from a ledge in the vicinity of Surprise Canyon, in the Panamint Mountains northeast of the old mining camp of Ballarat. So far as it is known, the Lost Chicken Bones Mine is still lost. **Map Code 15 I-9**

Inyo County — In September, 1849, a train of six or seven wagons of Mormons bound for the Mormon colony in San Bernardino made camp at a point about 7 miles northwest of what is now known as Death Valley Junction. In the party was a jeweler from Missouri, and he was carrying $6,000 and his eastern stock of jewelry and watches.

During the night, the party was attacked by Indians. Although the Indians were driven off, the emigrants lost their horses and the jeweler was killed.

The survivors dug two holes, one in which they buried the jeweler, and the other in which they placed his cash and jewels. Covering these, they wheeled the wagon they had to abandon over the jeweler's grave and set them afire. No other effort was made to mark the spot.

This place came to be known as Burnt Wagons, and as such, once appeared on some maps, but has completely disappeared in recent years. Inquiry in Death Valley Junction (State 190-127) might reveal the approximate site of old Burnt Wagons, and the treasure, if not already found, is almost certainly there. **Map Code 15 I-10**

Inyo County — Walter Scott ("Death Valley Scotty") died in his famed castle in January, 1954. Albert M. Johnson, Scott's partner and companion at the castle, had died previously in 1949, leaving the castle to the Gospel Foundation of California, the pet project of his wife.

Upon Johnson's death, Scott became a ward of the foundation with the right to live in the castle the remainder of his life.

Shortly after Johnson's death, Scotty announced that he and Johnson had weighed out 14,000 ounces of gold one night and divided it down the middle, and that Johnson had buried his share someplace near or on the grounds of the castle. At the same time, Scott announced that he (Scott) had $600,000 worth of pure gold hidden on the Death Valley Ranch, plus $10,000 in gold certificates.

When Internal Revenue agents asked Scott to pay the tax on this fortune, he had to confess that it was all a fib — that he didn't have anything. It had all but been forgotten that a federal judge had ruled officially in 1941 that Death Valley Scotty's famed gold mine was a myth. **Map Code 15 H-10**

<u>Inyo County</u> — Thomas Shannon was one of the original members of a party of mostly unmarried men who called themselves the Jayhawkers. They came west from Illinois in 1849 and dropped down into the then little-known and as yet unnamed Death Valley. Many of the young men in the Jayhawker party were from moderately well-to-do families, and Shannon was one of them. According to his own statement, he carried $6,000 in gold coins. This was no burden as long as there were wagons in which to carry it.

However, someplace on the floor of Death Valley, on or near the vicinity of Sage Flats, and at an unidentified place the Jayhawkers called Snow Camp, they found it necessary to abandon their wagons and strike out afoot in a desperate effort to save their lives. Shannon offered half his gold to any man who would carry it out. He had no takers, so it was buried with the expectation that he would recover it sometime later.

James B. Rood, a member of the ill-fated party, later said that they had pooled all their gold and buried it, but did not estimate its wealth. Some twenty years later, Rood and a party of men searched for the gold in a canyon on Tucki Mountain, near what he believed to be the site of Snow Camp. When they failed to find the gold, Rood concluded that it had been washed away by a cloudburst. Shannon, who went to the gold fields around Marysville, California, and mined six years with considerable success, never tried to recover his $6,000 in gold coins.

This is one of the best-documented of treasure stories, but the site of Snow Camp has never been definitely established, and it is within the boundary of Death Valley National Monument. **Map Code 15 H-9**

<u>Inyo County</u> — For almost a hundred years, western prospectors have been fascinated and baffled with the story of the Lost Breyfogle Mine. Generations of men have devoted their lives — and some have sacrificed them — in the search for this

elusive ledge of reddish ore richly laced with gold. Whether his first name was Jacob, James, Charles, or Herman — there certainly was a man named Breyfogle, and it is a fact that he emerged from the searing desert half crazed, clutching samples of fabulously rich gold-bearing ore.

Seldom ever is the claim made that Breyfogle never existed, or that his find was a hoax. Even the contemporary group of mining men who came to believe that Breyfogle's rich ledge existed only in his imagination, could not account for the gold-bearing quartz that he brought out of the desert. Where, and under what circumstances Breyfogle acquired this ore, is explained in a hundred different ways, but it must be concluded from all the available evidence that Breyfogle did find a rich ledge of gold ore somewhere in the region of northern Death Valley or in southwestern Nevada.

Even the Indians had their superstitions concerning this lost mine, and supposedly they knew its location as a place haunted by evil spirits, which further nourished the theory that it was located near a poison spring. There are many claims that the Breyfogle gold has been found, and a new claim is made almost every year. Whether this is true is anybody's guess, but it is true that rich finds have been made in searching for the Lost Breyfogle.

Here is the Breyfogle story reduced to its essentials, and based largely on the earliest writings on the subject. Early in 1862, silver was discovered in the vicinity of Austin, Nevada.

On hearing this news, three prospectors — McLeod, O'Bannon, and Breyfogle — left Los Angeles on foot for the new strike. They chose the shortest and most dangerous route — across the Mojave Desert, skirting the southern slopes of the Argus Mountains, across Panamint Valley, and into the Panamint Mountains.

One afternoon they made camp near a water-hole on the eastern slope of the Panamint Range, bounding Death Valley on the west. During the night, McLeod and O'Bannon were slain by Indians as they slept. Breyfogle, who was sleeping some distance from his companions, was awakened by their screams and fled barefooted down the slope. At dawn he found himself in Death Valley.

Although Breyfogle's later account of his actions were always confused, it appears that he, in some manner, managed to cross Death Valley and begin the ascent of the Funeral Range, which bounds Death Valley on the east. Part way up the mountain, he saw to the southward — and perhaps three miles distant — a green spot which he took to be the growth around a spring.

Half crazed with thirst, he started toward it, but about midway he came across a soft, gray float rock with gold showing through it, and seconds later he came upon a showing of reddish feldspar — the mother vein from which the gray rock had washed away in ages past. He filled his bandana with samples of the reddish ore; then pushed on to the green spot, which proved to be only a mesquite tree. Eating too freely of its beans, Breyfogle suffered a collapse and temporary loss of mind.

When Breyfogle recovered his senses, he was at Baxter Springs, Nevada, 250 miles to the north, having in his crazed condition crossed the Funeral Range and the Amargosa Desert. There he rested for a time, and then, after another long tramp, finally reached Austin, wasted in flesh, but still carrying with him his precious samples of ore.

His story found ready believers and the following winter, Breyfogle and a party of twenty men set out to relocate the deposit he had found. He was able to lead them to the mesquite tree where he had gorged on beans, but the lode of reddish feldspar eluded them. In the end, angry and disgusted, the party returned to Austin and a little later, Breyfogle disappeared from view. George Hearst, who made a great fortune in mining and was not taken in by wild schemes, kept prospectors in the field for a long period, searching for the Breyfogle lode.

Out of all that has been written about the Lost Breyfogle Mine, taking into consideration the many conflicting and confusing versions, these simple facts are known — a man named Breyfogle did find a rich ledge of gold-bearing ore someplace in the Funeral Range. He and many others spent months and years in searching for this vein, and their searches generally centered in the Funeral Range. There is no conclusive proof that the Breyfogle ledge has ever been found.
Map Code 15 H-10

<u>Inyo County</u> — The story is told of a man suffering from tuberculosis who came to the old mining camp of Ballarat and hired an Indian named Joe Button to take him to the driest spot he knew. The old Indian took the ailing man to a place in the Cottonwood Range on the west side of Death Valley and left him. After several weeks, the stranger showed up in San Bernardino for supplies. He had with him several sacks of rich gold ore. While in San Bernardino, the man worsened and

died. Relatives sold his gold ore for $7,200, but failed to locate its source. The well-known desert prospector, Shorty Harris, hired Joe Button to take him to the spot where he had left the tubercular, and while the remains of his camp were found, it was decided that a cloudburst had covered his placer. Harris finally gave up his search for the tubercular's lost mine, which was centered in Marble Canyon. **Map Code 15 I-9**

<u>Inyo County</u> — Jack Stewart, a veteran prospector who knew every inch of the Death Valley country, and had made several rich strikes, told a friend shortly before he died in 1947, of a rich strike he had made while traveling from Stovepipe Wells to Olancha (US 395) for supplies. He was moving through the Panamints, probably in the area of Calico Mountain, when he was caught in a sudden near cloudburst.

On the following morning, when the storm passed over, he observed a place where rushing waters had cut a channel through an old slide. Pieces of quartz at the bottom of the wash were shot through with gold. He reasoned that the landslide had carried the quartz into the wash, and that the ledge from which it came was up above. With his supplies running very low, he picked up what ore he could carry and continued on to Olancha, intending to return at some later date.

As happened to so many prospectors, however, he heard of other rich strikes and did not attempt to relocate the cloudburst ledge for several years. When he did, he failed to find it, and with his eyesight failing, he gave up. **Map Code 15 I-9**

<u>Inyo County</u> — It is generally accepted that Death Valley Scotty's claim to having a secret gold mine in Death Valley was more of a hoax than a fact.

But if Scotty had been less the prankster and a more serious prospector, he might have found a real lost mine close to his famed castle in the extreme northeastern portion of Death Valley.

When Crisanto Santavinas, a Peruvian living in the rich silver camp of Cerro Gordo, was a boy of 19, he accompanied Juan Reynas, a Mexican who built furnaces for the smelting of gold and silver ore, on a trip from Cerro Gordo to Lida, Nevada.

They crossed the Saline Valley and started to climb the Ubehebe Range, a northern extension of the Panamints. The Indian guide with them took the two into Colorado Canyon, the only one in the area that runs along the top of the mountain. Here the guide said they would find water by digging. While the Indian was digging for water, Juan Reynas took his gold pan to do a little prospecting. Presently, he returned and displayed a pan of sand heavily flecked with gold.

Turning to young Cris Santavinas, the Mexican said, "Cris, you come back here and get this gold. Up there in the wall of the canyon is a ledge of gold. That is where this has washed from. Each year the rains wash down a little more black sand and a little more gold. You come back and get it." This was in Colorado Canyon, and from its mouth one can see Scotty's Castle. When Cris returned to Cerro Gordo, he told his father of the Mexican's find and begged to be allowed to go back and locate the ledge of gold, but his father told him that he was too young, and that it was too dangerous to go into the canyon of the bad Indian. He was referring to Colorado, an Indian who had killed several men who had entered the canyon named after him. Although Cris lived to be more than 100 years old, he never returned to the canyon, nor did he tell this story until the later years of his life.
Map Code 15 H-9

Inyo County — Frank "Shorty" Harris, who has been mentioned previously, was a well-known character around several of the southern California mining camps, particularly in the Death Valley and Mojave areas. He made several rich strikes, the proceeds of which were generally spent on financing prolonged drinking sprees with friends. It was always Shorty's belief that when he was broke, he could go out and pick up another stake.

One day, Shorty made a rich find while camping in one of the tortuous canyons between the old mining camp of Skidoo and the floor of Death Valley. He said it was the richest gold ore he had ever seen. To mark the place, he stuck a pick in the ledge and traveled on to Skidoo to obtain supplies, and of course to wet his whistle in celebration of his good luck. By the time Shorty had sobered up a few days later, he had completely forgotten which canyon he had taken. Shorty Harris was known for the reliability of his word, and no one ever questioned this find, but of all those who tried, not one ever found the pick that marked the Lost Shorty Harris Mine. **Map Code 15 I-9**

- ## THE LOST GOLDEN EAGLE MINE

Inyo County — In 1902, an old prospector named "Alkali" Jones set out from Skidoo, in Death Valley, for Searchlight, Nevada. During the trip, he became lost in a furious sandstorm, and after the storm subsided, climbed a small eminence to secure his bearings. Here he discovered a vein of rotting quartz heavily sprinkled with native gold. Staking out a claim which he called the Golden Eagle, because one flew over at the time, he took several samples and proceeded.

An Old Prospector's Bones Near Smith Mountain

Inyo County Lost Golden Eagle Mine

MAP THIS ON A TOPO MAP —
www.1wbta.com/Inyo-County-Lost-Golden-Eagle-Mine

In Searchlight, he outfitted for the return trip, planning to stop and work his new-found claim. He was never heard of again.

Several years later, the remains of his camp was found by an Indian, and a skeleton nearby was identified as that of the old prospector. There was no indication as to how he had met death.

Detailing The "Alkali" Jones Story

Special note: The use of online USGS map sites provides the exciting ability to detail out your search. This is a close-up map of the Smith Mountain area.

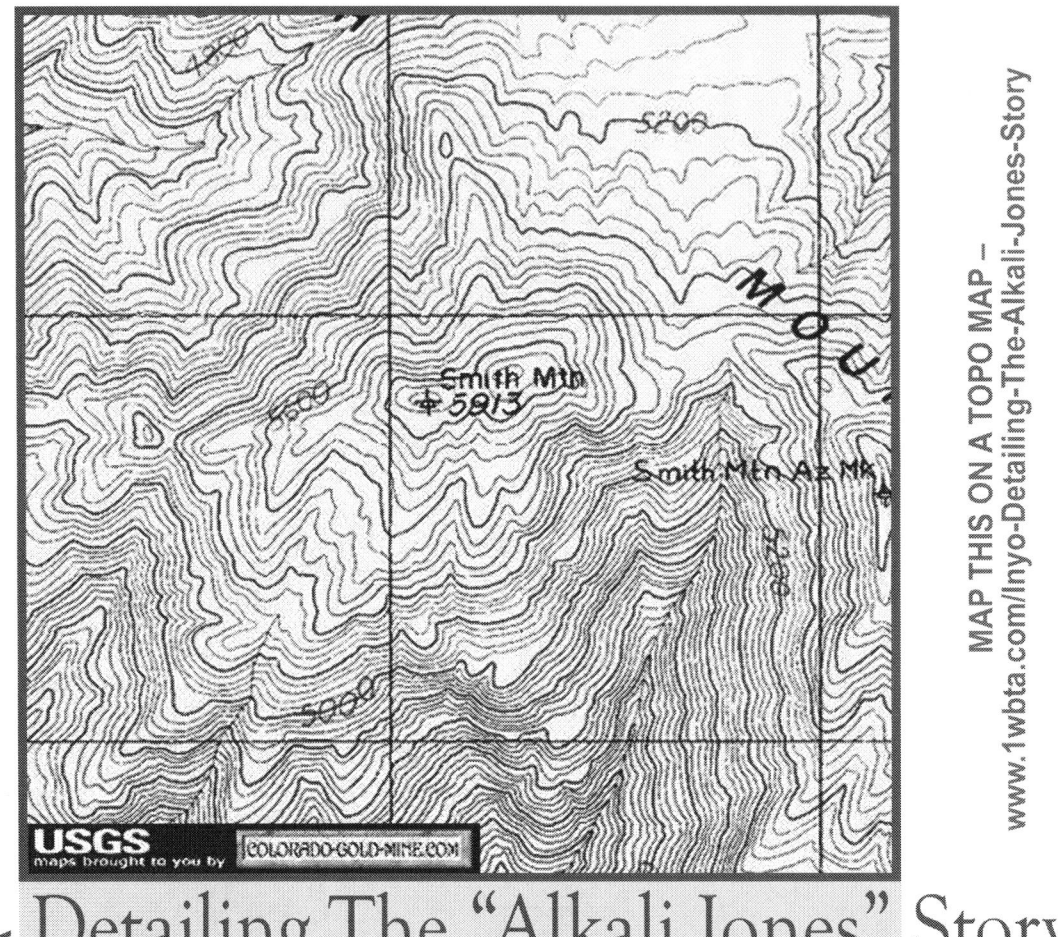

MAP THIS ON A TOPO MAP —
www.1wbta.com/Inyo-Detailing-The-Alkali-Jones-Story

Searches for the Lost Golden Eagle Mine are generally conducted in the area of Smith Mountain, in the lower section of the Black Mountains. **Map Code 15 1-10**

<u>Inyo County</u> — In the spring of 1861, Charles Alvord and Asa Bennett, with three or four others referred to as "the Mormons," entered Death Valley in search of the then widely-known Lost Gunsight Mine. About all is known of Alvord for certain is that he was from New York State, and that he had a little knowledge of prospecting. The claim that he was a member of the original Death Valley Forty-

Niners has not been conclusively proved. Traveling in a six-mule wagon, the Alvord-Bennett party entered the southern end of Death Valley, where they made camp, probably near Saratoga Springs at the southern tip of the Ibex Hills.

While the others made short prospecting trips near their wagon, Alvord took his gear and a supply of food and struck out north along the range of mountains fringing the western side of the valley. When he did not return after two weeks, the party was about to give up waiting for him and head back for Los Angeles. Then one day Alvord walked in, hale and hearty, and surprised that there should have been any concern over his absence. He carried with him samples of black ore shot full of gold. This aroused little excitement among the men, because Bennett had found what he believed to be rich specimens of silver. Alvord examined them and expressed his doubt.

In Los Angeles, Bennett's silver samples turned out to be lead, but Alvord's black ore was rich in gold. Shortly after this, Alvord, Bennett, and a man named William Stockton planned another trip to Death Valley to work the Alvord ledge. When the Mormons of the original party heard of this, they demanded the right to share in Alvord's find. Under pressure, Alvord finally agreed.

It was late in the year when the party reached Death Valley, and a mantle of snow lay over the high mountains. After a fruitless search, Alvord said that the snow changed the appearance of everything and that he could not retrace his steps.

Some members of the party accused Alvord of purposely failing to find the mine and threatened to hang him. Alvord, a remarkable man of 60 years at the time, simply stated that hanging him would certainly not find the gold.

After several days of bitter quarreling, the party, including Asa Bennett, abandoned Alvord to his own fate, leaving him but a scanty supply of food.

When Bennett reached Los Angeles he had second thoughts. He had once been stranded in Death Valley himself, and so he told William Lewis Manly, leader of the original Death Valley Forty-Niners group, of Alvord's predicament. Manly berated Bennett and the others for such an act and immediately organized a rescue party. Before reaching Death Valley, the party, including Asa Bennett and a storekeeper named Twitchell, camped one night beside a dry falls. As they sat around the campfire, Charles Alvord stumbled in. He had no food, but aside from being weary, he was in surprisingly good shape.

That night, the decision was made that, in as much as they were well supplied with food and water, they would enter Death Valley and search for lost mines. They penetrated the Panamints, crossed the Valley, and made camp for a prolonged stay. Then the decision was made that they would need more provisions, after all. It was agreed that Bennett and Twitchell would take the pack mules and return to Los Angeles for additional provisions, while Manly and Alvord would stay and prospect until their return.

The two prospectors did not become alarmed until Bennett and Twitchell were long overdue. They were reluctant to leave as long as their supplies held out, but they were beginning to run dangerously low and there was little native game to be had. Finally, it was decided that they would have to get out at once if they were to survive. For Alvord, it was the second time that year he had been stranded in Death Valley.

Manly and Alvord were about at the end of their ropes when a group of prospectors from Visalia, searching for the Lost Gunsight Mine, stumbled upon them. Again Alvord and Manly had cheated Death Valley, but the question burned Manly — why had Bennett, whose life he had once saved in Death Valley, deserted them? Manly never saw Bennett again, but 31 years later he met Twitchell in Santa Monica and asked him to explain.

Twitchell replied that there were three feet of snow when they reached the Coast Range, that they had a terrible time in getting through, and that it would have been six weeks before they could have returned. By that time, they figured Alvord and Manly would either be dead or would have made their way out, so what was the use of returning?

Manly later commented, "It required some grace to swallow that story."

While Alvord could cheat Death Valley, he wasn't so fortunate with his fellow men. With the party that had saved Manly and Alvord after their abandonment by Bennett and Twitchell was a man named Jackson, which is about all that is known of him. He later persuaded Alvord to join him in a coal prospecting trip in the region west of Buena Vista Lake, in Kern County.

When Alvord's distinctive gun showed up in the possession of a man named Caldwell, questioning revealed that it had been purchased from Jackson. Another miner revealed that he had purchased Alvord's burro, also from a man named

Jackson. A party of miners went to Jackson and Alvord's camp, determined to hang Jackson if Alvord were missing. The camp was deserted.

A search turned up Alvord's skeleton, its flesh stripped clean by birds and wild animals. Jackson had obviously lured Alvord into the country and had murdered him for his belongings. Jackson was never heard of again, but Alvord's name is perpetuated in the mountains south of Death Valley, where some think his ledge of gold is located.

The only known clue to the location of Alvord's Lost Mine is a hint given by Charles Alvord himself — and there were few who questioned this man's word. "It is within sight of a striped butte," he said. This butte is generally believed to be the striped butte after which Butte Valley is named. It is in the Panamint Range in the southwestern corner of Death Valley National Monument. **Map Code 15 J-10**

<u>Inyo County</u> — Manly Peak is near the western boundary of Death Valley National Monument, just to the southeast of the Park Service Summer Headquarters. Somewhere on the southwestern slope of Manly Peak, facing Redland Canyon, a piece of colored cloth was left to mark a place where gold ore was picked up that later assayed $15,000 to the ton. The colored cloth was left there by Asa M. Russell of Los Angeles, and Ernest Huhn, who was frequently known as "Siberian Red" because he had prospected in Siberia.

It was the habit of these two prospectors to leave a piece of different colored cloth at the spots where samples were collected, and to identify the samples with pieces of cloth of the same colors. When the assay of $15,000 to the ton showed on one particular sample, they returned to the indicated area, but failed to find the right colored cloth. So far as it is known, this mine is still there, but the piece of colored cloth has probably long since disappeared. **Map Code 15 I-10**

<u>Inyo County</u> — While freighting between Los Angeles and Salt Lake City, Gomer Richards is said to have found a rich ledge of gold in Boundary Canyon. Finding freighting very profitable at the time, Richards marked the ledge so that it could be found and worked at a more appropriate time. When he arrived in Salt Lake City and told Brigham Young of his find, the Mormon leader advised him to forget it as gold would only bring him misery and possible death. Being a good Mormon, Richards accepted Young's advice, but he left a map and description of the area with a grandson who tried unsuccessfully several times to locate the ledge. **Map Code 15 I-10**

<u>Inyo County</u> — In the 1870s, two clamshell bottom ferry-type boats, the Bessie Brady and the Mollie Stevens, transported bars of silver from the Cerro Gordo mine at Keeler Wharf across Owens Lake to Cartoga, where it was loaded on mules for transportation to Los Angeles. According to a persistent story, the Mollie Stevens sank in Owens Lake in 1878 with a cargo of silver bars, which has never been recovered.

Through the years, water in Owens Lake, bordering US 395 west of Death Valley, has gradually disappeared until only occasional water holes now remain in the basin. Evidences of a vessel of some nature under the dry surface of Owens Lake have been discovered, including an anchor believed to have belonged to the Mollie Stevens. **Map Code 15 I-8**

<u>Inyo County</u> — Along with the Dutchman and the Pegleg Smith, the Lost Gunsight Mine is one of the most famous in California and while there seems little doubt as to its existence, it has nevertheless been called a myth and a legend. In the opinion of the original Death Valley Forty-Niners who expressed themselves on the subject, the lost silver lode was located within a short distance of what is known today as White Sage Flats.

This is a region easily reached by automobile, but those who do not know the ways of the desert should not go into this region unless accompanied by someone who does.

In the winter of 1849-1850, several loosely banded parties, now known collectively as the Death Valley Forty-Niners, made a crossing of that strangely exciting valley called Death. Out of this crossing came two lost mine stories and one lost treasure. In the subsequent search for these, at least two more lost mine stories developed.

On December 29, 1849, four members of the so-called Georgia-Mississippi party — Captain Towne, James Martin, and two others whose names are in dispute — decided to strike out on their own directly across the Panamints. For three days they wandered aimlessly through the canyons and along the ridges at the base of Tucki Mountain. Passing a boulder, Captain Towne accidentally hit it with the muzzle of his rifle, knocking off the sight. He searched but could not find it among the small rocks, but he did pick up a piece of black substance and recognized it at once as being silver. The ground was covered with it. He looked about and found the ledge from which it had fallen. Martin confirmed that it was silver.

When the Martin-Towne party finally reached the settlements of California, the pieces of silver were widely displayed and aroused a great deal of interest. Almost at once, and in spite of the dreadful descriptions given the region by those who had just crossed it, men prepared to drop everything and search for the Lost Gunsight Mine. For a hundred years it was the lodestar of prospectors, and the search for it still goes on. **Map Code 15 H-9**

<u>Inyo County</u> — Not many years ago, the Southwest Museum of Los Angeles established that the rugged mountains in the supposed vicinity of this story's site was once the home of Pinto and Gypsum cavemen — perhaps as long as 8,000 years ago. When Frank Bishop prospected through the canyons of the Coso and Argus Mountains, he heard Indians make veiled references to a hidden canyon. Then he met an old Indian who showed him several large gold nuggets which he said had come from the hidden canyon in the Argus Range.

He drew a rough map of the area for Bishop, and described how the canyon could only be entered and left through a small rock crevice barely large enough to admit a man. He said the canyon had once been the home of "old people" who lived there in caves, and that one wall of the canyon was covered with Indian writing — petroglyphs.

After a year's search, Bishop found a canyon answering the description. One wall was covered with petroglyphs and there were caves, but all except one were too high on the ledge for Bishop to enter. There were signs of habitation in profusion — obsidian points, scrapers, and rock chips.

For some unknown reason, Bishop let five years go by before he attempted to return; then he found everything changed. He could not even locate the two peaks, a gray colored one on one side of the canyon, and a red cinder cone on the other, by which he had landmarked the canyon. After a prolonged search he gave up, but he never lost faith in the existence of gold in the "Canyon of the Old People in the Argus Mountains." It is pointed out that the Argus Range is largely located within the boundaries of the U. S. Ordnance Test Station. **Map Code 15 I-9**

<u>Inyo County</u> — High in the Funeral Mountains on the eastern edge of Death Valley, and in the general area of old Chloride, is said to be a cave containing placer gold in black sand, and in incredible quantities. The cave is said to have been discovered by two Paiute brothers, one of whom was killed while attempting to

swim across a pool of water in the cave. Following the tribal custom, none of the Indians would return to the cave where one had been lost, nor would they give any white men directions to the cave. **Map Code 15 H-9**

<u>Inyo County</u> — In the 1860s, a wealthy Mexican family and its wagon train of belongings and servants was passing through the Panamint Mountains on the west side of Death Valley when they were attacked by Indians. All of the party was killed with the exception of two small children, who were taken captive.

In time, the two captives escaped to tell the story of the massacre, and how the Indians took the gold coins found in the wagons and buried them in a crevice in the canyon where the massacre had taken place. Searchers for this treasure have concentrated their efforts around Emigrant Springs in Emigrant Canyon, which is in Death Valley National Monument. **Map Code 15 H-9**

<u>Inyo County</u> — When John Searles and Bill Parkinson were loading borax at Searles Lake one day, they looked up to see a man staggering across the flat from the base of the Slate Range. As he collapsed at their feet, they thought he was dead, but after a few swallows of water he regained consciousness. But the Chinaman was badly frightened and wanted desperately to get to Mojave, where he said friends would ship his body to China for burial, if he should die. When Parkinson left with his load for Mojave, he put the ill Chinaman aboard, together with the leather bag he carried. En route, the Chinaman, in thanking Bill for his kindness, withdrew a piece of ore from the bag. He said he wanted Bill to know where it came from.

The sick Chinaman had been working at the Harmony Borax Works in Death Valley. Ill and no longer able to stand the abuse of the foreman, he had started afoot for Mojave. Some friendly Indians had directed him to a short cut across the Panamints. In passing through a canyon, he had come upon a field of rich float and had placed a few pieces in his bag. He described the place as best he could. Before Parkinson left Mojave to return to Searles Lake, he heard that the Chinaman had died. Over the next five years, Parkinson and Searles made several trips into the Panamints in search of the Chinaman's lost gold mine, centering their efforts in Six Spring Canyon, which is located straight east of the old mining town of Ballarat. **Map Code 15 J-9**

<u>Inyo County</u> — Somewhere in the Avawatz Mountains northwest of Baker (Interstate 15), an unnamed Mormon, traveling alone and on his way from Utah to

join the Mormon colony at San Bernardino, lost his way shortly after leaving Las Vegas. Facing the unknown desert, he worked his two mules south and west until he reached the Avawatz Mountains at the southern extremity of Death Valley. Wearied by a long pull up a hill, his mules stopped and refused to move.

The Mormon picked up some rocks and filled his pockets. Occasionally pelting them at the mules, he proceeded on. When he finally arrived in San Bernardino, he bought a new suit of clothes from a merchant and left his old suit to be repaired. The merchant found a few remaining rocks in the pocket, and recognized that they were rich in gold.

The merchant informed the Mormon of his findings, and together they looked for the gold atop a hill in the Avawatz Mountains. They found many hills that fitted the Mormon's description, but they found no gold. Others have searched for the Lost Old Clothes Mine, but with no more success. Part of the Avawatz Range extends into the Fort Irwin Military Reservation, where public travel is restricted.
Map Code 15 J-10

<u>Inyo County</u> — In the fall of 1904, Alex Ramey (also spelled Ramie), an experienced prospector, while making a foray through Death Valley, made camp one night at the southern tip of the Last Chance Range. During the night, his mules broke their hobbles and wandered away, leaving him afoot.

As Ramey was making his way toward some tanks that afternoon, he stumbled over a protruding quartz ledge, and the quantity of gold throughout the ledge told Ramey that it was a bonanza. Breaking off a few samples, he wandered on, desperately in need of water. When Ramey finally collapsed he was found by friendly Indians and nursed back to health. But shortly after he reached civilization, he died.

Having a premonition of his death, Ramey had given a close friend, a fellow Frenchman, directions for reaching the ledge which had assayed almost half gold — one of the richest finds ever made in Inyo County. After making an extensive search for Ramey's lost ledge, the friend gave up with the conclusion that a cloudburst or an earthquake had so altered the land that Ramey's directions could no longer be followed. His search was centered directly to the north of Ubehebe Peak in Death Valley National Monument. **Map Code 15 H-9**

<u>Inyo County</u> — What little is known of John Goller's gold find in Death Valley comes from William Lewis Manly, who chronicled the epic crossing of Death Val-

ley by the original Forty-Niners shortly after he arrived in California. Manly wrote that Goller (the name is spelled variously, and is frequently confused with Goler, a German who found and lost a gold mine in the El Paso Mountains) and his German companion kept constantly together, often traveling some distance from the main party in search for water and game.

While engaged in this manner one day, one German called to the other, "Come here and see what I have found — gold!"

The man came to look, Manly wrote, but was not excited. "It is water and food I want," he said, "not gold." It was the universal attitude of the harried Forty-Niners toward riches at that time. Only food and water could save their lives. The two Germans pocketed some specimens and trudged on.

When Manly visited Goller in Los Angeles in 1862, some 13 years after the incident, he questioned him regarding the gold, and suggested that it might have been mica instead of gold. Goller replied strongly that he had seen plenty of native gold in Germany, and he was positive that what he had found was gold. Presumably, he had none of the samples at this time.

Goller operated a blacksmith shop in Los Angeles and prospered, but about 1876, he had financial reverses and dropped from view. No record has ever been found of his later travels or of his death. But there were friends who later told that Goller insisted that if he could find the spot again, he could pick up a wagon load of gold. John Goller was considered to be reputable and reliable. Few ever stepped forward to dispute his word.

There is little if any evidence upon which to pinpoint the place of John Goller's find, but the general consensus is that it is in the western confines of Death Valley, probably in the Panamint Mountains where the Jayhawkers emerged from Death Valley, at Towne's Pass. If this is correct, it is in the same general area as the Lost Gunsight Silver Mine. **Map Code 15 H-9**

<u>Kern County</u> — Piute Lookout lies north of Claraville and south of Lake Isabella, in the rugged wilderness of the Piute Mountains. A stagecoach carrying gold out of the Havilah-Bodfish mining area in the early days is said to have been robbed near what is now known as Miracle Hot Springs. The treasure secured was taken by the two bandits to Piute Peak, more than 8,000 feet elevation, where it was cached when one of the robbers was injured in a fall by his horse. The injured man was propped against a tree and made as comfortable as pos-

sible while the other rode away to secure help. The companion never returned (his fate is not known), and the injured man eventually died. Supposedly, this treasure is still cached on Piute Peak. **Map Code 15 J-8**

Kern County — Havilah, now almost a ghost town, was once the county seat and leading town in Kern County. There are several lost mine stories about the area, and the hundreds of people who have searched for them have, so far as it is known, come up with nothing.

This story concerns an unnamed miner from Havilah who, while walking from Delonegha Hot Springs across the mountains to Havilah, became lost in the fog that suddenly swept in. While wandering about on the mountain he stumbled upon a ledge of gold from which he took samples. When he finally reached Havilah, these were assayed and showed great richness. Figuring that he had crossed the mountains just to the north of Lightner Peak, he returned to the area and conducted an extensive search, but finally gave up without re-finding the ledge. **Map Code 14 J-8**

Kern County — A Frenchman whose name has long since passed from history, came to Bodfish, now a ghost town, and prospected Bodfish Creek, where he found a gold ledge of considerable value. He built a cabin and an arrastre. While walking from Bodfish to Havilah one day, he found another and richer ledge as he prospected along the way. He leaned his shotgun against the ledge so that he could identify the place when he returned to stake his claim.

In Havilah, he told of his good luck and celebrated with a drinking spree. When he started out for his cabin, he was in no condition to travel. Nightfall overtook him, and he became lost in the mountains. He was found several days later, frozen to death. Almost everybody in Havilah had heard about the ledge, and learning of the Frenchman's death, rushed out to find it. They found nothing.

About five years later a group of boys were exploring the mountains south of Bodfish, when one, Frank Vaughn, while separated from the others, found a rusted old shotgun. He took it home for a relic. The Vaughns had not been in the area very long and had never heard the story of the Frenchman's Lost Shotgun Mine. When they finally learned, young Frank could not guide them back to the spot. **Map Code 14 J-8**

Kern County — When Havilah was a booming mining camp, prospectors were too busy looking for gold to wash their own clothes, this chore being handled by a woman who took in washings. One day this unnamed lady took a specimen out of a miner's shirt pocket, and even she recognized that it was rich in gold.

She showed it to the miner when he came for his washing, and he said he could go right to the place where he had picked it up — and there was plenty more there. He had been on a prolonged binge and had completely forgotten the specimen. Apparently he had also forgotten his landmarks, for all his efforts to locate the ledge on Bodfish Creek failed. Supposedly, the Lost Washerwoman Mine is still there. **Map Code 14 J-8**

<u>Kern County</u> — About 1900, Sam Holmes, a Los Angeles pioneer, made a trip to Havilah to inspect some of the mining claims, with a view to prospecting if they looked promising. After staking out five claims, he boarded the stage for the return trip to Los Angeles, riding beside the driver. At Sam's feet was a box that aroused his curiosity. He asked the driver about it, and was told that he could find out when they got to the railroad, where the box would be transshipped.

Upon arrival at the railroad, two male passengers on the stage claimed the box. Holmes overheard them tell the express agent that the package contained two gold bars valued at $1,500 each, and he picked up enough other conversation to learn that the two men were taking this amount out of their claim every month.

When Holmes asked the strangers where their claim was located, one replied that they were not telling because they did not want the area swarmed over by an army of prospectors. Holmes later heard that one of the partners had dropped dead in Los Angeles, and the other was killed in a saloon fight. Holmes later searched the Havilah area for the secret mine, but never found it. **Map Code 14 J-8**

<u>Kern County</u> — Slim Winslow was running cattle in the Kern River country when he was impressed with all the searching for lost mines in the Havilah-Bodfish area and decided to do a little looking himself. He hardly knew what gold looked like, but he took sample upon sample, only to find them worthless. One night, Slim worked a bunch of samples from the Piute Mountains to the south of Bodfish, but failed to recognize that they were rich and threw them aside outside his cabin.

Years afterwards, a mining man happened to see them and told Slim they were very rich in gold. Winslow thought he could go right to the spot in the Paiutes where he had picked them up, but he had sampled a hundred or more places there and never found the right one. He finally gave up in disgust, but others still search for Slim Winslow's lost mine. **Map Code 14 J-8**

Kern County — During stagecoach days, the product of the mines around Mono and Bodie were shipped out to Los Angeles in the form of nuggets or smelted bars. One of the stage stations on this route was near a place now called Freeman Junction, a desert stop in the foothills of the Sierras, close to where the Los Angeles Aqueduct is crossed by State 178 coming down from Walker Pass. A stage carrying $25,000 in gold once made its change of horses here, but its departure was delayed by a threatening storm. As the driver and passengers relaxed in the dingy station, a sudden wall of water roared down upon them and swept the station and its passengers down the wash. Only one managed to save himself. Someplace in that wash is the wreckage of the stagecoach and an iron chest containing $25,000 in gold. It is believed to be less than a half mile from present Freeman Junction. **Map Code 15 J-9**

Kern County — Mission San Buenaventura, in the city of Ventura, consecrated in 1782, was the ninth mission established in California. Whether these missions possessed any great wealth in gold and coin is doubtful, but at the height of its prosperity, San Buenaventura's padres could boast of having 37,000 head of cattle, 600 head of horses, 200 yoke of working oxen, 30,000 sheep, and 200 goats. Certain treasured relics brought from Spain or Mexico graced all the missions. It is said that Indians, rebelling at San Buenaventura Mission, took the church treasures across the mountains and buried them near Lake Buena Vista in Kern County. We are in the dark as to what these treasures consisted of.
Map Code 14 K-7

Kern County — Old Fort Tejon, once a flourishing army post, is located on Interstate 5 just north of the town of Lebec. Padres from San Fernando Rey de España Mission frequently visited here, performing various ceremonies, and according to tradition, they operated a gold mine in the nearby mountains. A similar story places the San Buenaventura Mission Mine in the San Emigdio Mountains, which are in the same general area. Early pioneers in the region heard the stories of these mines from Indians and are said to have made many searches for them.
Map Code 14 K-7

Kern County — In 1867, a German named Goler (his first name is usually given as John, but this maybe because the name is frequently confused with that of John Goller, who prospected the same general area at about the same time) started out to prospect his way from Death Valley to Los Angeles. He followed a small canyon down to within 40 miles of the present site of Mojave (State 14-58), and continued on into the El Paso Mountains where he stopped at a spring to drink. Looking down into the water, he was amazed to see gold nuggets. He gathered a few, but fearful of an attack by Indians, soon hurried on. He was now anxious to reach Los Angeles, report his discovery, and to seek help in prospecting the region.

After leaving the spring, Goler decided to take a short cut, but soon learned that it was no short cut at all and that he was lost. Realizing that he could not take the time now to relocate the spring, he climbed a small hill, studied the surrounding region, and drew a rough map. To indicate the spot for the return trip, he stuck his gun in the ground. Several days later Goler reached Los Angeles, which was then filled with prospectors who drifted in from the gold excitement on the Kern River. Goler showed his nuggets around, but no one seems to have taken him seriously.

In some unknown manner, Goler met another German named Cuddeback, who agreed to finance a search for the spring. On this trip, Goler became lost again, and some in the party accused him of leading them on a wild goose chase. A second expedition proved as fruitless, but on a third search they found gold in Red Rock Canyon, an estimated 15 miles from where Goler had left his gun. They conducted mining operations here for several years, abandoning the search for Goler's spring in the El Paso Mountains. Eventually, John Goler disappeared entirely, and just as in the case of John Goller, was never heard of again.

Some 50 years after Goler's trip from Death Valley to Los Angeles, Will Munsey, one of the owners of the Lazy M Ranch north of Mojave, found an old Spencer repeating rifle stuck in the ground atop a small hill. Because of the dry climate, the works were well-preserved, and the dates on the rifle were 1867 — the year of Goler's journey from Death Valley to Los Angeles. It was generally assumed that this was John Goler's gun. The region in which it was found was about 20 miles north of Mojave, and this could have been on Goler's route from Death Valley to Los Angeles.

Gold was eventually found in the canyon where Goler was thought to have been, and the place is known today as Goler Canyon. A mining district here named Goler produced $1,000,000 in gold, but it has never been determined beyond question that this was really Goler's original discovery. Goler Canyon is in the El Paso Mountains, northwest of Randsburg and northeast of Mojave. If this was the site of the spring where Goler found the gold nuggets, his mine has probably been found. If not, the Lost Goler Mine may still yours for the finding. **Map Code 15 J-9**

Kern County — Cache Creek runs north of US 466 between the western end of Tehachapi Pass and the town of Monolith. According to an Indian legend, a wagon train reaching the western downgrade of Tehachapi Pass was suddenly attacked by Indians. Some of the settlers managed to flee up Cache Creek, where they buried $15,000 in gold coins before being overtaken by the Indians and slain.

The few who managed to escape knew that the gold had been taken up Cache Creek, but did not know where it was buried or hidden, and their efforts to find it later were unsuccessful. **Map Code 15 K-8**

Kern County — A story is told of a young Indian who had committed an offense against the tribe, and as punishment was taken into the mountains, tossed over a cliff, and left to die. Although badly injured, he was nursed back to health by a young girl who rescued him. Making their home away from the tribe, they roamed the hills for wild game on which they lived.

On one of these excursions, the young couple found a ledge of gold that was so rich that, even with the crudest of tools, they produced enough to trade for all of their requirements. It is said that this gold was traded at the post at old Fort Tejon (now a State Park on US 99 just north of Lebec), and pioneers thought the ledge was located in one of the small canyons in the Tehachapi Range, probably Little Sycamore or Cottonwood Canyon. **Map Code 15 K-7**

Kern County — In a small canyon near Boron (State 58) is supposed to rest the ashes and irons of an old Spanish carreta (long, narrow cart). In the carreta at the time it was attacked by Indians was a quantity of gold coins. After killing all in the small party, the Indians dug a shallow hole, placed the gold in it, rolled the carreta over the spot and set it afire. So far as it is known, this treasure has never been found. **Map Code 15 K-9**

Kern County — Just before the turn of the century, Kernville (north of Lake Isabella) was known as Whiskey Flat. At that time, a man named Yarborough and his partner worked a gold mine on the Kern River, nearby. When Yarborough was sent to prison for the murder of his partner, Mrs. Nettie Yarborough blew up the entrance to the mine, stating that it was cursed and that no one would ever work it again. Mrs. Yarborough was in her eighties when her husband died in prison. She then relented and tried to tell a friend of her husband's where the mine was located. About all she could remember was that it was a certain distance from a large pine tree, and that various tools would be found scattered around.

Repeated searches for the Lost Yarborough Mine have been unproductive, and although the claim has been made that it had been found, there is considerable doubt. **Map Code 15 J-8**

Kern County — The little town of Isabella is saved from being a complete ghost because it is located on State 178, a popular tourist and vacation route. Old-timers here tell the story of a miner who had considerable success and saved his money, which he buried in or near his small home just north of Isabella. It was assumed that the miner had accumulated and cached several thousand dollars before suddenly dying of blood poisoning. Those who have searched for this treasure have looked for the remains of a small cabin which had a stone fireplace. **Map Code 15 J-8**

Kern County — Redrock Canyon is a deep lateral gorge whose towering cliffs are of reddish-brown sandstone, carved into fantastic shapes. State 14 crosses it about 40 miles north of Mojave. It is said that an old Indian who had been befriended by a white man about 1925 attempted to repay his benefactor by telling him where the Indians used to gather placer gold in Redrock Canyon. The white man was to look for a lone tree standing in a triangle of three boulders. His years of efforts to locate the placer reportedly failed. **Map Code 15 J-8**

Kern County — There is little left in Garlock today except the railroad siding. Located on the southeastern slopes of the El Paso Mountains, it is in the heart of a country that has seen a great deal of mining activity. An old Indian used to come into the store at Garlock who always had a generous amount of gold nuggets to trade. When he sobered up from his usual long drunken sprees, he wandered away to the east.

Those who attempted to follow him to his secret mine were always lost as he turned north into Iron Canyon and vanished. Those who waited for him to return always saw him emerge from the same canyon, so it was assumed that the Indian's rich source of gold was someplace at the head of one of the small canyons running off of Iron Canyon to the northeast of the near ghost town of Garlock. **Map Code 15 J-9**

Kern County — George Ely, a partner of William Lynn, after whom Lynn Valley was named, was supposed to have accumulated a fortune during his stay in the Glenville (State 155) area. When Ely died, his fortune could not be found, and treasure seekers began a frantic search for it. In the 1920s, fearful that treasure hunters would open his grave in the old Oak Creek Cemetery, in the belief that the treasure might have been buried with him, relatives had a heavy concrete slab poured over Ely's grave. Inquire in Glenville for directions to his old headquarters. **Map Code 15 J-8**

Kern County — Freeman Creek and Greenhorn Creek come out of the Greenhorn Mountains to join at a point just above where they empty into the Kern River between Democrat Hot Springs and Miracle Hot Springs. At the junction of these two creeks, there once stood a store and saloon operated by a man who owned two producing gold mines in the area. He told relatives that he had buried more than $100,000 in various caches around his store. After he was killed by a mine cave-in, relatives searched and found $48,000 in gold dust and coins buried in tins and glass jars. So far as it is known, the remaining $52,000 or so has never been found. **Map Code 15 J-8**

Kern County — State 178 follows the course of Freeman Canyon, or Freeman Wash, as it is also known, from Walker Pass to where it joins State 14. About one-half mile west of Freeman Junction, the point where the two highways meet, State 178 crosses the Los Angeles Aqueduct. Near this point is a massive pile of rocks known as Robber's Roost (one of several in California), which overlooked the old road from the northern mines to Los Angeles. It was so named because outlaws preying on the treasure-carrying stagecoaches kept a lookout here for their targets.

A stage carrying $58,000 was once held up as it approached this spot, but the bandits were unaware that it was being followed by a party of soldiers. Seizing the treasure chest, the outlaws fled into the foothills as the soldiers rode up. In the ensuing battle, four of the bandits were quickly killed, but the fifth managed to hide or bury the treasure before he, too, was slain. A quick search was made for the chest at the time, but the urgency of getting a wounded soldier to a doctor in Mojave was more important. Subsequent searches made for the treasure failed so far as we know.

Presumably, the treasure of Robber's Roost is still there. **Map Code 15 J-9**

Lassen County — On the evening of Dec. 26, 1873, Tiburcio Vasquez and his band of outlaws made a bold raid on the little stage-stop town of Kingston, no longer in existence. The bandits succeeded in binding 39 men and robbing three stores before the alarm could be given. In their wild flight to their horses, left in a corral across the river, three of the bandits were killed. It is said that the one delegated to carry the loot was badly wounded, but managed to get across the river. Finding no horse waiting for him, he buried the money and attempted to escape afoot. A skeleton found years later was believed to have been his. **Map Code 12 C-5**

<u>Lassen County</u> — A man named Brockman was gathering up his horses in the fall of the year in the region just to the southwest of Horse Lake, when a bad storm blew up. Trying to outrun the storm, he tired his horse and stopped at a small creek to give it a drink of water. He noticed that the black quartz bank of the stream looked like it might contain gold, so he knocked off a piece and put it in his bag. The storm worsened so he gave his horse his head, thinking it would take him back to his camp, but the horse and rider ended up in Susanville instead. Here the piece of ore was analyzed and found to be rich in gold.

There was now too much snow on the ground to return to the stream, and by spring he could not locate the place. After spending many years searching for the stream with the black quartz banks, Brockman finally gave up, concluding that the heavy storms of that winter had changed the contour of the land. **Map Code 12 C-5**

<u>Lassen County</u> — The little town of Pittsville is located on the Lassen-Shasta county line just north of State 299. To the southeast a few miles, and above the bank of the Pit River, was Bloody Springs, so-named for the massacre that took place here when Indians ambushed an emigrant train.

The lone man to escape picked his way through the precipitous Pit River Canyon and finally reached Fort Crook. According to his report, the Indians, finding a great amount of $20 gold pieces in the wagons, lined up on the bank of the Pit and held a contest to see which of them could throw one of the coins across the river gorge. The contest ended only when all the money was in the river, or lodged in the almost inaccessible rocks on the gorge walls. An occasional $20 gold piece is still picked up in the area. **Map Code 12 B-5**

<u>Los Angeles County</u> — Eagle Rock is an enormous boulder visible from Eagle Rock Boulevard as it enters the suburb of Eagle Rock from Los Angeles. It is so named for the fancied fact that it resembles an eagle's head. It is said that just prior to the time Prudent Beaudry acquired the property on which Eagle Rock stands, Mexican bandits used a cave at the rock's base as a place to hide their loot. There have been many searches for it, but it is practically impossible to search now, because the area is surrounded with residences. **Map Code 16 B-3**

Los Angeles County — San Gabriel Wash runs between the towns of Monrovia and Azusa. It is dry except in times of heavy rain when it can be a flood threat. Fish Canyon empties into the wash a few miles above Azusa. Small quantities of gold are still recovered in this area by Sunday prospectors. For many years there has been a legend of a lost ledge of gold in this region, based partly on a story that an old Indian woman who herded goats in the vicinity periodically brought in specimens of moderately rich gold-bearing quartz, which she sold in Monrovia.
Map Code 16 B-5

Los Angeles County — Somewhere on the 5,000 acres of land that once formed the Repetto Ranch and is known as King's Hills — all now a part of the Los Angeles suburb of Monterey Park — is believed to be buried $40,000 in gold, if it has not been found. Alessandro Repetto was an Italian immigrant who came to California, and prospered.

On April 14, 1874 (the incident is a matter of public record), the Tiburcio Vasquez gang of outlaws swooped down upon the Repetto ranch headquarters, located in wooded rolling hills, and demanded Repetto's money on the threat of death. Repetto informed the bandits that he kept his wealth in a bank of Los Angeles, whereupon the outlaw leader ordered him to send someone to get it. Repetto sent a small boy into Los Angeles with a note to the bank to give him $800.

Suspicious that something was wrong, the bank called the sheriff and the boy revealed the holdup. Immediately, a posse was formed and rode off to the Repetto ranch. Meantime, still believing the main portion of Repetto's wealth was kept at the ranch, the old man was tortured until he produced two bags containing $40,000 in gold and silver.

After abusing the servants, ransacking the premises, and partaking of Repetto's excellent wine, the bandits heard the approach of the sheriff's party, mounted their horses, and rode off into the trees. A short time after the robbery, a traveler stopped at the Repetto house and reported that he had seen a group of riders dismounted and gathered under a tree. It seemed that they covered up something and then rapidly rode away.

Repetto always assumed that the bandits, fearing they could not flee with the burden of the treasure, hurriedly buried it among the trees on his property. For years, he searched in vain for his money, and when he sold his property, he reserved the right to continue to search.

A month after the Repetto robbery, an informer tipped off the sheriff's department in Los Angeles that Vasquez was holed up at Greek George's cabin located in what is now the heart of Hollywood. Vasquez was captured and later hanged. At the time of his arrest, he had very little money on him, and he implied that he could put his hands on plenty of money in return for his freedom.

It is not known that any of the Vasquez gang ever recovered the Repetto treasure, but in view of the close watch kept by old Alessandro Repetto, it seems unlikely. Many of the acres of the old Repetto Ranch have been graded away for the development of streets and residential areas, but some of the wooded acres remain almost untouched. Could the gold and silver coins be there?
Map Code 16 C-4

<u>Los Angeles County</u> — Raids such as that on the Repetto Ranch (see above) made Tiburcio Vasquez the most feared of southern California bandits in the 1860s and early 1870s. He roamed the country from the Bay Area south to Los Angeles, and left legends of buried treasure in more than a dozen different places. When operating in the Los Angeles area, one of his hideouts was a place now called Vasquez Rocks or Robber's Roost, located on a high ridge in Escondido Canyon about four miles northwest of the town of Acton. This interesting geologic formation of sandstone with embedded rocks of several kinds, is easily reached and the area is now a privately operated tourist attraction. It has been the scene of many treasure hunts, but it is doubtful that any has ever been found. **Map Code 15 K-8**

<u>Los Angeles County</u> — The Vasquez Caves are a series of small caves gouged out by wind and rain in the sandstone cliffs of Escondido Canyon about two miles from the Vasquez Rocks (see above). The caves were indeed used by Tiburcio Vasquez because their vast maze made it almost impossible for a posse to trail the bandits in the region, but the story that Vasquez also left buried treasure here seems doubtful. **Map Code 15 K-8**

<u>Los Angeles County</u> — Coehody Pass was an early road from San Gabriel to Los Angeles, but it is now practically a solid residential section. Tiburcio Vasquez is supposed to have cached a quantity of gold coins in the low hills of the pass. A Mexican boy is said to have found some loose gold coins there many years ago, but was unable later to show anyone the spot where he picked them up. There probably hasn't been a search made for the remainder of this treasure in many years. **Map Code 16 B-4**

Los Angeles County — Just to the north of busy State 118, and about a mile north of Chatsworth, is a natural rock formation known as Castle Rock. From its towering crest, a large part of San Fernando Valley can be seen. At its base during the early days was an Indian village where Tiburcio Vasquez and his band could always secure food and shelter because he shared his loot generously with the Indians. The area has been thoroughly searched for the treasure the bandit is said to have buried here. So far as it is known, none has ever been found.
Map Code 16 A-1

Los Angeles County — Another favorite hideout for Vasquez and his gang was in an area now known as East Chilao, in the timbered, rocky wilderness area north of Monrovia. It is now a popular recreational area. The long narrow valley of West Chilao, and nearby Horse Flat with its secret trail, both provided plenty of pasturage, and the great rocks of the area made an almost impregnable fortress. It is said that no posse ever attempted to follow the outlaws into this region, which is easily reached over Angeles Crest Highway (State 2). There has been much searching for the treasure Tiburcio Vasquez is said to have buried in the area.
Map Code 16 A-5

Los Angeles County — When a hill back of the Sisters of Immaculate Heart College administration building was gouged out by earth-moving equipment in 1957, a sharp watch was kept for a treasure supposedly buried there by the famous bandit Joaquin Murrieta.

Ever since the Sisters bought the property in the early 1900s, they have been besieged with treasure hunters armed with "authentic" maps. No one seems to know where the treasure maps come from, nor how it happened that Murrieta buried treasure here, but it is certain that no treasure was turned up by the power shovels. Immaculate Heart College is located at Franklin and Western Avenues in Hollywood. **Map Code 16 C-3**

Los Angeles County — Rancho Malibu, along the coast of California west of Santa Monica, was granted by the King of Spain in 1804 to Jose Bartolome Tapia. Tiburcio Tapia, who operated a store in Los Angeles and was one of the pueblo's leading citizens, owned an interest in Rancho Malibu.

Smugglers found the isolated coast at Malibu convenient for their operations from Catalina Island, and it is said that Tiburcio acted as their agent and custodian of the contraband goods which were eventually sent to Los Angeles by ox cart.

Tapia profited handsomely through his smuggling activities and is believed to have left part of his wealth buried at Malibu when he moved to his Rancho San Jose at Pomona.

In modern times, excavators for a building foundation dug up a kettle half filled with gold and silver coins. It was claimed at the time that this was part of Tapia's treasure, and that the remainder was still hidden on the old Rancho Malibu acres. The coastal section of Malibu is now lined with the palatial beach homes of television and movie stars, and back of them cuts the wide swath of busy Coast Highway (State 1). **Map Code 14 L-8**

<u>Los Angeles County</u> — Tiburcio Tapia's Rancho San Jose was along the foothills east of Los Angeles, about where the famous Cucamonga vineyards now grow. He made frequent business trips between Rancho San Jose and Los Angeles, usually in an ox cart and accompanied by an Indian helper.

When Governor Manual Micheltorena was sent to Alta, California to put down a threatened revolt by the Los Californios, who desired to form an independent republic, Tiburcio Tapia feared that his wealth might be seized. To avert this, he secretly loaded his money and jewels, packed in boxes, aboard an ox cart, and left Los Angeles for San Bernardino, accompanied by the faithful old Indian.

Near the eastern boundary of Rancho San Jose (now a part of the city of Pomona), he halted near a grove of trees and sent the old Indian on into San Bernardino with a message for the alcalde to come out and meet him. When the Indian returned, he noticed that the boxes containing Tapia's wealth were missing from the ox cart.

Shortly after this incident, Tapia was stricken with fever and his condition gradually worsened. Realizing he was going to die, he revealed that he had buried his wealth near the place where he had rested while the Indian was gone. He said it was directly under the elbow-shaped limb of a great sycamore tree, but these were the only directions he gave, and all efforts to recover his treasure have, so far as it is known, been unsuccessful. Today the area is built up and all sycamore trees have been gone for years. **Map Code 14 L-8**

<u>Los Angeles County</u> — On the evening of Feb. 8, 1950, a jewelry salesman named Cohen, of 1543 Veteran Avenue, West Los Angeles, was held up and robbed of $200,000 worth of platinum and diamond Masonic pins and other expensive jew-

elry, a shipment recently received from New York. About a week later, James A. Miller and a party from Anaheim were picking mushrooms in an old olive grove on the McNally Ranch when they saw two men trying to push an automobile from a mudhole in which it was stuck. Helping extricate the car, the mushroom pickers noticed a freshly dug mound of earth nearby, as it drove away.

They dug up and uncovered a battered jewelry sample case containing four lodge pins, all of platinum and set with diamonds. Police later identified this with the Cohen robbery and thoroughly searched the old McNally Olive Grove, but found nothing. The belief prevailed that the thieves had buried the remainder of the loot in another part of the grove.

The old ranch has now been subdivided and is partly occupied by the community of La Mirada. Only a small part of the original olive grove still stands.
Map Code 16 D-5

Los Angeles County — On the highest hill in the Los Angeles suburb of Manhattan Beach, there stood a 3-story frame house for many years. Built in the 1800s, the house stood in the approximate center of the old Duncan Ranch, comprising about 23 acres. On the side of the house facing Santa Monica Bay, there was a balcony, and the story prevailed that pirates used this balcony as a place to flash signals to their ships at sea. When the right signal was given, the ships landed their contraband goods at the foot of First Street. When this old house was demolished and the ground cleared for truck gardening, a search was made for a treasure supposedly buried there, but none was found. **Map Code 16 D-2**

Los Angeles County — Santa Catalina Island lies in the Pacific Ocean about 27 miles southwest of Los Angeles Harbor. Only part of the island is open to the public, the remainder being privately held. The existence of gold on Catalina was known long before the island was acquired by the United States. William Yount, a pioneer Californian, while hunting sea otter on Catalina, found some rich outcroppings, but placed little value in his find. After the discovery of gold at Coloma in 1848, Yount made three trips to Catalina in search of the outcropping, but met with no success.

Other prospectors took up the search for Yount's Lost Mine, and several small finds were made. In 1863, a mining district was formed, but the Union, fearful that the Confederates might attempt to seize the island, placed forces on Catalina and the miners were forced to leave. Troops were withdrawn from the island

in 1864, but by that time the interest in gold on Catalina had waned. The last official record of a claim was filed in 1865. There is little doubt that Yount's find was genuine, but exactly where it was made is not definitely known.
Map Code 16 G-2

<u>Los Angeles County</u> — In 1861, General Placido Vega, agent for the Mexican patriot, Benito Juarez, went to California and collected gold, silver, and precious stones with which to buy arms in the struggle with Emperor Maximilian. It is estimated that $200,000 was collected. For safekeeping, the treasure was taken by three trusted men and buried in the hills near San Bruno in San Mateo County. This burial was observed from concealment by a sheepherder named Diego Moreno.

After the strangers left, Moreno dug up the treasure and fled to Los Angeles. Here he stopped at a tavern operated by a fellow Mexican at what is now the approximate intersection of Cahuenga Boulevard and Highland Avenue — the south entrance to Cahuenga Pass. Moreno slipped out one night and buried the money and jewels in six separate holes around a Fresno tree, from which he took bearings.

On a trip into Los Angeles, Moreno suddenly took ill and was taken to the home of another Mexican, Jesus Martinez. While apparently recovering from his illness, and wishing to repay Martinez for his kindness, Moreno told him of the treasure buried in Cahuenga Pass, and offered to take him there as soon as he was able to travel. However, Moreno took a turn for the worse and died. Pretending to be woodchoppers, Martinez and his son went to Cahuenga Pass and attempted to locate the treasure. Just as the Fresno tree was located, the elder Martinez dropped dead. The boy, believing there was a curse on the treasure, fled the scene and never again attempted to recover it.

About 1885, a Basque sheepherder named Correo, investigating the barking of his dog at a particular spot, dug down and brought up one of the buckskin parcels of treasure. He immediately took his wealth and went to Spain.

In 1939, the County of Los Angeles issued a permit for two mining engineers to dig for the treasure in one of the parking lots of the famed Hollywood Bowl. Nothing was found. Other attempts to locate Moreno's hoard have all failed. In all likelihood, the area in which the treasure was buried is now completely built up.
Map Code 16 B-3

<u>Los Angeles County</u> — When Mrs. Angie Parra of Los Angeles was a little girl, she lived with her parents at 3157 Boulder Street. Back of the main house, her grand-

father, Manuel Montejo, a very aged man, lived in a little shack. He paid for all of his requirements with gold coins of which he seemed to have an inexhaustible supply. When he died suddenly in 1925, no money was found among his effects.

Soon thereafter, the Parra property was sold to the City of Los Angeles for an extension of the Malabar School, now at 3200 Malabar Street. Mrs. Parra always believed that her grandfather had buried his wealth someplace on the Parra property.

Several times she sought permission to dig on that portion of the Parra lot acquired by the Malabar School, but was not successful until 1954, when she received permission to dig with the agreement that the City of Los Angeles was to receive one half of anything found. She hired two professional treasure hunters who dug and probed as school officials looked on.

Nothing was found, but Mrs. Parra still believes that her grandfather's money is there. **Map Code 16 B-3**

<u>Los Angeles County</u> — Don Francisco de Avila was alcalde of the pueblo of Los Angeles in the early 19th century. In 1818, he built an adobe home at what is now 14 Olvera Street, now restored and a private museum.

Don Francisco was a wealthy man, and each year as he sold his sheep and cattle, he became even richer. There being no banks in the pueblo, after each sale he placed his gold in tin cans, sealed them, and buried them under a pepper tree on his estate, but never more than a single can in a location. When Avila died suddenly in 1831, the secret of his buried gold died with him. There is not the slightest clue as to where the pepper tree stood, but in all probability, the site is now built up or paved over. **Map Code 16 B-3**

- ## SECRET GOLD MINE ON MOUNT DISAPPOINTMENT

And... Big Payoff When Eating Wild Onions For Lunch!?

<u>Los Angeles County</u> — The first known discovery of gold in California was made not far from Los Angeles, six years before Marshall's electrifying discovery at Coloma, when Francisco Lopez pulled up a bunch of wild onions for his lunch and found particles of gold clinging to their roots.

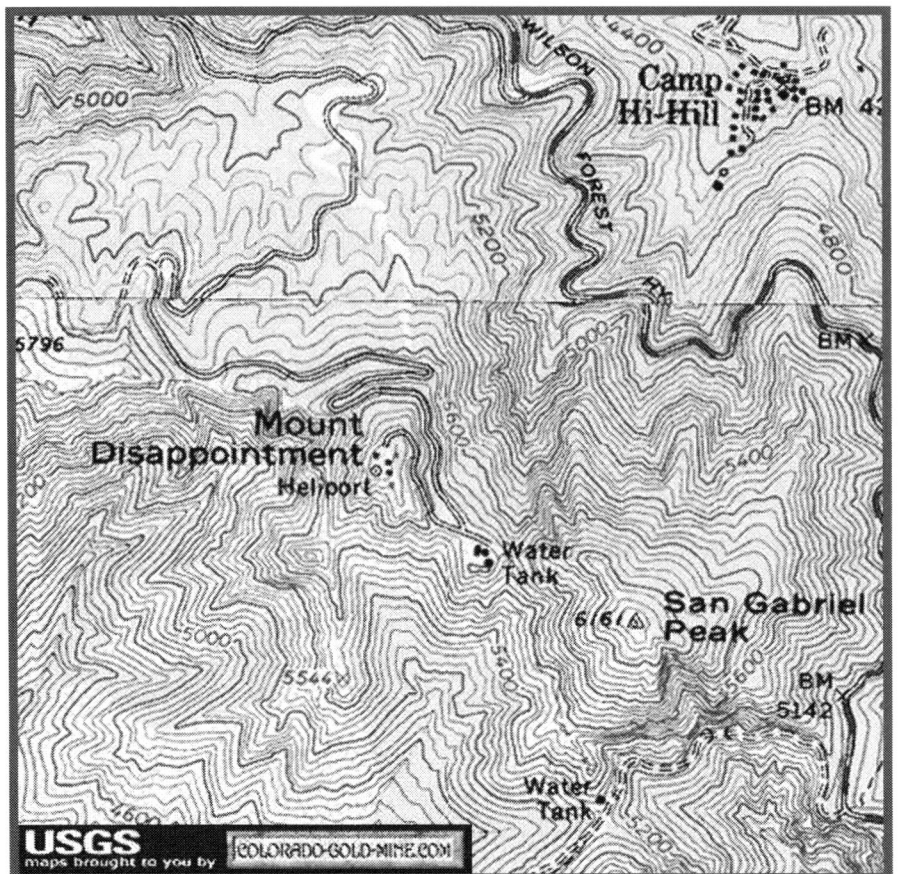

Los Angeles - Mount Disappointment

MAP THIS ON A TOPO MAP —
www.1wbta.com/Los-Angeles-Mount-Disappointment

Earlier unrecorded finds were undoubtedly made, and one of these may have been on Mount Disappointment, in the San Gabriel Mountains north of Pasadena, by an Indian who frequently brought a bag of gold into Los Angeles and always drank until it was gone.

Repeated attempts to follow the Indian to his secret mine failed, the pursuers always being lost in the foothills back of Pasadena. Finally, it was demanded of the Indian, upon threat of his life, that he take a party of white men to the mine. He refused and was killed. An occasional search is still made for the lost gold on Mount Disappointment. **Map Code 16 A-4**

<u>Los Angeles County</u> — In 1853, four bandits held up and robbed a stage at about what is now the site of Claremont. They secured an estimated $30,000 from the Wells Fargo chest. They fled up San Antonio canyon, but realizing that

a posse would soon be on their trail, decided to separate. The leader, with the money in his saddlebags, headed down the East Fork of the San Gabriel River to its junction with the main San Gabriel.

Three of the bandits were overtaken and killed at a site approximating the Rincon Ranger Station. The leader, after burying the saddlebags and their contents in a grove of oak trees at a site now believed to be Camp Oak Grove, maintained by the County of Los Angeles, was also killed. So far as it is known, this treasure has never been recovered. **Map Code 16 B-5**

<u>Los Angeles County</u> — A Catalina Island Indian chief named Turai was taken to the San Gabriel Mission on the mainland when he became ill. About to die, he told his friend, Sam Prentiss, who frequently hunted and fished on Catalina's shores, of a treasure buried along the shore at the base of a large tree. Prentiss moved to the island permanently and built a small cabin near Emerald Bay, where he concentrated his search for the treasure for almost 30 years.

Before Prentiss died, he told his secret to Santos Bouchette, son of the survivor of a ship wrecked on Catalina. Bouchette dug at the base of hundreds of trees, and while he did not locate the treasure, he did discover a vein of silver at Cherry Valley.

Finding this treasure will almost certainly be done by accident, as thousands of trees on Catalina were cut down for cordwood in the early days. **Map Code 16 G-2**

<u>Los Angeles County</u> — It has long been believed that the Indians of San Gabriel Mission worked a secret gold mine in the San Gabriel Mountains canyons north of Claremont.

There is no proof of this, but the area has long been prospected by Sunday hopefuls. Some color is found now and then, but no ore of any great value.

In modern times, one of the prospectors who turned up in the slopes above Claremont was a secretive German who built a crude shack in one of the low canyons and stayed to himself while he worked the surrounding area.

His supplies and provisions were brought to him by a friend who drove up Palmer Canyon and blew his horn. The German appeared from the brush — always from a different direction — picked up his supplies, and left, leaving no trail that anyone ever managed to follow.

One day, the strange German appeared at the camp of two other prospectors and displayed ore samples rich in gold. He revealed no information as to where the ore had been secured, and just as mysteriously, left. One day, the friend delivered a supply of provisions, and blew his horn in the usual manner.

The German did not appear nor did repeated blowings bring him. Later the canyons were searched, but the German seemed to have vanished completely. The mystery of his disappearance was never solved. Some speculate that he met with foul play or perhaps was killed in an accident.

Others believe that he had secured enough gold to satisfy his wants and simply walked away from his secret mine in the Claremont canyons. **Map Code 17 B-6**

<u>Los Angeles County</u> — Chatsworth (State 27) is a small town in the northwestern section of San Fernando Valley. In 1949, it was the scene of a search for $130,000 believed to have been buried near the home of an aged Mexican. The Mexican's young wife had run away from her husband in Mexico, and had accompanied an American man to Southern California. The aging Mexican husband converted his holdings to gold and followed, attempting to catch the fleeing pair.

His failing health, however, caused him to give up the chase, and he settled in a modest house in the then tiny settlement of Chatsworth. The fact that he always paid for everything in gold caused some speculation.

When he died in 1899, a freshly-dug empty hole was found at the base of a large tree near his home. Signs indicated that a heavy chest might have been dragged away, but rains had eliminated any possibility of following the trail.

It was believed that the old man, shortly before his death, had for some reason moved his gold to a new hiding place. Because of his physical condition, it was reasoned that he could not have taken it far. When his house was razed in 1949, the foundations were bulldozed in a search for the treasure, but nothing was found. Unless it has been found and never reported, this treasure is believed to still be where the aged Mexican placed it. **Map Code 16 A-1**

<u>Los Angeles County</u> — On April 27, 1863, the small steam tug Ada Hancock of the Banning Fleet was transferring passengers from the wharf at San Pedro to the steamer Senator, anchored in Wilmington Bay. Suddenly, the tug careened, admitting cold water to the engine room. The boiler exploded, demolishing the vessel. Twenty-six of the 53 passengers aboard were lost, including William

Ritchie, a Wells Fargo messenger who was carrying $10,000 in gold on his person, and Fred E. Kerlin of Fort Tejon, California, who was carrying $30,000 in greenbacks. So far as is known, none of this money was ever recovered. **Map Code 16 E-3**

Los Angeles County — The McDonnell Avenue Elementary School is located at 111 North McDonnell Avenue in East Los Angeles. On a vacant lot adjacent to the school is believed to be buried chests of jewels and currency, placed there about 1924 by a Mexican family said to have fled a political upheaval in their homeland. In 1962, a rotary digging machine was employed in a search for this treasure, but nothing was found. **Map Code 16 C-4**

Los Angeles County — When the United States declared war on Mexico in 1846, many Spanish families, fearful of the seizure of their wealth by the Americans, buried or hid their valuables and fled to the safety of Mexico.

Among those who fled Los Angeles was an unnamed Spaniard who is said to have buried a chest of treasure at Beaudry Avenue and Figueroa Terrace, near the heart of downtown Los Angeles. This is still an area inhabited largely by people of Spanish or Mexican descent. **Map Code 16 C-3**

Los Angeles County — An employee of the Governor Mine near Palmdale (State 14) knew that his employer was illegally hoarding gold, and that he kept it in a safe in the mine office, together with some other money.

Figuring that his employer could not report the theft of gold, the employee stole it and buried it nearby in five separate holes. However, the employer did report the theft and cast suspicion on the employee, who was eventually convicted and sentenced to prison.

After being released from prison, the thief tried to recover the gold, valued at $150,000, but found that he was under constant surveillance. He got into trouble again and was sentenced to a life term on a federal charge. In the prison hospital, the thief told a Mexican hospital attendant where the gold was buried and gave him a rough map. The Mexican enlisted the help of another man, and together they searched for the treasure, but with no success. **Map Code 15 K-8**

Los Angeles County — It is said that the Mission San Fernando Rey de España, in the San Fernando Valley section of Los Angeles, once shipped quantities of gold to Spain and that this gold came from "La Canada del Molino," which has been translated as

"Mill Creek." A creek by this name runs off the Big Tujunga northeast of the town of San Fernando, and because there has been some gold mining activity in this area, it is reasoned that the San Fernando Mission Mine was located in this area.

It is believed by some that the Monte Cristo Mine, found on Mill Creek off the Big Tujunga in the 1880s, is actually the rediscovered San Fernando Mission Mine. **Map Code 16 A-4**

<u>Los Angeles County</u> — Deadman's Cove is a slight indentation in the Pacific coast near Portuguese Bend and west of San Pedro. It has long been rumored that pirates once used the shelter of this cove in the Palos Verdes headland, and that they left a metal box here filled with Mexican gold, silver, and jewels. Several unsuccessful searches have been made for this treasure, the last of record being in 1952. **Map Code 16 E-2**

<u>Los Angeles County</u> — In the city of Pasadena, an unidentified mission treasure has been searched for, in the vicinity of Armada Drive and Zanja Street. Just where this treasure came from, and the circumstances of its hiding, are not explained by most writers on the subject. It is the opinion of this writer that the story has no basis in fact. **Map Code 16 B-4**

<u>Los Angeles County</u> — Near the prominent Huntington-Sheraton Hotel at 1401 S. Oak Knoll Drive in Pasadena, is said to be buried a cache estimated at $300,000. This treasure is said to have been buried by a Mexican family when fearful of an Indian raid, long before Pasadena was founded. **Map Code 16 B-4**

<u>Los Angeles County</u> — In downtown Los Angeles, a treasure of unknown origin has been sought in years past, at the end of Court Street just west of Flower Street. No details of this treasure are available, and if it exists, it will likely stay there because this area is completely built up or paved over. When E. A. Pruitt of Santa Monica sought permission from the Board of Public Works to dig for this treasure, he was turned down because he refused to divulge the origin and nature of the treasure. **Map Code 16 C-3**

<u>Los Angeles County</u> – Sanfrancisquito Canyon is in the western section of Los Angeles County, its lower extremity being between the towns of Newhall and Saugus. Part of its distance is traversed by a hard surface road, serving a popular recreational area. It was here that the first reported discovery of gold was made in California, by Francisco Lopez, in 1842.

A rancher living in the lower portion of the canyon carried on a small mining operation, and distrusting banks, buried an estimated $200,000 in gold coins near his adobe ranch house.

When he died without revealing where the fortune was hidden, his sons tore down part of the old adobe and found a quantity of gold coins concealed in various places. This started a search for the main portion of the treasure the sons believed their father had hidden. So far as it is known, it was never found.

When the Sanfrancisquito Dam broke above the ranch, drowning more than 400 people, what remained of the old adobe was completely washed away, and coins were scattered downstream, where they are occasionally found today. Whether or not the main cache was washed away, or merely covered with debris, has never been determined. **Map Code 14 L-8**

Los Angeles County — At an arson trial in Los Angeles in January, 1963, Fran Campbell of Burbank, self-styled "Queen of American Prospectors," testified that Spanish conquistadores buried millions in treasure in the area of Forest Lawn Memorial Park (a cemetery) in the Hollywood Hills. Miss Campbell also testified that Carlos Vasques, who robbed the San Fernando Bank about 1890, is supposed to have buried his loot in the same area. The judge did not allow Miss Campbell to elaborate on other treasures. **Map Code 16 B-3**

Los Angeles County — The town of Calabasas is at the far western end of Los Angeles County, just before it meets the Ventura County line. The area was once the hideout of outlaws, and the quasi-feudal domain of a Basque sheepherder, Miguel Leonis, who was once known as the "King of Calabasas." For many years, there have been periodic searches for the fortune that is supposed to have been buried to keep it from falling into the hands of outlaws. When the old sheepherder died, he left no directions to his treasure. The original adobe house of Miguel Leonis has been restored and is now open to the public. **Map Code 14 L-8**

Los Angeles County — According to an early California legend, there is a bullock cart full of gold buried in Santa Inez Canyon not far from where Sunset Boulevard meets the Coast Highway (State 1). About 1836, so the story goes, two padres accompanied by a few Indian servants were driving a cart heavily laden with gold, from San Fernando Mission to San Pedro. They were set upon by bandits as they reached the mouth of Santa Inez Canyon. As the Indians

fought off the attackers, the padres rolled the cart into a nearby marshy area where it slowly sank out of sight. Neither the priests nor the Indians were ever heard of again. Presumably they were killed by the frustrated bandits. When Sunset Boulevard was put through to the coast, the marsh was filled in.
Map Code 16 C-1

<u>Los Angeles County</u> — Wyatt Earp, of the famous Tombstone Earps, died in a bungalow court at 4000 ¾ West 17th Street in Los Angeles, in 1930. In the early 1960s, the Los Angeles Board of Education purchased the 7-unit bungalow court which was adjacent to the Mt. Vernon Junior High School. The bungalows were demolished.

At that time, an old lady who had lived in the court while Earp also was a tenant, revealed that she saw strange and rough looking characters visit him at night. Then she would hear what she thought was the floor boards being taken up, followed by the sounds of digging. This led to the suspicion that all or a part of the $80,000 taken in a stagecoach robbery in Arizona, which Earp was accused by some of participating in, might have been buried there. The site is now occupied by buildings and yards of the Mt. Vernon Junior High School.
Map Code 16 B-3

<u>Los Angeles County</u> — The little town of Duarte, in the greater Los Angeles area, was named after Andreas Duarte, who had a 4,000-acre tract on the site. He had a small adobe on his place, and is said to have buried his wealth nearby at the base of a sycamore tree that had an elbow-shaped branch. When American forces took over Los Angeles, Duarte fled south into Mexico, leaving his fortune behind.

In time, he returned to Los Angeles, and one of his sons lived on the old Duarte grant until about 1893, making many attempts to locate his father's buried fortune.

Apparently it was never found, for as late as 1918, freshly dug holes would often be found in the mornings, indicating that treasure hunters were at work during the night.

At that time, there were still many sycamores and oaks on the place, but later all were cut down when the entire grant was made into an orange grove.
Map Code 16 B-5

<u>Los Angeles County</u> — A party of shipwrecked Spaniards are said to have buried a chest of coins of unknown value at or near Reseda Boulevard and Eddy Avenue in

the Los Angeles suburb of Northridge. It is known that at least one search was made for this treasure before the area was built up, but if anything was found, it was not reported. No explanation is available as to why the treasure was brought this far inland for burial. **Map Code 15 L-8**

Los Angeles County — In the 1870s, E. A. "Doc" Bragg is said to have rediscovered a lost mission mine in the area of Sawmill Mountain, in the extreme northwestern corner of Los Angeles County. He reputedly took out a small fortune, keeping the location of the mine a secret. When he became involved in a shooting scrape with a neighbor, Bragg abandoned the mine and left the area.

According to Rose White, who searched for the twice-lost mine for many years, Bragg had told her father that he had taken $800,000 out of the mine, and gave directions for finding it. Rose's father had passed this information on to his daughter, who searched as long as she was able, but finally had to give up in defeat. **Map Code 14 K-8**

Los Angeles County — Griffith Park, in the City of Los Angeles, is a 3,761-acre slice of the easternmost of the Santa Monica Mountains, and is preserved largely in its original state. Pirates are said to have buried treasure here during the days when the Mexican regime enforced strict controls over the importation of foreign goods, with the result that smuggling became a thriving occupation in Los Angeles.

The park is under the control of the Recreation and Parks Commissioners, who have in the past been rather liberal in granting permission to search for treasures in Los Angeles parks. **Map Code 16 B-3**

Los Angeles County — Elysian Park, a 600-acre municipal recreational area in the City of Los Angeles, is the site of one or more rumored buried treasures, the origin of which seems to be obscure. One account places the value of the gold supposed to be buried in this beautifully wooded area at $6,000,000. It is said to have been buried there by a Mexican family fleeing a revolution in their homeland.

On three different occasions, the Los Angeles Recreation and Parks Commissioners have granted permission to dig for treasure in Elysian Park, with the City taking from 25 to 50 percent of anything found.

The last digging for this treasure occurred this year. So far as it has been reported, nothing has been found. **Map Code 16 B-3**

"Steamer Arriving At Santa Catalina Island," ca. 1909?
Published By Edward H. Mitchell, San Francisco

<u>Los Angeles County</u> — In May, 1919, J. M. Taylor of Los Angeles received a letter from his friend Guy Mayo in Buenos Aires, Argentina. Mayo sought Taylor's aid in recovering a buried treasure in Los Angeles. This is the story Mayo wrote.

On his deathbed, a friend told Mayo that he had become involved in trouble in Los Angeles in 1875, and had to leave the country in a hurry. He had had to leave $4,400 in gold which he had buried in the floor of a stable "about 84 feet west of Main Street, and about 90 feet north of High or Water Street." It is said that Taylor could never locate the site of the stable, and failed to recover the money.

In 1875, the area where the money was buried was largely undeveloped, but today it is completely built over and paved. If the money was uncovered during excavations, it seems never to have been reported. **Map Code 16 B-3**

<u>Los Angeles County</u> — Mission San Gabriel Arcangel, in the Los Angeles suburb of San Gabriel, was founded in 1771, and like most of California's missions, it has its treasure story. It is said that treasure allegedly worth millions was taken from the mission by Indians and carted to the hills in what is now the town of Monterey Park, where it was buried.

In the early 1930s, a party of men made a search for this treasure in the Coyote Pass area of Monterey Park, apparently without success. It is highly doubtful that any of the California missions possessed any "millions" to bury. **Map Code 16 C-4**

Los Angeles County — For many years a fabulous character known as "Louis the Fat" operated a popular French restaurant in Los Angeles, and accumulated a fortune, which he was never known to have banked.

On his death, a search was made of the restaurant, but his wealth was not found. It has been said that it was buried someplace in the vicinity of Main and Commercial Street, an area that is now completely occupied by buildings or is paved over.
Map Code 16 B-3

Vintage postcard, ca. 1900 to 1915?
The east face of Main Street between Arcadia Street and Commercial Street, which is from the Baker Block to Ducommun Corner (from the pioneer hardware merchant who originally had his shop near here). In the center, behind the street pole, is the St. Charles Hotel, originally the Bella Union Hotel, which was the main hotel in the 1850s. Commercial Street, formerly Commercial Row - was originally the very heart of the Los Angeles business community.

Los Angeles County — In the late 16th century, there began a two-way sea lane traffic between Acapulco, Mexico, and Manila in the Philippines.

From Mexico, went millions in gold and silver, and the returning galleons brought in silks, jade, antiques, and other products from China.

One of these "Manila Galleons" went down someplace off Catalina Island, and apparently some of the cargo washed ashore, for when Sebastian Vizcaino went ashore on Catalina in 1602, he was shown rich cloths from China by the Indians.

The value of this cargo has been placed at $2,000,000, although we do not know how this figure was arrived at. Supposedly this hulk lies off Seal Rock at the island's southeastern tip.

At least two other galleons in the Acapulco-Manila trade are said to have gone down off Santa Catalina. Both of these wrecks are said to rest off the southern side of the island, in Outer Santa Barbara Channel.

One is the Nuestra Señora de Ayuda, believed to have capsized in a storm in 1641, taking an estimated $500,000 in treasure down with it.

In spite of the fact that Spanish frigates were not used in the Pacific to escort treasure-laden galleons, there is a story that one went down off the northwestern tip of Catalina with a cargo of treasure valued at $1,300,000.

Frigates were used to escort some Spanish treasure fleets in the Atlantic, but in order to give them more speed, their cargoes were kept as light as possible.

In January, 1754, the Spanish galleon San Sebastian, loaded with $2,000,000 worth of Mexican gold and bound for Manila, foundered on submerged rocks about halfway between Santa Catalina and San Clemente Island, in what is known as the Outer Santa Barbara Channel.

It is said that the crew managed to get about half of the gold off before the vessel went to the bottom. At least two groups of skin divers have tried to locate the hulk of the San Sebastian, but without any reported success. **Map Code 15 M-8**

Counties M – P

Would one of you ladies stir that pot of chili? Nothing like some smoke flavor on beans and chili peppers! Alright, gather closer… I think this 'bout explains what happened to California in the Rush.

"When it was over, more than four hundred thousand men had tried their hand at digging for gold. Some starved, lost everything they came with, and returned home feeling as failures. Others found incredible wealth, and found their lives changed forever, for the better.

ut no matter how each man faced the end of the gold rush, each who lived through its trials had attained, whether returning home or staying on, a wealth of stories and experiences to share." (essortment.com)

You and I, good friends, are carrying this wealth of stories on into the future!

Marin County — In one of the old buildings of Rancho Burdell, near Novato (US 101), is an old adobe wall, once a part of the home of Camillo Ynitia, last chief of the Olompali Indians. Soon after, he sold the Olompali Rancho for $5,200, Ynitia was murdered by his brother, who believed that the gold had been hidden in the nearby hills. So far as it is known, this treasure has never been found. **Map Code 12 F-3**

Marin County — Angel Island, across Raccoon Strait from Point Tiburon, is the largest island in San Francisco Bay. In 1911, according to many accounts, the American steamer R. J. Cochrane sank off Angel Island in 16 fathoms of water. Aboard the vessel, and never recovered so far as it is known, was $100,000 in gold bullion and $14,000 in lead pigs. The above story has been repeated for years, but recently a careful treasure student points out that no R. J. Cochrane appears listed in the shipping registers at the time of the alleged sinking, but that there was an H. J. Corcoran which sank in San Francisco Bay in 1912, after colliding with another vessel. She is said to have carried a safe in which there was $30,000 in gold bullion. **Map Code 13 B-8**

Marin County — Point Reyes juts out into the Pacific Ocean south of the town of Point Reyes. It has been the scene of several shipwrecks, including that of the Manila galleon San Augustine, which is said to have gone down in 1595 with an unknown amount of treasure. The names of Spanish galleons frequently duplicated each other.

There are, for example, two other San Augustines reportedly wrecked off the Pacific Coast of America. **Map Code 12 F-3**

<u>Marin County</u> — Just south of the mouth of San Rafael Creek, and directly northwest of California Point, is Red Rock, a small island called Golden Point on some maps. It is an uninhabited area of one or two acres, and there is a tradition of a buried treasure here, although our research has not determined its origin. **Map Code 12 F-3**

- ## LOST GOLD VEIN ON THE MARIN SIDE OF GOLDEN GATE

Covered Up When The Golden Gate Bridge Was Erected!

❖ ❖ ❖

<u>Marin County</u> — In 1851, a rich quartz vein of gold was discovered on the Marin side of Golden Gate, and the Golden Gate Mining Company was formed.

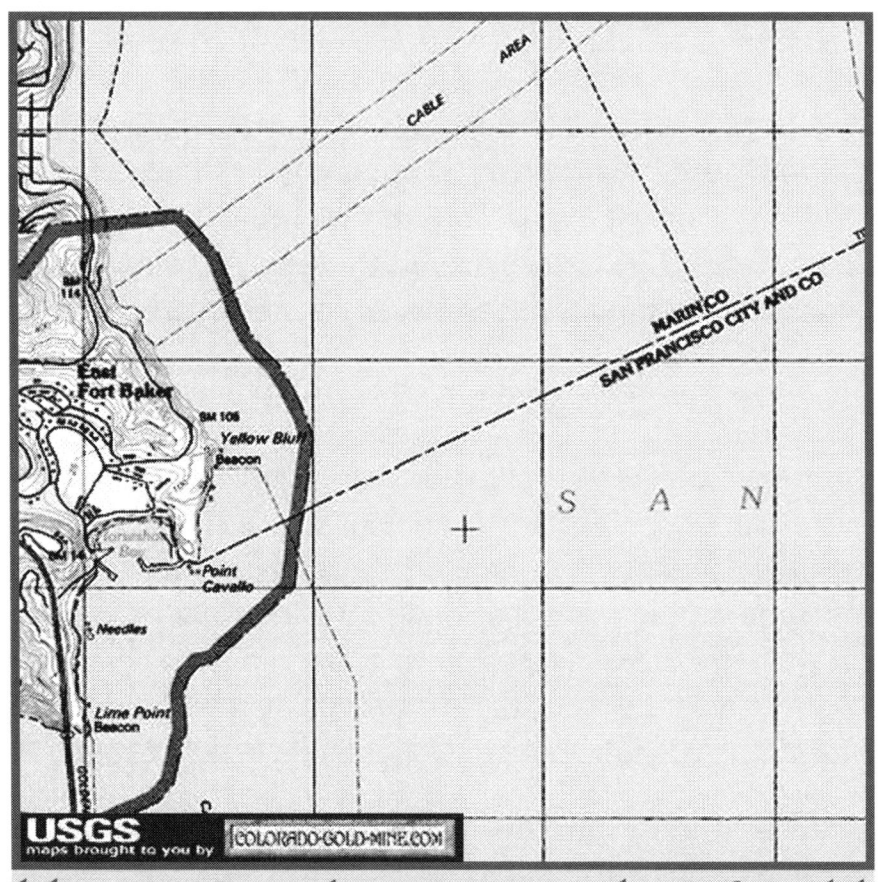

Lost Gold Vein On The Marin Side Of Golden Gate

MAP THIS ON A TOPO MAP —
www.1wbta.com/Lost-Gold-Vein-On-The-Marin-Side-Of-Golden-Gate

It was the cold and foggy season, and when the vein disappeared a few feet below the surface, the company abandoned the claim and walked away. Many have insisted that the vein merely pinched out and would reappear again. Efforts to locate the old vein have failed, and it is believed that it might have been covered up when the Golden Gate Bridge was erected. **Map Code 13 B-8**

Marin County — In July, 1595, Sebastian Cermenho was sent from Manila in the 200-ton galleon, San Sebastian, to search for a safe anchorage in northern California. The captain made land at Cape Mendocino and sailed down the coast, finally anchoring in what is now known as Drake's Bay, about 30 miles north of San Francisco. Ashore they found the Indians to be friendly. One day while most of the crew visited ashore, the clumsy, over-loaded galleon broke her anchor in a mild gale and drifted inshore where she capsized. The amount of treasure carried by the San Sebastian was moderate, as was the case with most of the eastbound Manila galleons. **Map Code 12 F-3**

Marin County — In 1957, a motorist stopped to repair a flat tire near the mouth of Corte Madera Creek on Drake's Bay. While doing so, he picked up a piece of black metal which he eventually took to the University of California for examination. Carefully cleaned, the plate revealed an inscription claiming all the land for the Queen of England, and it was signed by Francis Drake. After exhaustive research, scientists accepted this as the authentic "plate of brasse" as recorded by Francis Fletcher, chaplain aboard Drake's treasure-laden ship, the Golden Hinde.

This supported the story that Drake did bring the Golden Hinde into what is now known as Drake's Bay, in 1579, upon his return trip to the north, trying in vain to find the fabled Northwest Passage. He remained here for six weeks, reconditioning his vessel and gathering food for the renewed voyage. While here, it is said, Drake lightened the burden of the Golden Hinde by burying part of the treasure cargo ashore. **Map Code 12 F-3**

Mariposa County — On the morning of December 12, 1851, Joseph F. A. Marr, then the county treasurer of Mariposa County, left his home in Agua Fria, then the county seat, to collect taxes from the miners scattered at the various diggings in the Mariposa Hills. Before departing, however, Marr buried or hid, presumably in the vicinity of his home, 300 hexagonal gold slugs minted at Mount Ophir, then worth $15,000. This was money belonging to the county, and it was secreted in this manner because there were no banks in Agua Fria.

Late in the afternoon on that same day, Marr was overtaken by a heavy rainstorm that flooded the streams. As he attempted to cross Deadman's Creek, within sight of the Lewis Store on the main road between Mariposa and Legrand (Merced County), both horse and rider were swept away by the torrent of water. Marr's body was found on the following day, but the saddlebags containing the tax money he had collected could not be located, even after the flood waters subsided.

The amount of this money was never determined, but it could have been a considerable sum, as he was collecting a $20 head tax on each of the foreign miners.

Searchers for the Marr treasure immediately dug up the banks of Deadman's Creek, the hillsides around Agua Fria, Marr's garden, and ransacked the old courthouse itself, but not one of the $50 slugs, now valued by some as high as $10,000 each, has ever been found. Although nothing exists of Agua Fria today, the site is easy to locate. It was situated about six miles east of Mariposa at about the point where State 140 crosses Agua Fria Creek. **Map Code 13 G-6**

Mariposa County — When gold was first discovered in the bare-looking slopes around Bagby (State 49), it attracted many Chinese and the native population of Mexicans. There is a story here about a Mexican prospector who, injured in a fall on one of his many lone trips, stopped to rest near Bagby. Starting to move on, he noticed he had been sitting on a seam of quartz streaked with gold.

Marking the place in his memory as best he could, he moved down the long grade through "Hell's Hollow" and into the little town of Bagby, where he secured help. In a few days the Mexican miner was dying of complications, and directed that a letter be sent to his family in Mexico, telling them of the rich ledge and approximately where to find it. Prospectors soon heard the story and rushed out to find the dying Mexican's ledge. Supposedly it was never found.
Map Code 13 G-6

Mariposa County — The town of Bagby (State 49) was once known as Benton Mills and was the scene of much gold mining activity in the 1850s. On the Merced River near here is said to be a cave in which a Mexican stored several burro loads of rich gold ore which he presumably mined in the area.

Covering his shaft and the entrance to the cave, the Mexican returned to his native country to bring relatives back with him to assist in working the mine. While there he was killed, and no trace of the secret mine has ever been found.
Map Code 13 G-6

Mariposa County — California's fabled bandit, Joaquin Murrieta, frequented the early mining camps of the gold country and was seen many times around Bagby (State 49). Wherever Murrieta spent much time, there grew up a romantic but seldom documented story of his buried treasure. One of these stories concerns $60,000 he is said to have hidden in a cave near Bagby. It is said that the particular cave was selected because it contained many skeletons, and Murrieta reasoned that his superstitious countrymen would not enter the cave in search of his gold. **Map Code 13 G-6**

Mariposa County — When Coulterville (State 49) was a prosperous mining town of several thousand people, a Frenchman built a wood-burning smelter on the banks of Maxwell's Creek to extract the gold from the ore taken from his nearby mine.

Another Frenchman, employed at the mill, worked a secret placer in the same area and accumulated a sizeable fortune in gold nuggets which he buried in an iron bean pot near the old mill. Just before he planned to take his gold and return to France, he was killed by a falling beam. His bean pot of gold, so far as it is known, has never been found. **Map Code 13 G-6**

Mariposa County — In the 1850s, Mount Ophir was a thriving town, principally because of a rich mine nearby, and the private mint built here by J. L. Moffat. A marker along State 49, less than two miles northwest of Mount Bullion, marks the site. Near the ruins of the old mint is an arched stone vault, broken and ravaged by treasure seekers. Raw gold is said to have been stored here, and somehow the rumor started and spread that a treasure was hidden here, although there appears to be no explanation for it.

Moffat's mint, the first legally authorized by Congress in California, was famous for its $50 hexagonal gold slugs. Some of these could have been lost in the area, but there is no record of it. Extremely scarce today, these coins are said to bring as much as $10,000 each on the collectors market. **Map Code 13 G-6**

Mendocino County — The town of Mendocino (State 1) was named for Cape Mendocino. The Cape has been the scene of several shipwrecks, and the town of Mendocino was founded by a party seeking to salvage tea and silk from one of these wrecked vessels. One of the wrecked ships was believed to be carrying miners from Alaska and $65,000 in gold bullion. Before the vessel went down, the captain managed to get the ship's safe ashore and buried it within sight of State Highway 1. Just why the safe and its treasure were not later recovered is not explained, but there have been many searches made for it, most of them concentrated in the area just north of the town of Mendocino. **Map Code 12 D-2**

<u>Merced County</u> — Snelling, once a mining town and, until 1872, the seat of Merced County, is located on the Merced River in northeastern Merced County. In 1857, three young prospectors on their way from the northern mines to San Francisco stopped here for the night, and made camp in the timber along the river. Each man carried $5,000 in hexagonal $50 gold coins secured at Mount Ophir, and an estimated $60,000 each in raw gold, for a total of some $195,000. Before bedding down for the night, this treasure was taken to a nearby grove of trees and buried for the night for safekeeping.

Sometime during the night, people in Snelling heard gunshots along the river. Investigating, they found the three prospectors dead, apparently murdered in their sleep, as there were no signs of a struggle. This indicated that the killers knew nothing of the cache of gold, and that the motive for the murders was to secure the miners' horses and outfits. It is believed that this treasure has never been found, in spite of a great deal of searching for it. **Map Code 12 G-6**

<u>Merced County</u> — About 1855, the treasure chest secured in a stagecoach robbery was buried near Snelling (see above). It is said that the robber buried the chest in a shallow pit while he went into Snelling to a saloon to wet his whistle, intending to recover it and be on his way in a short time. He became involved in a brawl, however, and was killed.

Knowing that he was going to die of his wounds, he told of the buried chest, but gave only vague directions for finding it. It is believed that the chest may have been covered by a gold dredger. **Map Code 12 G-6**

<u>Merced County</u> — In the 1860s or 1870s, Basque sheepherders occupied Rancho Centinela, between the little towns of Centinela and San Luis Gonzoga. Rumors had it that one of the Basques sold his flock for a considerable sum of gold, which he buried somewhere near the two-story adobe structure in which they lived.

Shortly after this incident, he is said to have lost his mind and could never thereafter remember where he had hidden his wealth. The story spread and many treasure seekers were attracted. In a vain search for the money, they tore up the entire yard and a portion of a nearby field. The adobe structure was torn down in 1890 when the property was acquired by the Miller and Lux cattle interests. **Map Code 12 G-5**

Merced County — After robbing and murdering Chinese miners of the Mokelumne and Calaveras river mining camps, Joaquin Murrieta and his gang are said to have camped on the Merced River near Snelling. Here the bandit leader is said to have buried a small iron chest containing $30,000 in gold. It is not explained why this treasure was seemingly abandoned. It is said that in the 1930s, a dredge working on the river brought up a chest of this description, but before it could be recovered, it slipped and fell into a deep hole. Efforts to recover it by divers failed. **Map Code 12 G-6**

Merced County — West of the old Rancho Panoche is the pleasant little mountain valley of Saucelitos. At the lower end of the valley, Tiburcio Vasquez and his band of outlaws had a hideout.

It was here that Juan Soto, a member of the gang, is said to have buried his share of the Vasquez loot while he rode into the Pfiefer adobe to secure salt for the barbecue the outlaws were planning. Sheriff Henry Morse of Santa Clara County happened to be at the Pfiefer Ranch where a fiesta was in progress. He recognized Soto and killed him on the spot. It is believed that Juan Soto's treasure has never been found. **Map Code 12 G-5**

Modoc County — Alturas (US 395-299), the seat of Modoc County, is in a region whose history is one of violent and bloody Indian warfare. Captain "Holden" Dick was one of the more friendly Indians in the region. He frequently came into Alturas and traded large nuggets of gold for supplies. He seemed to have an inexhaustible source of gold.

One day two men decided to find out where Captain Dick's gold came from. They followed him out of Alturas, and neither was ever seen again. The Indian was accused of doing away with them, and on his next trip into Alturas, he was arrested and jailed.

One night, a "committee" broke into the unguarded jail, dragged Captain Dick out, and hanged him. Following Dick's death, his squaw was questioned as to the source of the gold. She refused to tell, and died suddenly under mysterious circumstances. After the squaw's death, a sheepherder began trading the same type of gold nuggets. It was suspected that he had stumbled upon Captain Dick's secret mine, and he was followed. No mine was found. Soon he, too, disappeared, never to be seen again. In spite of all the searches made for the Lost Holden Dick Mine, it has never been found. **Map Code 12 A-6**

- ## **WHITEMAN'S LOST CEMENT MINE IN THE BURNT COUNTRY**

Reddish Cement Holding Gold "Like Raisins In A Pudding"

❖❖❖

<u>Mono County</u> — No lost mine in the history of California created more excitement while it lasted than a vein of "cement" in which "lumps of gold," were set "like raisins in a pudding," according to those that allegedly saw the samples. No other California lost mine has been steeped in more mystery, or has left in the wake of its search more cold-blooded murders.

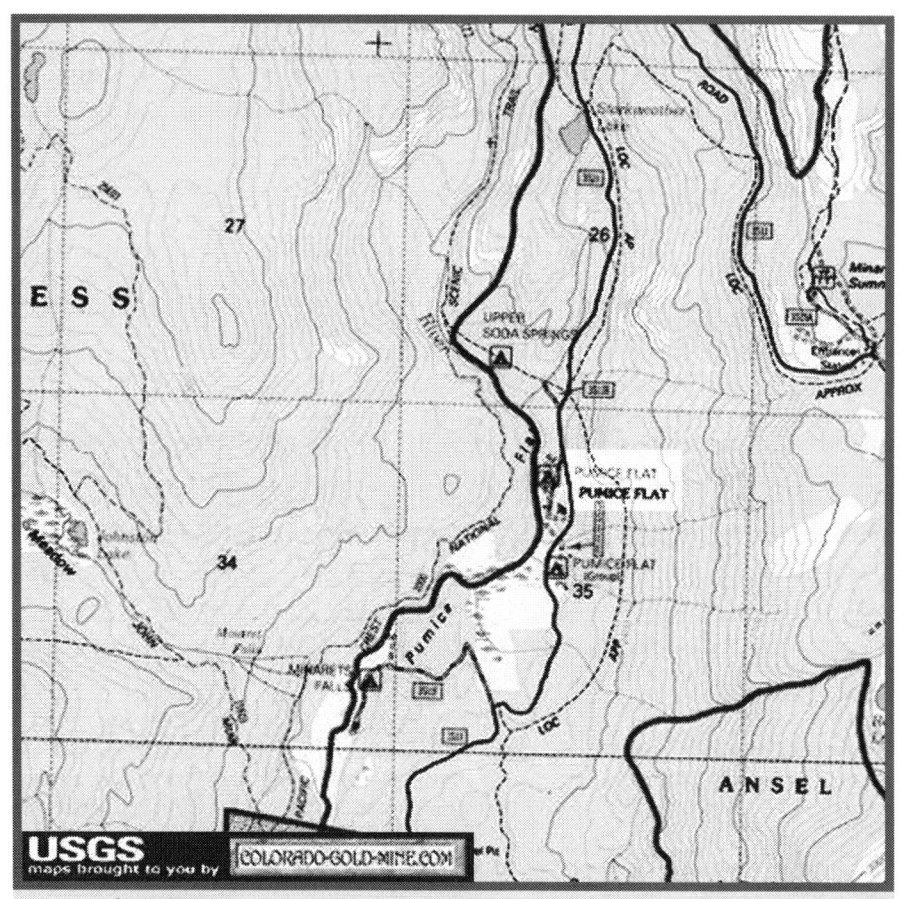

Whiteman's Lost Cement Mine In Burnt Country

MAP THIS ON A TOPO MAP —
www.1wbta.com/Whitemans-Lost-Cement-Mine-In-Burnt-Country

There are two versions of the manner in which the "Cement Mine" was originally found, but they vary little in basic detail. Three German brothers fled into the eastern slopes to escape a band of Indians. Here they found a peculiar "cement-like" substance which was rich in gold. They took out what they could carry and started for San Francisco. Along the way, one fell and broke his leg. He was either abandoned or killed by the others.

Detailing The Whiteman's Mine In Burnt Country Story

Special note: The use of online USGS map sites provides the exciting ability to detail out your search. This is a close-up map of the Pumice Flats area.

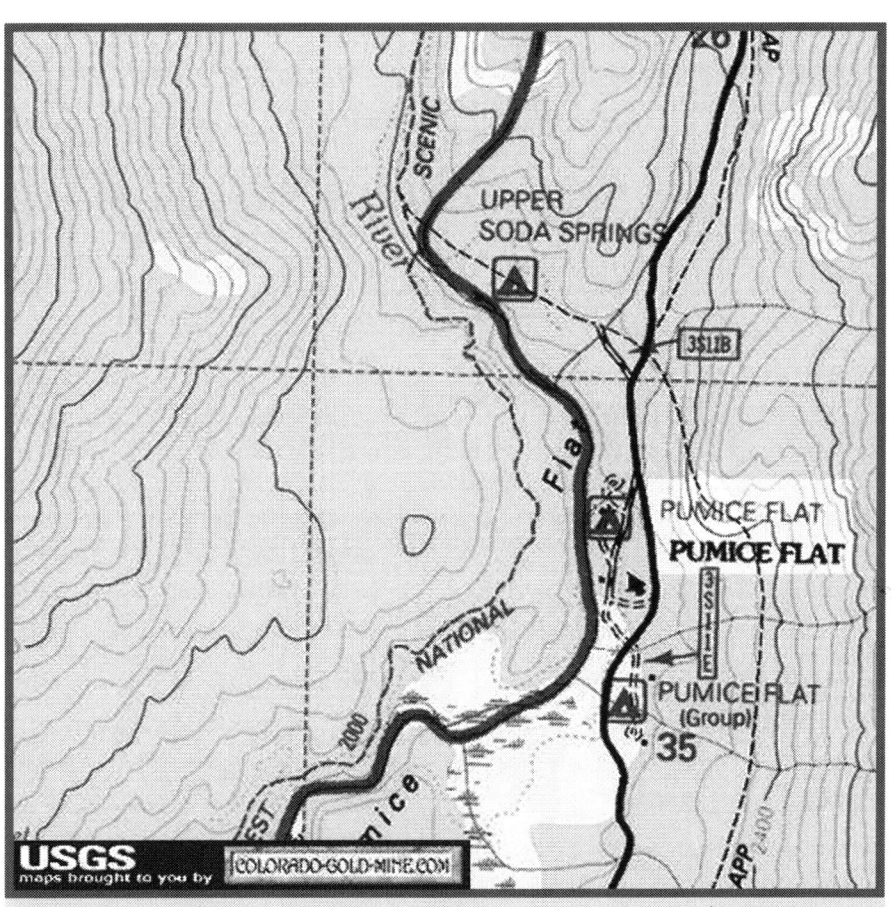

MAP THIS ON A TOPO MAP —
www.1wbta.com/Mono-Detailing-The-Whitemans-Mine-Story

The second brother died of natural causes before reaching his goal, and the third finally arrived in San Francisco in a sick and dying condition. He was treated by a Dr. Randall. When informed that he could not survive, the ailing man offered the doctor the ore samples and gave him a crude map of the region south of Mono Lake and at the headwaters of the Owens River. It was in what he called "burnt country," a region well known today as Pumice Flat, an area of gigantic ash heaps and pumice silt of past volcanic eruptions. Dr. Randall found the 10 pounds of ore given to him to be filled with pieces of free gold.

Just why Dr. Randall took four years to act on his good fortune is not known, but it was not until the spring of 1861 that he rode into Monoville to find the whole country excited over the news of some rich finds — not lost mines, but the real thing. Dr. Randall did not state his reason for being in Monoville, nor was he asked. He quietly hired two men to guide him to a forbidding stretch of wastelands known then and today as Pumice Flat, about 8 miles north of Mammoth Canyon, and dominated by Mammoth Mountain.

- ## THROWING THE COUNTRY INTO A FRENZY OF EXCITEMENT

There, Dr. Randall located and staked out 160 acres of land which was later duly recorded and became known in time as Whiteman's Camp. After this, Dr. Randall returned to San Francisco. No one thought much of his visit, but it was the beginning of an episode that was to throw the whole country into a frenzy of excitement within a few months.

In the summer of 1861, after Dr. Randall's short visit to the Mono area, a stranger who called himself Farnsworth appeared in Monoville and spread the news that he had discovered a deposit of rich gold-bearing cement while prospecting south of Mono Lake and near the headwaters of the Owens River. He had samples of ore to prove it. Farnsworth became friendly with Robert Hume, a well-known San Franciscan who was highly respected in the Mono region.

Before many days, they were outfitted and riding south out of town.

About two weeks later, Farnsworth rode into Monoville on a well-lathered horse. He was hatless and his clothing showed unmistakable signs of a fight. He said they had been attacked by Indians, and that Hume had been killed while he had barely escaped with his life. He pointed to the bullet holes in his coat, but some thought they looked like knife holes. People recalled that Robert Hume was known to have $700 on him when he had ridden out with Farnsworth. Plainly, Farnsworth was suspected of foul play. A self-appointed committee placed him under guard while others rode out to investigate.

They were able to trace the two men to a small stream, now known as Deadman Creek, from the incident. About four miles northeast of Pumice Flat, where Dr. Randall had staked out his mysterious quarter-section of land, they found a campsite. By tracing one man's tracks down to the stream, they came upon a small pile of rocks, underneath which they uncovered the head of Robert Hume. The rest of the decapitated body was found a short distance away, identified by the name inside a ring on its finger.

A rider was dispatched to Monoville with the news, and with instructions to strengthen the guard over Farnsworth. A few days later, Farnsworth managed to escape from under the nose of a snoozing guard. He was never seen again.

In the spring of 1862, Dr. Randall returned to Monoville and hired 11 men, including a cook named Van Horn, and a well-known miner named Gideon "Gid" Whiteman.

At this time, Dr. Randall assertedly showed samples of a reddish "cement" ore containing gold, and related how he had obtained them from the dying German. He stated that the 11 men would prospect every foot of his 160 acres until the main ledge was found.

- ## MYSTERIOUS LAND & MINE, MYSTERIOUS DISAPPEARANCES

After a few weeks, Dr. Randall, too, inexplicably disappeared, and he was never heard of again.

Using Monoville as his headquarters, Gideon Whiteman came and went mysteriously, causing a wave of excitement wherever he appeared. There were those who thought Whiteman had found Dr. Randall's mine without the doctor's knowledge, and had killed him to get the mine all to himself. The mystery deepened when Whiteman rode out of Monoville one day and joined the list of those figures associated with the now lost Cement Mine who were never seen again.

Other mysterious characters came to Monoville and Aurora, stayed a few weeks, and then departed with new-found partners in search of the Lost Cement Mine. Often, these newly-acquired partners were never heard of again.

In 1877, a man named McDougall was picked up in San Francisco in a dying condition. He is said to have confessed to a priest that he had been hired by a man named Kent who had found the Randall mine in 1869. The dying man said that together they had worked the mine and had taken out $400,000 in gold, which Kent had packed out and shipped to Chicago. Tiring of the operation, and afraid that the area was going to fill with prospectors, they had hid all traces of the mine and abandoned the project.

Perhaps no one will ever know how many of these stories associated with the Whiteman Lost Cement Mine are true, nor will anyone ever know how many expeditions have searched the "burnt country" for the reddish cement holding gold "like raisins in a pudding," but it is said that for many years, from one to 20 independent searches were made every year. And there are still those who believe Whitman's Lost Cement Mine will one day be found. ^{Map Code 13 G-7}

<u>Mono County</u> — Near the summit of the High Sierras, to the west of the town of Mono Lake (US 395), is said to be a lost gold mine originally found by a Mexican who was chasing a stray mule. It is said that the Mexican later took in a partner, and together they packed out four mule loads of gold ore. Both men were killed before they returned to the mine, and their rich deposit has never been found.
^{Map Code 13 F-7}

<u>Mono County</u> — High up in the Sierras at the north end of Mono Lake, an old miner is said to have found a rich ledge of gold. One day he came into a friend's camp at the edge of Mono Lake and complained that he was ill. The friend, another miner named Shepard, got him to a hospital in Carson City, Nevada. The sick man told Shepard if he didn't get well enough to come back to the mine, he would tell him exactly where the ledge was located. A few days later, Shepard received word that his friend had died. So far as it is known, the mine has never been located. ^{Map Code 13 F-7}

<u>Mono County</u> — Many soldiers serving in the west found a little time to prospect, and it is said that some even joined the army to get shipped west, gain a little experience, and then desert to become prospectors. When General Fremont camped about five miles west of Bridgeport (US 395), it is said that two of his soldiers, prospecting in their off time, made a rich strike.

When the command was ordered to move on, they deserted to work their claim, regularly bringing gold into Bridgeport. They were finally caught and placed in prison. It is speculated that they never again had the opportunity to work their mine, and supposedly it is still there. The region did produce a lot of gold.
^{Map Code 13 F-7}

Mono County — Saloons and gambling halls thrived during Bodie's wild boom as a gold camp after the discovery of gold there in 1852. Money was so free that miners threw $20 gold pieces to kids in the street, just to see them scramble. One miner accumulated a fortune of $25,000, which he is said to have hidden in or around his house at the edge of town. One night he was killed by a drunken fellow miner, and people practically demolished his house searching for his wealth. So far as we know, it was never found. **Map Code 13 F-7**

Mono County — Early in the year 1880, the stage from Bodie to Carson was held up shortly after it pulled out of Bodie. The bandits got away with $30,000 in gold bullion. A posse picked up their trail and soon overtook the two outlaws. In the fight that followed, one of the men was killed and buried on the spot, while the other was taken alive and placed in jail.

A day or two later, and before telling where the loot was hidden, he died, probably a suicide. Two miners, Frank Holmes and a man named McCullough, hunted for months for the cache, concentrating their efforts in a region about 20 miles north of Bodie and along the old stage road to Carson City. **Map Code 13 F-7**

Mono County — Sonora Pass over the High Sierras is located on State 108 at the common meeting place of three county lines — Mono, Alpine, and Tuolumne. In the late 1840s, a party of Mexicans discovered a rich ledge of gold ore near the summit of Sonora Pass. They mined the ledge and packed the ore out on burros to an arrastre they had built near the town of Sonora. On one of the pack trips out of the mountains, they were attacked by bandits and the entire group of Mexicans was killed. It is believed that this ledge has never been rediscovered. **Map Code 12 F-7**

Mono County — McGee Creek runs west off of US 395, west of Crowley Lake, and heads at McGee Lake in the High Sierras. Two Indians herded sheep in all the meadows around McGee Lake during the summer months. Once when they came down for the winter, they picked up some rocks with which to balance the slipping pack on one of the mules. When they unloaded the packs some time later, an old prospector named George Brown happened to see the discarded rocks. He recognized at once that the rocks were rich in gold. All efforts by Brown and the Indians to locate the place where the rocks had been picked up, failed.

It was their conclusion that the debris washed down by the snow run-off probably covered the ledge. **Map Code 13 G-7**

Monterey County — Dutra Creek is the northwest fork of Carpojoro Creek. The former is in Monterey County and the latter is in San Luis Obispo County. Near the headwaters of Dutra Creek, a few miles east of State 1, the padres of Mission San Antonio de Padua are said to have maintained a silver mine which was known locally as the "Priest Mine." It is said that Indians secured silver from the mines long before the arrival of the Spanish missionaries, and with the arrival of the padres, the ore was carried over a road to San Antonio de Padua Mission to the north.

Aged Indians described the location of the mine as being north of a pear orchard where the trail passed a pine tree. At this point, a distant view of the ocean was obtained. Prospectors of modern times have found traces of some excavations, but no silver has been found in the region. This is one of the more plausible of the several lost mission mines in California. The region is accessible only by rough trails. **Map Code 14 I-4**

Monterey County — When wealthy rancher, and alcalde of the little mission town of San Juan Bautista (San Benito County), Don Jose Maria Sanchez was apparently drowned in a flooded stream, his wealth, consisting of 17 sacks, each containing $5,000 in gold dust, was taken to Monterey by the administrator of the estate and secreted in a hole in the adobe foundation of the administrator's home.

When the alcalde's widow married, and the new husband was unable to secure the gold dust unless he paid what he thought was an unjust fee, it started a legal battle in which kidnapping and murder were featured. Finally, only one man knew where the treasure was after it was whisked away from the administrator's hiding place. He was Jerry McMahon, brother of Don Jose Sanchez's widow. When he was killed in an exchange of shots in a Monterey hotel, the secret hiding place of the Sanchez fortune in gold dust was known by none.

Where is it? Presumably in or around Monterey. **Map Code 14 H-4**

Monterey County — In the Ventana Primitive Area, southwest of Monterey (State 1), is Ventana Park, which legend says is the site of the Lost Mine of the Ventana. Indians are said to have mined gold there for the padres of the missions of Monterey and Carmel. This mine is also placed on Double Ventana Cone, which is still farther to the southwest.

Gold has been and is still mined to some extent in this general area, giving some credibility to the story. **Map Code 14 L-4**

Monterey County — On the summit of the old trail from Rancho San Bernabe up through Pine Canyon and down to Rancho Milpitas, is an immense pile of jagged rocks with a cave in them. This was frequently used by travelers in the early days as a night shelter. On top of these rocks, unseen until the steep ascent is made, is a flat piece of ground several acres in extent. This is said to have been the hidden pasture where Tiburcio Vasquez and his band of outlaws hid their stolen horses. There is the usual story of Vasquez leaving treasure in one of the small caves in the rocks. The area is just south of King City (US 101) and is difficult to locate without local assistance. **Map Code 14 I-5**

Monterey County — Hippolyte Bouchard, a French privateer sailing under the flag of Argentina, is the only pirate of note ever to molest the California coast. In 1818, he made a general nuisance of himself, raiding Monterey, Santa Barbara, and San Diego. It is said that when he entered Monterey on Nov. 20, 1818, the church treasures were quickly gathered up and hidden in the hills of Carmel Valley. Just why these treasures were not recovered and returned to Monterey is not explained. But maybe it was because, as the padres of Carmel Mission said, they were never taken there. **Map Code 14 H-4**

Monterey County — There is a legend that the Indians of Carmel Mission, working in the gold mine operated by the mission to the south, did not turn over all the gold they mined to the good padres, but secreted the fine gold on their persons and retained it. This would then be tamped into the hollow quills of seagulls and hidden in a cave near the mouth of the Carmel River. The reason for this larceny is not made clear, as it appears that the Indians did not use the gold for trading purposes. **Map Code 14 H-4**

Monterey County — It is an established fact that Francis Drake's ship, the Golden Hinde, carried a vast amount of pirated treasure when it navigated the California coast in 1579. Although there is a story that Drake took the Golden Hinde into Stillwater Cove, now a small yacht harbor about 14 miles north of Monterey, and lightened the vessel's cargo by carrying part of the treasure ashore and burying it, there is no substantiation for the claim. Yet people have searched in vain in the Stillwater area for the treasure Drake is said to have buried there. **Map Code 14 H-4**

Monterey County — In the 1850s, a lone bandit robbed an army payroll from the Presidio of Monterey and fled afoot. It is said that he was seen entering a cemetery. A short time later he was shot and killed, but no money was found on him. Whether he secreted the money in the hole of a nearby tree before he arrived at the cemetery, or hurriedly buried it in the cemetery, is still argued among the old-timers who heard their fathers tell the story. A mysterious church treasure is also said to be buried in the same cemetery. This listing does not infer that we advocate anyone molesting a cemetery in search of any kind of a treasure. **Map Code 14 H-4**

Monterey County — The Mission San Carlos de Borromeo at Monterey was the second in the California system of missions. In order to keep his acolytes away from the soldiers of the Presidio of Monterey, Father Serra moved the mission in 1771 to nearby Carmel Valley, and San Carlos de Borromeo became a Presidio Chapel, which it remains to this day. There is a legend that the Indians of the newly-moved mission picked up free gold in the black sand in the crevices of a sea cave under Point Lobos. **Map Code 14 H-4**

Monterey County — About 1845, a Spanish vessel carrying gold, silver, jewels, and supplies for the government and troops in Alta California, was en route to Monterey. Chased by pirates, the vessel reached and was about to enter Monterey Bay when it was attacked and sunk by gunfire. The ship is said to have carried about $9,000,000 in Mexican gold and an unknown quantity of silver.

In 1908 or 1909, a Captain Barstow, long familiar with the Monterey Bay area, is said to have located and seen mast stumps and certain parts of the high cabin believed to have been those of the treasure ship. For some unexplained reason, no effort was made at recovering the treasure. The vessel is probably now covered with sand or silt. **Map Code 14 H-4**

Napa County — An unknown amount of loot taken in the holdup of a Napa-Sacramento stagecoach is said to be buried at the summit of a slight hill about six miles northwest of Napa (State 29). It appears that the outlaws were about to be overtaken by a posse at this point and hurriedly buried the loot. Of the three bandits participating in the robbery, one was killed on the spot by the stage's messenger, and the other two were captured, but one soon died of his wounds. The lone survivor denied that he knew where the treasure had been secreted by his companions. He later died in prison. **Map Code 12 F-4**

Nevada County — In the fall of 1853, Francis Lingard, well-known around the Feather River mining camps, walked into John Carrington's store at Nelson Point and paid for $100 worth of provisions and supplies with a single gold nugget. At the gasp of surprise from the spectators, Lingard displayed several other nuggets of equal size. Lingard returned a second time to Carrington's store, made more purchases, and again paid for them with nuggets. But on his third trip to the store, Lingard made no purchases, and when the opportunity arose, he told Carrington that he was flat broke. This is the story Lingard told.

While looking for water in the High Sierras the year before, Lingard had found a small stream where it fell over a ledge into a lake. Kneeling at the lake's edge, he noted that the bed of the stream's channel, and for some distance out into the lake, was covered with large nuggets of pure gold. Obviously they had been carried there by the stream from some source above. All he had to do was pick the nuggets up.

That night, Lingard made camp near the bed of gold, gathered all he could carry the next morning, and headed to Nelson Point for supplies. Along the way, he found he had more gold than he could carry and cached most of the nuggets at the base of a large pine tree. When he returned to the region after his first trip to Carrington's store, he could find neither the lake nor the cache of nuggets at the pine tree. Nor could he find them on his second return, made necessary because he had to go to Nelson Point again for supplies.

Carrington believed Lingard and grubstaked him for a third search for the bed of gold. He continued the search until winter forced a halt. The following spring, Lingard led a party of half a dozen men in search of the golden lake and the cache of nuggets. After several weeks of failure, the search was abandoned. Lingard guessed that the heavy rains preceding the organized search had raised the level of the lake to a point where it concealed the bed of gold. The fate of Lingard is unknown, although some claim he was killed by the angry gold seekers. Although searches for Lingard's storied lake of gold have all but ceased, the region searched in the past has generally been in the lakes area of eastern Nevada County. **Map Code 12 D-5**

Nevada County — Before going to Nevada City (State 20-49) for supplies, an unnamed miner is said to have buried an unknown amount of gold near his cabin which stood close to the present site of Lake Vera Lodge. The miner disappeared mysteriously and so far as it is known his treasure has never been found. **Map Code 12 D-5**

Nevada County — Nevada City has always drawn its wealth from gold mining. In 1850, between 10,000 and 35,000 miners worked every inch of land within a three-mile radius. One of the early prospectors here was Jefferson A. Casserly. When he died in Nevada City in 1936, he named his granddaughter, Miss Jean Kuster of San Francisco, his heir. In his strongbox was found a single gold nugget worth $5,000. Miss Kuster had not taken him seriously, but after his death, she recalled that her grandfather had once taken her to a spot along Deer Creek and said, "Remember this spot. When I am gone, it will make you rich." Certain that her grandfather had buried the bulk of his wealth there, she conducted an extensive search, but found nothing. Miss Kuster was recently quoted as saying she still thinks the treasure is there, if she could only locate the right spot. **Map Code 12 E-5**

<u>Nevada County</u> — Located in the rough country northwest of Nevada City (State 20-49), and accessible only over rough and unimproved roads, is the remains of the old mining camp of Bloody Run. It is said that a miner named Mayberry took more than $40,000 worth of gold out of his claim here and buried it near his cabin. When robbers attempted to force Mayberry to tell where his fortune was hidden, he resisted and was killed. It is believed that Mayberry's treasure has never been found. **Map Code 12 E-5**

<u>Orange County</u> — In 1859, a California pioneer named Daniel Sexton secured permission to dig near the ruins of San Juan Capistrano Mission for several bags of gold he swore he knew was buried there, but declined to give any details. When he dug so extensively beneath one house that the owner feared it would cave in, he was denied the right to dig further. Sexton died insisting there was gold there, and a lot of people guessed he knew what he was talking about, else he wouldn't have done all that digging. **Map Code 15 M-9**

<u>Orange County</u> — Somewhere in the mountains east of San Juan Capistrano Mission is said to be a lost gold mine once worked by mission Indians. In 1812, the mission was partially destroyed by an earthquake, which killed 29 persons and closed the entrance to the mine, trapping some Indians inside. Because the Indians refused to work the mine after this disaster, it is said the mine was never reopened. **Map Code 15 M-9**

<u>Orange County</u> — The Mission San Juan Capistrano was started in 1796 and completed in 1806. During its early days the village of San Juan Capistrano declared war on Mexico because of the harsh treatment inflicted upon the Indians by Mexican officials. It is said that, at this time, a group of trusted Indians were delegated to carry certain church treasures into the hills and bury them.

This was done, but when it came time to bring the treasures back to San Juan Capistrano, the Indians refused to do so, nor would they reveal where the treasures had been buried. In 1935, a search was made for these church treasures just to the east of the town of Santa Ana. It was said at the time that nothing was found, although there was some talk that this was a cover-up. **Map Code 15 L-9**

<u>Orange County</u> — For years, a succession of treasure hunters have searched the first site of Mission San Juan Capistrano for a treasure supposedly buried there when an Indian attack forced the padres to flee to the safety of the mission in San Diego. As the story goes, they buried their wealth under the foundations of an old building. When they returned to the mission, this treasure was left undisturbed for some reason. Later, the old building was demolished. When the second mission site was selected about 5 miles away, the treasure seems to have been forgotten. Almost nothing remains today of the mission's original foundations. **Map Code 15 M-9**

<u>Orange County</u> — One day in 1868, the northbound Los Angeles-San Diego stage was held up by five men in a tree-lined draw, inland from what is now the resort town of Corona del Mar. After throwing down the strongbox, the stage driver was waved on and raced into the little town of Santa Ana to spread the alarm. A posse quickly gathered and rode out for the Santa Ana Mountains, where it was presumed the outlaws would flee.

The bandits, however, guessing the posse would head for their old haunts in the Santa Anas, made camp near the scene of the holdup. As the disappointed possemen were returning to Santa Ana on the following day, they came upon the outlaws quite by accident, still stretched out in their blankets. The lawmen opened fire without warning, killing all five bandits.

In their eagerness to kill the bandits, the posse completely overlooked the necessity of keeping at least one of them alive to reveal where the treasure was hidden. A search was made of the region around the camp, but not a trace of the treasure was found.

It has long been reasoned that the loot must have been hidden someplace on the huge 93,000-acre Irvine Ranch, stretching from the Pacific Ocean across the coastal foothills and into the Santa Ana Mountains. Because the region is so readily accessible to treasure hunters, it is said that hundreds have searched for this treasure which is estimated to be worth about $30,000 in today's values.

But that part of the ranch on which the treasure is generally believed to have been buried is now the campus of the Irvine branch of the University of California. **Map Code 15 M-9**

Placer County — In 1850, two prospectors, John Scheuneman and Harry Woolridge, made camp near the headwaters of the American River. At night, small articles began to disappear, but left in their place would be a nugget of gold. The experienced men knew the exchange was being made by packrats. After days of careful observation, they traced the packrats to their nest in the crevice of a high ledge, reached by the animals over the limb of an overhanging tree.

The snow of an early winter hindered their efforts to follow the packrats to their source of gold, so they returned the following summer. They found the overhanging tree and the crevice, but there wasn't a packrat in the area. Apparently their disturbance of the region had frightened the colony away. So far as it is known, the source of the packrat's gold has never been found, and is still believed to rest someplace along the American River southeast of the town of Gold Run (Interstate 80). **Map Code 12 E-5**

Placer County — Prospectors poured into this area by the tens of thousands in 1849 and 1850, and a network of trails radiated into the camps in the hills and ravines as the turnpikes became choked with stagecoaches, freight wagons, and horseback riders. Tunnel mining was popular in this area, and the story is told of an old German prospector who took a fortune from a tunnel on the American River just below Auburn (Interstate 80).

Before taking a trip to the east, he closed the entrance to his mine, intending to return to it. For some unknown reason he never came back to Placer County, and it is believed that the entrance to his tunnel has never been found. **Map Code 12 E-5**

Placer County — Yankee Jim is nothing more today than the hard-to-find site of an old mining camp on a ridge between the Middle and North forks of the American River. It was named after a seaman who deserted his ship at the start of the gold rush and found a gold mine of great riches. He is said to have traded chunks of pure gold when other miners offered nuggets and dust.

Some thought he had found the true Mother Lode.

The only man who ever came near seeing the sailor's source of gold was Jim Currier. Promised to be taken in as a partner, Currier was to see the mine on an appointed day, but on that very day, Yankee Jim disappeared and was never seen again. His famed mine is believed never to have been found. Directions to the old camp of Yankee Jim can probably be secured in Auburn. **Map Code 12 E-5**

Placer County — The tragic story of the Donner party's ill-fated trip is well known, and it is a matter of record that one or more of the party buried wealth when hopelessly trapped in the snows of the High Sierras near what is now known as Donner Lake, in October, 1846.

The Donners are known to have left Illinois with $10,000 in gold. Both George and Jacob Donner died while the party was stranded in the deep snows, and both left the care of their wealth to Tamsen Donner.

She also died before rescue came, and what became of the gold is a mystery that has never been solved. It is assumed that this treasure was buried or hidden in the camp at Donner Lake, along with other smaller amounts by other members of the party. In 1891, some 191 silver coins were found and identified as those buried by Mrs. W. C. Graves. Donner Lake is located almost exactly on the Placer-Nevada county line, and north of Interstate 80, 10 miles west of Truckee.

MAP THIS ON A TOPO MAP —
www.1wbta.com/Nevada-Placer-Donner-Party-Tragedy
Map Code 12 E-6

Plumas County — An old miner lying near death in a hospital tried to reveal the location of his secret mine to a friend. He had called the mine the White Mule because it had been discovered while chasing his straying animal of that color. He said that it was located at a point where one could see Taylorsville, Greenville (State 89), and one other town ending in "ville," but he couldn't recall the rest of the name. Prospectors of the time were puzzled over this description because they couldn't find another town name ending in "ville" in the area. Although a legend now, there was a great deal of searching for this mine at one time. **Map Code 12 C-5**

Plumas County — Sometime in 1850, a prospector named Marks came into one of the camps around Marysville and told a strange story. He said that he and his partner had been told by friendly Indians of a stream northwest of Marysville whose banks were lined with rich gold-bearing ore.

Marks and his partner set out in search of the stream. When his partner became ill and had to give up the search, Marks continued on and eventually located a stream where great masses of free gold lined its bank. But no sooner had he located the golden stream than he was attacked by unfriendly Indians and driven away.

In Marysville, Marks enlisted a party of 30 men and they headed eastward toward Sierra Valley, turned northward, and began a search for Mark's stream of golden banks. They scoured Last Chance, Humbug, and Red Clover valleys without success, and then Marks led the party westward to the junction of the Middle Fork of the Feather River and Nelson Creek.

Here the group, running low on provisions, broke up in disgust and Marks was lucky to get away with his life. Those who did believe in Mark's story, and listened to his description of the stream, concluded that it was located in the vicinity of Camel Peak, and possibly near what is now known as the village of Rich Bar. **Map Code 12 D-5**

Plumas County — In the fall of 1850, an unnamed scout found a rich ledge of gold in the Brown Hill district near the village of La Porte. As winter was coming on, he was unable to start work on the mine, so he placed a blaze mark on several trees in the vicinity to guide him back to the spot the following spring. The ledge, he told friends, extended 14 inches above the ground and was brownish in color. In the spring, he and others started a search for the ledge that lasted for many years. It was finally concluded that the trees had been consumed by a forest fire and that the winter weather had collapsed the ledge. **Map Code 12 D-5**

- ## FRENCHMAN HENRY GORDIER'S BURIED GOLD

Murder, Mayhem & Four Unsavory Characters Hanged

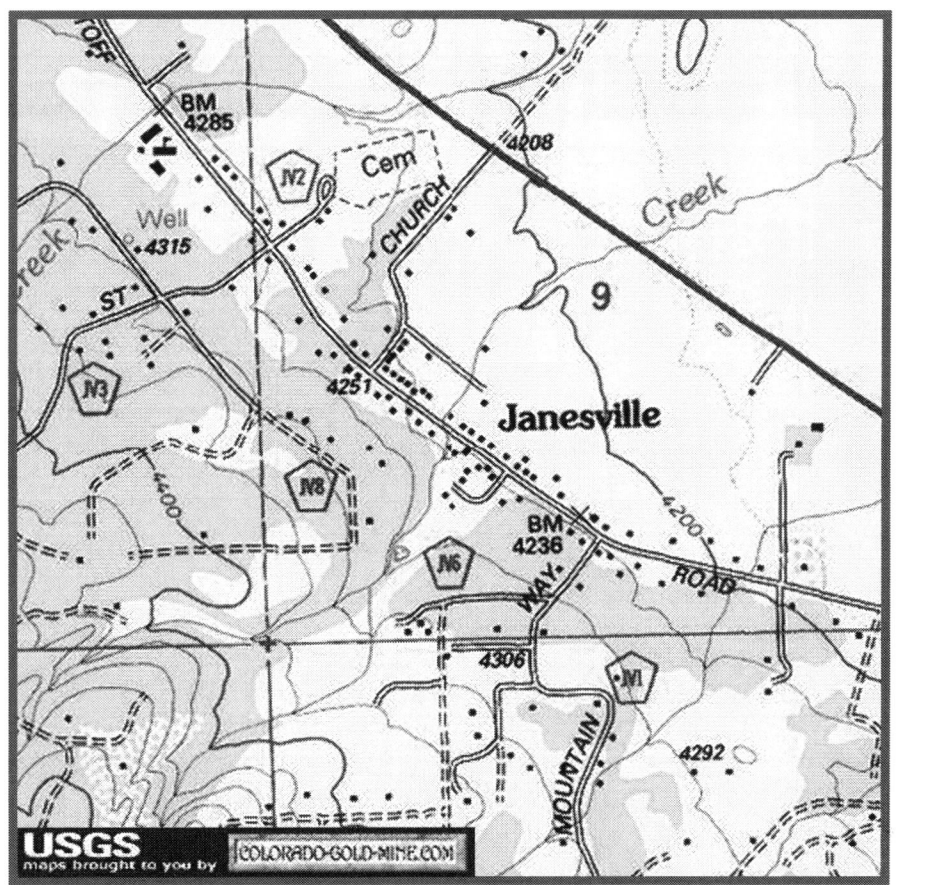

Lassen Frenchman Henry Gordier's Buried Gold

MAP THIS ON A TOPO MAP —
www.1wbta.com/Lassen-Frenchman-Henry-Gordiers-Buried-Gold

Plumas County — Henry Gordier accumulated a sizeable fortune as the prospecting partner of Isaac Coulterhurst in the California diggings. Retiring from mining, Gordier bought a herd of cattle in the fall of 1857 and settled down on a farm along Baxter Creek, on the north side of Honey Lake, and not far from the town of Janesville (US 395). Gordier was respected and well liked. When he turned up missing early in 1858, his neighbors became alarmed and organized a search. They were especially suspicious of three unsavory characters that had moved into Gordier's cabin, saying they had purchased the property and that Gordier, a Frenchman, had returned to his native country.

Special note: The original book by Penfield lists this tale in Plumas County. However, upon research on the locations given, this was located to the north, in Lassen County. These locations include: Baxter Creek, Honey Lake, Janesville, and the Susan River. Willow Creek and today's Wildlife Area are about 16 miles north of Susanville on Hwy. 139.

When Gordier's weighted body was found by divers in a pothole on the Susan River at the mouth of Willow Creek, the strangers occupying his ranch were immediately arrested by vigilantes. It was common knowledge that Gordier was a moderately wealthy man, and it was presumed that he kept his fortune in gold coins and nuggets buried someplace near his cabin on Baxter Creek. When freshly-dug holes were discovered in the vicinity, it was guessed that Gordier had not only been murdered for his real property, but also for the gold he was believed to have buried. The amount of gold was estimated by Gordier's best friends to have been about $40,000.

After a hurried vigilante trial, four men were hanged for the murder of Henry Gordier. All went to their deaths declaring their innocence, and each denying that he had found any of Gordier's gold. An extensive search for the Frenchman's fortune by neighbors failed to reveal a thing, and it was concluded that Gordier's gold was still buried or hidden someplace near his cabin, now demolished.

Fort Janesville - In 1860, after the Battle of Pyramid Lake (also known as "The Ormsby Massacre"), settlers built a loopholed stockade for protection from an Indian attack that never materialized. The fort, which had a bastion, or block house, in its southwest angle, was less than a mile from the town of Janesville. The site of the fort is now a California Historic Landmark.

In 1877, a Miss Mary Dunn and a small party of searchers found several gold nuggets in the vicinity, one of them worth $240, but the remainder of Henry Gordier's wealth is apparently still there. This is one of the best authenticated of all California treasure stories, and the area is very accessible to searchers. A few years ago the postmaster of Janesville pin-pointed the Gordier cabin site, although the property itself at that time was involved in some sort of litigation. **Map Code 12 C-6**

Counties Q – S

 I am certain you've noticed that one of our regular treasure tellers is not here tonight. Are you ready for this? He is treasure hunting in Scotland! Now THERE is a wise man! Nothing like a full moon from a different land full of more ancient tales. I am reminded of this: "Knowledge is the treasure of a wise man." (William Penn). Yes, always remember that a great legend isn't much good if you don't do your research! Okay, did you hear that? The coyotes are telling us to hurry up and get on with the stories!

❖❖❖

- ## PEGLEG SMITH AND HIS RICH BLACK NUGGETS OF GOLD

A Field Day With The Lost Pegleg Smith Mine Story!

<u>Riverside County</u> — The Lost Pegleg Smith Mine ranks with the most famed in America. There is no question of the fact that Thomas L. "Pegleg" Smith found rich black nuggets of gold. Many people in San Bernardino saw them.

In 1828 or 1829, Pegleg and a companion named Le Duc, or some variation thereof, left the Colorado River at Yuma Crossing, bound for the pueblo of Los Angeles.

Somewhere in their travels they ran short of water, and Pegleg climbed one of a group of three small buttes, knowing that if there was any water in the area it would be in the hills.

It was here that he found the small nuggets he thought to be copper. The butte was yellow at its base and black on top, and Pegleg said it was carpeted with the black nuggets, which he later discovered were gold.

Hundreds have searched for those black nuggets of gold, some have lost their lives, and writers have had a field day with the Lost Pegleg Smith Mine Story.

Where is the black butte covered with gold?

If you draw an imaginary line from Palm Springs straight south to the Mexican border, and another straight line east from Palm Springs to the Colorado River as the eastern boundary, and the international boundary as the southern border, you have defined an enormously large stretch of desert and mountains. Someplace in this area is the Lost Pegleg Smith Mine.

For what it is worth, and based upon years of research into the subject, it is the writer's opinion that the most likely spot for the Lost Pegleg is in the Chuckwalla Mountains, somewhere in the area of Guilliday Well.

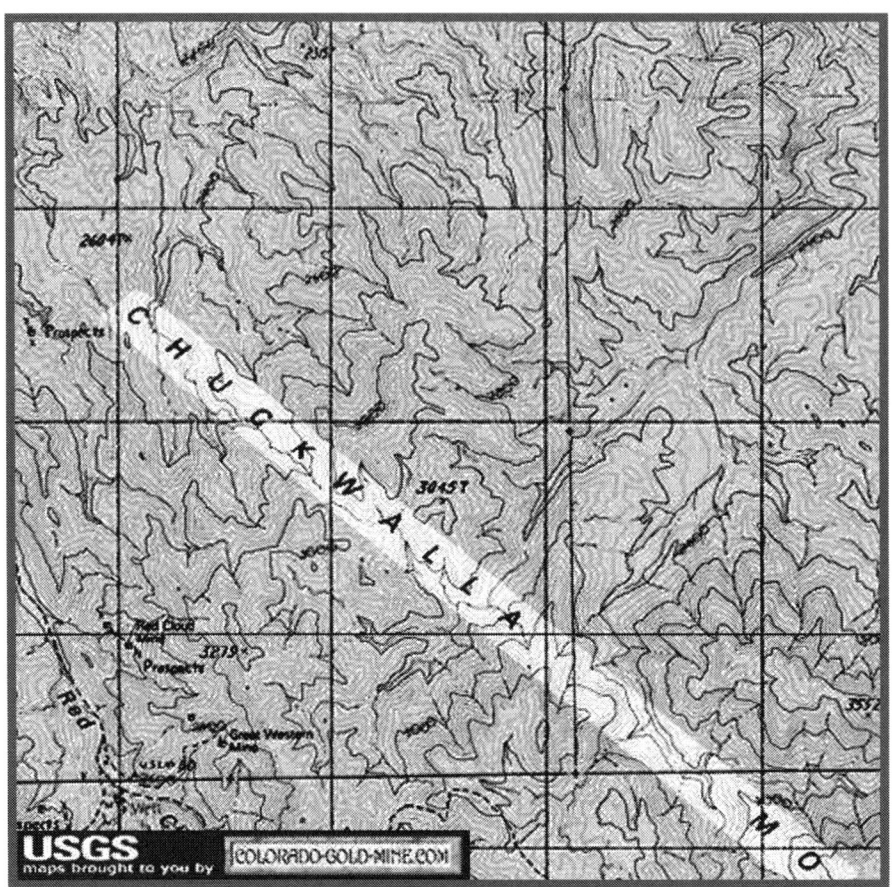

MAP THIS ON A TOPO MAP —
www.1wbta.com/Riverside-Lost-Pegleg-Chuckwalla-Mountains

Good luck with this one, folks! Treasure leads cover a huge area of land! The California Treasure Atlas lists possible sites for Pegleg's Gold:

- In the Chuckwalla Mountains in the area of Guilliday Well
- West of the Salton Sea
- SW of the Salton Sea
- NE of the Salton Sea
- Across the Colorado River near Picacho and towards the Cargo Muchacho and Chocolate Mountains
- In the Imperial Valley between San Bernardino and the Chocolate Mountains
- 20 miles E of Niland near the Chocolate Mountains
- In the Santa Rita Mountains
- Between Mecca and Blythe, S of I-10
- 3 miles E of Jamacha

Source: www.1wbta.com/US-Treasure-Atlas-Vol-2-California-Colorado

Map Code 15 M-12

Riverside County — It is said that someplace within a 12-mile radius of Indian Wells, just south of State 111 between Palm Desert and Indio, a British remittance man known only as "Endless Ed" turned bandit after his remittance was cut off. It is claimed that Ed buried $9,000 in gold coins, and then killed himself near the spot, in remorse over his crimes. **Map Code 15 L-11**

Riverside County — Originally there were only two palm trees at Dos Palmas, but now there are many at this desert oasis east of the northern end of the Salton Sea. Without any apparent basis in fact, there has persisted for many years the tale of a Spanish galleon wrecked in the prehistoric Gulf of Mexico, its hulk now resting beneath desert sands as the waters of the gulf receded and silt replaced it. The site of this wreck is usually placed at or near Dos Palmas. The two original palms were visible for miles across the comparatively level desert floor, and served for centuries to guide travelers to this always dependable source of water. **Map Code 15 M-11**

Riverside County — Cottonwood Spring is a small oasis in the dry hills of the most southerly part of Joshua Tree National Monument, easily reached by a road running north off of US 60-70 between Indio and Desert Center. In the early 1900s, a San Francisco man regularly camped here, making daily trips into the Cottonwood Mountains and returning every night with a small load of high grade ore.

When he had accumulated about 300 pounds, he would haul it out in his buckboard, and ship it to San Francisco. One day his body was found miles away from his camping place, and it was assumed that he had been killed by robbers. A fortune in gold was later recovered from his San Francisco home, but his rich mine in the Cottonwood Mountains is believed never to have been found. **Map Code 15 L-11**

Riverside County — Much of the Coxcomb Mountains lie within the northeastern boundaries of Joshua Tree National Monument. In 1902, a worker with a survey crew in this area picked up the trail of a bighorn sheep while out on a hunting trip. He followed the sheep's trail along a ledge that gradually became so narrow that he could no longer safely make his way along it.

In turning around, he faced the wall and saw a vein of dark rose quartz heavily sprinkled with gold. He pried off a small sample and put it in his pocket. On the opposite wall, he noticed a blotch of coloring that was much lighter than the rest.

It was roughly in the form of a star, and this he memorized as a guide to later locate the place. Around the campfire that night, he told of his experience and everyone agreed it would require a fortune to mine a ledge on a sheer wall such as this. Discouraged, he forgot about the find, but later tried unsuccessfully to locate it. **Map Code 15 L-12**

<u>Riverside County</u> — Someplace in the Hexie Mountains northeast of Indio (Interstate 10), a land where the heat can be unbearably scorching, and water can be scarce, Indians told of an immense body of gold scattered about the floor of what is believed to be an extinct volcano. Two men are said to have once located this gold, and to have taken about $10,000 worth of it, but after a trip to San Francisco, they were never able to locate it again. The Hexie Mountains are located within the boundaries of Joshua Tree National Monument, where mining rights are leased to individuals in certain areas. **Map Code 15 L-11**

<u>Riverside County</u> — Papuan was the last of a little band of Papago Indians who lived along the Colorado River in Western Arizona. When his tribe had been decimated by the Apaches, he moved northward and joined a friendly band of Mohaves, eventually marrying into the tribe. Keeping mostly to themselves, Papuan and his old woman bride would frequently slip away for several days at a time, always returning with gold nuggets which they freely shared with the tribe. They crossed the Colorado at Blythe and it is believed that they traveled to the southern slopes of the McCoy Mountains, where the gold was secured. Most of this gold eventually found its way to Ehrenberg, where it was traded at a store operated by Bill McCoy, after whom the mountains were named. McCoy once estimated that in a two-year period, Papuan and his people traded $75,000 worth of gold at his place.

In 1886, Papuan was killed by Apaches and his secret gold mine was all but forgotten until 1906, when a man named Hartman, learning that Papuan's widow was still living, attempted to secure the location of the mine from her. All he could learn from the tight-lipped old woman was that she and Papuan's adopted son, Chinkinnow, were the only people in the tribe who knew where the gold came from. Hartman's efforts to secure the secret from the boy also failed, except that Chinkinnow did tell him that the gold came from the McCoy Mountains. Hartman eventually gave up, and so far as it is known, the secret of old Papuan's Lost Mine is still intact. **Map Code 15 M-12**

<u>Riverside County</u> — In the vicinity of Grapevine Creek, northwest of the northern tip of the Salton Sea, is a lava bed covered with a fortune in gold nuggets. The gold is said to be tarnished black like the rock in which it is found. Two white men

are supposed to have followed an Indian trail into the desolate area, where they came upon the skeletons of several Indians who are presumed to have died of thirst and heat. According to the story, the white men took out a fortune in gold, but never went back because of the intense heat in the region.
Map Code 15 M-9

Riverside County — The desert town of Sage is located on State 79 between Radec and Hemet, in southwestern Riverside County. Juan Chavez, a lieutenant of the bandit Juan Murrieta, made camp here one night while en route to Mexico with a pack train of mules carrying an estimated $200,000 stolen from the northern California mines. During the evening, while most of the men were engaged in gambling, the man assigned to guard the pack mules led them up a canyon, still carrying their packs. Quickly removing the gold from the packs, he buried it at the foot of the tree and started back with the mules. Before he reached the camp, however, the mules were missed and a party went out in search of them. When they were found, Chavez killed the disloyal guard, unaware that he had removed and hidden the gold. Not until Chavez and his party had traveled many miles to the south was it discovered that the gold was missing, and by this time, none of the party could retrace their steps to the campsite and make a search for the buried gold. Presumably, the treasure is still there at the base of a tree marked with a cross. **Map Code 15 M-9**

Riverside County — Fig Tree John was an Indian recluse who lived for many years on the shores of the Salton Sea near a place called Traventine Point, just west of US 99 where it crosses the Riverside-Imperial county line. He was a familiar character in the early days of the Coachella Valley, and it is well-known and authenticated that he disappeared at intervals only to return with his pockets filled with gold nuggets. He roamed the Santa Rosa Mountains and let it be known that he considered the region his private property, occasionally chasing white men out with his rifle.

Fig Tree John had a son, Johnny Mac, who, when questioned about his father's secret mine, would only mutter, "Maybe so, maybe no." But some of the older tribesmen openly admitted that Fig Tree John indeed had a source of gold in the Santa Rosas, and said that he had killed several people in protecting his secret. Fig Tree John died in 1927 at the reported age of 135 years. Most of the searches for Fig Tree John's lost mine are concentrated in the area of Rabbit Peak, almost on the Riverside-Imperial county line and west of the northern tip of the Salton Sea.
Map Code 15 M-11

Riverside County — Legend says that the desert Indians once worked a rich emerald mine in the Santa Rosa Mountains, and that they had a trade route for the gems to Mexico. Robert Thompson, a mining engineer employed in Colombia, South America, heard this story from a Mexican who worked for him. The Mexican claimed that his grandfather had worked in the mine, and had heard so much of the area that he could take Thompson to it. In time, Thompson accepted the offer.

The men arrived in the Santa Rosas and made camp at the site of Rock House in Rock House Canyon. The search was made along the rocky slopes beyond. The Mexican said the marker they would look for would be a large stone shaped like a wolf's head. This was found toppled from the wall into a deep ravine, where it was half-covered by a tangle of boulders and stones, obviously the work of an earthquake. A search of the area revealed pottery shards, traces of old campfires, and Thompson found a piece of green rock which he declared to be emerald. There were bits of a pale green mineral, beryl, the substance emeralds are found in.

Thompson was certain they had found the Lost Emerald Mine of the Santa Rosas, but after a long search, he concluded that the entire area had been changed by a massive earthquake, and that it would take someone else to uncover the mine.
Map Code 15 M-10

Riverside County — Sometime in the early 1900s, a prospector named Nicholas Schwartz found a sizeable gold nugget in the lower reaches of Rock House Canyon, some distance north of the Riverside-San Diego county line. Digging down, he took out $18,000 worth of gold. He later told a friend that he had placed his pick and shovel in the hole, covered it, and walked away. He said that too much money was no good, and he didn't need any more. Although he gave the friend a crude map of the location, he refused to take him to it. It is said that the friend was never able to find the Lost Schwartz Mine. **Map Code 15 M-10**

Riverside County — There's a lot of desert area between Tabaseco Tank and Dos Palmas Springs in the desert valley between the Orocopia and Chocolate Mountains at the northeast corner of the Salton Sea. But, someplace in that vast area is a stretch of reddish earth filled with gold. One day when Tom Clark was working his claim at Mesquite Springs, at the southern tip of the Chocolates, a young prospector appeared out of nowhere. He was broke, hungry, lost, and suffering from tuberculosis. Clark had prospected for years and knew what it was to be hungry and broke. He took pity on the stranger and gave him a grubstake.

The stranger moved on and it was the last Clark heard of him until he received a letter containing a crude map and the repayment of the grubstake. The stranger wrote that he knew he was going to die, and he wanted Clark to have the rich find he had made while on his way from Mesquite Diggings to Dos Palmas. The letter was from Dos Palmas, and Clark rushed there, but the stranger was dead upon his arrival. In his last delirious days, Clark was told, the stranger had talked about his find, and from what could be pieced together, it was concluded that he had stopped at Tabaseco Tank, and had found the gold sometime after leaving there, and before arriving in Dos Palmas. Tom Clark's search for the reddish earth containing gold went on for years, but he never found it. **Map Code 15 M-11**

San Benito County — Gabilan Peak is the highest (3,169 feet) in the Gabilan Range near Hollister (State 156). For more than 150 years, this area has been searched for the fabled silver mine said to have once been worked by the Indians of Mission San Carlos Borromeo del Rio Carmelo. The location of the mine has been unknown since it was closed by the padres when Fremont entered the area on his way to Monterey, in 1852. The mine was never reopened. From time to time, some rich silver tailings have been reported found in the Gabilan Mountains, and it is believed by some that these are from the old padres' silver mine. **Map Code 14 H-5**

San Benito County — National Park Service officials at Pinnacles National Monument state that visitors frequently ask about a treasure supposedly buried there. The story persists that California's "muy caballero" bandit, Tiburcio Vasquez, buried treasure in one of the caves in the Monument, but Park people say that they have never found any trace of it and doubt that it exists. It was about 25 miles from the Pinnacles that the Vasquez gang committed their most murderous deed, when they raided the small village of Tres Pinos. Here they robbed the store and murdered three helpless men, after which they fled to the Pinnacles.

There is no record of the amount of money secured at Tres Pinos, but it is believed to have been in the neighborhood of $5,000. Tradition says that this is buried in Old Cave in Big Bear Gulch. The fact that old guns and other rusted articles were once found here has given credence to the story. Don't attempt any digging here without permission, however, which is doubtful of being granted. **Map Code 14 L-5**

San Benito County — On State 25, a few miles south of Hollister, is the little town of Tres Pinos (see above), named for the three stunted pines that once stood on the banks of Tres Pinos Creek. In the early days, the place consisted only of a general store and a few houses. In August, 1873, the Vasquez gang raided the town, killed three defenseless men, and robbed Snyder's store of an estimated $5,000. It was this crime that Vasquez was later hanged for, in San Jose. The loot taken in this robbery was probably never buried at all, but tradition gives it three separate hiding places — in Pinnacles National Monument, along Tres Pinos Creek near the scene of the crime, and in a grove of willows near the little town of Paicines (State 25). **Map Code 14 H-4**

- ## THE STORY OF KOKOWEEF MOUNTAIN'S CAVE OF GOLD

<u>San Bernardino County</u> — Kokoweef Mountain lies in the northern part of the Ivanpah Range, and is located just south of the hamlet of Wheaton Springs (US 91-466). In recent years, Kokoweef Mountain has been the scene of the most publicized lost mine story to come out of California.

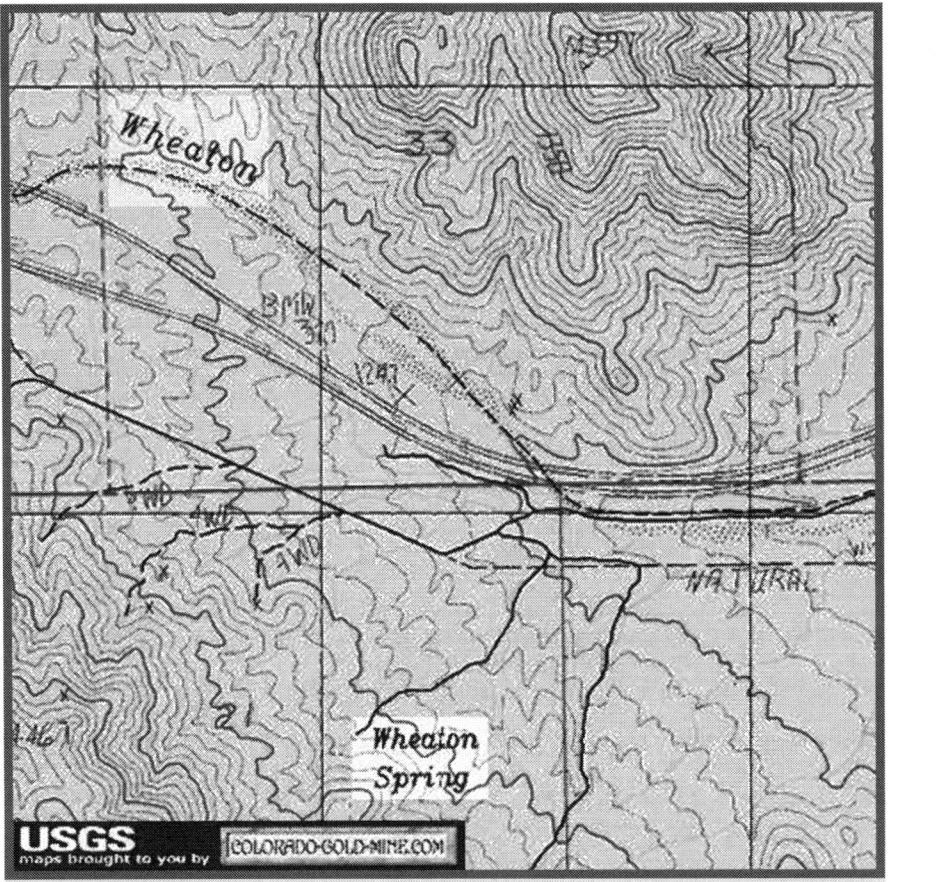

San Bernardino Kokoweef's Cave Of Gold

MAP THIS ON A TOPO MAP —
www.1wbta.com/San-Bernardino-Kokoweef-Cave-Of-Gold

It all started with a young boy named Earl P. Dorr, who lived on his father's ranch in Colorado. They were friendly with the Indians who passed their way, and one day one of the Indians gave young Dorr a map and told him this story.

Long years ago, three Indian brothers had found a cave, the entrance to which was atop a mountain. They entered and explored the vast cavern, finding it filled with black sand. Probing into the sand, they found it to be rich in gold nuggets. They carried away a quantity to show to their tribe. Many times the brothers returned to the cavern, until one of them fell one day from a high precipice in the cave and was killed. From that time on the Indians were forbidden to enter the cave.

With the presentation of the map to young Dorr, the giver told him that one day he could find great riches in the cave of the black sands. Although young Dorr treasured the old map given him by his friend, he thought the story to be another Indian legend. As he grew to manhood, however, he thought more and more of the cave of gold and wondered if it could possibly be true. He determined to find out.

In 1927, accompanied by a mining engineer who is not named, Dorr said he followed the map and found the entrance to the Indian cave atop Kokoweef Mountain in the Ivanpah Range. They descended 2,000 feet into the cave and found a canyon 3,000 to 3,500 feet deep, with many rooms branching off from it. At the bottom of the canyon was a flowing river they estimated to be about 300 feet wide and of great depth. They remained in the cave long enough to determine that the water rose and fell, suggesting to them that it was part of a vast subterranean system connected with the Pacific Ocean, and that the rise and fall of the water was actually the Pacific tides.

When the tides were out, there was exposed on both sides on the canyon a beach of black sand from 100 to 150 feet wide, and ranging in depth from 4 to 11 feet. In this sand, just as the Indian had told Dorr as a boy, they found gold nuggets. Exploring up the canyon, they traveled a distance of 8 miles, stopping only when they came to a sheer drop of 3,000 feet. Taking about 10 pounds of gold, they left the cave.

Up to this point in the story of Kokoweef Mountain's Cave of Gold, most accounts are in more or less agreement, but from here on the story becomes confusing and contradictory. One account states that when the men were leaving the cave, the mining engineer had a heart attack and had to be helped out by Dorr. On the surface, other prospectors appeared, and some of the nuggets were accidentally spilled, revealing the find.

To protect the cave, Dorr climbed down and set off dynamite charges, sealing the entrance. The rushing winds inside the cave suggested to Dorr that the cave had a second entrance which he determined they could find later, but some thought he was taking quite a gamble.

Another version of the story says that the mining engineer died on the spot, and that Dorr staked out a claim which included the area of the blocked-up entrance. So great was his faith that he could find the second entrance that he failed to keep up his claim on the original entrance and lost it by default to another prospector who staked the claim and later sold it to a mining company.

Earl Dorr continued his search for the second entrance the remainder of his life, and hundreds of others have searched with no more success. So far as one can determine, the mining company in control of that part of Kokoweef Mountain encompassing Earl Dorr's plugged-up mine entrance has never made an effort to reopen it. Perhaps that is because they don't believe the Kokoweef Mountain story any more than we do.

But if Earl Dorr's story is acceptable, the cave of gold is indeed a storehouse of vast wealth. Estimates of the value of the gold resting in the black sands of Kokoweef Mountain range as high as $10 billion, based, it is said, upon the assay of Dorr's samples and his description of the extent of the black sand beaches. **Map Code 15 J-12**

<u>San Bernardino County</u> — In the early 1930s, two robbers held up a bank in Needles, California, and fled with the loot in an automobile. Near the little town of Oro Grande, just north of Victorville (Interstate 15), their car broke down and they hastily buried the loot and fled afoot. Suspicious of the car being abandoned, Victorville police picked the men up as they tried to hitchhike a ride. While the robbers were being held for investigation, the police heard of the bank robbery over the radio. Sentenced to prison, one of the men was killed in an attempted escape and the other died. Both had consistently refused to tell where the loot was hidden, except that it was along the Mojave River just to the north of Oro Grande.
Map Code 15 K-9

<u>San Bernardino County</u> — The southeastern end of Van Duzen Canyon can be reached from State 18 about midway between Big Bear Lake and Baldwin. Unlike so many lost mine sites in this section of California, this one is rather easy to reach. In 1860, the first mining claim was staked out in Holcomb Valley north of Big Bear Lake, and thousands of hopeful prospectors flocked into the area.

Among these was a man named Van Duzen who had a working knowledge of mining and geology. In some manner, he acquired a partner and together they built a little cabin in what is now known as Van Duzen Canyon. In the months that followed, they prospected in a systematic manner, and then they began turning up in the trading centers with gold in such quantities as to attract attention. They were tight-lipped and careful that they were not followed. But Van Duzen did confide in a friend that they had struck it rich, and that their accumulated gold was stored preparatory to packing it out to San Bernardino.

When a considerable time elapsed and neither of the men showed up in their usual haunts, nothing much was thought about their absence. But when Van Duzen's companion was observed leaving the canyon with their pack animals, apparently headed for San Bernardino, there was some concern. A group of Holcomb Valley miners rode out to the Van Duzen cabin to investigate. They found his body in the cabin, apparently murdered by his partner. The news of the suspected murder stimulated interest in finding the secret mine, and extensive searches were made in the upper reaches of Van Duzen Canyon. Not a trace of the mine was found.

In the summer of 1868, there showed up in Holcomb Valley a middle-aged Frenchman and a young man named Stebbins. They appeared to be partners, yet the Frenchman went on prospecting forays, leaving Stebbins to shift for himself. The Frenchman centered his activities in the upper reaches of Van Duzen Canyon, and before long, it was apparent that he, too, had struck it rich. Prospectors and merchants said the gold he traded was amazingly similar to that traded by Van Duzen. There was speculation that the Frenchman had found Van Duzen's mine. Then, suddenly and without apparent reason, the Frenchman vanished. Young Stebbins was suspected of foul play, but stubbornly denied any knowledge of his partner's disappearance, and there was no real evidence against him. After a few weeks, Stebbins, too, mysteriously dropped out of sight.

Fifty years or more passed and the Van Duzen and Frenchman incidents were all but forgotten, when there appeared in Holcomb Valley an aged man who said his name was Stebbins — the same Stebbins who had worked with the Frenchman.

He left for Van Duzen Canyon almost immediately, with the announced intention of searching for the Lost Van Duzen Mine, which he said he believed the Frenchman had found. He searched for months but failing health finally forced him to give up.

The activities of Van Duzen and his unnamed partner, and the Frenchman and Stebbins are fairly well established, and all this would certainly indicate that Van Duzen Canyon holds the secret of one, maybe two, lost mines. **Map Code 15 L-10**

<u>San Bernardino County</u> — Near the small town of Yucapai, east of Redlands (Interstate 10) a few miles, is said to be the tailings of an old mine once worked by Indians under Spanish masters. The tunnel or shaft to this gold mine has never been found, but it is claimed that pieces of high grade ore from the mine have been picked up in the area. **Map Code 15 L-10**

<u>San Bernardino County</u> — In 1898, the brothers Roy and Jim Morrow discovered turquoise on the south slope of Slocum Mountain, about 30 miles north and a little west of Barstow (Interstate 15). They worked the mine for about one month and then abandoned it because turquoise had little value in those days. Many years later, the four Morrow brothers made repeated attempts to find the mine, but without success. The mine is believed to be located just within, or just outside, the southern boundary of the U. S. Naval Ordnance Test Station, a dangerous high explosive detonation ground. Permission to enter the area must be secured from the N.O.T.S. Security Officer at China Lake, Calif. (US 395). **Map Code 15 J-9**

<u>San Bernardino County</u> — Ed Shaw, a veteran desert prospector, told of a father and son from Pasadena who prospected around the southern base of the Bullion Mountains, to the north of Twentynine Palms (State 62). They found a vein of gold which appeared to be rich and extensive. They intended to stake their claim the next day, but in the morning found their mule had pulled its tethering stake and wandered away. Leaving their equipment in camp, they went in search of the animal, its tracks leading them in the direction of Daggett some 50 miles to the northwest. Short of water, and unfamiliar with the searing heat of the desert, they finally arrived in Daggett more dead than alive. Once they had recovered, they were so disgusted with the desert that they took the train for home and never again tried to locate their lost ledge, which is marked today by the remains of their camping equipment. The entire Bullion Range is located on the U. S. Marine Corps Training Center. **Map Code 15 L-10**

<u>San Bernardino County</u> — About 1872, Johnny McCloskey, of Bishop, California, went to his birthplace in Texas to be married to his childhood sweetheart. A few years later he and his wife and small daughter decided to return to Owens Valley. They set out in a light wagon drawn by two good horses. At Marl Spring, in the Marl Mountains north of Kelso, one of their horses died suddenly, leaving them

with no choice but to take what possessions they could carry and set out afoot. One evening they camped on the Amargosa River about 30 miles above the Amargosa Mine. Here they found cool water and a ledge that Johnny sensed might contain gold. He panned what he could with a household pan and was astounded with the color he found.

Their supplies were running desperately low and the heat was becoming intense. They dared not tarry any longer. Johnny was an experienced desert man, and was certain that he could find his way back to the ledge. After settling his family in their Inyo County home, Johnny retraced his steps, accompanied by another experienced prospector. McCloskey was certain that they had located the right ledge, but there was no gold. Presumably devastating cloudbursts had changed the course of the river channel. When they arrived at Marl Spring, Johnny found that his wagon and remaining possessions had been taken by thieves. The site of Johnny's lost ledge of gold is believed to be near Salt Spring, which is about 30 miles north of Baker. **Map Code 15 J-10**

San Bernardino County — About 1900, a young Basque sheepherder stumbled upon a rich deposit of gold in a lava bed on the southern slopes of the Argus mountains southeast of Trona. He carefully marked the place in his memory, but unaware that there were several lava beds in the area, he was never later able to find the right one. The Argus Range is almost entirely within the boundaries of the U. S. Naval Ordnance Test Station. **Map Code 15 J-9**

San Bernardino County — In 1850, Louis Rubidoux purchased the Rancho Jurupa along the Santa Ana River north of what is now the city of Riverside. In time, he built a winery and gristmill, and dealt in land. Fearful that his fortune, kept on the ranch, might be lost in one of the Indian raids, he is said to have taken a large chest of gold and buried it on the south slope of Slover Mountain, just south of the city of Colton. It is pointed out that Rubidoux was never to have banked any money, and no great amount of money was found when he died. **Map Code 15 L-9**

San Bernardino County — Whipple Wash, in the Whipple Mountains, runs into the Colorado River about 14 miles above Parker Dam. As late as 1935, an unnamed German prospector was known to be taking a considerable quantity of gold out of his secret mine believed to have been located near a spring at the upper end of Whipple Wash. He traded his ore in Needles and Yuma. One day he announced that he had enough gold to last him the rest of his life. He intended to return to his native Germany and take it easy.

"But just in case," he said, "I'll keep the mine a secret, in case I have to come back to it." He left and was never seen again. **Map Code 15 K-13**

<u>San Bernardino County</u> — California is not generally considered to be a diamond producing state, but there are records of more than 600 diamonds being found in various parts of California. In 1942, an unidentified man picked up a diamond weighing between two and three carats about one mile beyond the outskirts of San Bernardino. This led to the revelation by a San Bernardino woman that her grandfather had found many diamonds about a mile outside San Bernardino, and that she knew approximately where to look for them. Because of this concentration of finds outside San Bernardino, it is believed by many that a field of diamonds exists somewhere on the periphery of San Bernardino. **Map Code 15 L-9**

<u>San Bernardino County</u> — Kelso is located on an unnumbered road running north out of Bagdad (US 66), and at the southeastern extremities of the Kelso Mountains. It is in one of the most desolate areas of southern California. Near here, a legend says, an old prospector's burro strayed away during the night. In the morning, the old miner wandered into the Kelso Hills looking for the animal. He stumbled upon a rich ledge of gold and took samples before plodding on in search of the missing animal By nightfall he was completely lost and was never able to find his way back to the ledge — nor did he find his burro. **Map Code 15 K-11**

<u>San Bernardino County</u> — "Old Man" Lee was a well-known prospector around San Bernardino in the 1870s. He is said to have made lone prospecting trips into the vast desert expanses to the south and east of San Bernardino, and one day he came into town to file a mining claim. He supposedly hired a man to help him sink a shaft and the two left town together. Some time later, Lee began showing up in San Bernardino with bullion to sell. Unlike most old prospectors, Lee apparently made little effort to conceal the location of his mine, stating that it was in the Bullion Mountains to the east of San Bernardino. But those who tried to follow him soon found the old man had given them the slip.

One day, Lee came into San Bernardino for supplies and provisions, telling a storekeeper that he had to return to his mine in a hurry because his partner was about out of food. He left town that night and the following morning his body was found a few miles east of San Bernardino, a bullet through his head. Robbery was ruled out as the motive when his watch and money were found on his person. The mystery of his death was never solved.

A group of concerned citizens, carrying a supply of provisions, started out in search of Lee's helper, probably hoping to learn the location of Lee's mine at the same time. They failed to locate either, and the hired hand was never seen again. It was speculated by some that Old Man Lee had sold an interest in a mine that never existed, and that the purchaser, learning this, had killed Lee. Others disbelieve this and have sought the Old Man Lee lost mine in the Bullions, which are mostly contained within the borders of a U. S. Marine Corps Training Center. **Map Code 15 K-11**

San Bernardino County — Many years after Pegleg Smith's famous find, two men set out from San Bernardino in a buckboard pulled by a pair of mules. Their announced goal was the finding of the black butte, covered, as Smith said, with black rocks containing gold. After two or three days of travel they indeed came to a black butte. At its base, they came upon a skeleton and an empty water gourd. They were about to move on when a small pile of yellow nuggets caught their eyes.

Looking about, they found the ground covered with black rock which revealed gold when the surface was scratched off — the same as Pegleg Smith's gold, but Pegleg's was found at the top of the butte and this was at the base. As they picked up the gold, winds constantly whipped up swirls of dust, making it difficult to breathe. After a time, it burned their throats and irritated their perspiring bodies. They concluded this was what had killed the man whose bones lay there, and decided that they must leave at once. Loading all the gold they had collected — they estimated it at $65,000 worth — they left. By the time they arrived in San Bernardino, both men were choking and the skin was peeling from their exposed flesh. It was months before they were completely recovered, and neither man ever went back to the butte with the choking yellow dust, somewhere in the Bullion Mountains. **Map Code 15 K-11**

San Bernardino County — Gold was discovered in the Big Bear region in 1860, followed by a brief gold rush which was all but over by 1880. During this period, an unnamed party is said to have buried a large fortune in coins near the ruins of an old Spanish fort believed to have been located in the vicinity of Big Bear City. There are no records of a fort of any significance being built in this area, but it is possible that the Spanish erected a temporary stockade here, although no trace of one has ever been found. **Map Code 15 L-10**

San Bernardino County — L. O. Long and an unnamed partner made a rich gold strike in the northern slopes of the Sheep Hole Mountains. The partner became ill and returned to San Francisco, leaving Long to work the mine alone. Eventually, the partner died. On his last trip out of the Sheep Holes, Long fell and injured his side and leg. Finding his shotgun too much of a burden to carry, he cached it and some other things near the mine. In San Bernardino, Long's condition worsened, and shortly before his death he wrote a letter in which he stated that his placer mine was located about 15 miles west of the southern tip of a dry lake. He described the mine as being in a brushy canyon where there was a stream. There are few brushy canyons — and fewer springs — in the Sheep Holes. A combination of the two is not known. The dry lake referred to by Long is believed to be Bristol Dry Lake, located to the south and east of Amboy (US 66). **Map Code 15 K-11**

San Bernardino County — Calico, once a booming mining camp north of US 91-466 between Barstow and Yermo, became a ghost town, but is now rebuilt and being operated as a tourist attraction. When Pat Hogan and Wong Lee lived there, they teamed up to beat the roulette wheel in Lucky Joe's Gambling Palace by using Wong's system based upon a reading of the stars. Pat left the gambling den with most of his winnings and went to his shack in Wall Street Canyon back of Calico.

Wong Lee stayed on for further play, but got into an argument with Lucky Joe and was killed. Joe then went up Wall Street Canyon in search of Pat, determined to recover the gold he had lost. He shot Pat and left him for dead, but failed to find the gold. But Pat was only wounded. A few days later, he showed up in Las Vegas where he, too, got into a fight and was fatally wounded. With his last breath, he gasped, "The gold — it's buried in Calico — three feet from the big rock." So far as it is known, no one has ever been able to determine which big rock Pat meant. The cache is guessed at being worth $20,000. **Map Code 15 K-10**

San Bernardino County — An unnamed prospector is said to have found a large nugget of gold in Minnelusa Canyon, and after much searching, located its source. Later he is reported to have displayed large quantities of gold around the saloons and dancehalls of Holcomb Valley, but he was too clever to allow anyone to follow him to his secret mine. After the prospector's sudden death, members of his family are said to have found a crude penciled map among his effects. Apparently it was intended for his use only, for it contained undecipherable symbols. A search was made, but without success. Minnelusa Canyon's lower extremities can be reached from State 18 north of Big Bear Lake. **Map Code 15 K-10**

San Bernardino County — In the early 1900s, a desert figure known only as Hermit John came into the Santa Fe Railroad freight station at Amboy (State 66) and dumped six sacks of ore on the station platform to be shipped to San Francisco.

One of the sacks broke open and a group of idlers were amazed at the ore's incredible richness. One of the men present happened to be John D. Mitchell, who later became a well-known writer of southwestern lost mine lore. Mitchell wrote that he talked to Hermit John, and the old miner told him that the ore came from a location in the Sheep Hole Mountains northeast of Dale Lake (dry) and Cadiz Lake (dry). He said it was an old shaft once worked by Mexicans or Spaniards, judging from an old arrastre and the mining tools scattered about its entrance. Two or three old graves indicated to Hermit John that its former owners had been killed or died and were buried there. On the day following the Amboy incident, Hermit John left and was never seen or heard of again, and his mine has never been located. **Map Code 15 L-11**

San Bernardino County — The Avawatz Mountains at the southern tip of Death Valley National Monument extend from the southeast to the northwest. A portion of their center is included in the Fort Irwin Military Reservation. While hunting sheep in the Avawatz Range one day, Bob Black, a friend of Death Valley Scotty, found quartz float rich in gold, but he couldn't locate the ledge from which it came. Later, he and Scotty returned to the place where the float had been picked up, but a recent cloudburst had changed Bob's landmarks and washed the float away. Several later attempts were made to find the ledge, but without success. **Map Code 15 J-10**

San Bernardino County — The Lost Mohave Mine may be the oldest lost mine in California. It appears to have been worked by both the Hualapai and Mojave tribes hundreds of years ago. Gold from the Mohave (the name is usually spelled with an "h" in California, and with a "j" in Arizona) is said to have been circulated by the Indians along the Colorado before the first white men came to California.

The location of the mine was a strict tribal secret which only a few tribesmen shared. So strictly was this secret kept that eventually only one old Indian chief, Arataba, knew its exact location and he alone brought out the gold the tribe needed.

In 1892, an old miner named George Nay, while following a faint Indian trail through the southwestern slopes of the Mohave Mountains, across the Colorado River from Topock, Arizona, was certain that he had come upon this long lost mine. But when he later attempted to return to it, he failed to find any of the landmarks he had placed in his memory. So far as it is known, the Lost Mohave Mine is still lost. **Map Code 15 K-13**

San Bernardino County — The name San Bernardino was bestowed by a party of missionaries, soldiers, and Indians from the San Gabriel Mission in Los Angeles, who entered the valley on the feast day of San Bernardino of Siena. There is an old Spanish legend that the missionaries from San Gabriel moved to that area to seek a lost silver mine, which they had learned about from some of the converted Indians. It is believed that this mine has never been found. The Mormons who later founded Rancho San Bernardino here are said to have sought this lost silver mine. **Map Code 15 L-9**

San Bernardino County — In 1866, a party of Mormons led by a man named Adams worked a rich gold mine in the northern reaches of the Clipper Mountains east of Essex (US 66). In the dirt floor of their cabin they are said to have buried their accumulation of gold. One day a band of Indians raided the camp and killed all except one or two who managed to escape. The nameless survivors were never later able to locate the concealed mine nor the cabin, which the Indians are believed to have burned to the ground. One of the survivors revealed that the covered shaft of the mine was located at the intersecting point of diagonal lines drawn between the burnt stumps of four juniper trees.

Many years later, a rancher named Bert Smith was thrown from his horse as he was riding through the northern slopes of the Clippers. As he picked his way out of a tangle of undergrowth, he found what he thought to be a cover for an old mine shaft. He removed it and dropped rocks into the hole, which he guessed to be about 20 feet deep. Nearby, he picked up a few pieces of ore which later proved to be very rich. As he recovered from his injuries in Barstow, he heard of the Lost Mormon Mine for the first time, and was sure that his horse had dumped him right into it. All later attempts to locate the spot were failures, however.

This lost mine is frequently referred to as the Lost Adams Diggings, and is often confused with the Lost Adams Diggings in Arizona or New Mexico, and with the Lost Adams Mine in New Mexico. **Map Code 15 K-11**

San Bernardino County — The Southern Pacific Railroad from Los Angeles to Yuma and the southeast goes through Colton and then swings southeast through San Timeteo Canyon and into Beaumont.

Sometime in the early days of the railroad, Indians are said to have held up a train in San Timeteo Canyon and made away with two chests of gold coins. A rapidly organized posse is said to have overtaken the fleeing Indians and forced a fight at or near what is now known as El Casco, to the southeast. The Indians were all killed, but no money was found on them or in their saddlebags. It is thought that the Indians, upon seeing the posse approaching them, hurriedly buried or hid the loot. **Map Code 15 L-9**

<u>San Bernardino County</u> — While working on the Santa Fe Railroad at Danby, California, in 1894, it was Tom Scofield's job to develop a spring in the Clipper Mountains to the northwest and pipe the water down to the station at Danby. On one of his excursions into the Clippers, Scofield followed a dim trail out of pure curiosity. He passed through a large split rock and came out on a high flat surrounded with steep rock walls. All about him was evidence that this had once been a mining camp. There were shredded pieces of tent, a bed of dried boughs covered with remnants of an old blanket, and rusted cooking utensils including an old iron Dutch oven.

At the far end of the flat, Scofield found the shaft, and nearby was the dump. He examined it and later pronounced it the richest gold ore he had ever seen. Accidentally, he kicked over the Dutch oven to find it half-filled with gold nuggets. Unable to believe that he had found a lost mine of such richness, Scofield hurried back to Danby and caught a train to Los Angeles, where he went on a long drinking spree.

When it was all over, he was broke and it was two years before he could raise a grubstake or find a partner with finances. When they went into the Clipper Mountains, they failed to locate the Lost Dutch Oven Mine. **Map Code 15 K-12**

<u>San Bernardino County</u> — Amboy Crater, also known as Amboy Volcano, is visible from US 66, south of the highway and west of the hamlet of Amboy. It rises 200 feet above the craggy lava beds and a footpath leads to the side of the cone of dark gray pumice and lava. There are two stories of gold being found here, but neither can be confirmed.

In the 1920s, a small girl, daughter of the Santa Fe Railroad agent in Amboy, is said to have found a black lava rock appearing to bear gold. When her father had it assayed, it proved to be rich, but he could not locate the ledge from which it was picked up. From what his daughter could tell him, it came from the west side of Amboy Crater, or from around the edges of Amboy Dry Lake. The second story concerns two unnamed men who supposedly found a small crater near Amboy. The bottom of the crater was filled with gold nuggets — and the skeletons of two men. They are said to have taken out $10,000 in gold, but were unable later to return to the place. **Map Code 15 K-11**

San Bernardino County — Bernard McFadden, the health faddist, is reported to have buried several caches of money across the nation, the most publicized being in New York State. When he owned the Arrowhead Springs Hotel at Lake Arrowhead, California, he is supposed to have buried a sum of money there, and this is attested to by his wife in her book *"Barefoot in Eden."* So far as it is known, this cache has never been found. Lake Arrowhead is a popular resort reached by State 18 out of San Bernardino. **Map Code 15 L-9**

San Bernardino County — There is an unconfirmed story that a gold brick valued at $25,000 was stolen from a shipment of gold bars in Barstow (Interstate 15), and buried near a pile of rocks along the Mohave River near Barstow. An old miner is said to have confessed to the robbery when he solicited the aid of another prospector in attempting to recover it. **Map Code 15 K-10**

San Bernardino County — In the late 1880s, a band of four or five outlaws held up the Bradshaw Route stage office in Beaumont (Interstate 10), then known as San Gorgonio, and made off with $20,000 in gold coins. Heading west across the Moreno Badlands, they holed up in a mesquite grove on the outskirts of the little town of Moreno. On the following morning, they were surprised by a posse and all killed. No gold coins were found on their bodies or in the area searched, so it was presumed that the treasure was buried or hidden some distance away from where they made camp and were killed. **Map Code 15 L-10**

San Bernardino County — About 1932, a long freight train was slowly pulling across the desert between the way stations of Homer and Bannock. From the cab window of the locomotive, the engineer saw the figure of a man stretched out in the sparse shade of a bush along the rails ahead. Obeying the custom of trains stopping to give aid to people in distress in the desert, the engineer brought the freight to a grinding halt. The unconscious man, near death from heat and exposure, was taken aboard and hospitalized in Barstow when the train reached that point. Without ever speaking a word, he soon died. When his heavy knapsack was opened, officials found 35 pounds of black silver ore.

An immediate effort was made to trail the dead man from the spot where he had been picked up. Along the seven miles the trackers were able to follow, other pieces of the same ore were found, apparently discarded to lighten his burden. Eventually his trail was lost among the rocks in the mountains to the north, where he is believed to have made his find on the slopes of Homer Mountain. All efforts to locate the source of this rich silver ore have failed. **Map Code 15 K-12**

San Bernardino County — The Turtle Mountains lie to the north of Rice and west of US 395, in the southwestern corner of huge San Bernardino County. Somewhere in the northeast extremities of these mountains is a stone arch which is the key to the location of a lost mine, which was originally found by a party of Mexicans who are said to have taken out $30,000 worth of gold before the waterholes in the region dried up and forced them to leave. When they later returned, the placer could not be located. Several people have since reportedly seen the arch and have explored the area, but with similar lack of success. Others have claimed from time to time to have found the Lost Arch Mine, including an old-timer from San Bernardino, who offered to take this author to it, for a fee. **Map Code 15 L-12**

San Bernardino County — There are three different Table Mountains in California. The one involved in this story lies to the east of Gold Valley, which flanks the Providence Range northeast of Kelso. Prospecting partners Bert Smith and Bob Holliman had a falling out in this region.

One day, Smith went out in search of boundary markers with which to settle the argument with Holliman. While making his way down the short but steep side of a mountain, he slipped and fell until his hands caught hold of an object. He was able to hold on to it just long enough to learn that it was a piece of iron partially closing the entrance to a cave or tunnel.

As he tumbled to the bottom, the thought came to him that he had heard the story of a lost gold mine in this area, the entrance to which had been closed by an iron door. He was too exhausted to investigate further, but he still clung to a piece of ore that had rolled down with him. This later proved to be reasonably rich in gold. The incident brought the partners together in a later search for the Table Mountain "Mine with the Iron Door." To our knowledge, they failed to locate it. **Map Code 15 J-2**

- ## A WASH TUB OF GOLD NUGGETS IN THE TURTLES

San Bernardino County — In 1883, it is related that a man named Jamison married a squaw in a tribe of Paiute Indians then living on the Nevada side of the Colorado above Fort Mohave. Jamison's motive, it is said, was to learn the secret location of a gold mine worked by the Indians. After a year or two with the tribe, the squaw's brother showed Jamison where the mine was located.

Having the information he wanted, Jamison left the tribe and brought a friend named Fields out from the east to work the mine with him. Starting out from

Homer Siding on the Santa Fe Railroad, the two men traveled about 40 miles in their buckboard, bringing them, it is believed, to the northern stretches of the Turtle Mountains where the mine was located.

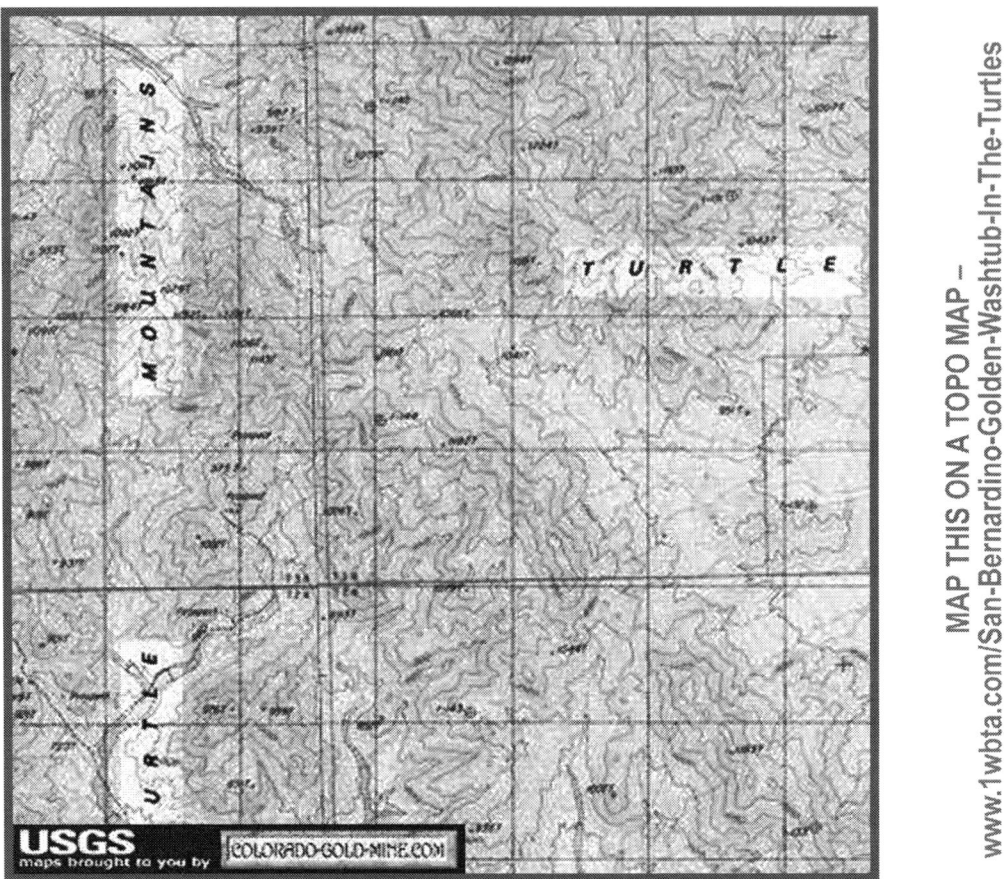

San Bernardino Golden Washtub In The Turtles

MAP THIS ON A TOPO MAP —
www.1wbta.com/San-Bernardino-Golden-Washtub-In-The-Turtles

According to the story, nuggets were so thick on the surface of the ground that all they had to do was to pick them up, and in two days' time they had a wash tub half full of gold. Running short of water, they hid the tub of gold in a little cave in one of the canyons near the mine and started out at night for Homer. During the night, they became hopelessly lost. Abandoning their mules and buckboard, they stumbled on afoot, eventually coming to the little town of Blake on the railroad.

A few days later, a prospector found the wandering mules and brought them and the buckboard into Blake. On the floor of the vehicle was a bag containing $15,000 worth of gold nuggets. In bad health, Jamison went to Needles to recuperate, while

Fields traveled east to secure financial aid to develop the mine. Jamison soon died of fever, and Fields was never again able to locate the lost mine in the Turtles, nor the cave containing a wash tub half-filled with gold nuggets. **Map Code 15 K-12**

<u>San Bernardino County</u> — The finding of a skeleton near Old Woman Springs southeast of Lucerne Valley about 18 miles, and an alleged murder were associated with a search for this lost mine during its early history. When a man appeared who claimed to know where the mine was located, he agreed to lead an organized search party to it.

Camp was made near old Woman Springs. On the following day, the guide asked permission to scout the country alone. He went into the hills west of the spring and was gone all day. Thinking they had been tricked, the search party was about to give up when their informant appeared, carrying a bag of rich silver ore. On the next morning, however, he refused to take anybody to the mine or tell where it was located. When threats failed to budge him, the party gave up in disgust. Those who still thought they had been duped could offer no explanation for the bag of silver.

J. A. Delameter, the man who designed and built the famous Twenty Mule Team wagons, was a strong believer in the existence of this lost mine and spent a lot of time and money in trying to locate it. He thought the mine was located in the southeast portion of the Granite Mountains, a point to which a man could walk to from Old Woman Springs and back in one day. **Map Code 15 K-10**

• SAN LUIS REY MISSION – $10,000,000 IN SPANISH GOLD

<u>San Diego County</u> — A cache of Spanish gold said to be worth as much as $10,000,000 has been the search object of many treasure hunters in San Diego County over the past 30 years. As much as $250,000 of this vast treasure has been found in scattered places in the vicinity of the Mission San Luis Rey, situated inland about four miles from Oceanside (State 1). The origin of this treasure, and the circumstances of its burial in San Luis Rey Valley, is shrouded in mystery, but the general opinion is that it was buried by Francisco de Ulloa, a trusted lieutenant of the Spanish conquistadors, Hernando Cortez, conqueror of Mexico.

Dr. Joseph J. Markey, Oceanside physician and an avocational archaeologist, claims to have heard this story in Paris in 1947 from a Spaniard whose name was Miguel de Ulloa, a direct descendant of Francisco de Ulloa.

According to Miguel, after the sacking of Mexico by Cortez, he heard of the fabulous Seven Cities of Cibola far to the north and commissioned Francisco de Ulloa to sail up the west coast of America, travel inland, and make a search for them. Ulloa said the galleon Trinidad sailed with a crew of 21 men, and in the holds of the vessel were stored about $10,000,000 worth of gold, packed in pitch-covered wooden boxes. The gold was evidently part of the loot taken in Mexico, and was not only intended to finance the trip, but to be kept safe from other greedy conquerors arriving in Mexico.

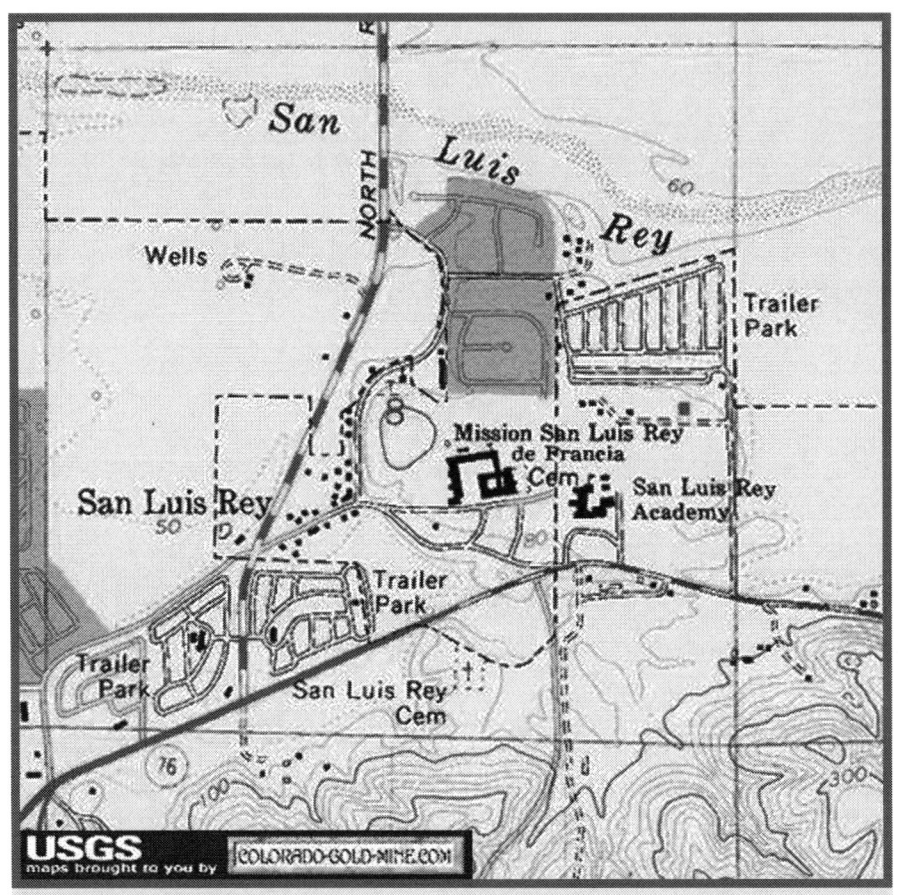

San Luis Rey Mission - $10M In Spanish Gold

MAP THIS ON A TOPO MAP —
http://www.1wbta.com/San-Luis-Rey-Mission-10Million-Spanish-Gold

The Trinidad finally arrived at the mouth of the San Luis Rey River, at what is now the town of Oceanside, and dropped anchor. Leaving three men aboard the vessel, Ulloa and the remainder of the crew transported about half the gold ashore and carried it inland in three separate trips, where it was buried.

While living among the friendly Indians in San Luis Rey Valley, Ulloa and his men contracted scurvy and all died. Supporting this incident is the fact that a mass grave was found inland from Oceanside in 1937. The skulls had no teeth nor roots, the mark of men who die of scurvy. Bits of armor, a few buttons and other artifacts of Spanish origin were found, strengthening the belief, when the story of the treasure was learned later, that these were the remains of Francisco de Ulloa and his crew.

One of the three men left aboard the Trinidad was the historian of the voyage, Pablo Salvador Hernandez. He left behind the records on which this story is said to be largely based. After weeks of waiting for the return of Ulloa and his men, the three seamen gave them up for dead and decided to return to Mexico. Because they could not handle the Trinidad alone, they constructed a longboat and finally made their way back to Mexico in that.

The abandoned galleon eventually broke her anchor, drifted a short distance south, and capsized with the remainder of the treasure, an estimated $5,000,000. Some historians do not agree with Dr. Markey that Ulloa died in California, and say he also made his way back to Mexico. But Dr. Markey is more concerned with the fate of the gold. As a member of the San Luis Rey Historical Society, he has spent a lot of money in searching for it, and there are vague hints that some of it has been found. **Map Code 15 M-9**

San Diego County — After the abandonment of the galleon Trinidad (see above), the ship broke its anchor in a storm and drifted about two miles to the south. Evidence brought up by divers is said to indicate that the hulk might lie off the mouth of Loma Alta Creek and the 1600 block of Pacific Street in Oceanside. Coins have been washed ashore here, leading to the belief that the hulk is breaking up, although it is recognized that this may be the remains of a vessel other than the Trinidad. If and when the identification of the ship is established, divers with modern gear may be able to recover the Trinidad's $5,000,000 in gold. **Map Code 15 M-9**

San Diego County — In the extreme southeastern corner of San Diego County, the San Diego & Arizona Eastern Railroad swings north from Jacumba, skirts the Jacumba Mountains, and turns southeast to Dos Cabezas Station and on into Imperial County. There are many tunnels in the area, each being numbered. Tunnel 21 is some 35 miles northeast of Dos Cabezas. In this vicinity, in 1910, an old Indian is known to have taken out several sacks of gold ore from a secret placer operation. All efforts to locate the placer in recent years have failed. The area is within the southern extremity of Anza-Borrego Desert State Park. **Map Code 15 N-11**

<u>San Diego County</u> — Coyote Creek is located in upper Anza-Borrego Desert State Park, just south of the Riverside-San Diego county line. Indians native to this area frequently told that two German prospectors from Los Angeles mined several burro loads of gold ore in the vicinity of Coyote Creek, packed it out, and never came back.

Much later, a Los Angeles schoolteacher, on summer vacation, approached veteran prospector Charles Knowles in Oak Grove and hired him to serve as her guide in a search for a mine once worked by her German father. He had left her a map of the location, $4,200 in gold taken from the mine, and some rich samples of ore. Her map called for a large flat stone on which was carved a spearhead. Near this stone would be found the arrastre in which the ore was crushed. After a fruitless search of 10 days or more, Knowles gave up, and the schoolteacher returned to Los Angeles. Knowles never saw her again.

Some years later, Knowles found a stone arrastre in the Coyote Creek region. Certain that he was on the right trail to the lost mine of the two Germans, he searched in vain for the flat stone carved with a spearhead. Many believe that the Lost Two Germans' Mine and the Lost Schoolteacher Mine are one and the same.
Map Code 15 M-10

<u>San Diego County</u> — El Cajon Mountain lies almost due south of the town of Ramona (State 78), and west of El Capitan Reservoir. According to a generally accepted story, an Indian appeared in Los Angeles with a burro load of silver ore which he sold to a silversmith. On a second trip to Los Angeles with another load of ore, the Indian was killed in a fight, and the story of the dead man's silver mine created wild excitement.

Years later, the silversmith who had purchased the ore from the Indian, revealed that the Indian had told him his mine was located on El Cajon Mountain. It is believed that a Mexican later worked it before he disappeared. An Indian legend says that the padres of Mission San Diego de Alcala had earlier worked the same mine. One of California's better-known lost mines, this one is known by five different names —

- The Lost El Cajon, because of the mountain it is supposed to be located on;
- The Lost Wadham, after a San Diego pioneer named Wadham, who owned the Barona Ranch adjacent to El Cajon Mountain;
- The Lost Barona, because of the prevalence of the name "Barona" in the area;

- The Lost Indian Silver Mine, because of the unnamed Indian who worked the mine and first brought it to wide public attention; and,
- The Lost El Capitan Mine, because that was once the popular name for El Cajon Mountain.

Map Code 15 M-10

San Diego County — One night, Charley Helm and a party of cowboys, driving a herd of cattle through Earthquake Valley, made camp at a spring. Young Harry Yarnell, a rider with the outfit, struck up a conversation with another rider, an Indian named Julian Cabrias. Taking a liking to Yarnell, the Indian told him that his people had taken much gold out of the area, and displayed some nuggets to prove it. The following morning the Indian took Yarnell up to the mouth of a small canyon and told him that there was plenty of gold up there about half a mile. To mark the place, Yarnell erected a small cairn, intending to stop on his way back after the cattle were delivered to El Centro.

In El Centro, Yarnell was offered another job that was too good to turn down, and it was spring before he got back to Earthquake Valley. The cairn was missing, probably washed away by a sudden rush of water from a cloudburst. Yarnell searched the area for years without finding the canyon, nor were his efforts to locate the Indian who knew the secret, Julian Cabrias, any more successful. He had simply vanished. The locale of this lost mine is generally placed west of Julian and south of Scissors Crossing (State 78). **Map Code 15 M-10**

San Diego County — Since the 1920s, people have been studying the "Bluebeard" Watson murder case for a clue to the hiding place of $200,000, bilked from the wealthy wives he married as a bigamist. It is almost certainly buried someplace in the Borrego Desert, and possibly near the place Watson indicated to the district attorney's office.

James P. "Bluebeard" Watson, before he died in San Quentin Prison of tuberculosis in 1939, confessed to the slaying of as many as 14 of his 25 wives. He married, either as a bigamist or as a fake husband, wealthy women, bilked them out of their wealth, and then disposed of them. When he was finally brought to justice, it is believed that he made a deal with the Los Angeles district attorney.

In return for the confession of the murder of an Idaho girl in California, and for showing the district attorney's office where her body was buried, Watson is believed to have been promised life imprisonment instead of the death penalty. Watson was wanted on a murder charge in Washington at the same time, and the penalty there would almost certainly have been death.

Watson took officials to a remote place in the desert where the girl's body was dug up. Watson was then tried, convicted, and sentenced to life imprisonment. He is supposed to have told the district attorney's office "approximately" where he had buried $200,000, believed to have been near Borrego Springs. Although officials never admitted that this money was found, there were many at the time who believed that it had been. **Map Code 15 M-10**

<u>San Diego County</u> — Ramona (State 78) is a small community in Santa Maria Valley in the back country of San Diego County. One of the Indian legends of this valley tells that a large treasure of gold and silver and church possessions, brought from a mine and mission in Arizona, was stored in a cave here, awaiting transshipment to San Diego, where it was to be placed aboard a galleon and shipped to Spain. The entrance to the cave was concealed with an iron door over which was thrown rocks and debris. According to the Indians, after the treasure was hidden, they were sent back to Arizona, and the padres in charge of the treasure were killed by other Indians. Several articles have been found in the area to indicate the presence of Spanish in the area at one time, and several marks found on trees and rocks have been interpreted as treasure symbols. **Map Code 15 M-10**

<u>San Diego County</u> — In 1682, according to tradition, the pirate ship of Jesus Arroa was wrecked in a great storm off San Diego. Those of the crew who survived went inland and are believed to have reached Sheep Head Mountain, south of Mt. Laguna, although there is no uniformity of opinion on this location. Here the shipwrecked men lived off the land and wild game, and found placer gold. A great quantity of gold dust and nuggets was gathered and stored, with the hope of someday getting it back to the coast and on a passing ship.

One day, a band of Indians swarmed down upon the seamen. Seeing the attack coming, Jesus Arroa hurriedly wrote a note describing their situation, placed it in a metal case and buried it. Above it he placed a crude cross bearing instructions to dig below. Then all were killed. It is said that this cross and note were found by a Spanish prospector in 1873, and that a search was made for the stored gold and its sources, but nothing was ever found. This story has many conflicting versions and locations. **Map Code 15 N-10**

San Diego County — Signal Mountain looms up just south of the international border, west of Calexico-Mexicali. Travelers in the early days sometimes passed it on the Mexican side of the border, and sometimes on the California side. Indian attacks in this area were frequent and all the members of at least two wagon trains were annihilated in the area. One of these trains consisted of a party of Sonorans returning from northern California to their homeland, and carrying an undetermined amount of gold. Just before the Indians swarmed upon them, they pulled their wagons into defensive formation and hurriedly buried their gold. It is believed that this massacre probably took place at what is now an abandoned gravel pit almost on the border and directly north of Signal Mountain. When the pit was being worked, remains of old wagons were found in the area, but if any gold was found, it seems never to have been reported. **Map Code 15 N-11**

San Diego County — A Portuguese prospector named Antonio Joseph, working across the border in Mexico, came upon a badly injured Indian boy. Placing the boy on one of his burros, he took him to the nearest Indian village. In appreciation, the lad told Joseph where the Indians secured much gold, to the north. Starting at Signal Mountain, the prospector followed the boy's directions to Coyote Mountain in the northeastern corner of what is now Anza-Borrego Desert State Park. Years later, the skeletons of two mules, both loaded with gold, were found in this area. Presumably they belonged to Antonio Joseph, and the gold was secured via the Indian boy's directions. The prospector was never heard of again, and so far as it is known, neither his bones nor the source of the gold has ever been found. **Map Code 15 M-10**

San Diego County — In the booming days of the mining camp of Banner (State 78), a man who called himself Jim Green, but was better known to the miners as "Nigger Jim," worked at odd jobs. When Louis Pindree came to town to buy supplies with gold taken from the secret mine he worked in partnership with George Le Ponde, he was shot one night by an unknown assailant as he left a saloon.

He died in the arms of Jim Green, who tried to save the Frenchman's life.

Shortly after this incident, Green, who was normally broke, seemed to have an unlimited supply of gold. He explained it by saying that the dying Pindree had given him his share of the mine worked in partnership with Le Ponde, and Le Ponde verified it. When Le Ponde later disappeared, it was suspected that Nigger Jim had murdered him to get the mine for himself. Then Jim Green mysteriously vanished, and the mine he called the "Phantom" became lost.

It was believed to have been located in the vicinity of Yaqui Well, a short distance to the north of State 78 in the Anza-Borrego Desert State Park. **Map Code 15 M-10**

San Diego County — The Indians had known of the existence of gold in the back country of San Diego County for many years, and they were quick to learn of its value in terms of trading it for the white man's goods. Once learning this, they were extremely close-mouthed about the sources of their gold. Carmelita was a squaw who became accustomed to the nice things gold would buy. After her husband was killed, she moved to Banner and took a job as a servant in a rooming house. Under the guise of visiting her tribe, she made frequent trips into the desert, always going alone and always returning with enough gold to satisfy her needs. All Carmelita would tell when questioned was that the mine worked by her husband was on San Felipe Creek. San Felipe runs from the little town of San Felipe, southeast to Scissors Crossing. It is a large expanse of desert to search, but someplace along its course is the source of Carmelita's gold. **Map Code 15 M-10**

San Diego County — During the early 1930s, an Indian known only as Charlie lived with his squaw near Imperial (State 86), and frequented the rodeos, boxing matches, and other sports events in the Imperial Valley towns. He was notorious for the large amounts of money he wagered on these events, and was known to have lost heavily, sometimes as much as $20,000 at a time. This never seemed to concern Charlie. When he was out of money, he and his squaw would mount their horses and ride out toward San Felipe Wash. On their return, they would be carrying large amounts of placer gold. Attempts to follow them always failed. When the two disappeared, an extensive search was made for the placer, but without success. It is believed now that the mine is probably covered with debris washed down by a cloudburst. **Map Code 15 M-11**

San Diego County — A party of Mexicans who had served with the bandit Joaquin Murrieta were attacked by a band of Indians just east of Carrizo as they were fleeing California. Hopelessly outnumbered, the Mexicans were all slain. Many years later, an old Indian whose father was supposedly the leader of the attack, said that after the slaughter, the Indians gathered up the treasure carried by the outlaws, placing it in large ollas (pots), and hid them in a small cave under an overhanging ledge in the nearby hills. **Map Code 15 N-11**

San Diego County — Entering a narrow ravine with steep rocky sides in Fish Creek Canyon where it penetrates Split Mountain, a half-breed Indian known only as Indian Joe was trying to recover his canteen, which had fallen into the ravine by accident. As he struggled down the wall, his eyes were attracted to an outcropping that appeared to be rich in gold. As he pried off several large pieces for samples, the wall suddenly collapsed, revealing a dark cavern. Indian Joe enlarged the opening and entered, finding it to be a crude man-built vault made of stones. Finding nothing in the vault, Indian Joe took his samples and headed for Banner. In a few weeks he announced that he was making another trip to the vault, and after that was never seen again.

Many years after Indian Joe's disappearance, an old Indian related that Joe had been killed by his own people for the gold he carried. According to the old man's story, the Indians knew that Joe had not only found a rich ledge of gold, but that the vault had contained a stagecoach strongbox filled with gold bars, only a portion of which Joe managed to get out before being killed. Supposedly, the gold bars are still there, and some credence is given to the story because the Butterfield Overland stages were frequently robbed in this region. **Map Code 15 M-11**

San Diego County — In 1818, the padres at San Diego Mission established an *assistencia* at Santa Isabel, 40 miles inland, to care for the Indians who could not keep in close touch with San Diego. Into the Santa Isabel Valley there came three Missourians in 1851. Indian runners observed that they carried a heavy bag. As they camped that night, a quarrel broke out over the division of the contents of the bag — gold dust and nuggets. One of the men killed the other two and then was killed by the Indians. The bag of gold was taken to the Indian village and turned over to the chief. That night, a council was held, and afterward, the chief carried the bag of gold across the valley, and later returned without it. So far as it is known, this treasure, in a buckskin bag the size of a watermelon, still lies buried in the foothills west of Santa Isabel Mission. **Map Code 15 N-10**

San Diego County — A Dutchman named Dietz was a persistent searcher for the Lost Pegleg Smith Mine, concentrating his efforts in the north end of Blair Valley in almost the geographical center of San Diego County. From time to time he brought in ore samples to be assayed, but always they were found to be worthless. One day, Dietz was found to be absent for a longer period of time than usual, and a worried friend went out in search of him. He was found on the desert, ill with fever. While he was hospitalized in San Diego, a report on his latest samples showed them to be extremely rich in gold. Dietz could not recall where they came from, except that the area was near a cave out of which flew a black crow as he passed it. The Lost Black Crow Mine is believed to be located in the north end of Blair Valley. **Map Code 15 M-10**

San Diego County — Yaqui Well is located on State 78 and within the boundaries of Anza-Borrego Desert State Park. To the west of Yaqui Well, the highway goes through Sentenec Canyon and past Grapevine Mountain. At the southern base of Grapevine Mountain, two men searching for Indian artifacts found a reddish clay substance from which they picked out several gold nuggets. Believing they had all the nuggets, they left, never expecting to return to the place. In Julian sometime later, they happened to relate this story to an old Indian who told them that the Indians used to gather nuggets over a large area at the southern base of Grapevine Mountain. All efforts of the men to later locate the rich placer deposit failed. **Map Code 15 M-10**

San Diego County — Late in 1852, or possibly during the early months of 1853, a single heavy wagon with six or seven riders on mules made camp one night a short distance south of Borrego Springs in the Borrego Badlands, now a part of the Anza-Borrego Desert State Park. Attacked that night by hostile Indians, the travelers were picked off one by one until all were dead. It is said that the travelers were wealthy, and that before the attack, they had buried their gold and the campfire was built over the spot, a not too uncommon practice in those days. Many have searched for this treasure, and the remains of their burned wagon, but neither has ever been found. **Map Code 15 M-10**

San Diego County — Coyote Mountain is in the northern part of Anza Borrego Desert State Park, northeast of Borrego Springs and east of Clark Dry Lake. It is known locally by some old-timers as Butler Mountain, after an old prospector of that name. One day, Butler came into the camp of Fred Clark at Clark Well, where he was running some cattle, and told him that he was very sick and wanted to get to a hospital in San Bernardino. Clark explained that he couldn't leave the cattle, and asked the old man to go to his tent and rest.

A short time later, two men arrived in an automobile from San Diego — one of the first to enter Borrego Valley. They talked to the sick man, and he told them that he had a rich gold mine on Coyote Mountain. He stated it was imperative that he get to the hospital in San Bernardino, and that he had a feeling he would not come out alive. He had a map to the mine, and this, he told the men, was theirs if he did not survive. If he pulled through, they could still have a half interest in the mine for their trouble. The men agreed, and took Butler to San Bernardino, where he soon died. True to his word, there was a crude map among his effects, and this was given to his two benefactors. After a search of Coyote Mountain lasting several months, the men gave up, unable to follow the map's rough directions. **Map Code 15 M-11**

San Diego County — About 1900, an Indian girl came into a railroad construction camp at Indio, carrying a quantity of gold nuggets which she freely displayed. When two prospectors loafing at the camp asked her where they came from, she said she couldn't tell them, but she would take them there. Arriving at a point in the northern end of the Borrego Mountains, she pointed to a ridge to the southeast and said the mine was there, but she refused to go further. Alex McCloud, a veteran San Diego County prospector, was always of the opinion that this was the famed Lost Pegleg Smith Mine, and he searched long and hard for it in that region. The area is in the northwest portion of the Anza-Borrego Desert State Park. **Map Code 15 M-10**

San Diego County — Warner Springs (State 79) has been a popular resort area since stagecoach days when it was known as Warner's Ranch. Not far north of Warner's Ranch was a roadside and saloon which prospered with the tide of travelers passing its door. On being told that a party of Mexicans planned to rob him, the saloon's owner took his savings of $8,000 and buried it in the basement of the old building.

One night, the bandits arrived as predicted, and in the battle that followed, the innkeeper was killed. The Mexicans searched for the money, but failed to find it. The old building has now completely disappeared, but a shallow depression marks the spot where it once stood. If this treasure was ever found, the fact has not been made public. **Map Code 15 M-10**

San Diego County — The name Williams turns up in southern California lost mine lore almost as frequently as that of the "Dutchman" or "Frenchman." Usually there is no record of a first name. This story concerns a certain Williams who was shown a rich deposit of silver by some Indians he had befriended. The location of this deposit is often placed in the mountains back of San Diego, generally in the Alpine (US 80) area. Williams is said to have taken out all the silver he would need for the rest of his life, and went east to live a life of ease.

The Indians covered the mine to keep it a secret, and supposedly it is still there.
Map Code 15 N-10

- ## THE BUCKSNORTS' BUCKSKIN BAG OF GOLD NUGGETS

San Diego County — In the early days of Warner's Ranch, an old Indian used to sit in poker games, always well supplied with a buckskin bag of gold nuggets. All efforts to determine where the Indian got his gold, failed. The Indian's squaw worked as a domestic for Mrs. Wilson, wife of the storekeeper at Warner's Ranch. Out of gratitude for nursing her back to health after a serious illness, the squaw offered to take Mrs. Wilson to the source of her husband's gold.

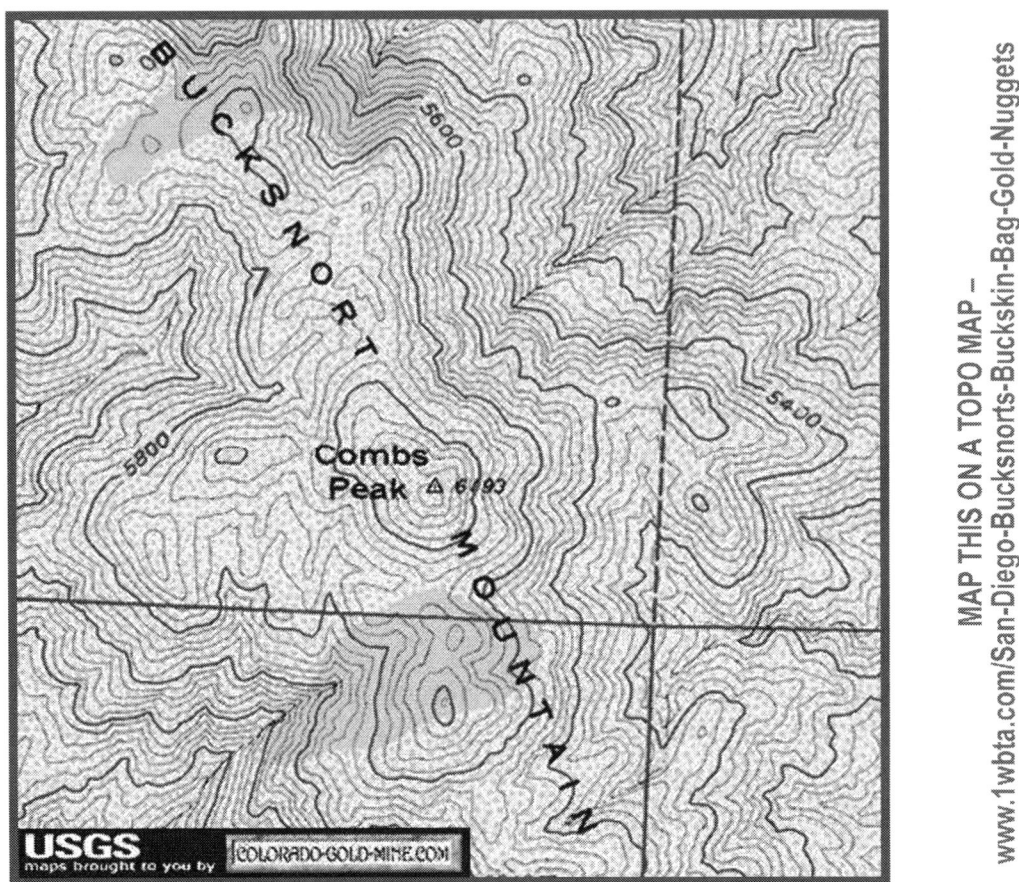

San Diego Bucksnorts Buckskin Bag Gold Nuggets

MAP THIS ON A TOPO MAP —
www.1wbta.com/San-Diego-Bucksnorts-Buckskin-Bag-Gold-Nuggets

At the edge of a group of small hills known as the Bucksnorts, to the east of Oak Grove, the two women were overtaken by the squaw's angry husband, who ordered them back. Soon the Indian took his woman and left the country, but the squaw had managed to tell Mrs. Wilson that the mine was in the Bucksnorts.
Map Code 15 M-10

<u>San Diego County</u> — In the late 1880s, a stranger who gave his name as Bell stopped at Warner's Ranch for several days. When leaving, he announced that he was going to head afoot for Yuma and search for the Lost Pegleg Smith Mine along the way. Apparently not knowing the country, he strayed far north of the

route to Yuma. One day, he stumbled into a camp of miners in the upper ridges of the Cargo Muchacho Mountains. He was out of water and in a desperate condition. Little hope was held for his recovery, but the camp cook took a liking to the stranger and eventually nursed him back to health.

In appreciation, Bell took the cook into his confidence and told him this story. A few miles east of the Vallecito Stage Station, Bell had seen a group of riders approaching in the distance. Knowing that the country was full of bandits, he had detoured into a small canyon to wait until they had passed. While there, he kicked aside some rocks and found them so full of yellow metal that he thought it impossible that it could be gold, but he put some specimens in his pockets.

As Bell displayed the samples, the cook exclaimed that this was the richest gold ore he had ever seen. The decision was made not to tell the miners lest everyone would want to rush to Bell's hideout canyon. One day when the miners were all away from the camp, Bell and the cook took two horses and a wagon and made a secret departure. They were never seen again. Some years later, the wagon and the skeletons of the two mules, still in harness, were found near the southern base of Fish Mountain. The fate of Bell and the cook is a mystery today, as well as the location of Bell's Lost Hideout Canyon Mine, which is believed to be somewhere in the southern slopes of the Vallecito Mountains. **Map Code 15 M-11**

San Diego County — In 1934, the Vallecito Stage Station on the old Butterfield Stage Line was restored, and the area on which it stands is now designated as Vallecito Stage Station County Park. All types of travelers passed through here in the early days because it was on the busy main route from Los Angeles to Yuma. It is said that a party of Mexican bandits carrying $80,000 in gold, taken in their raids in California, stopped here on their way to Mexico. Planning to stay overnight, and aware that a posse might catch up with them at any time, the leader took the gold into a nearby small canyon and buried it. Returning to the stage station, the bandit was ambushed by a party of lawmen and killed. The remaining Mexicans fled, and presumably their buried gold is still there. **Map Code 15 M-11**

San Diego County — Another story associated with the Vallecito Stage Station is that of the bandit who operated in the area, and specialized in robbing the Butterfield stages. It is said that he was so successful, and accumulated so much loot, that he placed it in *ollas*, took the *ollas* into the nearby hills, and concealed them in a small cave. It is claimed that after the bandit was eventually killed, his widow spent many years searching for his cache. **Map Code 15 N-10**

San Diego County — Somewhere along the old Butterfield Overland Mail Route through Vallecito Wash, and probably between the ruins of the old stage station at Carrizo and the restored station at Vallecito, which are 17 miles apart, is an iron chest containing $65,000 in gold. There are two versions to the story.

- One is that four men held up a stage in this area and secured the chest of treasure. When all were killed a short time later, the chest could not be found.

- The second version has it that a lone bandit held up the stage, and finding the chest too heavy to make off with, hurriedly buried it near the scene of the holdup. About to ride away, the bandit was confronted and killed by the stage driver he thought was dead.

Map Code 15 N-10

San Diego County — Of the 10 stage stations built in San Diego County by the Butterfield line, only three remain today — Vallecito, Oak Grove, and Warner's. The San Felipe Station, located in San Felipe Valley about midway between Vallecito and Warner's, has entirely disappeared, and even the site is difficult to locate. Two prospectors waited here for a stage one night, hardly concealing the fact that they had just struck it rich and had a fortune of gold with them.

A lone bandit suddenly entered the little adobe station, seized the gold and left. Recognizing the bandit, the station keeper went to the door and called him by name. There was no answer, and the keeper returned to the station. Minutes later, the bandit reappeared, ordered the station keeper to procure a shovel and start digging his own grave. Waiting his chance, the station keeper swung at the bandit's head with the shovel, dealing him a fatal blow, but as he was falling, the bandit fired, killing his opponent. Because the prospectors' gold could not be found after the killings, it is presumed that the bandit took it some distance away and buried it before returning to kill the station keeper. **Map Code 15 M-10**

San Diego County — In the 1820s, according to an old legend, a Spanish messenger named Rubio, while carrying a dispatch from Monterey to Mexico, became lost and wandered around until his supply of water ran out. He was finally found by friendly Indians and taken to Vallecito, where he stayed until he was able to resume his journey. While there, he told the Indians that he had found a deposit of gold high up in the mountains to the northwest. The Indians told him they knew it was there, and that they gathered it from time to time for trading purposes. In later years, the Indians of the Vallecito area said this gold was in the Vallecito Mountains. **Map Code 15 N-11**

San Diego County — About 1850, a party of emigrants westward bound camped at Vallecito overnight. Before resuming the trip the following morning, a man named Williams left the party after having a disagreement, and struck out by himself, headed for San Diego. It is believed that he traveled down Storm Canyon and entered the Laguna Mountains. When he arrived in San Diego, he had a large number of diamonds. He said the diamonds were found in a blue clay-like substance, and that they covered a large area. After selling the diamonds, Williams disappeared and was unheard of again. Whether or not he returned to the field of diamonds is not known. The Laguna Mountains are traversed by a road running off US 80 at Laguna Junction. **Map Code 15 N-10**

San Diego County — A man known only as Wiley or Williams is said to have located a rich ledge of gold near Vallecito Spring. He built a crude arrastre and worked the place until his supplies ran out. Finding he had more gold than he could carry out with him, he took what he could carry and cached the remainder in a crevice between two large rocks, one of which could be swung from its place by using a bar as a lever. He returned to his mine to find a band of Indians camped at the spring. They ordered him to leave and he refused. He was promptly killed. It is believed that his mine and cache of gold are still there. **Map Code 15 N-10**

San Diego County — About 1870, when Julian was the mining center of San Diego County and riding the crest of a boom, an unnamed Frenchman came into the camp with a burro load of rich gold ore. After selling the ore, he proceeded to get on a roaring drunk, telling all who would listen that he had a mine in the Tierra Blanca Mountains directly south of Vallecito. After recovering from his drunk, he left to return to his mine, but was met and killed by an Indian whose sister he had offended. So far as it is known, this mine has never been found. **Map Code 15 N-11**

San Diego County — Old Town was the original Spanish settlement in what is now San Diego. There have been persistent rumors that the padres of San Diego Mission, originally located in Old Town, buried their treasures here when they were expelled from the country. One story has it that the padres dug a tunnel from the mission to the bottom of a nearby canyon to assure a supply of water should they be besieged by Indians, and that the church wealth was concealed in this tunnel.

Another story relates that when word came to vacate the missions, the San Diego Mission padres decided to transport their accumulated gold to Los Angeles. Two priests rode ahead of the several mules loaded with the mission gold. As they were in one of the canyons just north of San Diego, the scouts saw signs of Indians ahead, and fearing an attack, hurriedly unloaded the gold and concealed it in a cave. According to this version of the story, the entire mission party was killed by the Indians and the gold still rests in a cave, its entrance now concealed by a cave-in. **Map Code 15 N-10**

San Diego County — Black Mountain (1,500') lies directly to the north of San Diego and west of US 395. A Mexican tradition says that the padres of San Diego Mission, fearful that they were going to be forced to leave the mission, had their treasures taken to Black Mountain where they were hidden in a mine shaft from which gold and silver had been mined by the mission. It is a matter of church record that the California missions and the Mexican civil authorities were often at odds, and there is evidence that some mining activity occurred in the mountains around San Diego long before the arrival of Americans. Furthermore, when the Franciscan Fathers were expelled from the country, they took no treasure with them. If they had any treasure, what happened to it? **Map Code 15 N-10**

San Diego County — According to tradition, two oxcart loads of gold and mission church valuables are hidden in the depths of a rich silver mine once worked by the padres of the San Diego Mission in the area of Starvation Peak, west of Ramona (State 78). The treasure is said to have been placed there by the padres when Mexico threw off Spanish rule. **Map Code 15 M-10**

San Diego County — In 1956, a skin diver announced that he had found what appeared to be a wrecked Spanish galleon off Solano Beach (Interstate 5). It was speculated that the ship might have been one of the vessels of the Francisco de Ulloa expedition sent out to discover a river passage to the fabled Seven Cities of Cibola. The vessel is in 60 feet of water, and scientists at the Scripps Institute of Oceanography said the description of the condition of the wood in the hulk ruled out the belief that it was a Spanish galleon of that period. They said wood borers would have long ago made sawdust of the vessel. **Map Code 15 N-9**

San Diego County — The Spanish galleon Madre de Dios is said to have gone down off Carlsbad (Interstate 5), about two miles south of Oceanside and 13 miles north of Solano Beach, in an area where other galleons are said to have gone down. It is guessed that this, too, may have been one of Francisco de Ulloa's vessels (see above). It is reported that $150,000 was recovered from this wreck, but efforts to secure a confirmation of this claim have met with no success. **Map Code 15 M-9**

- ## **FIVE LOST MINES RIGHT IN THE HEART OF SAN FRANCISCO**

San Francisco County —

Mine #1 – Strange as it seems, there are five lost mines right in the City of San Francisco. These were discovered when San Francisco was building up in its early days, and at a time when so much gold was being taken out of the Mother Lode country that nobody paid much attention to a vein right in the city.

Except for its parks, San Francisco is a solid mass of buildings and pavement. While there is little chance of ever finding one of these San Francisco lost mines, their locations are listed here for the record.

San Francisco Mine #1 - Telegraph Hill

MAP THIS ON A TOPO MAP —
www.1wbta.com/San-Francisco-Mine-No-1-Telegraph-Hill
Attribution: http://commons.wikimedia.org/wiki/User:Dr. Blofeld – CC-BY-SA-2.0

- ◆ **#1 –** Gold was discovered at the base of Telegraph Hill by the young daughter of Governor McDougal while she was playing along a bank that had caved in.

Mine #2 – Nob Hill is one of San Francisco's 44 hills, and one of its original "Seven Hills." The effects of the Gold Rush were substantial. With ships, equipment, and merchandise, and 1000s of sea-faring Argonauts flooding into California through the Golden Gate, San Francisco straight away became the very center of the Gold Rush.

No other city grew larger or more rapidly. Its populace in January of 1848 was 800; by 1853, it had blossomed to over 50,000, with even more pushing through, to and from the mines. San Francisco quickly became the most culturally and ethnically diverse place in the world.

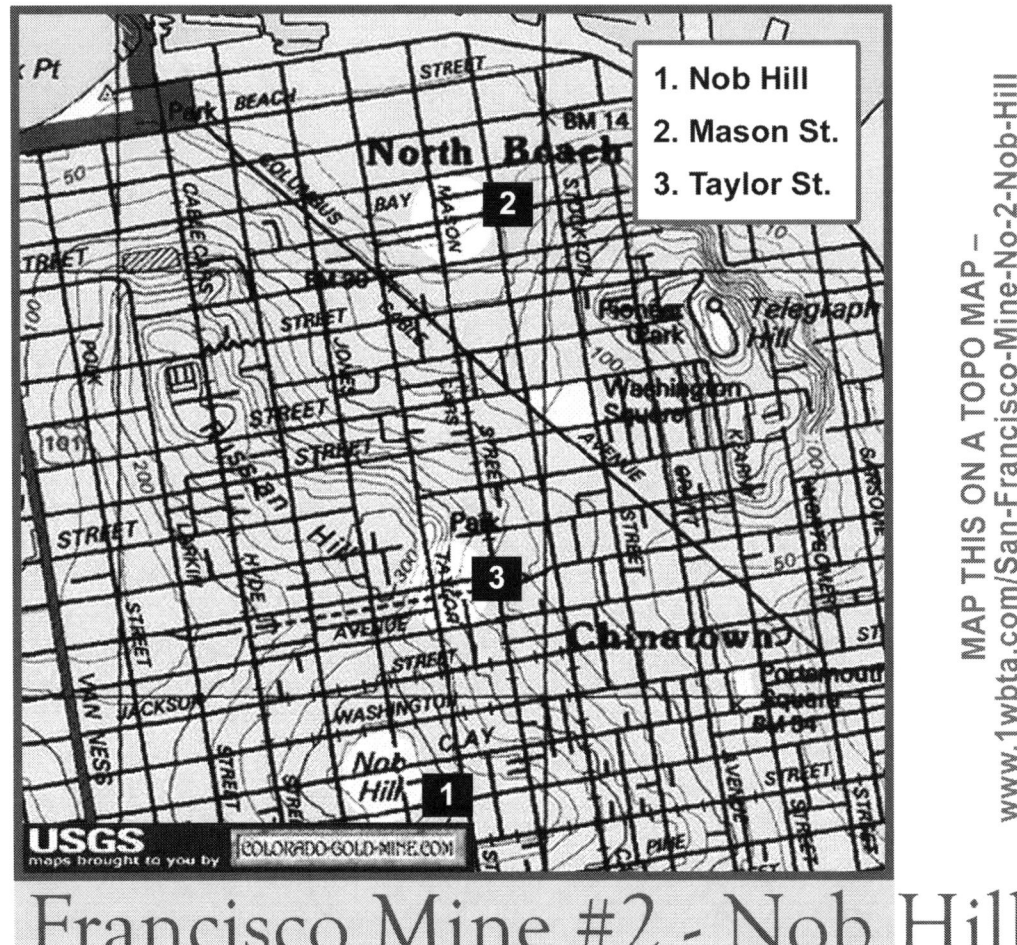

San Francisco Mine #2 - Nob Hill

MAP THIS ON A TOPO MAP —
www.1wbta.com/San-Francisco-Mine-No-2-Nob-Hill

- ♦ **#2 –** Another find was made on Nob Hill between Mason and Taylor Streets. This was actually worked by two miners for a time, but when they returned after a Fourth of July celebration, they found the property closed off to them. Leland Stanford, who owned the property, was accused of closing off the property because he wanted it for building sites.

Mine #3 – Portsmouth Square is a one-block park in Chinatown, San Francisco, California, that is bounded by Kearny Street on the east, Washington Street on the north, Clay Street on the south, and Walter Lum Place on the west. Portsmouth Square is located on the site of the first public square established in the early 19th century in the Mexican community of Yerba Buena, whose name was changed to San Francisco in 1847.

During the Mexican-American War, Captain John Berrien Montgomery of the USS Portsmouth was ordered to seize Yerba Buena. On July 9, 1846, the first American flag was raised near the Mexican adobe custom house in the plaza that would be named Portsmouth Square, in honor of Capt. Montgomery's ship.

San Francisco Mine #3 - Portsmouth Square

MAP THIS ON A TOPO MAP —
www.1wbta.com/San-Francisco-Mine-No-3-Portsmouth-Square

- **#3** – In 1851, a foot-wide vein of high quality gold was found near the surface at Broadway and Grant Avenue, pinching out at Portsmouth Square. Again, the desire to build was greater than the desire to recover the gold. San Francisco was bursting at the seams for room.

Mine #4 – ✪ Green Street – Running from the Embarcadero to the Presidio, Green Street was named in William Eddy's 1849 survey of San Francisco. Talbot Green came west in the spring of 1841 in the first immigrant party to travel over the Sierras to California.

✪ Stockton Street – Named for the city. Muddy streets and a keen entrepreneurial spirit defined Stockton, California, back in 1849. Before long, this bustling town and its waterways turned into a gateway for supplies needed in the nearby gold mining communities. Although the gold rush ended by 1855, Stockton businesses prospered from their ability to process and transport agricultural products to the markets of the world.

✪ Grant Avenue – A one-way street for cars bound northward. Grant begins its 1.6 mile gambol from Market St. to Pier 39 in high fashion style. The Chinatown section is as congested as a Hong Kong side street. Upper Grant Ave. often looks as if there's a flea market or street fair in progress, whether there is or not. Consequently, the best way to experience this many-faceted thoroughfare is on foot.

Fisherman's Wharf Nearby, ca.1847

At The Foot Of Green Street In San Francisco

♦ #4 – In 1853, on Green Street between Grant Avenue and Stockton, a citizen digging a well because he was tired of paying the high prices charged by water carriers, brought up seven gold nuggets from a depth of 30 feet. But the water was worth more to him than the gold and he kept digging until the water flowed freely.

Mine #5 – ✪ Vallejo Street – Named after Mariano G. Vallejo, a distinguished native Californian, born in Sonoma July, 1808. He was one of the founders of Benicia. He was once State Senator. The town of Vallejo was also named after him. He was one of the delegates to the convention that framed the first constitution of this State.

✪ Powell Street – Said to be named after Doctor Powell of the United States sloop of war Warren, Captain Hull.

✪ Market Street – Thrown in for good measure… Supposed to be so-called after Market Street in either Philadelphia or Baltimore, or both, though about the time this one was named, the latter was changed to Baltimore Street. This street took its present direction because it was laid out parallel to Mission Street. Sand hills fifty or more feet high stood on it from Kearny street west, up until about 1859 or 1860.

Resource: http://www.sfgenealogy.com/sf/history/hgstr.htm

Artist: Continent Stereoscopic Company ~ Publisher
Title: St. Ann's Building, Market and Powell Streets, San Francisco, Cal.
Market & Powell Location Is Very Close To Here - Date Created: ca. 1880

San Francisco Mine #5 - Vallejo & Powell Streets

Image Source: www.1wbta.com/San-Francisco-Mine-No-5-Vallejo-Powell-Street

- **#5 –** In 1854, an inch-wide vein of rich gold-bearing quartz, running in a zig-zag course near the surface, was found at Vallejo and Powell Streets. Its irregularity called for hard digging, and no miner in those days wanted to dig when panning was much easier. **Map Code 13 B-8**

San Francisco County — Bela Clarke came to San Francisco from Maine in 1890, seeking a chest of treasure he claimed to have buried in 1864 near what is now known as Ocean Beach. Building a house above the beach, Clark was surprised one morning to see the hulk of an old vessel washed up on the beach by a gale. A few yards from the hulk was a large iron chest, barely protruding from the sand. Fearing robbers, Clarke buried the chest on the spot. Soon after his house was completed, Clarke sold it and moved to Nevada, unexplainedly leaving his treasure chest behind. His attempts to recover the chest and its presumed treasure contents in 1890 failed, as did subsequent efforts. **Map Code 13 B-9**

San Francisco County — In 1834, the authorities in Mexico secularized the California missions. Padres of several of the missions are reported to have hidden or buried their treasures rather than surrender them to the Mexican government. The priests of Mission Dolores, in San Francisco, are said to have placed their treasure in chests and then transported them to a vessel for shipment to Spain. The ship is said to have capsized in a squall on the north shore of Yerba Buena Island, now a stepping stone on the San Francisco-Oakland Bay Bridge. The treasure chests were later recovered, taken ashore, and buried. Presumably they are still there. **Map Code 13 B-9**

San Francisco County — A pirate named Martin Thierry, about whom little is known, is said to have buried a sizeable fortune on Angel Island in San Francisco Bay before sailing away for an extended voyage. He became involved in trouble in Russia, and later died in Java without having had a chance to recover his buried loot. It is reported that Mayor James Rolph of San Francisco received a letter from a French detective in 1926, asking his support in making a search for the treasure. According to a news item of the time, Mayor Rolph wasn't impressed. **Map Code 13 A-8**

San Francisco County — The problems of recovering treasures buried in metropolitan cities are almost insurmountable if those treasures happen to be under concrete. Such would be the case with the Furman treasure supposedly buried at Montgomery and California streets in San Francisco. Henry Furman stated in 1926 that when his mother and grandmother arrived in San Francisco from Mexico in 1850, they brought a fortune with them in Mexican gold and jewels.

The two women camped in tents, there being no other accommodations in those hectic gold rush days. Frightened by a group of thugs at one site, they hastily buried their money and jewels and moved to another.

When they returned to recover their wealth some time later, it was covered with tons of rock and debris in the midst of a building area. Workers refused to remove the rocks for the pleading women. When the building erected there was demolished in 1926, Henry Furman was on hand to claim the family treasure, but none was found. He claimed the gold and jewels were scooped up in a steam shovel, dumped in trucks, and hauled away. **Map Code 13 B-8**

San Francisco County — The Farallones, a chain of rocky islands about 32 miles west of San Francisco, are nevertheless included in the County and City of San Francisco. Noonday Rock, marking the northern end of the chain, was named for the clipper ship Noonday, which struck it and sank in 1863, carrying a small but undetermined amount of treasure. In 1883, the schooner Bremen was wrecked in a fog on the south shore of Southeast Farallon Island, going down with a complete cargo of scotch whiskey. **Map Code (off map)**

San Francisco County — There is an unconfirmed story of a great Mexican treasure buried on Angel Island. About 1870, a dying Negro man told of coming to California in the early 1850s as a servant of a wealthy Mexican family. The old Negro related that he had helped bury the Mexican's great treasure someplace on Angel Island, but died before he could give explicit instructions for recovering it. **Map Code 13 A-8**

San Francisco County — There is some controversy as to whether or not a sailing vessel named the Valparaiso went down about three miles outside the Golden Gate in the late 1870s. Some accounts report the loss of the vessel with $5,000,000 in gold bullion, while others deny it. Shipping records do not support the story. **Map Code 13 B-8**

San Francisco County — In August of 1888, the City of Chester sank about three miles outside Golden Gate, and this sinking is confirmed by old shipping records. Supposedly, the hulk lies under some 90 feet of water, and is thought to be completely covered with sand or mud. All efforts to locate the wreck have failed. The value of the cargo carried by the City of Chester ranges Lip to $30,000,000 in gold bullion, but it seems likely that it was very much less than that. **Map Code 13 B-8**

San Francisco County — On February 22, 1901, the Pacific Mail liner, City of Rio de Janeiro, was engulfed in a sudden fog as it was about to enter Golden Gate en route to San Francisco. The vessel struck a submerged rock and went down with the loss of about 130 lives. Estimates of the value of the gold bullion and other treasure carried by the vessel range up to $11,000,000. All attempts to locate the hulk have failed, and it is believed by some that the heavy tides in the area may have carried it out to sea, where it is possibly covered with mud or sand. **Map Code 13 B-8**

San Francisco County — In the 1850s, an American whaling vessel found itself in Callao, Peru, during a political uprising. Some wealthy Peruvian families persuaded the whaler's captain to take aboard chests of valuables for safekeeping until the trouble subsided. Deciding he could not wait for the revolution to end, the captain of the whaler put to sea and headed for San Francisco, a stop on its way to the Arctic whaling grounds. Here the chests were taken ashore and buried on Yerba Buena Island. It was the captain's intention to pick up the chests on his return trip and deliver them to their owners in Callao, but the vessel was lost at sea. It is supposed that this treasure is still there. **Map Code 13 B-9**

San Joaquin County — Woodbridge is a small town just north of Lodi (State 12). In the 1870s, a man named Therien had a small cabin here, in which he lived when on hunting trips. No one suspected that Therien used this place as the hiding spot for an estimated $50,000 in gold. In 1926, two men who claimed to be sons employed a steam shovel to excavate the ground around the old cabin. So far as it is known, this search and many others that followed produced nothing. No trace of the cabin remains. **Map Code 12 F-5**

San Joaquin County — Corral Hollow can be reached over Corral Hollow Road one mile west of Tracy (US 50). Two miles beyond Corral Hollow is Castle Rock, a sandstone formation containing many small caves. Tradition says this was used as a hideout by Joaquin Murrieta and his gang, and that they left buried treasure here. This same story is told of the several places in California where Murrieta is said to have hidden out. **Map Code 12 F-5**

San Luis Obispo County — About 1907, two brothers, William and John Herd, were employed by the padres of Mission San Luis Obispo to tear up an old floor. In the process of doing so, they found six silver bars under the floor. Where did the silver come from?

Elderly Mexicans said the mission once operated a silver mine, and one, a man named Vegas, claimed to have worked in it. He said that workers in the mine were taken there blindfolded and under escort. When they came to a certain place in a canyon, the first escort was replaced by a second. During their turn to work in the mine, the laborers were never allowed to leave it, and when taken out they were also blindfolded. Slag from the mine was carefully scattered, and relays of mules took the ore out, so that a minimum number of people would know where the mine was located.

It is said that when General Fremont approached San Luis Obispo in his conquest of California, the padres of the mission had all traces of the secret mine obliterated so the Americans could not find it. According to tradition, the mine was located to the northeast of the mission. **Map Code 14 J-5**

San Luis Obispo County — The town of San Luis Obispo grew up around the Mission San Luis Obispo de Tolosa (Saint Louis, Bishop of Toulouse), which is said to have been so named because two pyramidal peaks northwest of the mission suggested a bishop's mitre. When the padres learned of Fremont's approach in a pelting rain in November of 1846, they are said to have taken all the church valuables up to one of the volcanic peaks, which is now known as Bishop's Peak. Here it was hidden in a cave, and the lone Indian helper was sworn to secrecy. The Indian is said to have later turned traitor, and to have removed the treasure and concealed it in a second cave a short distance away. **Map Code 14 J-5**

San Luis Obispo County — There is a story of an unnamed Chinaman who made frequent and mysterious trips from San Luis Obispo. After being gone for several days, he always returned with plenty of gold to spend. All attempts to follow him failed, and the Chinaman seemed to enjoy flaunting his pursuers.

One night, the Chinaman became involved in an argument and was killed. A search of his room in a little hotel turned up a rough map with some cryptic symbols. After an examination of the map, the most experienced miners in the area guessed that the Chinaman's mine was located in the La Panza Range between Mariana and Navajo Creeks. **Map Code 14 J-6**

San Luis Obispo County — Whether or not Sir Francis Drake landed at Pirate's Cove on the coast near San Luis Obispo, and cached a fabulous treasure from the Golden Hinde, is disputed by historians and will probably never be settled until some original documents pertaining to the voyage are discovered. To lighten the Golden Hinde's cargo, Drake is said to have removed $25,000,000 worth of treasure, a truly fantastic sum for a vessel with a capacity of nearly 100 tons. Historians are in agreement that Drake sailed the Golden Hinde into what is now known as Drake's Bay in Marin County, and there is the similar story of lightening the vessel's burden by removing the treasure. **Map Code 14 J-5**

San Luis Obispo County — Cave Landing is located about two miles northwest of San Luis Obispo and a half mile east of the tiny seaport town of Avila. A path leads down the side of a cliff to a curving beach, from which can be seen the great Arch

Rock and the mouth of Robber's Cave. Not visible from passing ships, it is said that pirates and robbers used this spot as a hideout and left treasure concealed here. Much digging in the past has failed to uncover it. **Map Code 14 J-5**

<u>Santa Barbara County</u> — Early in the 1880s, the French pirate Hippolyte de Bouchard, in the pay of Argentina, conducted several raids on the coast towns of California. After sacking Monterey and raiding the Rancho del Refugio in Gaviota in 1817, he dropped down to Santa Barbara the following year and threatened to burn the pueblo. Most families who had the opportunity, buried or hid their valuables, and the women and children fled across the mountains to Santa Ynez Mission.

One of those who tried to protect her jewels and money was Dona Josefa Boronda de Cota. She threw them down the public well that stood across Anacapa Street from the county courthouse, an area that is now all paved over.

The well was then 60 feet deep, and after the pirate had departed, no one could be found who would go down and recover the treasure. The money and jewels were reported still there when Dona Josefa, then the wife of James Burke, died in 1882. Gradually, the well filled with debris, and in recent years, a parking garage was built on the site.

This treasure, it can be assumed, is well beyond the reach of treasure seekers, but on tiny Skeleton Island, eight miles west of Santa Barbara, Bouchard is said to have paused to bury treasure while on his way to San Diego. Skeleton Island was then an Indian pueblo, and the pirate is said to have placed the bodies of a few Indians over the treasure pit before it was covered. Years later, the Indians are said to have recovered their dead, but left the treasure undisturbed. **Map Code 14 L-6**

<u>Santa Barbara County</u> — Mt. Solomon is visible to the west from US 101 between Los Alamos and Santa Maria, as it goes up through Solomon Canyon. It was named for Solomon Pico, who used the mountain as a base for raids on stagecoaches operating between Santa Barbara and San Luis Obispo in the 1850s. Solomon, from a good Mexican family, turned to outlawry as a protest against the invasion of California by Americans. The stretch of road through Solomon Canyon was considered the most hazardous in southern California.

When Solomon Pico retired to Baja, California, his place was taken over by Jack Powers. His holdups became so frequent and flagrant that a band of vigilantes from San Luis Obispo finally drove him out of Santa Barbara County. Both Pico and

Powers are said to have left treasure buried in their hideouts on Solomon Mountain, but no one knows exactly where they were located. **Map Code 14 K-6**

Santa Barbara County — There are probably more tales of treasures and lost mines associated with Santa Barbara Mission than any other in California. One story has it that Indians brought a sack of gold into the mission at Santa Barbara, and the padres, fearing other Indians would desert the mission to seek the gold, told the Indians there was a curse on the gold and they must take it back where it came from. This, the superstitious Indians did, and the padres tried to follow them, but failed. It is believed that this gold came from the area around Zaca Lake north of Los Olivos (State 154). **Map Code 14 K-6**

Santa Barbara County — The San Rafael Primitive Area lies along the headwaters of the Sisquoc River, with its southernmost tip less than 15 miles north of the city of Santa Barbara. At its northern end is a region known locally as the Hurricane Deck Country, because of the fierce winds that sweep across its lonely and extremely rugged vastness. It is a region infrequently penetrated by man. Here, in the Hurricane Deck region, are supposed to be the legendary gold mines worked by the Indians under the padres of Santa Barbara Mission. Whether there is any truth to the story or not, a number of early Californians once combed the area in search of the fabulous Lost Padre Mine, and an occasional tight-lipped treasure seeker still goes there. There is a road of sorts into this area, out of Santa Ynez (State 154). **Map Code 14 K-6**

Santa Barbara County — Not far from the coast, on the western outskirts of Santa Barbara, is Veronica Springs, on Arroyo Burro and just to the west of Los Positas Road. Pirates are said to have buried a chest of treasure near the springs when pursued by a Spanish vessel. There appears to be no explanation as to why the treasure was never recovered. **Map Code 14 L-6**

Santa Barbara County — Mission Santa Ynez, established in 1804 as the nineteenth in the California mission system, is located in Santa Ynez Valley on the outskirts of the little town of Solvang.

When the Franciscan padres were expelled from California, the padres of Santa Ynez are said to have taken 15 mule loads of gold and silver coins in rawhide bags and buried them near the bases of two giant oak trees. Into these trees, as markers, were then driven the pointed ends of miners' candleholders. Many years later, a rancher, not knowing the significance of the candleholders, pulled them out.

It has long been said that these two oaks stood on what is now the Aliso Ranch, a popular resort area. Since mission days, many oak trees in this area have been cut down. **Map Code 14 K-6**

Santa Barbara County — There is a tradition that an old Indian regularly appeared at the Santa Ynez Mission with large nuggets of gold to trade. No amount of persuasion would induce him to tell where they came from, but he would always say that there was plenty, plenty more. Those who tried to trail him were always eluded along a branch of the Santa Ynez River to the north of Solvang. **Map Code 14 L-7**

Santa Barbara County — San Marcos Pass was the summit of the Santa Ynez Mountains over which stagecoaches between Santa Barbara and Los Olivos (State 154) operated until 1901. The four relay stations (all are still standing) between the two points were the scene of many early day stage robberies. The loot from one holdup is said to be cached in a canyon near Slippery Rock, where bandits frequently holed up in a cave. Signs of digging for this treasure can still be seen, although the area is now fairly well covered with brush. Another bandit treasure is said to be buried near Cold Springs Tavern, about halfway down the summit of San Marcos Pass to Santa Barbara. The building where passengers stopped for their noon day meal is still standing. **Map Code 14 K-6**

Santa Barbara County — Before dying in prison in 1909, a member of Joaquin Murrieta's gang confessed to burying a quantity of $20 octagonal gold coins "at the creek fork south of San Marcos Pass summit." The only place in the area fitting that description was Pat Kinevan's apple orchard. Tom Kinevan plowed up a $20 octagonal gold coin minted in 1849, but with this exception, no other coins have been uncovered in the area, although treasure hunters have excavated extensively at the creek fork. **Map Code 14 K-6**

Santa Barbara County — Ranger Peak lies to the north of Lake Cachuma and northeast of Los Olivos (State 154). It is an area hard to reach over unimproved roads. Indians of Santa Barbara Mission are said to have worked a gold mine here under the direction of the padres. Fearful that something bad would happen to them if they revealed the location of the mine, the Indians kept silent, but two prospectors are said to have tortured one old Indian until he revealed that the mine was at the base of Ranger Peak. **Map Code 15 K-7**

Santa Barbara County — Point Arguello juts into the Pacific Ocean west of Lompoc (State 1), and may be reached by an unnumbered road from that place, or from

Surf to the north. Because of prevalent fogs in the area, and the number of vessels that have met with disaster here, it is known as the "Graveyard of the Pacific."

On September 28, 1854, the 1800-ton sidewheeler steamer Yankee Blade sailed from San Francisco with about 800 passengers and a steel vault holding gold bullion estimated in value at between $100,000 and $2,000,000.

Among the passengers, bound for Panama where they would be shuttled across the isthmus by wagon and board another steamer on the Atlantic side, was a band of criminals known as the Turner Mob. Their specialty consisted of boarding a steamer as innocent passengers, seizing controls at sea, and then beaching the vessel along a lonely stretch of coast where the cargo and passengers could be looted at will.

Whether or not the Yankee Blade was taken over by the Turner Mob and deliberately beached on the rocky north side of Point Arguello, or whether the vessel crashed on the rocks in dense fog on the afternoon of October 1, 1854, as the result of a navigational error, has not definitely been established. The steel vault of the Yankee Blade was reported to have been found in 1948, and then lost. As far as it is known, all efforts to salvage the vessel have failed.

Also off Point Arguello is said to be the hulk of a Spanish "Capitana" galleon, which went down in 1610. Bound from Mexico to Manila, the galleon is supposed to have been carrying about $5,000,000 in gold and silver. **Map Code 14 K-5**

<u>Santa Barbara County</u> — Uninhabited San Miguel Island, most westward of the Channel Islands, is a place of mystery, a barren, windswept graveyard of prehistoric tribes, of shipwrecked sailors and Swiss Family Robinsons who sought seclusion in its lonely hills. It is also the burial place of the discoverer of California, the Portuguese explorer Juan Cabrillo, whose grave has never been found. Buried with him when he died on San Miguel is his famous diamond-studded sword.

In the centuries following Cabrillo's discovery of the island, shipwrecks have been frequent off Point Bennett, western extremity of the island. It is said that if divers were able to search offshore reefs, the remains of wrecked vessels from Manila galleons to early 20th century schooners would be found. One wreck and its treasure cargo is said to be buried in the sand hillocks on the south side of the island. Of all the Channel Islands, Santa Catalina is the only one that may be visited without permission of the leasee or owners. **Map Code 14 L-6**

Santa Clara County — Still standing near Santa Teresa Spring, immediately south of San Jose, is the stonework of an old vat where a French saddle maker, Changara, was allowed to tan hides from some of the cattle slaughtered on the Rancho Santa Teresa. Changara lived in a small cabin on the ranch and his saddles were in great demand, requiring that he make frequent trips to take orders.

On his return, it was his habit to bury the money he collected in the vicinity of his cabin. On one of these journeys he was murdered, probably for the money on his person. So far as it is known, his cache has never been found. **Map Code 14 G-4**

Santa Cruz County — During the northern California Bear Flag Revolt of 1846, a member of the rebels named Pickett, fearing the seizure of his wealth by the Spanish-Californians, buried $40,000 on the Old Augustin Rancho near Santa Cruz (State 1). It is not known why Pickett never reclaimed his treasure, and supposedly it is still where he placed it. **Map Code 14 H-4**

Santa Cruz County — Someplace in the Ben Lomond Mountains of western Santa Cruz County is said to be a lost gold mine once worked by the padres of three different missions. When the Indian laborers in the mine threatened to revolt, it is believed the padres permanently closed the mine by filling in its entrance. **Map Code 14 H-4**

Shasta County — During the early 1860s, two miners with $40,000 in gold were attacked by Indians along Beegum Creek, near the present hamlet of Wildwood, which is in the extreme southeastern corner of Shasta County. The miners were killed and the Indians were later tracked down and captured by a posse.

They said they placed the gold in a pool of water in a limestone cave along Beegum Creek. When they refused to take their captors to the cave or better identify it, they were all hanged. The treasure has never been found. **Map Code 12 C-4**

- ## LOST TREASURE CHEST BETWEEN REDDING & FRENCH GULCH

Shasta County — In May 1892, the southbound Shasta-Redding stage moved slowly up a grade five miles north of Redding. Beneath the feet of the messenger, George Suhr, was the treasure chest picked up at French Gulch. The driver, John Boyce, was being extremely alert. Four days earlier, the stage had been held up at Blue Cut just ahead.

Inside the coach was another guard, Buck Montgomery. As the coach entered the Blue Cut, a man stepped from the shadows and leveled a double-barreled shotgun at the driver and guard. Montgomery fired from inside the stage and dropped the bandit, Charles Ruggles, to his knees.

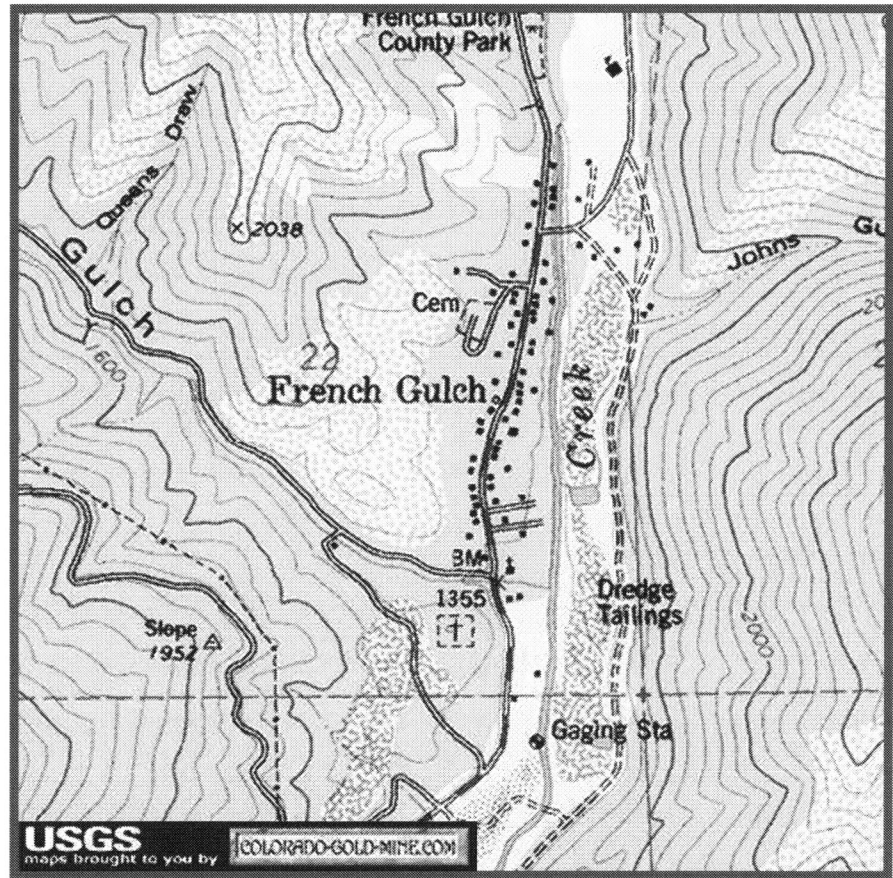

Shasta Lost Treasure Redding And French Gulch

MAP THIS ON A TOPO MAP —
www.1wbta.com/Shasta-Lost-Treasure-Redding-And-French-Gulch

From across the road, a second bandit, John Ruggles, fired a blast into the stage, wounding the driver and both messengers. The express box was seized and dragged off into the bushes. Buck Montgomery died soon after the stage reached Redding.

Members of Company E, California National Guard, took up the chase. They came upon the battered and opened treasure box. It was empty. Some say it carried $17,000 in gold bars. Others contend that it contained between $25,000 and $75,000 in gold coins. A few days later, Charles Ruggles was found crouched in the bushes. Badly wounded, he was taken without a struggle. About a month later, John Ruggles was captured in a restaurant in Woodland. Both were jailed in Redding. Before the bandits could be brought to trial, an angry mob stormed the jail, took the men out to a pine tree, and demanded to know where the treasure was concealed.

John averred that Charles didn't know where the gold was, and offered to tell them if they would agree to spare brother, Charlie. The men would have none of it and hanged the bandits forthwith. So far as it is known, the treasure has never been found, and it is believed to be hidden or buried not far from the scene of the holdup in Blue Cut. **Map Code 12 C-4**

Shasta County — When Clay Taylor decided to run for district attorney in Redding, he hired "Old Man" Waite to prospect his mining claim. When Waite reported there was no gold on it, Taylor sold the claim to Jerry Coughlin, who incorporated it into his ranch, which later became known as the Buckeye Ranch outside Redding. When Jerry Coughlin died, his son Steve took over the ranch. Many years later, Old Man Waite told Steve that he had found a fabulously rich pocket of coarse gold nuggets on Taylor's claim, but instead of taking out the gold, he caved a bank in on it, hoping to later acquire the property for himself.

Ill and very aged, Waite told Steve that his conscience bothered him and that he would try to make restitution by taking Steve to the spot where the gold was covered. Steve delayed the trip for a few days, and in the meantime Old Man Waite came down with pneumonia and died. Steve's efforts to locate the gold failed, and as far as it is known, it is still there on the old Buckeye Ranch. **Map Code 12 C-4**

Shasta County — An old unnamed prospector worked his way to the head of Cow Creek near the present town of Belle Vista (State 299). Here he found rich gold-bearing ore, and filled two gunnysacks with it, and headed his two mules toward Redding. He sold the ore, purchased provisions for a long stay, and headed back to his secret ledge. In his efforts to find it, he spent all of his money and two grubstakes provided by a barber. On one of his search trips, the prospector disappeared, but his mules were later found wandering about. His fate, and the location of the Lost Donkeys Mine, have never been determined. **Map Code 12 C-4**

Shasta County — Bear Creek is an eastern slope tributary of the Sacramento River a few miles north of the Shasta-Tehama county line, and southeast of Redding. In this general area, an unnamed prospector once came upon a cave which aroused his curiosity. Crawling through its narrow entrance, he found himself in a large room, the floor of which was strewn with relics, gold, and a large fortune of an undescribed nature. Removing all he could carry, he concealed the entrance to the cave and headed for Redding, marking a trail behind him. When he attempted to return to the cave and recover the remainder of the treasure, he could not locate it, nor have others who have searched for it. It is presumed that the contents of the cave had been stolen by Indians and hidden there. **Map Code 12 C-4**

Shasta County — In the spring of 1881, Alvey Boles was in Shasta City with a string of mules loaded with merchandise for one of the mining camps to the north. Just before his departure, three strangers mounted on good horses appeared and asked if they could join his train. Boles looked them over and agreed. That evening Boles and one of the strangers remained in their camp while the other two went out to flush a deer.

Alvey later heard the double crack of rifles and supposed they were having success. But when darkness came and the men did not return, Boles went out in search of them. When morning came and there was no sign of the strangers, Boles concluded they had been killed by Indians. Boles continued to Yreka where he sold his goods. He had all but forgotten the incident when, a year or two later, he met the two missing men. They told this story of their disappearance.

They had flushed a deer and brought it down. While they were dressing the deer, a dog ran up and barked. Then four men appeared and ordered the two hunters to follow them. The leader stated that they had found gold a short distance away and didn't want the news to leak out and cause an inrush of miners. Therefore, they were going to hold the two strangers until they had taken out all the gold they wanted. They could join in the work and share in the gold if they wanted to, but they couldn't leave.

The captives had begged the miners to take in the other two, but they would have none of it. The diggings had been so rich that the deer hunters had forgotten all about their captivity. After several months of hard work, the mules were loaded with the accumulated gold, the mine concealed, and the party headed for Sacramento.

Boles said it was hard to swallow the story, but he apparently believed in it enough to make a search for the spot himself. The placer from which the gold was taken remains unknown to this day. **Map Code 12 B-4**

Shasta County — Castle Crags, just south of the Shasta-Siskiyou county line and near Dunsmuir (Interstate 5), is a gigantic pile of gray-white granite, rearing its jagged spires a sheer 6,000 feet above forested slopes. When an army mule train carrying gold coins said to have a value of $200,000 was held up and robbed by Modoc Indians near what later became the Castle Crags railroad station, they carried the bags of gold into the crags and concealed it in a cave. Many searches have been made for this treasure, but it is believed that it has never been found. Castle Crags proper is now a State Park. **Map Code 12 B-4**

Shasta County — Sometime during the early days of California, an army payroll detachment was attacked by Indians while en route from Redding to Weaverville. In the attack, which is believed to have taken place near French Gulch, all the soldiers were killed except one, and he was badly wounded. In spite of his wounds, he managed to bury the payroll and stuck his rifle in the ground to mark the spot. He crawled away some distance before being found and taken to French Gulch for aid. Before he died, he managed to tell the story. Although many have searched for the treasure marked by the army rifle, it is believed that it was never found. Many years later, two deer hunters, unaware of the story, found an old army rifle in the area of French Gulch, but were unable to show exactly where it was picked up. **Map Code 12 C-3**

Shasta County — Another of the several reported places where Joaquin Murrieta and his followers are said to have buried treasure is in one of the Volcano Caves in Lassen Volcanic National Park, a weird, lava-devastated region surrounding the dormant volcano, Lassen Peak. There have been no reported treasure searches made here since the area became a national park in 1916. **Map Code 12 C-5**

Sierra County — In the fall of 1849, a stranger stumbled into a tent saloon at Downie's Flat on the North Fork of the Yuba River. He was half frozen and near collapse. When thawed out with whiskey, he said his name was Robert Stoddard, and he told this harrowing tale.

He and his partner left their wagon train to go out in search of game. They became hopelessly lost and wandered for several days. They came to a small stream and decided to follow its course downward. Eventually it brought them to a lake, which Stoddard guessed was 10 to 15 square miles in area. As they knelt to drink its waters, the two men saw at once that its bed was literally covered with gold nuggets as far out as they could see. They observed, also, that its shores were lined with incredible rich deposits of gold. They gathered what they could carry and left, noting the landmarks in the area so that they might return.

Following the course of another stream out of the lake they traveled that night, and on the following morning were attacked by Indians. Stoddard was wounded in the leg by an arrow. He became separated from his partner and never saw him again. Working his way downstream and desperately in need of food, he threw away all the gold except that which he could carry in his pocket.

Stoddard's story created a wave of excitement, and especially after showing the wound in his leg and displaying the gold nuggets, almost every man in the camp was willing to pay Stoddard to lead them to the lake of gold. But winter was setting in and Stoddard said he wanted to go to San Francisco. In the spring, he promised to return and lead a party to the lake with the golden bed.

Much to the surprise of some, Stoddard did return in the spring, and organized a party of about 25 to search for the gold. The project was supposed to be kept a secret, but when they took off, an army of about 1,000 men followed along. From Nevada City, the band headed westward toward Sierra Valley. Intentionally, or by accident, Stoddard led them to an area where there were dozens of glacial lakes, but he couldn't find the right one. They wandered on, and finally Stoddard pointed to a lake in the distance and declared that was the one. But when the rushing mob reached its shores, there was no gold.

Somewhere in the vicinity of the town of Beckwith, the angry searchers gave Stoddard 24 hours in which to produce the lake of gold or dangle at the end of a rope. During the night, Stoddard managed to escape the guards appointed to keep watch over him, and slowly made his way back to the settlements, where he persisted in his story and even tried to raise money for a second expedition. Some declared him to be a fraud, while others supported him.

Whatever he was, he gave northern California a wave of excitement that was remembered for years. Believe it or not, men still search for Stoddard's "Lake of Gold," and a small lake on the northern border of Sierra County is called Gold Lake after Stoddard. But if there is any gold there, it has long since vanished. **Map Code 12 D-6**

<u>Sierra County</u> — The tale of a golden lake is an ancient story, and one which Caleb "Old" Greenwood may have tried to exploit in northern California. Greenwood, ex-trapper and squawman, and his half-breed son drifted into Sutter's Mill one day in 1849, where men were picking up nuggets of gold. When Greenwood asked what the stuff was, and was told that it was gold, he replied that he knew where there was a lake whose shores were lined with gold. He told that he had

camped there one time with his children, and they picked the stuff up and played with it like marbles. When they left, they simply threw the gold pebbles away.

Where was this lake? Old Greenwood said his son John would lead a party there in exchange for new outfits, and a sum of cash — paid in advance. Thirteen men searched for a month and finally arrived back at Sutter's Mill, hungry, disgusted, and footsore. They had found no gold, but Old Greenwood insisted that the lake was sure enough there, but that John had simply missed it. From Greenwood's description, it was finally concluded that the lake was what is known today as Weber Lake in Sierra County, but was originally called Greenwood's Lake of Gold. Weber Lake's shores may have been lined with gold when Old Greenwood camped there, but there is no gold there today. **Map Code 12 D-6**

<u>Sierra County</u> — After their disappointing experiences with Stoddard and Greenwood, one would have thought the miners of the area would have looked upon the next lake of gold story with considerable skepticism. Such was not the case. In May, 1850, J. Goldsborough Bruff, a prominent California pioneer, was surveying lots at Benton City when he met a young Bostonian named Gibbs, who was down on his luck.

Gibbs told Bruff that he and an uncle, traveling westward from the Pit River, had discovered a lake about five miles long, deep set and towered over by three buttes. Around the shores of this lake, Gibbs said, they found gold nuggets ranging in size from marbles to walnuts. They gathered up about $5,000 worth before they were forced to flee by hostile Indians. Gibbs further said that he had made a rough map of the area, but later lost it. His uncle had returned to Boston to secure mining machinery. He had not heard from the uncle and presumed that he had met with some misfortune.

Bruff, a man with some geologic experience, and Peter Lassen, who knew more about northern California than anyone of his time, formed a search party to locate Gibbs' lake of gold. Lassen had previously been told by an Indian of a lake with three buttes rising above it whose shores were lined with gold. The Bruff-Lassen party explored the Sierra lakes for more than a month and finally returned to Benton City, unable to believe that Gibbs had lied to them... because they had found a lake perfectly answering the description — except that its shores were not lined with gold nuggets.

That lake is known today as Sardine Lake, because of its shape, and it is towered over by three buttes — the Sierra Buttes. It lies just to the north of Sierra City. **Map Code 12 D-5**

Sierra County — And yet the search for the lake of gold was not over. In the spring of 1851, two plausible characters drifted into Placerville, showing papers and maps to prove that a lake existed to the north, its bottom and shores covered with gold nuggets. James Summerfield, a Placerville miner, listened and was convinced. He recruited a company of men and struck out to the northeast. At Union Valley, the party became lost and confused, as the earlier searchers for the lake had before them. Floundering through 25 feet of snow, they were finally attacked by Indians and gave up. The lake of gold indicated by the maps in this case was in the area of Sierraville. **Map Code 12 D-6**

Sierra County — Gold was discovered on the creek below Allegheny in 1850, and the area is still producing. In the late 1870s, a farmer named Cornish, while gathering up his stray mules, made a fabulously rich strike. He gathered up about $3,000 worth of nuggets, rounded up his mules, and drove them back to his farm from the opposite direction of his strike. While putting the mules in their stalls, he was kicked in the stomach and shortly died. When the gold was found in his pockets, prospectors tried to locate its source by trailing the path taken by the mules, but this proved fruitless. A claim has been made that the Ironsides Mine, located some years later at the head of Jim Crow Canyon, was really the Cornish find, but others believe that Cornish made his strike northeast of Allegheny and near the old Hennis Pass Road. **Map Code 12 D-5**

Sierra County — Johnny Dodge, Bill Haskins, and an unnamed third party worked a rich mining claim in Castle Ravine, near Downieville (State 49). After taking out $50,000 worth of gold, including a single nugget of immense size, they concealed their claim and went to San Francisco, where they took a boat for New York. For various reasons, none of the three ever returned to clean out the remainder of the pocket. So far as it is known the Lost Castle Ravine Mine has never been found. **Map Code 12 D-5**

Sierra County — The old mining town of Allegheny can be reached from Goodyear's Bar, about 11 miles to the north, or from North Columbia, about 18 miles southwest. The Goodyear's Bar approach is recommended unless you want to see some of the most spectacular miles of mountain highways this side of the Swiss Alps. The road is a marvel of engineering skill, cut deep into the face of a stupendous precipice high above the deep gorge of the Middle Fork. Nearing Allegheny, one can see a few of the active gold mines, some still producing millions each year.

According to authentic records, one chunk of pure gold found in this region weighed 163 pounds and brought $27,000 from the mint. And from a single pocket as much as $80,000 was taken. Some of these rich deposits have become lost because of faulty surveys, or because of the sudden caving in of a tunnel. Others have been relocated, as happened in the case of the Red Star Mine, from which $85,000 was taken in a single shot in 1912. Hopes of recovering such leads are continually alive and modern treasure hunters can do much worse than follow the quest for treasure in this region. **Map Code 12 D-5**

<u>Sierra County</u> — At the old mining camp of Poker Flat, in 1861, a storekeeper named Jerome Peyron was killed in a battle wih a group of Mexicans who demanded to know where his wealth was hidden. Peyron was known to have made frequent night trips into the hills back of his store, and was believed to have cached his accumulated money there. The site of Poker Flat will require inquiry in Downieville (State 49). **Map Code 12 D-5**

<u>Siskiyou County</u> — In the summer of 1852, a party of five men (only the name of one, Hawkins, is known) left Yreka, then known as Shasta Butte City, and headed for the Shasta mines some 135 miles to the south. On the third night they made camp near a falls on the McCloud River, at a spot believed to have been about 7 miles east of the present town of McCloud (State 89). A short distance north of this place, they established a permanent camp and started extensive prospecting. They soon located a rich ledge. Because the Indians in the area were very hostile, they had to work with extreme caution. Every night, the gold they had accumulated during the day was buried within their camp.

One night Hawkins was some distance away, tethering their horses. He heard shots, and looking back towards the camp, saw a band of Indians kill his four partners. Hawkins succeeded in hiding out until after nightfall, but he was afraid to return to the camp for the accumulated gold lest the Indians hear him. Swimming the McCloud River, Hawkins finally reached the settlements and told his story. He later searched diligently for the mine and the gold stored there, but was never able to find it. He concluded that the Indians had erased every trace of it. It was not long after his last search that Hawkins died in a Shasta hospital. His story aroused a great deal of interest and many people searched for the Lost Hawkins Mine and treasure. It is believed that it has never been found. **Map Code 12 B-4**

<u>Siskiyou County</u> — Somesbar (or Some's Bar), located at the junction of the Klamath and Salmon Rivers, began as a mining town, but is now a year-round popular fishing resort. In the early mining days here, a teamster is said to have found a rich mine in the mountains to the northeast and taken out a considerable amount

of gold. He boasted in the Somesbar saloons that he would take out $100,000 and then give directions to the mine's location to his drinking pals. One day, his body was found along a trail believed to lead to his secret mine, but all searches failed to find it and his cache of gold. **Map Code 12 B-2**

<u>Siskiyou County</u> — On May 17, 1859, the Lassen-to-San Francisco stage was held up at Weed (Interstate 5). It was carrying two separate boxes of $50 gold coins consigned to Wells Fargo, their value at that time being placed at $128,000. Killing the driver and guard, the robbers loaded the gold into saddlebags, cut the stage horses loose, and rode away. Sheriff Spencer and a posse from Shasta City, on the trail of another outlaw, came upon the horse-less stage a half hour later, and took off in pursuit of the stage robbers. On the western slopes of Mt. Shasta they came upon two pack animals, their saddlebags empty. It was reasoned that the treasure, too heavy for a fast getaway, was buried in this area. Three miles beyond this point, they overtook the outlaws and all were killed. Part of the posse searched the area a week for the gold coins, but they were never found. **Map Code 12 B-4**

<u>Siskiyou County</u> — A man named Anderson is said to have found gold in a canyon on the western slope of Mt. Shasta. He told that there was a spring on the side of the canyon which formed a waterfall 30 feet high. The gold nuggets were found scattered about in a hole at the base of the falls, but the only access to the area led by a bed of rattlesnakes. In attempting to take out as much gold as he could carry, Anderson was bitten by one of the snakes and later died. **Map Code 12 B-4**

<u>Siskiyou County</u> — In 1931, a book called *"Lemuria — the Lost Continent of the Pacific"* was published in San Jose, California, by the Supreme Grand Lodge of the Mystical Order of the Rosae Crucis. The name of the author was given as W. S. Cerve, which was supposed to be the nom de plume of Dr. H. Spencer Lewis, first Imperator of the Rosicrucian Order of North and South America. Basing his information, the author said, on rare old manuscripts found in China and Tibet, the book covered the ancient history of the submerged land mass called Lemuria, and its people.

The last chapter, *"Present Day Mystic Lemurians in California,"* started a lot of commotion in northern California and touched off innumerable treasure hunts. It presented the theory that some of the Lemurians escaped submersion and found a new home in northern California, bringing their vast treasures with them.

The people of Dunsmuir, Weed, and Shasta City apparently enjoyed the publicity, and no doubt the income from tourists who flocked into the area was welcome, but it finally got to be old stuff and some establishments resorted to posting signs saying that absolutely no questions pertaining to treasures or Lemurians would be answered.

But the people kept coming until about the end of the 1930s, and some actually claimed to have made contact with the Lemurians. Natives say there is plenty of gold in the region, but it wasn't put there by the Lemurians. The gold may be there, but there hasn't been a report of anyone seeing a Lemurian for many years. **Map Code 12 B-4**

Solano County — On the night of August 5, 1901, the vault of the Selby Smelting & Refining Works at Vallejo Junction on San Pablo Bay was robbed of $283,000 in heavy smelted gold bars. Suspicion finally pointed to John Winters, employed as an assayer by the company. Confronted, Winters confessed that he had indeed committed the "impossible" crime alone by tunneling into the vault and taking the bars out one at a time on a bicycle to a point on the beach nearby, where they were buried under the mud at the water's edge at low tide. All bars except $150,000 worth were recovered. Winters was sent to prison, and died in a railroad accident shortly after his release. It is believed that the remaining bars were never recovered. **Map Code 12 F-4**

Stanislaus County — Oakdale (State 108) sits on a plateau above the Stanislaus River. On the banks of the Stanislaus near here is said to be buried the treasure of an outlaw band. Before he died, the only surviving member of the band tried to tell where the loot was hidden, but his directions couldn't be followed. Searches are still occasionally made for this treasure. **Map Code 12 G-5**

Stanislaus County — Someplace between the towns of Oakdale and Knight's Ferry, both on the Stanislaus River, may repose a safe containing an estimated $95,000. In 1872, a torrent of flood water rushed down on Knight's Ferry, then the seat of Stanislaus County. Many buildings were washed away and one of them was a store in which the safe, containing gold from the mines around Columbia and Sonora, went along with it. As the river swept wide of its normal banks, it is believed that the safe might have been deposited on land after the flood waters receded. There is no record of the safe ever having been found, however. **Map Code 12 G-5**

Stanislaus County — The site of Hawkins Bar, near the head of the Tuolumne River, is not exactly known today. "Old Hawkins," who discovered the site, is said to have filled bottles with gold taken from his claim, and to have buried these in separate caches around his cabin. At the time of his death, neighboring miners were prospering too much to look for Old Hawkins' gold. The camp eventually died, but it is believed that the cache of gold is still there. **Map Code 12 F-6**

Counties T – Z

Pass around some of those sodie pops from the cooler! We have covered miles of territory tonight, and we've got miles yet to go, and that's thirsty-making! We are a peculiar people, folks! Risk-takers, each and every one of us! Tracking down treasure takes skill but it takes real heart to launch out on ventures ignored by others. Here, good friends, is what California has given us…

It's been observed: "California presented to people a new model for the American dream – one where the emphasis was on the ability to take risks, the willingness to gamble on the future." (H.W. Brands, Historian)

Trinity County — Somewhere in the vicinity of the headwaters of the North Fork of the Trinity River, which is just about on the Trinity-Siskiyou county line and southwest of Weed (US 97), three prospectors named Cox, Compton, and Benedict, discovered a rich gold strike in a pit where a grizzly bear they killed had fallen. Here they built two small cabins and mined the strike until being driven out by the approach of winter.

Taking the proceeds of their summer's work with them, they started out to San Francisco, carefully marking part of their trail with blazed trees. In San Francisco, Cox and Benedict decided they had enough gold for the remainder of their lives and returned east, giving Compton full ownership of the mine. Before the winter was over, however, Compton came down with cholera and died, leaving directions to the mine to a friend named Mason. An army of men searched for the mine and failed to find it. This lost mine has gone down in legend as the Lost Double Cabin and the Lost Grizzly Bear Mine. **Map Code 12 B-3**

Trinity County — In 1863, Lt. Jonas Wilson and six soldiers had just received seven months back pay when they were sent out on patrol against some reported hostile Indians. Camping for a day's rest at the lower end of Haman Ridge, in the extreme southwestern corner of Trinity County and southeast of the town of Xenia, the soldiers passed the time by playing poker. At the end of the day, Lt. Wilson had most of his troopers' long overdue pay. Rather than carry it with him in battle against the Indians, he placed it in a leather pouch and secretly buried it at the base of a tree that bore the marks of a stroke of lightning. On that same day, the troops met the Indians and Lt. Wilson was killed by an arrow. So far as it is known, his poker winnings were never found. **Map Code 12 C-2**

- **DAVENPORT'S LOST TREASURE ON THE TRINITY RIVER**

❖ ❖ ❖

<u>Trinity County</u> — In 1849 or 1850, a man known only as Davenport selected a bar on the Trinity River about nine miles west of the present town of Helena, and the place virtually became known as Davenport's Bar. According to some accounts, Davenport took out as much as $500 worth of gold a day, and employed a Negro named Good and a Scotsman whose name is unrecorded.

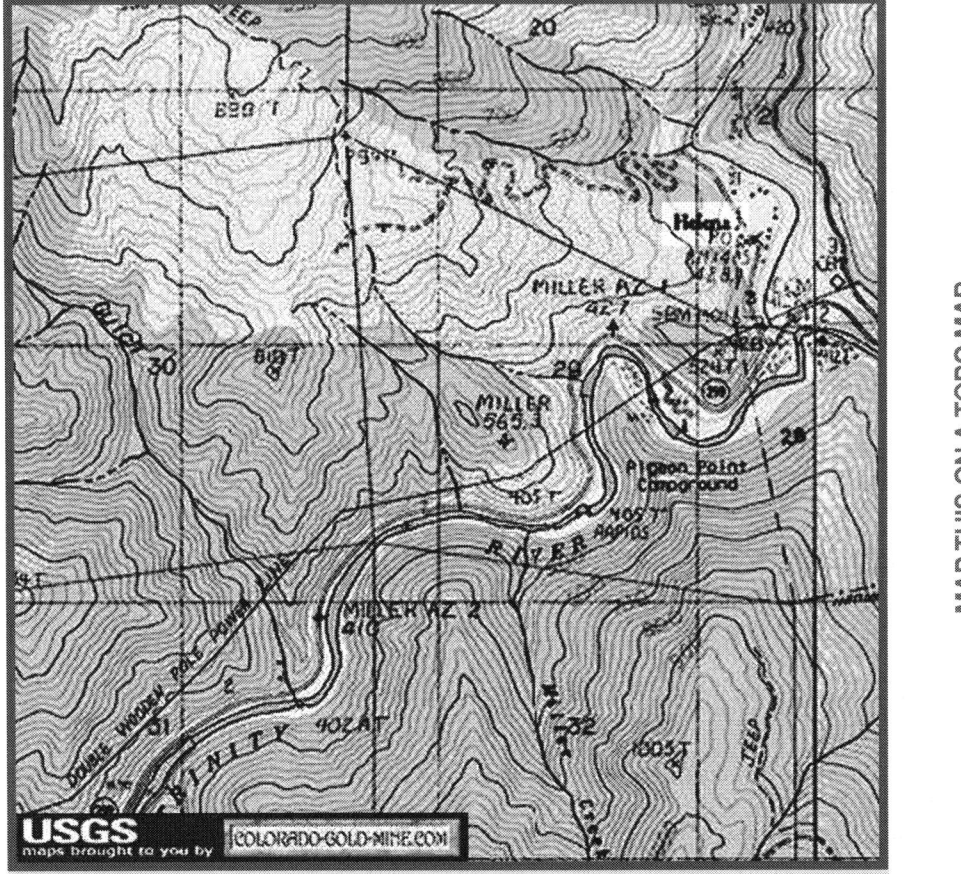

Trinity Davenport's Lost Treasure On The Trinity River

MAP THIS ON A TOPO MAP —
www.1wbta.com/Trinity-Davenports-Lost-Treasure-On-Trinity-River

Both men knew that Davenport cached his gold somewhere around their camp and they plotted to kill him for it.

One day, Davenport went to his pasture to get his horses for a trip to Sacramento. It was the last he was ever seen. His two workers were questioned, but not held.

A year or more later, Davenport's buried body was uncovered by accident. His skull was crushed. By this time, the two workers had vanished and were never seen in the region again.

About 15 years after the murder of Davenport, a man in Salt Lake City, said to have been the Scotsman, confessed that he and the Negro had killed Davenport for his gold, estimated to have been worth $50,000. They dug up the gold and re-buried it, intending to recover it at a later date, but were always afraid to do so because of the strong local suspicion that they were the murderers of Davenport. It is believed that this treasure has never been recovered. **Map Code 12 B-3**

Trinity County — Canyon Creek empties into the Trinity River at Junction City (State 299). Near here, in the richest mining days of the region, three partners worked a valuable placer claim. They were frugal men and hoarded their accumulation of gold against the day the placer would play out. Concerned with its safety after acquiring a considerable quantity of gold, each placed his share in a large copper can in which tea was shipped, and each hid his share in a location unknown to the others. When one of the partners, Frank Howell, died of a rattlesnake bite, the others could not locate his cache of gold, estimated to have been worth $125,000, and so far as it is known, it has not been found to this day. **Map Code 12 B-3**

Trinity County — In March, 1856, a Wells Fargo packtrain consisting of four men and a number of mules left Yreka headed south down a mountainous trail. Packed in the saddlebags slung across the mules was $80,000 in gold from the Yreka area mines. Solomon D. Barstow, in charge of the train, was to pack the gold through to Shasta where it would be picked up by a Wells Fargo stage.

On the third day out, with the morning sun about to break through and illuminate the slopes of Trinity Mountain, the train was suddenly held up by a group of men dressed in red shirts and red underdrawers. The ease with which the gold-filled saddlebags were secured astonished even the bandits.

That evening, the weary packers reached Shasta and spread the alarm. Barstow rode out with the rapidly organized posse because his reputation as a Wells Fargo guard was at stake and he badly wanted to recover the gold. Twelve miles north of the scene of the holdup, at the head of Clear Creek, the party came upon a pile of discarded saddlebags and blankets, indicating that this was the spot where the bandits had unloaded the pack mules and turned the animals loose. After investigating the scene, the posse rode on, unsuspecting that some of the bandits — and the treasure — were resting nearby.

The robbery had been carefully planned by Richard H. Barter, who was better known as "Rattlesnake Dick" because of the time he had spent prospecting at Rattlesnake Bar in Placer County. Failing at this, he had drifted into cattle stealing and now packtrain and stage robbery. Barter had reasoned that Barstow's mules would be wearing the Wells Fargo brand, and that it would be unsafe to use the mules to pack the gold out of the mountains once it was secured. The first gang was to go in and secure the gold, chase Barstow's mules away, and then go into hiding until a second gang brought up fresh and unbranded mules.

The plan seemed to be working smoothly until Barter's gang with the fresh mules failed to show up at the appointed time. Huddled in the rocks, the holdup gang managed to evade the posse. They waited throughout that night and the following day, and still Barter did not appear with the mules. The men became apprehensive and decided it was time to move out.

But how were they to get the gold out? George Skinner, one of the bandits, decided that. Taking half the loot, $40,000, he disappeared into the timber and buried it. The remainder was divided between them and placed in their saddlebags. This being done, they mounted their horses and rode south toward Auburn where they knew Rattlesnake Dick had planned to steal the mules.

That night, the outlaws unexpectedly encountered a second posse out in search of them. George Skinner was killed instantly. The others were captured and later sent to prison. All the gold was recovered except the $40,000 buried by Skinner. Only he knew where that was, and he was dead.

The area where the saddlebags were previously found was thoroughly searched, but no treasure was found. Rattlesnake Dick Barter was later killed in Auburn. When the imprisoned men were finally released, they were trailed for months by Wells Fargo agents in the belief that one of them might return to Trinity Mountain to recover Skinner's share of the loot. When this failed to develop, it was concluded that the dead Skinner had been the only one to know where the $40,000 in gold was buried.

This treasure, which is almost certain to be there if it hasn't been found, is somewhere on Trinity Mountain, part of which is in Trinity County, with the major portion in Shasta County. The holdup scene was right on the Trinity-Shasta county line, at the head of Clear Creek, but the treasure was buried an estimated 12 miles south of there, making it possible for the treasure site to be in either county. **Map Code 12 C-3**

Tulare County — The eastern front of the Sierra Nevada Mountains — or the Sierras, as they are commonly called in California — rises abruptly from the desert floor of arid Owens Valley. The Sierras in this region are pierced by access roads which lead to trails one can take to the crest of the range. One of the access roads, leaving US 395 south of Olanche, leads to Sears Pack Station. Here one can take a trail that will go in a roundabout way to the general area of a legendary lost mine.

According to an Indian legend, tribesmen once worked a rich gold mine in this section of the Sierras. Spaniards traveling through the region heard of the mine and purposely made friends of the Indians to learn its secret location. Accomplishing this, they simply appropriated the mine and were soon packing out burro loads of gold. One night, the angered Indians sneaked up on the camp and murdered all the Spaniards and a few Indians accused of giving away the secret.

Soon after the recovery of the mine, the Indians abandoned it, claiming that strange sounds came from the ground where its entrance had been concealed. It is said that the few white men who have tried to locate the mine have been frightened away by unexplainable sounds. The mine is traditionally placed near Deer Mountain, high on the eastern slopes of the Sierras, in Tulare County. **Map Code 15 1-8**

Tuolumne County — An old house near the town of Tuolumne is said to have been the headquarters of Joaquin Murrieta and his gang when operating in this section of California. Before the house was razed in the early 1920s, it was the scene of an extensive treasure hunt for a chest of treasure supposed to have been hidden in the house or buried outside it by the bandit gang. No treasure was reported found in or near the structure, long known as "Murrieta's Haunted House." **Map Code 12 F-6**

Tuolumne County — Yankee Hill, an old mining camp to the east of State 49 between Sonora and Columbia, exists today largely in memory. During the hectic mining days here, two brothers struck it rich and converted their gold bullion into coins. One moved away to San Francisco with his share, built a large home and shortly died. The survivor built a large home at Yankee Hill, and while it was under construction, he secreted his hoard of coins in a corner of the house.

One night, he accidentally knocked over an oil lamp, and the house soon went up in blazes. The old prospector escaped from the fire, but was badly injured. A neighbor came to his aid, but he refused it, asking instead that he dig in the ashes at a corner of the house. The neighbor obliged, raked out a tub full of coins, and then went for help. When he returned, the old man was near death and the tub of coins was missing. It is presumed that the injured man managed to haul the coins some distance away and bury them just before he died. All searches for this treasure, as far as it is known, have failed. **Map Code 12 F-6**

Tuolumne County — Grateful for the use of a cattleman's cabin near Yankee Hill (see above), an old prospector attempted to thank his benefactor by taking him to a large pocket of gold ore which he had found years before and once secretly worked, but eventually abandoned because of ill health. Accompanied by the cattleman, he searched for the ledge but was unable to find it, saying that a certain body of water he had planted in his memory as a landmark had dried up. **Map Code 12 F-6**

Tuolumne County — Except for the presence of Mark Twain's cabin, a shrine to American literature, Jackass Hill would be known merely as a natural stopping place of the early days along the Robinson's Ferry-Tuttletown Trail. Under the site of another old log cabin, here is supposed to lie a fortune in gold, buried there by a man before being murdered for it. Jackass Hill is near Columbia (State 49). **Map Code 12 F-6**

Tuolumne County — Columbia (State 49) was once known as the "Gem of the Southern Mines" for the amount of gold produced here. During those days it was the richest, noisiest and most wicked camp in the Mother Lode. With money rolling into the camp as fast as gold could be picked up in the surrounding hills and gullies, almost everyone had money to hide or bury.

A story is told of a rancher who lived just to the east of Columbia. He kept his wealth in an iron kettle, a fact a lot of people were aware of. One day he disappeared and his body was later found stuffed into a clump of bushes. Everything indicated that the murderer was seeking the rancher's wealth. An Indian was later tried and convicted of the crime, but just before he was hanged, he swore by his tribe that he had not committed the murder. People said the Indian would not have lied in the face of death, and that the treasure is still there. **Map Code 12 F-6**

Tuolumne County — Tom Davis arrived in Columbia about the time the gold there was playing out, although its brush-covered hills had produced something like $87,000,000. Although Davis managed to take out $5,000 in a relatively short time, more experienced prospectors were leaving the area for richer fields, especially the gold strike just made in the Fraser River country of British Columbia. Friends finally talked Davis into joining them to have a go at the newest gold rush.

Not needing his hoarded $5,000, Davis carried it out one night and selected a spot in a grove of pine trees. Here he buried the treasure, careful to mark three pines that enclosed the site. Two years of absence produced nothing but hard work and discouragement for Tom Davis. Broke, he returned to Columbia to recover his gold, only to find that all the trees in the grove had been felled. Day after day he returned to the area, and dug and probed between every trio of stumps. But he never found his $5,000, and presumably it is still there. **Map Code 12 F-6**

Tuolumne County — Nobody knew the Portuguese miner's name. He was secretive and kept to himself except when he came into Columbia to trade his gold for supplies or to convert it into coins. He always waited until nightfall to leave and was careful to see that no one followed him. Everyone knew that he had a rich mine back in the brush-covered hills near Columbia, but no one could pinpoint the location because his coming and going was always from different directions. Then he disappeared, and it was assumed that he had left the country.

Weeks later his body was found. There were no wounds to indicate he had met a violent death. In the pocket of his jacket a note was found, written in Portuguese and addressed to someone in Portugal. When interpreted by a Portuguese sheepherder, the note revealed that he had buried $100,000 in his mine and sealed the entrance. "I am a sick man," the writer said, "and I am going to die. I want you to have the mine and the money." There were no directions. Presumably, he had died before the letter was finished. **Map Code 12 F-6**

Tuolumne County — The town of Big Oak Flat (State 120), 49 miles west of Yosemite Valley, was named for an enormous oak tree that once stood on the site, but toppled over when miners dug the earth from around its roots to secure the gold it held. There is an unconfirmed story that a rich cache of high grade ore is buried here, and there have been many searches among the yards of the dilapidated old buildings, but so far as is known nothing of value has been found. **Map Code 12 G-6**

Tuolumne County — The area around Big Oak Flat (State 120), founded as Savage Diggings by James Savage, who accumulated a fortune by having Indian women gather placer gold and bring it in to his trading post to be exchanged for trinkets, was famous for its rich pockets of high grade ore. Two workers are said to have discovered a rich ledge here while building a road to a mine property. They secretly marked the vein and covered it with rocks and brush, hoping to work it someday when gold ore on the property was thought to be depleted. But the wait was too long. One man died and the other left the area. It is believed that this rich ledge is still waiting. **Map Code 12 G-6**

Tuolumne County — While camping at Big Oak Flat in the early 1920s, and hunting deer in the surrounding hills, Joe Thompson, who had been born in the Mother Lode country and knew something of gold, found a rich ledge on the south slope of Crocker Ridge. As Joe returned to his camp, the first snow of the winter set in, and it was the following May before he could again return to the ledge of gold. He was unable to locate his markers and searched for it unsuccessfully until his death in 1927. **Map Code 13 G-6**

Ventura County — Long before the Spanish padres arrived in Santa Clara Valley, the Indians had for many generations told strange legends of gold deposits in the mountains near the headwaters of Piru Arroyo, or Piru Creek, as it is also called. Piru Arroyo is reached over an unimproved Grade Valley Road out of Ojai (State 150). Independent of the legend, it is believed that comparatively modern Indians took gold from Piru Creek, and small quantities of gold are still in this region. Of the several lost mines associated with the California missions, there are many who believe that the true Lost Padre Mine is in the Piru country. **Map Code 14 K-7**

Ventura County — Sespe Creek is to the north of Fillmore (State 124) and at the southern base of the Topatopa Mountains. There has long been an Indian legend that the mission padres secured gold in this region. When early pioneers questioned the Indians about this, they said it was "taboo," and refused to give any information. **Map Code 14 K-7**

Ventura County — Juan Chavez often allied himself with the outlaw band headed by Tiburcio Vasquez; otherwise, he operated with his own gang. A hideout frequently used by Chavez was at the head of Agua Blanca Creek near the base of Stewart Mountain. Here he had a stockade made of stones, but the main protection was the ruggedness and isolation of the region which was seldom penetrated by lawmen. It is said that Chavez hid or buried more than 100 pounds of gold coins and bullion near here, at a place where three large oaks and a boulder formed a square. Before this treasure could be recovered by Chavez, he was captured and hanged. So far as it is known, this treasure still lies in the same burial site, which is extremely hard to reach. **Map Code 14 K-7**

Ventura County — Reyes Peak lies north of Ojai (State 150) and its base can be reached by a dirt road running east from Pine Summit on State 33. There is a story that an aged Mexican once worked a rich gold ledge somewhere along the slopes of Reyes Peak, trading his gold in Ojai for supplies and provisions. He was once persuaded to take the storekeeper to his mine, which he did only after the storekeeper agreed to being blindfolded. Shortly after this, the Mexican disappeared and the storekeeper's many efforts to locate the mine all failed. **Map Code 14 K-7**

Ventura County — The Topatopa Mountains lie straight north of Santa Paula (State 150). It is said that the Indians of Mission Buenaventura once worked a silver mine in these mountains. In order to keep the Indian workers close to the church, the padres built a small chapel near the mine. When Mexico secularized the mission, the padres of Buenaventura ordered the mine closed and the little chapel destroyed. If this mine existed, then its location in the Topatopa Mountains should be marked by the remains, if any, of a little Franciscan chapel. **Map Code 14 K-7**

Ventura County — On December 2, 1946, a DC-3 with six persons aboard, on its way from Burbank Airport to Salt Lake City, crashed on the side of White Mountain (6,253'), west of Interstate 5 and south of Gorman. The plane hit the mountain near its peak and exploded, killing all aboard. Although it has not been confirmed, one of the passengers was said to be carrying $100,000 worth of diamonds and they are not known to have been recovered. **Map Code 14 K-7**

Ventura County — Santa Susana Pass straddles the Ventura-Los Angeles county line northwest of the town of Chatsworth. It was just on the Ventura County side of the pass that California's "muy caballero" bandit, Tiburcio Vasquez, is said to have buried three chests of gold taken from a stage holdup. The treasure amounted to $60,000 in gold coins and was hurriedly buried to prevent its recovery by a hard-pressing posse. Before Vasquez could reclaim the chests, he was captured in Los Angeles and taken to San Jose, where he was tried, sentenced to death, and hanged. **Map Code 14 L-8**

Ventura County — Red Mountain lies to the northwest of the city of Ventura (US 101), and south of Casitas Reservoir. It has been the lure of treasure seekers for many years. Joaquin Murrieta, California's most romanticized bandit, once held up the Olivas Rancho southeast of Ventura and departed with bags of gold and other treasure said to have totaled $40,000. When one of the last members of the Murrieta gang was dying in San Quentin Prison more than 50 years ago, he stated that Murrieta had buried the treasure on Red Mountain.

The search is always for the three live oaks on the brow of a hill, for the dying prisoner is reported to have said, "Pass over the brow of a hill to a spring. Look to the south and locate three live oaks about 25 yards apart. Under the first, pistols and spurs will be found, and under the second, a chest with treasure will be found." **Map Code 14 L-7**

<u>Ventura County</u> — The walls of the old Olivas adobe stood until a few years ago at least, on the old Rancho San Miguel, a short distance southeast of the city of Ventura. For many years, the walls and floors of the adobe showed the efforts of Don Ramon Olivas' heirs to find his hidden fortune. It was rumored that Don Ramon kept a large sum of money in a vault in the structure, but after his death this was not found. It was then recalled that after a band of robbers had invaded Rancho San Miguel, and made away with part of the rancher's wealth, he removed the treasure from the vault and buried it. All efforts to locate this rather authentic treasure have apparently failed. **Map Code 14 L-7**

<u>Ventura County</u> — Wheeler Hot Springs (State 33) is a popular recreational resort north of Ojai (State 150). Near here is a small canyon in which Three-Finger Jack, a lieutenant of Joaquin Murrieta, is supposed to have buried $20,000 — his share of the loot from several holdups. Jack never got around to recovering the treasure because he was killed in 1853, along with Murrieta. **Map Code 14 K-7**

<u>Ventura County</u> — Frazier Mountain is almost on the Ventura-Kern county line, west of Gorman (Interstate 5). There has been some active mining here for many years, and the area has been rather thoroughly prospected by amateurs because of its easy access from Los Angeles. Many searches have been made in the area for a lost gold mine, the entrance to which is said to be covered with a piece of rusted iron.

The origin of this mine is vague, but it is said to have been discovered by a deer hunter who covered the iron with debris, intending to return when the winter snows were gone. He was never able to locate the old tunnel again, however. **Map Code 14 K-7**

Ventura County — Anacapa Island is the smallest of the Santa Barbara Channel Islands, and the closest to the mainland, lying about 12 miles southwest of Hueneme Light and about 32 miles southwest of the city of Santa Barbara.

Anacapa and Santa Barbara Island, about 30 miles to the south and east, form the Channel Island National Monument. Permission must be secured from the National Park Service to land on either. The shore line of Anacapa is lined with caves, the largest of which is said to have been used by early pirates as a hideout and base of operations. Tradition says the pirates left treasure buried on the island when they sailed away one day, never to return. **Map Code---off map**

Ventura County — The paddle-wheeler Winfield Scott, loaded with miners and millions of dollars in sacked gold, crashed on the rocks off Frenchy's Cove, Anacapa Island, in the 1850s. There is no record that any of this treasure was ever recovered, or even that the wreck was ever located. **Map Code--off map**

Ventura County — There are three treasures associated with San Nicholas Island, 76 miles southwest of Los Angeles Harbor and the most remote of the Channel Islands from the mainland. There are vague stories of treasure buried here by the Portuguese explorer, Cabrillo, and by Sir Francis Drake, but there appears to be no supporting evidence in either case.

There are also stories that pirates buried treasure in one of the many sea caves. Treasure or no treasure, you probably won't be going to San Nicholas Island anyway. It is under the jurisdiction of the Navy Department. **Map Code---off map**

Ventura County — An unidentified Spanish galleon is said to have gone down off San Nicholas Island in the 1730s. The vessel, according to some unconfirmed accounts, was carrying $1,000,000 in Mexican gold. **Map Code---off map**

• X Really *Does* Mark The Spot In Yuba County!

Yuba County — On a ridge back of Camptonville (State 49), Billy Snyder had a Title cabin on a placer claim he worked on a branch of Oregon Creek. He took out a considerable amount of coarse gold and dust, and then came down with such a bad case of dysentery that he had to quit work. He worsened and felt that he would die if he didn't get to a doctor in Nevada City.

But there was his gold — $30,000 worth of it. It would have to be hidden. One night, he happened to notice the moonlight shine through a small grove of sugar pines on a little flat above him. It was exactly 10 o'clock and he noted that the moon cast a shadow in the form of an X caused by two pine trees. What a place to bury his gold, for he knew that on the same day of another month, at exactly the same hour, the moon would cast the same shadow. On the night of July 21, he dug a hole where the X was cast at 10 o'clock. There he cached his gold.

From Nevada City, the doctor sent Billy Snyder to another doctor in Sacramento. The Sacramento medico sent him to still another doctor in San Francisco. It was six months before Snyder was healed and able to return to his little cabin.

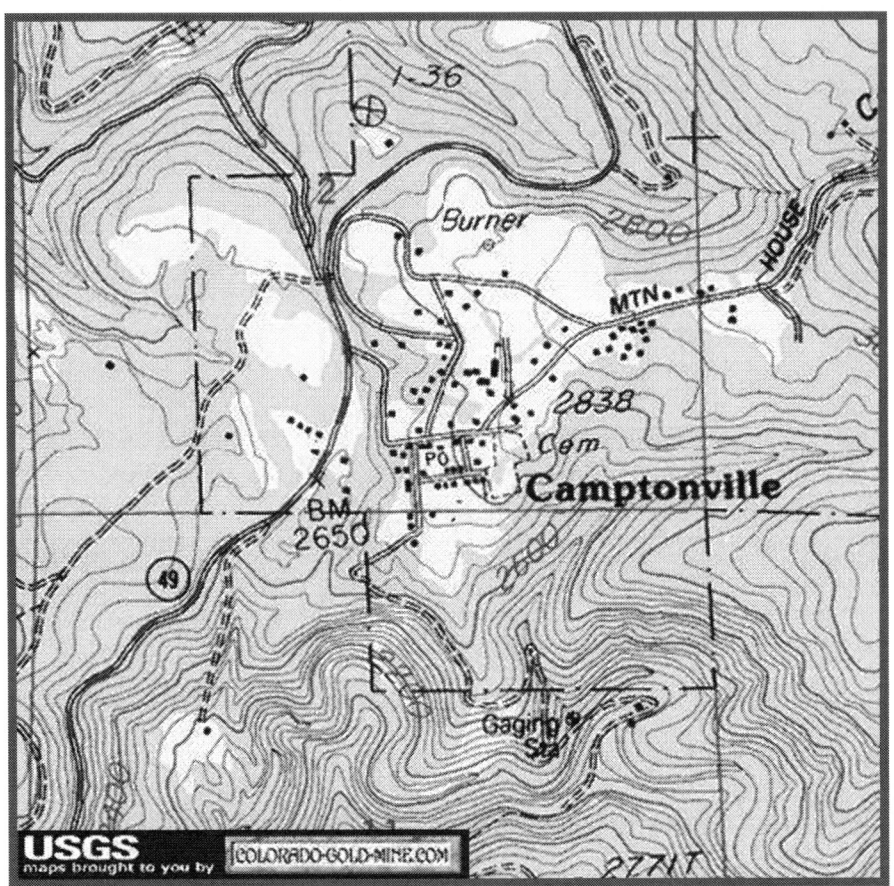

X Really Does Mark The Spot In Yuba County!

MAP THIS ON A TOPO MAP —
www.1wbta.com/Yuba-County-X-Marks-The-Spot

On the flat stood a sawmill, and every pine tree on the place was cut down! When Billy Snyder cashed in his chips, he was still trying to figure out where the moonlight had cast the figure X that marked the burial place of his treasure. **Map Code 12 D-5**

Chapter 5: Metal Detector Sites Of California

Illustrated: Metal Detecting For Mines, Finland, WWII

"There is nothing like looking, if you want to find something.
You certainly usually find something, if you look, but it
is not always quite the something you were after."
~J.R.R. Tolkien – English Writer and Author
of the richly inventive epic fantasy,
"The Lord of the Rings."
(1892-1973)

Illustrated: The Power Of Magnifying The Advantages

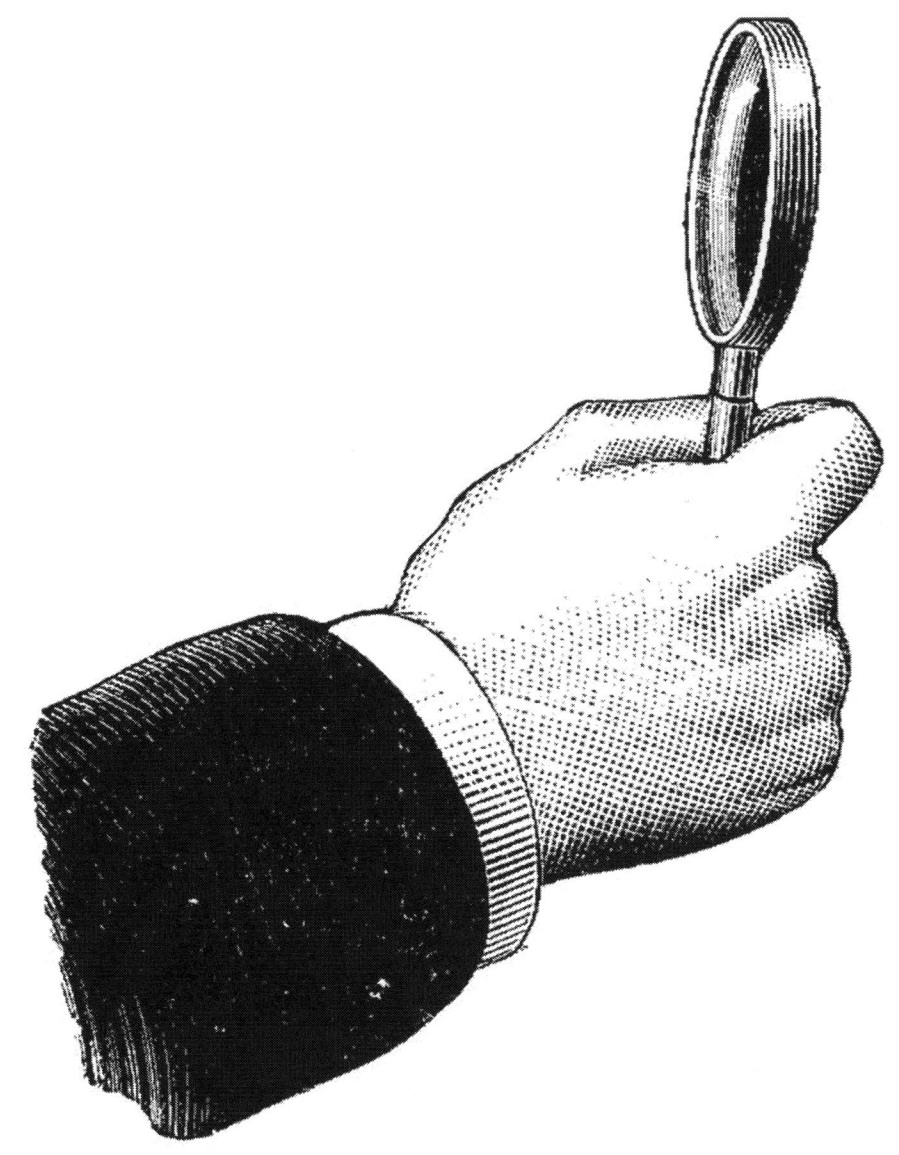

"Few enterprises of great labor or hazard would be undertaken if we had not the power of magnifying the advantages we expect from them."
~Samuel Johnson

"Keep on the lookout for novel ideas that others have used successfully. Your idea has to be original only in its adaptation to the problem you're working on."
~Thomas Alva Edison

Chapter 6: Metal Detector Sites By County

Counties A – D

So many of the gold seekers were men and women of integrity. We've heard tonight about those helping others along the gold rush path. Listen to the truth in that moaning wind… "A kind man who makes good use of wealth is rightly said to possess a great treasure; but the miser who hoards up his riches will have no profit." (Buddha). Well, of course, if miners hadn't hoarded treasures, then we'd have few stories to tell! But if you rumble back through tonight's tales, you will see that many evil or just plain selfish people buried or hid their goods, and never saw that treasure again!

Alpine County — Inquire in Markleville (State 89) for directions to the site of Loope, a hamlet on Monitor Creek, west of Monitor Pass. Loope is actually the site of the old mining camp of Monitor, which boomed in the 1860s and 1870s and was once large enough to have a newspaper. **Map Code 12 E-6**

Alpine County — Two miles above Loope Canyon from Loope (see above) is the site of the old mining camp of Mogul, of which practically nothing remains today. The mines in the Mogul-Monitor district produced silver, copper, and some gold. **Map Code 12 E-6**

Alpine County — The main strike at Silver Mountain was made in 1863, but by the mid-1880s, the camp was deserted. What little remains of Silver Mountain — the old jail and a few homes — are located on Silver Creek a few miles south of Markleville (State 89), where directions to the site should be sought. **Map Code 12 E-6**

Amador County — Inquire in Plymouth (State 49) for directions to Fiddletown, located about 6 miles to the east. Some of the historic old buildings remain. At one time, the camp's name was changed to Oleta because a sensitive citizen was ashamed of Fiddletown. Later, civic pride in the original name forced a change back. **Map Code 12 F-5**

Amador County — Make inquiry in Pine Grove (State 88) for directions to Volcano. This village of 150 inhabitants was once one of the richest and most populous towns of the Mother Lode country. Many of Volcano's old buildings are well preserved, but others are in ruins. In the surrounding hills once stood other mining camps, their sites and names now forgotten. A diligent search often turns up the remains of one of these. **Map Code 12 F-5**

Amador County — Inquire in Jackson (State 49) for directions to the sites of the following camps which are located nearby: Clinton, about 6 miles to the east, has some old buildings still standing; Slabtown, about 5 miles east of Jackson, exists only as a site; Irishtown, about 8 miles to the north, has all but vanished. It is hard to imagine how thick these old camps once stood in this region. Every once in a while, the remains of one is found. **Map Code 12 F-5**

Amador County — Amador City (State 49), although not completely a ghost (population 200), is little more than a row of decaying stone and frame buildings. It became a camp in 1849 when 3 ministers found gold-bearing quartz at the bottom of Amador Gulch. **Map Code 12 F-5**

Amador County — A mile or 2 south of Jackson on State 49 are the remains of the old Ginoochio Store, now a roofless shell with stone walls. This is all that remains of a forgotten mining town of the 1850s that once stood here. **Map Code 12 F-5**

Amador County — South of Jackson (State 49), crosses the Mokelumne River over Big Bar Bridge. At each end of the bridge stands an old inn, each now used as a dwelling. Camps once stood at every bar and flat along this stream, many of their sites and names now forgotten. Other camps once standing in the area are now submerged under the waters of Pardee Reservoir. **Map Code 12 F-5**

Amador County — Just south of Mokelumne Hill ("Mok Hill" to the miners), an old mining camp which still has a few hundred inhabitants, State 49 passes the ruined walls of several buildings and the burned-out site of a once extensive Chinatown. Among the ruins here are the remains of the great 3-story Hemminghoffen-Suesdorf Brewery. **Map Code 12 F-5**

Amador County — On State 49, about 3 miles north of Amador City, is Drytown. With a small population today, this place was once a much larger camp. Minor camps, all traces of which have now been lost, once occupied the gulches around Drytown. These included Blood Gulch, Murderer's Gulch, Rattlesnake Gulch, and Lower Rancheria. If you like to rough it, all these sites bear checking out because they are off the beaten path. **Map Code 12 F-5**

Butte County — Ask in Oroville (State 70) for directions to the site of Forbestown, located in a mountain cove to the east. This was a lively mining town for about 4 decades after its founding in 1850. Today, it is a ghost town of heaped debris, crumbling rock foundations, and stone and wooden walls. **Map Code 12 D-4**

Butte County — Ask in Oroville (State 70) for directions to the site of Bidwell's Bar, near the South Fork of the Feather River. A stone monument marks the site. Gold was found here in 1848, and by 1853, the camp had a population of 2,000. All that is left of the town today is an old stone store and some foundation traces. When the diggings were exhausted here, the entire population flocked to Oroville, where a new boom was in the making. **Map Code 12 D-4**

Butte County — Inquire in Oroville (State 70) for directions to the site of Cherokee, atop Table Mountain, about 11 miles to the north. A mining center in the 1860s, Cherokee gained brief fame with the discovery of diamonds in the placer diggings. It is claimed that several hundred diamonds have been found here in recent years, before the organized mining operation was mysteriously halted. From time to time, Cherokee is the home of a few people who live here among the old ruins. **Map Code 12 D-4**

Butte County — Pulga, on State 70 at the entrance to Flea Valley, was once a large mining camp known as Big Bar. Practically every river in California had its Big Bar, so when the railroad arrived here, it changed the town's name to Pulga. Little remains of the old camp except a few ruined buildings. **Map Code 12 D-5**

Butte County — On a bend of the Feather River, about 14 miles north of Marysville, a monument marks the site of the old gold camp of Hamilton, nothing of which remains today. Just above the site of Hamilton is the abandoned mining camp of Columbus, once populated mostly by Chinese. **Map Code 12 D-4**

Butte County — Inquiry in Oroville (State 70) may reveal some information as to the sites of the following abandoned mining camps, all of which were located in the vicinity: Long's Bar (only the cemetery remains), Bagdad, Adamsville (now in total ruins), Potter's Bar, Kanaka, Ohio, Berry Creek, Huff's Shores, Lindsay,

Bartee's Island, Big Kemshaw, Little Kemshaw, Wild Yankee Ranch, Deadwood, Concow, Blairown, Chub Gulch, Jordan Hill, Hermitage, Toad Town, Stone House, Oregon City, Oregon Gulch, and Spanish Town. These and many other California mining camps have simply vanished. **Map Code 12 D-4**

- ## CARSON HILL: RICHEST DIGGINGS IN THE ENTIRE MOTHER LODE

Calaveras County — The half-deserted village of Carson Hill is on State 49, a few miles south of Angel's Camp. Above Carson Hill was the richest diggings in the entire Mother Lode. More than $20,000,000 in gold was produced here.

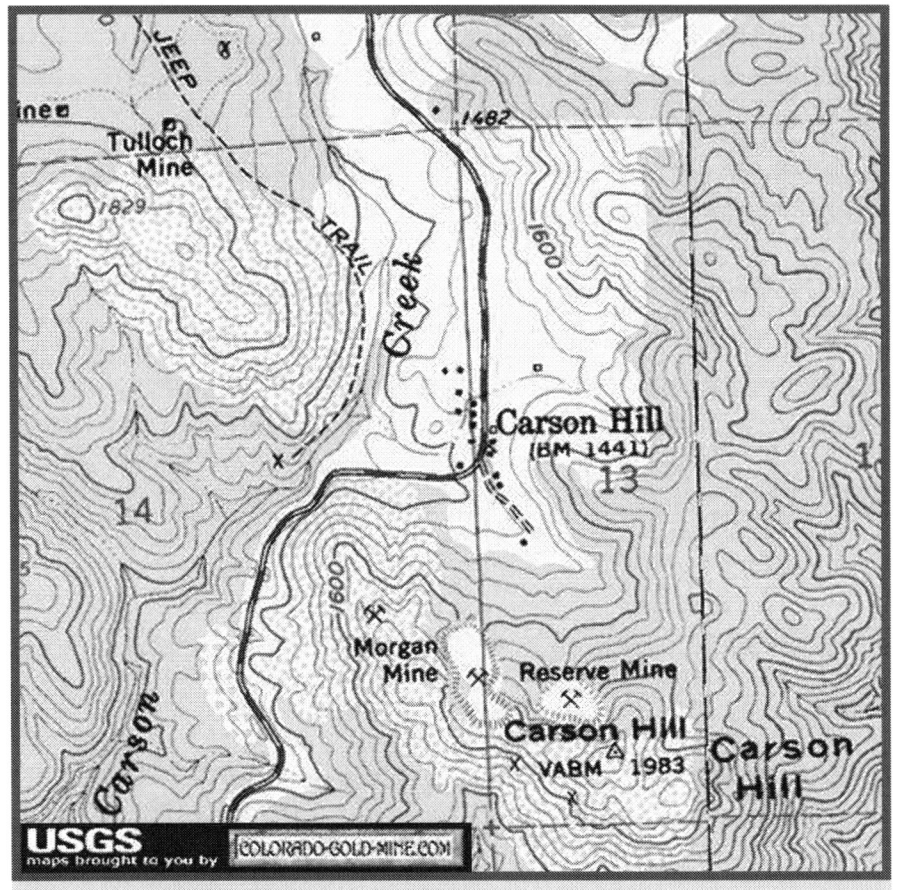

Calaveras County - Carson Hill

MAP THIS ON A TOPO MAP —
www.1wbta.com/Calaveras-County-Carson-Hill

Here was found the largest gold nugget ever mined in the United States – a solid mass of gold weighing 195 pounds troy weight. The remains of many old buildings are scattered over this area, and occasionally someone picks up a gold nugget that was overlooked by the gold seekers. **Map Code 12 F-5**

Calaveras County — On Albany Flat, just off State 49 between Angel's Camp and Carson Hill, stands the remains of the Romaggi Building, built in 1852. This combination store, saloon, and hotel was heavily patronized by travelers on the road to the camp of Joaquin Murrieta on Arroyo de los Muertos. Local tradition says that Murrieta left treasure hidden here, but this is said of every place in California that the bandit ever visited. **Map Code 12 F-5**

Calaveras County — Inquire in San Andreas (State 49) for directions to the site of Double Springs. Although this town was once important enough to serve as the seat of Calaveras County, hardly anything remains today, except a couple of rotting structures. **Map Code 12 F-5**

Calaveras County — Located on a dirt road just west of San Andreas (State 49), Camp Seco was once a wealthy copper mining center. Today only a few rock walls and ruined adobe houses stand amid the few occupied dwellings. **Map Code 12 F-5**

Calaveras County — Inquire in Mokelumne Hill (State 49) for directions to the hamlet of Camanche (originally, Limerick; also, Clay's Bar), located on the North Fork of the Mokelumne River, still to the west. Several old stone structures stand here as reminders of the camp's gold rush past. **Map Code 12 F-5**

Calaveras County — Ask in Mokelumne Hill (State 49) for directions to the ghost camp of Jenny Lind, located just south of State 26 to the west. Named for the famed Swedish singer, this old mining camp is marked by the remains of a few old buildings. **Map Code 12 F-5**

Calaveras County — Ask in Angel's Camp (State 49) for directions to Sheep Ranch, a hamlet that was once the gold mining camp where the foundation of the Hearst fortune was laid. An old frame hotel and some smaller buildings still stand. **Map Code 12 F-6**

Calaveras County — Inquire in San Andreas (State 49) for directions to an unnumbered mountain road, running roughly parallel to and several miles east of State 49. This road passes through the sites of several old mining camps including Dogtown, Scratch Gulch, and Brandy Flat. Little tangible evidence is left of any of these once important camps. **Map Code 12 F-5**

Calaveras County — Copperopolis is located on State 4 to the southwest of Angel's Camp. Founded as a stagecoach center, it boomed during the copper craze of the 1860s. Some of the ruined buildings here are made from bricks brought from the fading town of Columbia. **Map Code 12 F-5**

Calaveras County — The once lively camp of Vallecito (do not confuse with Vallecito in San Diego County) is rapidly disappearing. Only a few old buildings are left from the era when the Murphy brothers discovered the placer diggings here in 1849. For directions to Vallecito, inquire in Angel's Camp (State 49). **Map Code 12 F-5**

Calaveras County — Douglas Flat, once a rich gold producing camp, is located on State 4 a few miles east of Vallecito (see above). A few people still live here amid the ruins of old buildings of gold rush days. **Map Code 12 F-5**

Calaveras County — Inquire in Altavilla (State 49) for directions to the nearby site of Calveritas, once a hustling camp of Mexican placer miners. Little remains except some moldering old adobe walls. **Map Code 12 F-5**

Calaveras County — Inquire in Mokelumne Hill (State 49) for directions to the sites of the old mining camps of Jesus Maria, Whiskey Slide, and Happy Valley. The latter was originally an important French camp. All these are located a few miles to the east, and very little remains of any of them. **Map Code 12 F-5**

Calaveras County — A few miles south of Mokelumne Hill, State 49 runs through Chile Gulch. Here, American and Chilean miners fought the "Chilean War" in 1849. An old cemetery is about all that remains of the old camp of Chile Gulch. **Map Code 12 F-5**

Colusa County — Inquire in Maxwell (Interstate 5) for directions to the Stone Corral, about 6 miles distant. This enclosure of rough stone was erected by John Steele in 1855, and used as a holding pen for cattle. Indian vaqueros and others made this point their favorite camping place. **Map Code 12 E-4**

Contra Costa County — On the northeast approach to Mt. Diablo, a peak visible for miles around, a number of coal mining towns flourished from the mid-1850s to the mid-1880s. Among them were Nortonville, Somersville, Judsonville, and Stewartsville.

When the mines eventually closed, most of the buildings in these towns were torn down and hauled away. Only the old foundations mark their sites. **Map Code 12 G-4**

Contra Costa County — Inquire in Concord (Interstate 680) for directions to Pacheco, a small village laid out in 1857, but virtually abandoned after the earthquake of 1868, when most of the villagers moved to Concord, where they were offered free home sites.

Although Pacheco revived to a certain extent, it never reached its former size. Evidence of all ruins have disappeared. **Map Code 13 A-11**

- ## PORT COSTA: THE GOLD WAS IN THE GRAIN

Contra Costa County — Inquire in Martinez (State 21) for directions to Port Costa, once an important port from which grain was shipped direct to Europe.

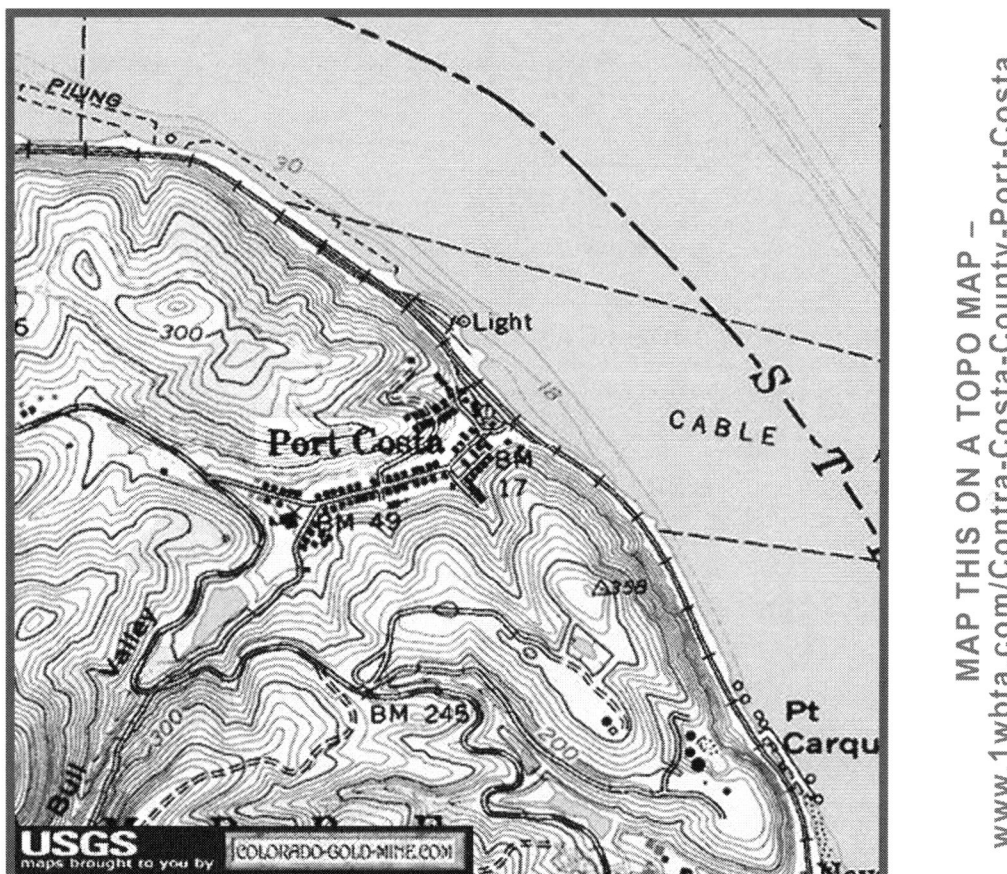

MAP THIS ON A TOPO MAP —
www.1wbta.com/Contra-Costa-County-Port-Costa

Today the town is almost abandoned. **Map Code 12 F-4**

Del Norte County — The village of Requa is just to the west of US 101, south of Crescent City. Founded in 1851, the camp grew rapidly in size, but just as quickly declined. A number of abandoned buildings still stand. **Map Code 12 A-2**

- ## CALAVERAS COUNTY – CARSON HILL MINE IN MELONES

Melones (also, Robinsons Ferry and Robinson's) is a former settlement in Calaveras County, now submerged beneath a reservoir named New Melones Lake. It lay at an elevation of 955 feet. Melones was founded on the site of a ferry operated in 1848 by John W. Robinson and Stephen Mead. The town initially took its name from the ferry. The first post office opened in Robinsons Ferry in 1879, the name was changed to Robinson's in 1895, and to Melones in 1902. The post office was closed in 1932, re-established in 1933, and then closed for good in 1942.

For more information on Carson Hill, see page 218.

Counties E – H

A thought just fluttered through my brain… about how much we learn at our campfire sessions! So wonderful, so painless! We all remember times in our schoolin' where the learnin' was not so painless! And all we needed as kids was a mountain top, a golden moon, and stories that set yer' teeth on edge! "Learning is a treasure that will follow its owner everywhere." (Chinese Proverb)

El Dorado County — The town of El Dorado (formerly Eldorado, Mud Spring, and Mud Springs) (State 49), boomed in the 1850s as a mining camp and still boasts of a few inhabitants. Most of the town's abandoned stone buildings were demolished in 1956, but a few walls remain to mark their sites. Many hoards of gold coins have been found in the walls and floors of these old buildings as they have been demolished. No one knows how many more remain to be found. **Map Code 12 E-5**

El Dorado County — The site of Logtown, once a humming mining camp, is located on State 49, about 3 miles south of El Dorado (see above). Here stands the ruins of a stamp mill where quartz was crushed to extract the gold. Almost nothing else remains. **Map Code 12 E-5**

El Dorado County — Georgetown (State 193) is not a ghost town, but it is one of the most interesting towns at the northern end of the true Mother Lode. At one time it was the trading center for some 10,000 miners in more than 100 surrounding camps, all of which have now disappeared. Among these were Mamaluke Hill, Sailor's Slide, Divine Gulch, Spanish Dry Diggings, and Volcanoville. Inquiry in and around Georgetown might lead to the sites of some of these and others. **Map Code 12 E-5**

El Dorado County — Shingle Springs, on US 50 east of Placerville, was once a popular stopping place for weary gold seekers. In the 1850s, the gulches were filled with miner's cabins, all traces of which have now disappeared. **Map Code 12 E-5**

El Dorado County — Inquire in Placerville (State 49) for directions to the site of Weberville, on Weber's Creek. It was here that Captain Charles M. Weber set up a store and traded goods to the Indians for the gold they brought in. Nothing at all remains of the settlement. **Map Code 12 E-5**

El Dorado County — On US 50, about 17 miles west of Stateline, is Toll House Flat, the site of Swan's Upper Toll House. Long lines of wagons use to wait here to pay their tolls. The entire site is vacant today. **Map Code 12 E-6**

- ## THE 1848 MAD RACE TO THE CALIFORNIA GOLD FIELDS

El Dorado County — Coloma (formerly, Colluma and Culloma) (State 49), on the South Fork of the American River, is where James Marshall made the discovery in 1848 that touched off the mad race to the California gold fields. It is now a State Park.

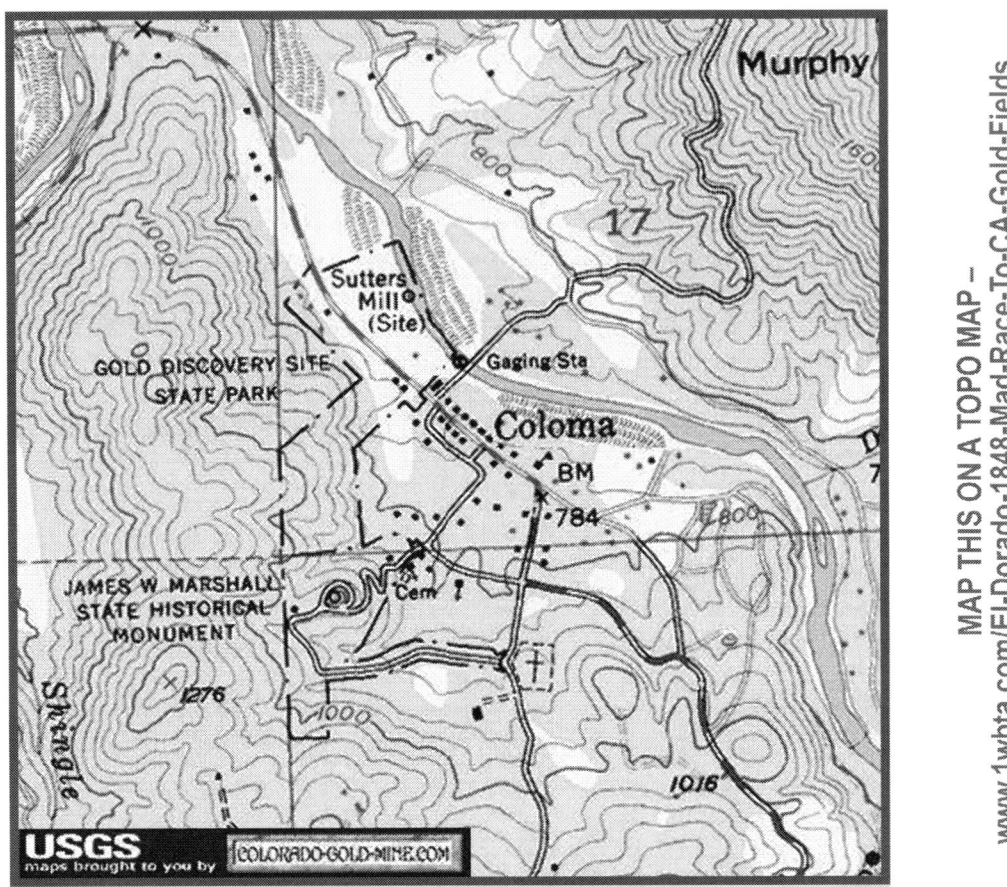

El Dorado - 1848 Mad Race To CA Gold Fields

MAP THIS ON A TOPO MAP —
www.1wbta.com/El-Dorado-1848-Mad-Race-To-CA-Gold-Fields

Inquire at Coloma for directions to Kelsey, the remains of a small town originally called Kelsey's Diggings. Nearby stands what is left of Lotus, originally called Marshall and then Unionville. A few old abandoned buildings stand at the edge of each town. **Map Code 12 E-5**

El Dorado County — Diamond Springs, on State 49, was a flourishing mining camp in the 1850s. A few structures of the gold rush period are still standing in this almost abandoned town. **Map Code 12 E-5**

El Dorado County — Two miles to the south of Toll House Flat (see above), at the base of a cliff called Lover's Leap, is the site of the Slippery Ford House. Located on one of the most important early roads into California, this was a busy wagon train and emigrant stop. **Map Code 13 E-6**

El Dorado County — Inquire at the Pyramid Ranger Station, on US 50 about 24 miles from Stateline, for directions to the Strawberry House. Now serving as a small summer resort, this house was once a popular stagecoach stop. The large barns still standing are reminders of the heavy wagon traffic that once passed this way. **Map Code 13 E-6**

El Dorado County — Inquire at the Pyramid Ranger Station (see above) for directions to the site of Leon's Station, known in pioneer days as Mother Weltie's. Nothing remains to indicate that this was once an important stagecoach stop. **Map Code 13 E-6**

El Dorado County — Inquire in Kyburz (US 50) for directions to the site of Sugar Loaf House. This was yet another important wagon and stage stop when present US 50 was an early emigrant road along some stretches. Nearby is also the site of Perrin's Toll House. Nothing remains of either. **Map Code 12 E-6**

El Dorado County — Riverton, on US 50, was called Moore's Station when it was a stop on Baker's Stage Line. The deserted old hotel stands in a grove of trees at the river's edge. **Map Code 12 E-6**

El Dorado County — Smith's Flat, located on US 50, has a population of only about 150 people today, but was once a rich mining camp with several times this many inhabitants. There are few visible remains of its early days. **Map Code 12 E-5**

El Dorado County — The ruins of Clarksville are on US 50, about 9 miles east of Folsom. With a population of about 25 today, this was a much larger town during placer mining days. There are several interesting ruins here. **Map Code 12 E-5**

El Dorado County — White Rock, on US 50, about 6 miles east of Folsom, was once a stage stop known as White House Rock, but is now merely a flag stop on the railroad. Inquiry here should lead to some interesting ruins. **Map Code 12 E-5**

Humboldt County — Orleans (State 96) was originally called Orleans Bar and was large enough to be the seat of Klamath County (no longer existing) for 20 years. Very little of the old town remains. **Map Code 12 B-2**

Humboldt County — Trinidad (US 101), with more than 250 population today, was once a town of more than 3,000 inhabitants, and an important distribution point for Trinity County miners. There are boarded-up and abandoned buildings, remains of offices, vats, and refineries of an old whaling firm. **Map Code 12 B-2**

Humboldt County — Trinidad Island, the largest of several islands in Humbolds Bay, was the scene of a massacre of Indian women and children in 1860 by white settlers. **Map Code 12 B-2**

Humboldt County — Overlooking the bay at the southern outskirts of Eureka (US 101) are the remains of Fort Humboldt. This outpost was used as protection against the Indians from 1853 to 1865. It was while stationed here before the Civil War that General Grant resigned from the army. Only one of the buildings still stands and it is operated as a private museum. **Map Code 12 B-2**

Seth Kinman (1815-1888) was an early settler of Humboldt County, California, a hunter based in Fort Humboldt, a famous chair maker, and a nationally recognized entertainer. He stood over 6 ft tall and was known for his hunting prowess and his brutality toward bears and Indians. Kinman claimed to have shot a total of over 800 grizzly bears, and, in a single month, over 50 elk. He was also a hotel keeper, barkeeper, and a musician who performed for President Lincoln on a fiddle made from the skull of a mule.

Known for his publicity seeking, Kinman appeared as a stereotypical mountain man dressed in buckskins on the U.S. east coast and selling cartes de visites of himself and his famous chairs. Inspired by the 1856 election of James Buchanan, a fellow Pennsylvanian, to the presidency, Kinman built his first presidential elkhorn chair and brought it to Washington.

The President was so pleased by the present that he bought Kinman a rifle and two pistols in return.

Presidents so honored include James Buchanan, Abraham Lincoln, Andrew Johnson, and Rutherford Hayes.

"I kill deer and elk meat up in Humboldt County. My range is from Bear Valley into Oregon. This winter I killed considerable meat so I thought I would take it easy and set about to make this cheer with a view of sending it on to Washington for Old Buck. After I got it finished, though, the boys up in our parts thought it enough to travel on; so I thought I would try and go on with it to Washington myself, leaving my mother and four children behind, and started with nothing but my rifle and powder horn. Nobody has yet sot in this cheer, and never shall till after the President."
~Seth Kinman

Counties I – L

> *This will bring shouts from that pile of kids over there! There are two things in life that I love so much... good stories and sticky chocolate brownies! Somebody pass around that plate of brownies! And speaking of fun stuff, here's a bit from the animation King himself... "There is more treasure in books than in all the pirate's loot on Treasure Island... and best of all, you can enjoy these riches every day of your life." (Walt Disney)*
>
> *Books. Books! They say everyone has a book inside them. Guess I should take these tales and write a book! Good friends, what do you say?*

Imperial County — The old mining camp of Picacho is located on the west bank of the Colorado River, about 25 miles north of Yuma, Arizona. It can be reached by a road of sorts out of Winterhaven (US 80), across the river from Yuma. Mexicans located the first placers here in 1862, and a pueblo of Spanish atmosphere flourished here in the early days, complete with fiestas and bullfights. The old main street of Picacho was within a stone's throw of the Colorado. With but a few buildings still standing, the town has now all but vanished. **Map Code 15 M-3**

Imperial County — Early in the 1900s, the mining camp of Tumco (initials of the United Mine Company) had a population of 3,000. Four saloons and buildings stood along its Stingaree Gulch. All that remains today are ruined adobe walls, stone foundations, and some mining structures. Tumco is located in the Cargo Muchacho Mountains, about 4 miles north of Ogilby Station on the Southern Pacific Railroad. **Map Code 15 N-12**

Imperial County — Coyote Wells, little more than a service station stop in the southwestern corner of Imperial County, was for many years a watering and camping place for emigrant trains. Various artifacts have been found in the area. **Map Code 15 N-11**

Imperial County — The Araz Stage Station, located on Interstate 8 about 5 miles west of Winterhaven, was once a busy way station for freight wagons, but now serves as a gas and food stop for motorists. Metal detectors used in the surrounding area have made some interesting relic finds. **Map Code 15 N-13**

Imperial County — Inquire in Plaster City (US 80) for directions to the site of the old Butterfield Stage Station on Carrizo Creek. Frequently known as the Carrizo Station, it is located almost on the Imperial-San Diego County line. Nothing more than a pile of weathered timber and crumbling adobe marks the site. **Map Code 15 N-11**

- ## IMPERIAL COUNTY: KANE SPRING'S TREASURE GALLEON

Imperial County — Inquire in Brawley (State 78-86) for directions to Kane Spring (formerly Cane Spring, Kane Springs, and San Anselmo), 150 feet below sea level.

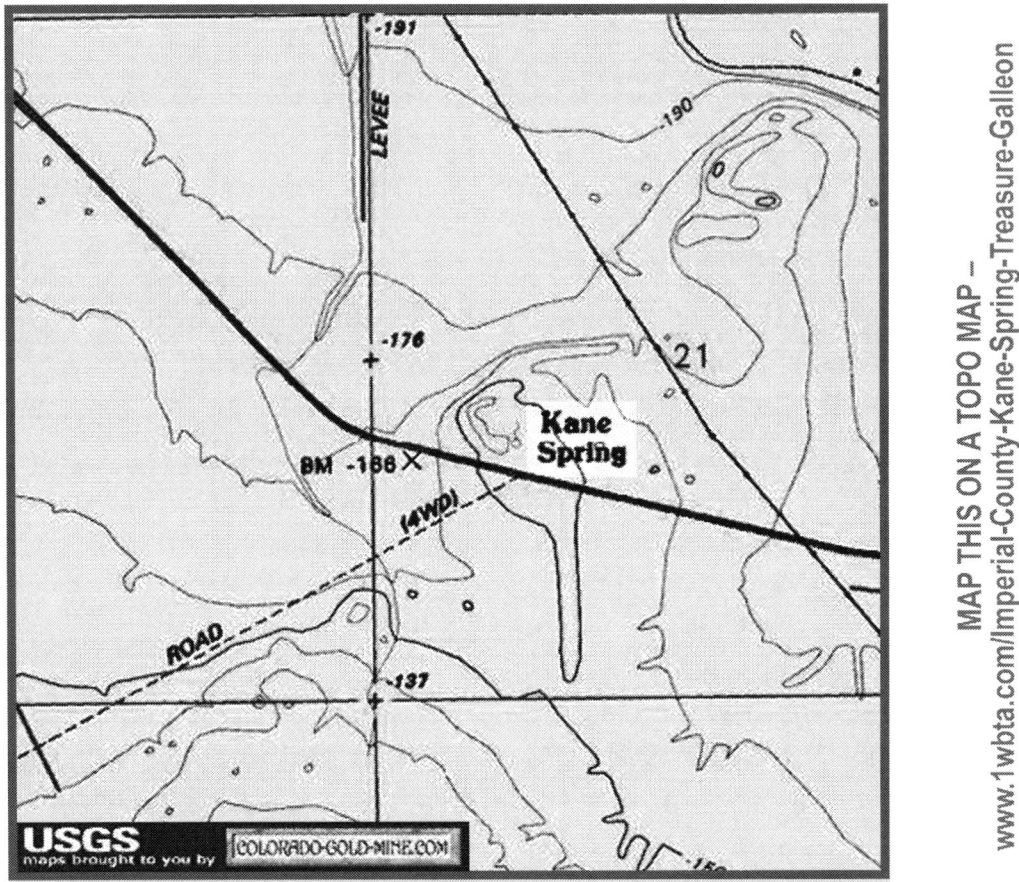

Imperial County - Kane Spring's Treasure Galleon

MAP THIS ON A TOPO MAP (See more on Kane Springs on page 63) — www.1wbta.com/Imperial-County-Kane-Spring-Treasure-Galleon

This is the oldest known waterhole on the Colorado Desert, and was long used as a camping ground by Indians and desert explorers. Many artifacts have been found in this region, including early Spanish armor. Kane Springs is also the locale of lost mines, buried treasures, and even a sand-covered treasure galleon. **Map Code 15 M-11**

Inyo County — Inquire in Death Valley junction (State 127-190) for directions to Greenwater (formerly Ramsey, The Camp, and Kunze), which is located on the eastern side of the Funeral Mountains and just outside the boundaries of Death Valley National Monument. Gold and silver were discovered here in 1884, but the settlement did not become active until 1905, when copper was found. The population then jumped from 70 to more than 1,000 in a single month. In its day, Greenwater had a newspaper, banks, and numerous saloons. Now only a scattering of beer bottles, some weathered boards, and stone foundations remain. Most of the lumber in its shacks was hauled to Shoshone when the camp died. **Map Code 15 I-10**

Inyo County — Panamint was one of the wildest of the early southern California mining camps, rivaling Bodie in the north for that distinction. It is located in the Panamint Range, just outside the western boundary of Death Valley National Monument. For directions to the site, make inquiries in Randsburg (US 395). A few skeleton frame houses stand amid the juniper and mesquite bushes, while the thick stone walls of former saloons and gambling halls speak of the camp's gay days. **Map Code 15 I-9**

Inyo County — Some distance up the Owens River from Kearsarge (across the river east of Independence) is the site of the old mining camp of Riverside. Once known as Graham City, the site will be difficult to locate without the assistance of an old-timer in the area. **Map Code 15 H-8**

Inyo County — Bell's Mill was the first flour mill in the Owens Valley and served a vast area. The ruins stand on Oak Creek, near the road leading from US 395 to the Mt. Whitney Trout Hatchery west of Lone Pine. **Map Code 15 H-8**

Inyo County — Chrysopolis was an early mining camp that flourished in the 1860s. It was located on the east side of the Owens River, and south of the Aberdeen Station on the abandoned branch of the Southern Pacific Railroad from Laws to Keeler. Inquire about the site in Big Pine (US 395). **Map Code 15 H-8**

Inyo County — Inquire in Independence (US 395) for directions to the site of Fort Independence. A decaying log cabin, once the officers' quarters, is all that remains. Established in 1862, it was maintained until 1877, and played an important part in keeping the Indians in check in this region. **Map Code 15 H-8**

Inyo County — Just to the east of the village of Cartago (US 395) was an employee's town, once considered a model housing project. It has been virtually abandoned since the lime, soda, and borax plant closed here several years ago. **Map Code 15 I-8**

Inyo County — The silver camp of Lookout once flourished on the top of Lookout Mountain in the Argus Range. About 40 buildings in various stages of decay still remain, including some with the walls still standing. The camp served the Modoc Mine, the remains of which still stand on the east side of Lookout Mountain about a mile away, and the Minetta Mine, which was on the south side of Lookout Mountain. Attention is called to the fact that the site of Lookout is just within the boundaries of the Naval Ordnance Test Station and is closed to public travel. **Map Code 15 I-9**

<u>Inyo County</u> — The site of Millspaugh lies to the south of Maturango Peak in the Argus Range. Almost nothing remains of this short-lived camp which is located within the boundaries of the Naval Ordnance Test Station. Sites within the Naval Ordnance Test Station are listed herein because it is speculated that the facility may be abandoned. **Map Code 15 I-9**

<u>Inyo County</u> — The roofs of Ballarat are mostly gone and its walls are crumbling away, but a few people still dwell here from time to time in the few remaining shacks. Ballarat's heyday was between 1895 and 1907, when it was a bustling supply center for Panamint Valley prospectors, and a link between the borax mines of Death Valley and the outside world. Ballarat is located on the western slope of the Panamint Range, 26 miles north of Trona. **Map Code 15 I-9**

<u>Inyo County</u> — The site of White Mountain City can be reached out of Big Pine (US 395) over Westgard Pass Road. It started with a five-stamp mill, and several buildings, some of stone, still stand. Among the strangest features of White Mountain City are the extensive stone corrals running in a zigzag for hundreds of feet. Very little is known about the early history of the place, but its proximity to a good highway has attracted many bottle collectors and its bones have been picked clean. There is also some evidence that the site has been dug extensively. **Map Code 15 G-8**

<u>Inyo County</u> — The site of Lee is located in the Funeral Mountains, just inside the California border and about 24 miles southeast of Death Valley junction (State 127-190). The site contains only a few remains, and part of the road to it, winding in and out of California and Nevada, is negotiable only by 4-wheel drive vehicles. **Map Code 15 I-11**

<u>Inyo County</u> — The site of Owensville is on the east bank of the Owens River about 4 miles northeast of Bishop (US 6-395). This was at one time the most important settlement in the northern part of the Owens Valley. By 1871, it was deserted and not a thing remains today except faint markings to indicate where the town once stood. **Map Code 13 G-8**

Inyo County — The mining camp of San Carlos, started in 1862, was located on the east bank of the Owens River near the mouth of Oak Creek, and a few miles north of Independence (US 395). The site is marked by the stone foundations of old houses and a lone smokestack where the mill once stood. **Map Code 15 H-8**

Inyo County — The site of the old mining camp of Bend City is near the Owens River about 5 miles east of Independence (US 395). The ruins of the old town may still be seen near Kearsarge Station on the abandoned branch of the Southern Pacific Railroad from Laws to Keeler. **Map Code 15 H-8**

Inyo County — Through the mid-1860s, the camp of Kearsarge (not the same as above), flourished on the west side of Kearsarge Peak. By 1865, it was of considerable size, but it came to an abrupt end on March 1, 1867, when an avalanche of snow destroyed most of its buildings. That night, the people of Kearsarge moved down to Owens Valley. **Map Code 15 H-8**

Inyo County — The site of the mining camp of Galena is on the Owens River not far from the Kearsarge Station, but its exact location is completely lost. You could make an important contribution to western history if you could locate this once ambitious camp. **Map Code 15 H-8**

Inyo County — Inquire in Keeler (State 136) for directions to Cerro Gordo, an old mining camp still producing silver, lead, and zinc, but now is only a shell of its former self when it had a population of 1,500. Here are the remains of a smelter, an old hotel, several buildings, and many half-caves and half-shacks where miners once lived. Visitors to the area are cautioned to beware of the caved-in entrances to old mines in the vicinity. **Map Code 15 H-9**

Inyo County — Just off State 136 near Keeler, and located near the old shoreline of Owens Lake (now dry), are the crumbled remains of an old brick smelter, the only reminder left of the once active mining camp of Swansea. **Map Code 15 H-9**

Inyo County — Inquire in Olancha (US 395) for directions to the site of Darwin, in the Coso Range to the east. The town was named for Darwin French, who found silver and lead ledges here while searching for the Lost Gunsight Mine. By the end of 1875, Darwin had 2 smelters, about 400 frame houses and more than 700 population. Today, the remains of Darwin consists of a collection of ruined shacks. **Map Code 15 1-9**

Kern County — The mining camp of Old Coso is located about 7 miles southwest of Darwin (see above). This century-old ghost town has extensive ruins of stone and adobe dwellings, foundations, arrastres, and rusted machinery. Right now, however, the site is not available to the public because it is located inside the boundaries of the Naval Ordnance Test Station. **Map Code 15 I-9**

Kern County — Inquire in Johannesburg (US 395) for directions to the site of Goler. This wild and rough camp flourished from 1893 to 1896 and then died overnight. Very little remains today to mark the site. **Map Code 15 J-9**

Kern County — The ghost town of Atolia is located about 5 miles southeast of Randsburg. Inquire there for directions to the site. Founded in 1907 because of the rich deposits of tungsten ore in the area, it had a population of about 2,000 during World War I, when tungsten was in great demand. Nothing remains of Atolia today. **Map Code 15 J-9**

Kern County — About one mile south of Johannesburg (US 395) is Red Mountain, which was first called Osdick. The camp came into being in 1919, when a rich silver strike was made here, and was for many years the trading center for prospectors from miles around. Although it is still found on some maps, very little remains of it today. **Map Code 15 J-9**

Kern County — Inquire in Bakersfield (US 99) for directions to the old mining town of Claraville, founded in 1866. While the town still has a population of about 100, and there are none of the original buildings left, there are many rock foundations and timbers hidden from view by sagebrush on the north side of the road just west of Landers Meadow. The pine-covered slopes to the north are pocked with old mining shafts and can be a real hazard to those not aware of their presence. **Map Code 15 J-8**

Kern County — About 9 miles northeast of Claraville (see above), and over a rough unimproved road, is Sageland, still occupied by a few families. The remains here include some old foundations and crumbling picket fences. Across a hillside to the northeast are the remains of the old diggings. **Map Code 15 J-8**

Kern County — Willow Springs was once a famous stage station and one of the earliest and best-known watering places on the Mojave Desert, a place of great importance to early explorers and travelers. It was the main station on the old Horsethief Trail, and an important stop for the wagons bringing the fabulous silver from Cerro Gordo to Los Angeles. Today, a few families still live here, but most of the remains of the early town have disappeared.

Willow Springs is located northeast of Rosamond (State 14) and can be reached over good roads. **Map Code 15 K-8**

Kern County — The ghost town of Cantil is located on State 14 northeast of Mojave. About all that remains of this old camp are some weathered and boarded-up old buildings. **Map Code 15 J-9**

Kern County — Inquire in Freeman Junction (State 14-178) for directions to the site of old Coyote Wells, a stage station robbed by Tiburcio Vasquez in 1874. Nothing remains except the site, and there have long been stories that part of the loot was buried in the rocks near the site. **Map Code 15 J-8**

Kern County — Inquire in Johannesburg (US 395) for directions to the ghost town of Garlock, originally called Cow Wells. On the road to the site of Garlock one goes through Randsburg, one of the best preserved mining towns on the desert. Although certainly not yet a ghost, Randsburg was once much larger. Garlock was founded in 1895 when an 8-stamp mill was erected here to work ore from Rand Mountain. Four years later, Garlock had a population of several hundred, but when the mills opened in Randsburg, Garlock became a ghost. Little is left in Garlock today, except a family or two and the Southern Pacific Railroad siding. **Map Code 15 J-9**

Kern County — Inquire in Bodfish (State 178), itself an old mining town, for directions to nearby Havilah, which was once important enough to be the seat of Kern County. Both towns grew up in the gold rush of 1880, and then all but vanished.

The old cemetery is about all that remains of the original town of Havilah, although there are many ruined miners' shacks in the nearby hills. The area is rich in stories of lost mines. **Map Code 15 J-8**

Lake County — Inquire in Lakeport (State 175) for information regarding the islands in Clear Lake. The Pomo Indians lived on these islands before they ran afoul of the white man's law, and were finally evicted after a short battle.

Most of the islands are now privately owned. **Map Code 12 E-3**

Lassen County — Buntingville (US 395), located just north of Janesville, consists of nothing more than a few widely scattered houses and a gas station. After A. J. Bunting opened a store here in 1878, the town grew rapidly for a few years and then fell into decay. Some old foundations are all that remain to indicate the town has seen better days. **Map Code 12 C-6**

Lassen County — Sixteen miles south of Adin (State 299) is the old mining camp of Hayden Hill. So little is left at the site that it is difficult to find. Inquire in Adin for directions. **Map Code 12 B-5**

Lassen County — While Janesville (US 395), with some 200 inhabitants, is not exactly a ghost town, it has several abandoned stores and houses from early and better days. These might bear checking out. **Map Code 12 C-6**

Los Angeles County — In the early 1860s, a small mining camp named Soledad was located in Soledad Canyon northwest of Los Angeles. Some remains of the old gold camp exist on the hillside across the canyon from Ravenna. Soledad Canyon is traversed by a well traveled road, so the area may be well picked over. If directions are necessary, inquire in Acton.

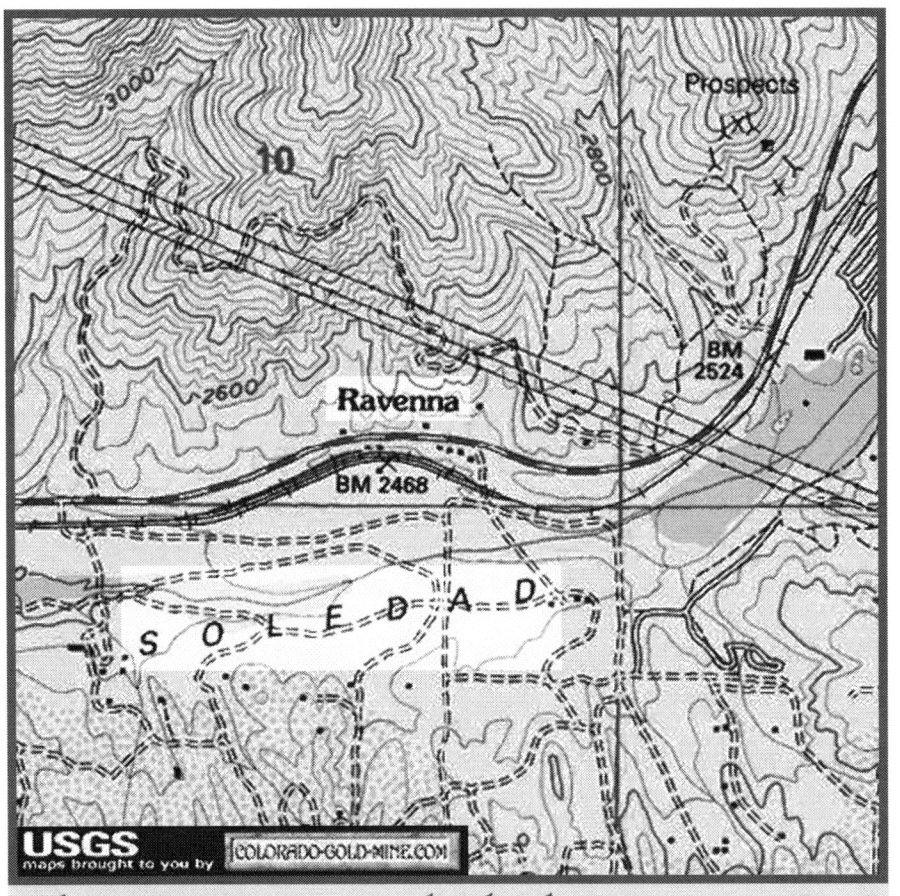

Los Angeles County - Soledad Canyon & Ravenna

MAP THIS ON A TOPO MAP —
www.1wbta.com/Los-Angeles-County-Soledad-Canyon-Ravenna
Map Code 15 K-8

Counties M – P

Good treasure tellers… Some of my best lessons in treasure hunting come from the stories we hear and then pass along. Here we find what TO do, as well as what NOT to do. Like the great rivers rolling along, picking up the sands and silt of ages and the gold contained there… we must ease our way along, picking up the nuggets of knowledge. We must make research a prime part of our searches. Otherwise, it is all too easy to fail.

"Sutter's friend, James Marshall, died the same way; penniless from a few bad investments and from having his land pillaged by thousands upon thousands of others who came looking for easy wealth. Having been the first to find the gold, Marshall never once made any money off his incredible discovery." (essortment.com)

Marin County — Just off State 1, at Bolinas Bay, is the site of the Bolinas Lighter Wharf. During the 1850s, ox drawn wagons hauled lumber to the wharf for trans-shipment on lighters to cargo vessels anchored in Bolinas Bay.

Haulers camped here, and might have lost or left many articles that could possibly be recovered with a metal detector. **Map Code 12 G-3**

Marin County — The jagged rocks of Duxberry Reef, stretching seaward 100 feet below the cliff-edged tableland of Duxberry Point, west of the town of Bolinas, is the graveyard of many ships.

The Panama-to-San Francisco vessel, Lewis, was battered to pieces here in 1853, with the loss of all freight and the narrow escape of 400 passengers. **Map Code 12 G-3**

Marin County — On State 4, about 4 miles south of Olema, are the ruins of a lime kiln in a ravine near the roadside. **Map Code 12 F-3**

Mariposa County — Inquire in Mariposa (State 49) for directions to the sites of two nearby old mining camps, Mormon Bar and Bootjack. Only some crumbling walls half-hidden among the trees and boulders mark the sites of these once lively gold camps. **Map Code 13 G-6**

Mariposa County — The site of Agua Fria is located on State 140 about 6 miles west of Mariposa. This once prosperous camp was at one time the seat of Mariposa County. Only a historical marker and a few rock foundations exist to indicate the site. **Map Code 13 G-6**

Mariposa County — Originally called Banderita, Coulterville (State 49) was once an important town of several thousand people. Suffering several disastrous fires, most of Coulterville's original buildings have been razed, and only some roofless walls remain. **Map Code 13 G-6**

Mariposa County — Bear Valley, on State 49, north of Mariposa, now almost deserted, was built by Gen. John C. Fremont as headquarters for his Mariposa Mines. The ruins of his company store and home are still visible. **Map Code 13 G-6**

Mariposa County — Located on State 49 about 5 miles north of Mariposa is the site of Mt. Bullion, first known as La Mineta and then as Princeton. This was once one of the most important camps in Mariposa County, with more than 2,000 miners living in the area. A few old foundations are all that remain. **Map Code 13 G-6**

Mariposa County — Inquire in Mariposa (State 49) for directions to Hornitos, once a wild and reckless Mexican camp with a population of about 15,000. This camp shipped $40,000 daily in gold from the Wells Fargo Express office. Many ruined buildings and foundations still remain. **Map Code 12 G-6**

Mariposa County — About 7 miles north of Mariposa (State 49) is Mount Ophir, where the remains of an early private mint are prominent among a number of old stone foundations. Hexagonal $50 gold slugs were minted here during the early 1850s. It is said that one or two of these have been found at the site, which is indicated by a marker on State 49. **Map Code 13 G-6**

Mendocino County — Albion, on State 1, is a small town overlooking the cove at the mouth of the Albion River. There is an abandoned lumber mill here and a number of half-ruined lumber company shacks. **Map Code 12 E-2**

Mendocino County — Elk (State 1) was originally called Greenwood and is sometimes still known by that name. Although it has a population of about 200, it has a string of frame store buildings going to ruin since lumbering operations ceased here in 1931. In the debris-littered gravel bottoms south of town are the rusting and rotting remains of the lumber mill. **Map Code 12 E-2**

Mendocino County — Gualala (State 1) is located at the mouth of the Gualala River. With a population of about 15 today, this was a booming lumbering town in the 1860s and 1870s. The abandoned sawmill at the river's mouth was operated until 1920, however. **Map Code 12 E-2**

Mendocino County — Novo (State 1) is no ghost, having a population of about 600, but there are many ruined buildings and tumbled-down warehouses in this old lumbering town. **Map Code 12 D-2**

Mendocino County — Caspar, on State 1 at the mouth of Caspar Creek, has a population of about 250, but it was once a much larger town. There are many old ruins here, if vandals have not by this time completely hauled them away. **Map Code 12 D-2**

Mendocino County — Navarro (State 128), with a population of 150 today, has many old weathered and empty houses to remind visitors of its lively past as a lumbering center. **Map Code 12 E-2**

Mendocino County — Rockport (State 1) is essentially a Georgia Pacific lumber camp today, a bleak array of weather-beaten shacks and crumbling buildings. **Map Code 12 D-2**

Modoc County — Fandango Pass Road, from a point just north of Fort Bidwell, to Willow Ranch on US 395, was used by many emigrant trains and was the scene of several Indian attacks. Arrowheads and other artifacts are still found in the area, and there are some rustic old abandoned farmhouses in the region. An historic massacre took place here in the 1850s at a site believed to be near a spring a short distance to the west and south of the Pass. Skulls were found here in the 1930s, and in 1966, an old wagon bed was found with an arrow embedded in the weathered wood. For directions to this site, make inquiries in Fort Bidwell. **Map Code 13 A-6**

Modoc County — Fort Bidwell, at the upper end of Upper Dry Lake, and north of Cedarville (US 299), was established in 1865 and abandoned in 1892. It has but a single store and many empty buildings. However, it is located on the Fort Bidwell Indian Reservation and permission to search here will have to be secured from the local council. **Map Code 13 A-6**

Modoc County — Inquire at Fort Bidwell for directions to the site of High Grade, located about 3 miles northwest of Mount Bidwell. Gold was discovered here in the rugged Warner Mountains in 1905, and the camp experienced three separate booms before it finally withered and died. It is now completely deserted. **Map Code 13 A-6**

Modoc County — At the edge of Alturas (US 395) is the town's most imposing building, built at a cost of $60,000 to serve as headquarters of a narrow-gauge railroad line. It has been deserted for many years. **Map Code 12 A-6**

Modoc County — Inquire in Alturas (US 395) for directions to the Infernal Caverns Battleground. In this seemingly impregnable fortress of caves and rocks, and in the meadows around it, occurred a battle between Gen. George Crook's forces and a band of about 100 Shoshone, Paiute, and Pit Indians. After a two-day struggle, the Indians were finally cornered and defeated. Many artifacts have been found in the area. **Map Code 12 B-6**

Modoc County — While Cedarville (State 299), with a population of 750, is not a ghost town, there are many old and abandoned buildings here. The town, originally a small trading post, once did a thriving business with Oregon-bound emigrants and Surprise Valley settlers. **Map Code 13 A-6**

Modoc County — Eagleville, south of Cedarville (State 299), and at the tips of Middle Dry Lake and Lower Dry Lake, is little more than a store and gas station. There are many boarded-up and abandoned houses here. **Map Code 13 B-6**

Modoc County — Lake City, 10 miles north of Cedarville (State 299), is practically a ghost town with but a single business building. Abandoned here is a huge flour mill and other buildings. **Map Code 13 A-6**

Modoc County — Goose Lake is skirted by US 395 in the extreme northeastern corner of Modoc County. Once 10 miles long and 28 to 40 miles wide, the lake was dry when Oregon-bound emigrants drove their ox-drawn wagons across its bed. The lake later refilled, but went dry again in 1924. Traces of campfires and abandoned wagon beds are still found along the old road across the lake bottom. **Map Code 13 A-6**

Modoc County — Davis Creek, a hamlet on US 395 north of Alturas, is a mere handful of ramshackle houses and abandoned store buildings. Unlike some sections of California, this region has not been searched extensively by metal detector fans. **Map Code 12 A-6**

Mono County — Near the foot of the Conway Grade on US 395 north of Mono Lake is the site of Monoville. Gold was discovered here in 1850 and within a few months the camp had a population of 750, large enough to challenge the right to be the county seat. Monoville thrived as the starting point for those seeking the Lost Cement Mine, but almost nothing remains today of this once booming camp.
Map Code 13 F-7

Mono County — The site of Dogtown, one of the earliest mining camps in the Mono region, is located a few hundred yards off US 395 and just south of the turnoff to Bodie. A few remnants of stores and houses are all that remain. In 1859, the population, lured away by more attractive prospects, moved en masse to Monoville, leaving behind piles of placered sand in Dogtown Creek. **Map Code 13 F-7**

Mono County — At the end of State 203, which turns off of US 395 north of Bishop, is a region of lakes and resorts known collectively as Mammoth Lakes. Ask for directions here to the site of Mammoth City. It is easy to reach by a short hike, but the many stone foundations and a few stone walls are hidden by a thick growth of manzanita. In its heyday as a mining camp, Mammoth City had a population of 2,500, but by 1881, it was almost deserted. **Map Code 13 G-7**

Mono County — Pine City, another of the camps which mushroomed during the Mammoth gold rush, was situated alongside Lake Mary near the junction of Lake Mary and Lake George Roads. Practically nothing remains of it and that is rapidly being taken over by the spreading Mammoth Lakes resorts. **Map Code 13 G-7**

Mono County — The site of Mill City is located in a clearing among the aspens and pines of the Mammoth Lakes resort area. Here are the sunken foundations of many homes, and the ruins of the Mammoth Mining Company's 40-stamp mill. Ask for directions in the town of Mammoth. **Map Code 13 G-7**

Mono County — The little town of Benton is on US 6, about 34 miles north of Bishop. Inquire here for directions to the site of the original mining camp of Benton, located about 4 miles away. Still remaining at the original Benton are a few historic buildings and the old cemetery. **Map Code 13 G-8**

Mono County — Inquire in Leevining (US 395) for directions to Lundy Lake, a few miles from Mono Lake. Near the west end of Lundy Lake is the site of the gold mining camp of Lundy. The site contains a number of old stone and frame buildings and rock foundations. High up on the mountain nearby may be seen the remains of the May Lundy Mine which produced $2,000,000 in gold before being shut down in 1898. **Map Code 13 F-7**

Mono County — The gold camp of Cameron, which flourished in 1882-1883 and then suddenly died, was located about 12 miles north of Bridgeport (US 395) and about 4 miles up Fryingpan Canyon, just inside the California line. Other nearby camps, all reached only by trail, are Star City, about 2 miles northwest of Cameron; Clinton, about 3 miles north of Cameron and near the mouth of Ferris Canyon; and Belfort, in Boulder Flat, about 3 miles west of Star City. **Map Code 13 F-7**

• MONO COUNTY – BODIE "THE WILDEST" & THE BODIE JAIL

Mono County — Ask in Bridgeport (US 395) for directions to Bodie, about 13 miles. This is one of the best-known and best-preserved mining camps and ghost towns in the west. Bodie was at its height from 1876 to 1880, when its inhabitants numbered between 10,000 and 12,000, and it was known as the wildest of all California mining camps.

Bodie is a ghost town in the Bodie Hills east of the Sierra Nevada mountain range in Mono County, about 75 miles southeast of Lake Tahoe. It is located 12 miles east-southeast of Bridgeport, at an elevation of 8379 feet. As Bodie Historic District, the U.S. Department of the Interior recognizes it as a National Historic Landmark.

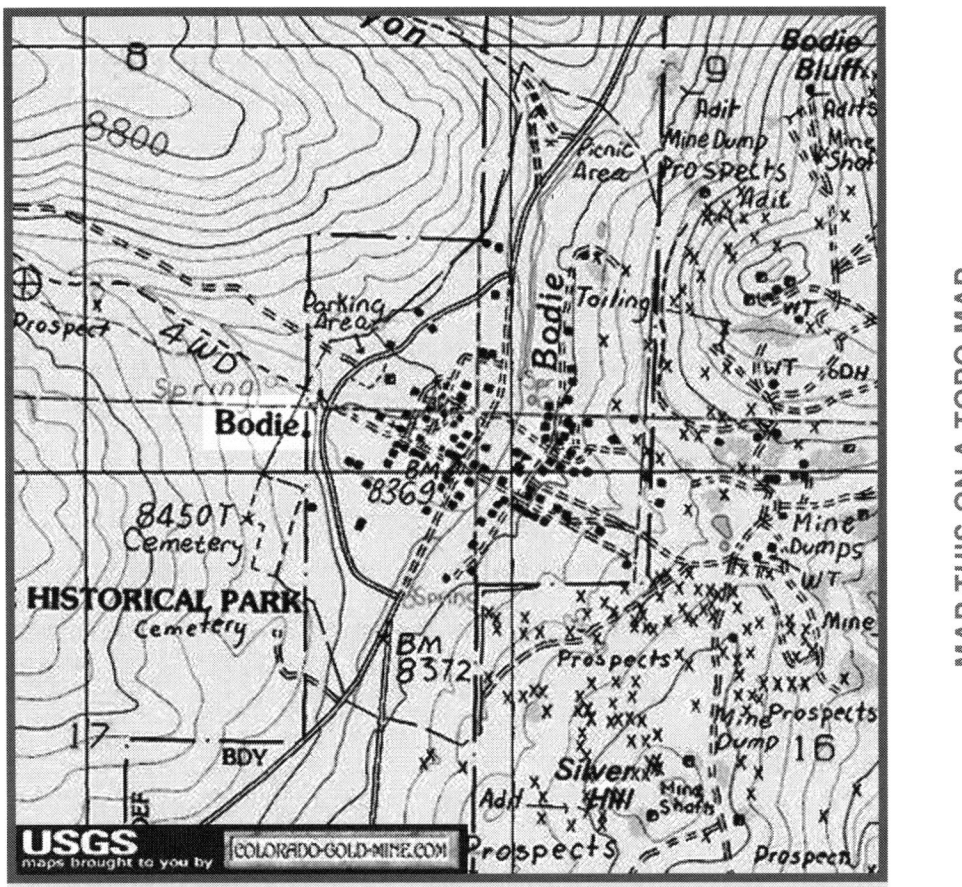

Mono County – Bodie & Bodie Jail

MAP THIS ON A TOPO MAP —
www.1wbta.com/Mono-County-Bodie-And-Bodie-Jail

The ghost town had been administered by California State Parks since becoming a state historic park in 1962, and receives about 200,000 visitors yearly. Starting in 2012, Bodie is administered by the Bodie Foundation, which uses the tagline *Protecting Bodie's Future by Preserving Its Past*.

Discovery Of Gold – Bodie began as a mining camp of little note following the discovery of gold in 1859 by a group of prospectors, including W. S. Bodey (first name uncertain). Bodey perished in a blizzard the following November while making a supply trip to Monoville (near present day Mono City), never getting to see the rise of the town that was named after him.

According to area pioneer, Judge J. G. McClinton, the district's name was changed from "Bodey," "Body," and a few other phonetic variations, to "Bodie," after a painter in the nearby boomtown of Aurora, lettered a sign "Bodie Stables." Gold discovered at Bodie coincided with the discovery of silver at nearby Aurora (thought to be in California, later found to be Nevada), and the distant Comstock Lode beneath Virginia City, Nevada. But while these two towns boomed, interest in Bodie remained lackluster. By 1868, only two companies had built stamp mills at Bodie, and both had failed.

In 1876, the Standard Company discovered a profitable deposit of gold-bearing ore, which transformed Bodie from an isolated mining camp comprising a few prospectors and company employees to a Wild West boomtown. Rich discoveries in the adjacent Bodie Mine during 1878 attracted even more hopeful people. By 1879, Bodie had a population of approximately 5000-7000 people and around 2,000 buildings.

As a bustling gold mining center, Bodie had the amenities of larger towns, including a Wells Fargo Bank, four volunteer fire companies, a brass band, a railroad, miners' and mechanics' unions, several daily newspapers, and a jail. At its peak, 65 saloons lined Main Street, which was a mile long. Murders, shootouts, barroom brawls, and stagecoach holdups were regular occurrences.

As with other remote mining towns, Bodie had a popular, though clandestinely important, red light district on the north end of town. From this is told the unsubstantiated story of Rosa May, a prostitute who, in the style of Florence Nightingale, came to the aid of the town menfolk when a serious epidemic struck the town at the height of its boom. She is credited with giving life-saving care to many, but was buried outside the cemetery fence.

Resource: http://en.wikipedia.org/wiki/Bodie,_California – **Map Code 13 F-7**

Creator: Historic American Engineering Record/Historic American Landscapes Survey - Bodie Jail, Bodie, Mono County, CA - Bodie State Historic Park - Exterior, View From Southwest, Front
Significance: The town of Bodie was the result of a gold rush in 1859. By 1879, Bodie reached its pinnacle with Main Street being approximately one mile long. The typical building was a poorly constructed one or two story frame structure. By 1883, the main veins had been exhausted and the people left as suddenly as they had come.
~Courtesy LOC.GOV, Library Of Congress, USA

Mono County — Inquire in Bridgeport (US 395) for directions to the site of Masonic, on the north slope of Masonic Mountain. Gold was discovered here in 1902 and the town grew up in three separate clusters of buildings.

A number of buildings are still standing, some in fairly good condition, but most are filled with debris and vines and are ready to collapse. The enormous old mill and ore tram are now in complete ruins. **Map Code 13 F-7**

Monterey County — Inquire in Salinas (US 101) for directions to Natividad, about 6 miles east, on a paved road. This was once a thriving station on the Coast Stage Line, but fell into ruin after the railroad and main highway passed it by.

Here, in 1846, was fought the battle of Natividad between 70 Americans ("Yankees") and 150 native Californians. **Map Code 14 H-4**

Monterey County — Just off State G16, between Carmel and Greenfield, is the hamlet of Jamesburg, founded in 1867 by John James. Once an active and much larger town, it is today little more than a country store surrounded by several deserted and tumbled-down buildings. **Map Code 14 I-4**

Monterey County — In the village of Notley's Landing, on State 1 south of Monterey, are the ruins of Notley's Landing, where timber and tanbark were brought on muleback to be loaded on waiting vessels. There are a few other old ruins here. **Map Code 14 I-4**

Monterey County — On the edge of the cliff above the mouth of Bixby Creek, at the Rainbow Bridge on State 1, are the ruins of Bixby's Landing where, in the early 1900s, lime from inland quarries was carried in huge buckets over a tram down to the pier. Little remains but the site. **Map Code 14 I-4**

Monterey County — In the village of San Simeon (State 1) is a handful of old deserted frame buildings, occupied by Portuguese whalers between 1865 and 1890. **Map Code 14 J-5**

Monterey County — Whaler's Cove, in Point Lobos State Park, reached by State 1 from Carmel or Monterey, was once the scene of whaling activity by Portuguese (see above), when the place was known as Carmelite Cove. The whalers had their cottages in a curve facing the bay, but all the buildings are now gone.

Just west of Whaler's Cove, at Cannery Point, Japanese engaged in abalone canning from the early years until 1928. These buildings have all been demolished. There are numerous spots in the vicinity where Indians are believed to have had seasonal campgrounds. Some artifacts have been recovered in the area, but bear in mind that this is State Park property. **Map Code 14 H-4**

Napa County — Inquire in St. Helena (State 29) for directions to the nearby old Bale Mill. Now being restored, this mill was built in 1846 by Dr. Edward Bale. The wheel was 40 feet in diameter and the main building was a 2-story structure. The place was long a meeting ground for crowds of all kinds. **Map Code 12 F-3**

Nevada County — North San Juan (State 49), with a present day population of less than 200, once boomed with 10,000 gold seekers when it was headquarters for the rich hydraulic workings on San Juan Ridge. The area around North San Juan is unusually rich in mining artifacts and in remnants of forgotten camps. Many of these sites are completely lost, but local investigation might reveal clues to some locations. To the best of our knowledge, little effort has been made to locate the sites of some of these relatively minor camps. Ask about the old camps of Foster's Ferry, Stoney, Rock Island, Succor, Slate Range, Cut-Eye Foster's, Kanaka, Winslow, Missouri, Condemned, and Frenchmen's. These were all in the general area of North San Juan and there are many others whose names have been forgotten. **Map Code 12 D-5**

<u>Nevada County</u> — Boca, on Interstate 80 near the Nevada line, was once a roaring lumber town. Today it is a mere handful of ramshackle shanties around a railroad station. Due to their accessibility, most of the ruins here have been fairly well picked over. **Map Code 13 D-6**

<u>Nevada County</u> — Inquire in Soda Springs (Interstate 80) for directions to the site of Last Chance. When gold was discovered here in 1850, the camp grew into a lively town, even boasting of having three lodge halls. All that remains to indicate it once existed is an old hotel and some scattered and deserted cabins. **Map Code 12 D-6**

<u>Nevada County</u> — Inquire in Grass Valley (State 49) for directions to the site of the old mining camp of Timbuctoo, which flourished in the 1850s. Nothing remains today except the shell of the old Wells Fargo Express office. **Map Code 12 E-5**

<u>Nevada County</u> — Along State 49 in Nevada County, and extending into Yuba County as it follows the North Fork of the Yuba River, are the sites of numerous old mining camps including Gold Range, Celestial Valley, Oak Valley, Dad's Gulch, Indian Springs, and Pike City. Local inquiry in the larger towns along State 49 in Nevada-Yuba counties might reveal information as to the location of these sites and others. **Map Code 12 D-5**

<u>Nevada County</u> — Somewhere in the area between Truckee (Interstate 80) and Hobart Mills, a few miles to the north and possibly near the confluence of Alder and Prosser Creeks, the families of George and Jacob Donner were stranded by heavy snows in October, 1846.

Lagging behind the rest of the Donner party because of a broken axle on their wagon, they made camp in crude huts made of boughs banked with snow, cut off from their fellow travelers camped at Donner Lake by 5 miles of snow drifts. The exact site of the George and Jacob Donner camp has never been located. When found, it will probably yield valuable historical relics. See more information on <u>page 135</u>. **Map Code 13 D-6**

Nevada County — About 5 miles west of Grass Valley (State 49), and on State 20, is the old mining camp of Rough And Ready where a few people still live. The Rough And Ready Diggings are half hidden by high chaparral, as are the ruins of some deserted buildings at the edge of town. **Map Code 12 E-5**

Nevada County — Inquire in Nevada City (State 49) for directions to an unnumbered mountain road up San Juan Ridge to Bowman Lake. This road will take you through Tyler, called Cherokee through the mining boom, now only a handful of weathered houses. The next town is North Columbia. Some of the old homes here are still occupied, but others, as well as some office buildings, have long since been deserted.

Continue to Lake City, a complete ghost consisting of little more than two or three deserted houses and an abandoned and sagging hotel. The next town is North Bloomfield where a few people still live. Here was located the greatest hydraulic mining operation on San Juan Ridge, and here the Malakoff Mine reduced its gold to bars for transportation to San Francisco. To foil holdup men, one single bar weighed a quarter ton and was valued at $114,000. Farther on is the site of Snow Tent, now completely vanished. **Map Code 12 D-5**

Orange County — Just south of Tustin (Interstate 5) is Red Hill, known to the early Spaniards as Cerrito de las Rancas (hill of the frogs). This was for many years a landmark and camping place for Indians, missionaries, and Spanish and Mexican travelers. Many artifacts have been found in the region, which will soon be completely built up. **Map Code 16 E-6**

Placer County — Inquire in Nevada City or Grass Valley, both on State 49, for directions to Dutch Flat, an old mining camp that played an important part in the history of the northern California mines. Founded in 1851, it was a prominent stage and freight stop. When hydraulic operations took over, Dutch Flat died.

China Store, a massive, fortress-like structure, is all that remains of Dutch Flat's Chinatown that housed more than 1,000 coolies during railroad construction days. Across the Bear River from here are the sites of the mining camps of Little Rock, Red Dog, and You Bet. Nothing at all remains of these once important camps. **Map Code 12 E-5**

Placer County — Gold Run, just off Interstate 80 between Auburn and Truckee, is not exactly a ghost town, but it is vastly smaller than in its active mining days in the 1860s and 1870s. All ruins here have been rather well explored. **Map Code 12 E-5**

Placer County — Inquire in Colfax (just off Interstate 80 south of Gold Run) for directions to Iowa Hill. All about this old mining town are signs of the treasures taken out of the hills since gold was first discovered here in 1853. The tremendous hydraulic operations later all but washed the town away. Only a few traces of ruins remain. **Map Code 12 E-5**

Placer County — Inquire in Auburn (Interstate 80) for directions to Ophir. In 1852, this was the largest town in Placer County. Among the nearby orchards and vineyards are the scars of old diggings, abandoned mining pits, dumps, and the foundations of an old stamp mill. **Map Code 12 E-5**

Placer County — Inquire in Auburn (Interstate 80) for directions to Foresthill, located on an unnumbered road to the northeast. The area around Foresthill is thick with the sites of old mining camps, including Yankee Jim's, once a large town but today only a cluster of buildings, and Michigan Bluff, a complete ghost but once the center of a vast hydraulic operation. The wrecks of a few stone and frame buildings are still here, but are rapidly being picked apart. Other sites in this immediate area are Shirt Tail Canyon, Ground Hog's Glory, Hell's Delight, Miller's Defeat, Ladie's Canyon, Devil's Basin, Hell's Half Acre, Bogus Thunder, Last Chance, Deadman's Bar, Rattlesnake Bar, Frytown, Milk Punch Bar, and Drunkard's Bar. **Map Code 12 E-5**

Plumas County — Ask in Oroville (State 70) for directions to La Porte, originally known as Rabbit Creek. Once the scene of great hydraulic operations, La Porte today has only a few inhabitants. A number of old brick ruins and rock foundations are remindful of its golden past. **Map Code 12 D-5**

Plumas County — Rich Bar (State 70), with a present day population of about 50, was several times larger when it was known to the Mexican miners as Barra Rica. Some mining day ruins are still to be found. **Map Code 12 D-5**

Counties Q – S

We all need heroes. Amazing heroes have cropped up in tonight's legends and lore! But, do we ever think of ourselves as heroes? Probably not, but we need a new mindset, for we ARE the stuff of heroes! I've heard it said, "Heroes take journeys, confront dragons, and discover the treasure of their true selves." (Carol Lynn Pearson)... and that is what they did in the gold days, and that is what we are doing today!

Their dragons were high mountains and deep ravines. Our dragons are of softer stuff... until you spend hours in research, and feel the bite of THAT kind of dragon!

Now that we've determined what hardy, heroic men and women we are... please pass around those marshmallows! It's time for some Storyteller S'mores!

Riverside County — Aguana (State 79) is almost on the San Diego-Riverside County line, and is no more than a store and a service station. Inquire here for directions to the ruins of the Aguana Stage Station, a wooden structure that once served the Butterfield Overland route. **Map Code 15 M-10**

Riverside County — Inquire in the town of Desert Center (Interstate 10) for directions to Corn Springs, an ancient Indian campsite in the Chuckwalla Mountains. Shards and artifacts are still picked up here. **Map Code 15 L-12**

Riverside County — Inquire in Hemet (State 74) for directions to Sage. Located near the California Division of Forestry's station at Sage is the site of old Sage, now abandoned and with only a building or two still standing. Farther south a short distance is the site of Radec (cedar spelled backwards). Important at one time because it was located on the Butterfield Overland route, nothing at all remains of Radec today. **Map Code 15 M-10**

Riverside County — Ask in Mecca (State 111-195) for instructions to reach Hidden Springs, an oasis in the Orocopia Mountains. At one time, the Cahuilla Indians frequently gathered here to hold powwows, and many artifacts have been found in the region. **Map Code 15 M-11**

Riverside County — Two miles from Hemet (State 74), and in the vicinity of the Ramona Bowl, is the site of the Indian village of Pahsintah, once the largest in the region. Scores of *metates* (corn-grinding holes) mark the site. **Map Code 15 L-10**

Riverside County — Temecula (Interstate 15) has far fewer buildings today than in 1882, when it was founded on the railroad connecting San Bernardino and San Diego. Ten years later, a torrential rain washed out the tracks and they were never replaced. Temecula declined rapidly. A few old ruined buildings remain. **Map Code 15 M-10**

San Bernardino County — Cajon Junction is at the intersection of State 138 and US 395. Inquire here for directions to the Rock Candy Mountains at the mouth of West Cajon Valley, a short distance away. This strange rock formation, scattered on both side of State 138, and across the Lone Pine Canyon Road, was formerly known as Mormon Camp Rocks because a caravan of Mormons camped here in 1851. Relics of the period have been found here. **Map Code 15 L-9**

San Bernardino County — Bagdad is a community of about 20 inhabitants on US 66 between Needles and Barstow. This was once a roaring mining camp. The few buildings that escaped the disastrous fire of 1918 are rapidly falling into ruin. According to weather scientists, this is the second driest spot in the United States. **Map Code 15 K-11**

San Bernardino County — Calico, just to the north of Interstate 15 near Barstow, is not listed herein as a ghost town because it has been rebuilt and now serves as a popular tourist attraction. However, about one-half mile from Calico, through Odessa Canyon, is the site of the genuine ghost town of Bismarck, of which very little remains. **Map Code 15 K-10**

San Bernardino County — Soda Lake lies just to the south of Baker (Interstate 15). On the dry surface of this lake, in 1860, dragoons of the U. S. Army fought a battle with Indians. The army maintained a camp on the bed of the dry lake until 1866. No visible evidence of the site remains. **Map Code 15 J-11**

San Bernardino County — Inquire in Needles (Interstate 40) for directions to the site of the ghost town of Barnwell. From here a dirt road goes east 9 miles to the ghost town of Hart, located less than 5 miles from the Nevada border. There are a few remains of old buildings in Hart, nothing at all in Barnwell. **Map Code 15 J-12**

San Bernardino County — Located just south of the town of Ludlow (Interstate 40) are the remains of the old camp of Stedman, originally called Rochester. Vandals have destroyed most of the remaining buildings. **Map Code 15 K-11**

San Bernardino County — The small mining camp of Doble, now almost completely vanished, is located east of Holcomb Valley and near the eastern end of Big Bear Lake. Inquire for directions to the site in the town of Big Bear Lake.
Map Code 15 L-10

San Bernardino County — Goldstone boomed with the discovery of gold there in 1915. It was located about 33 miles north of Goldstone Lake, and practically all that remains today are a few old buildings in various stages of collapse. The lake itself is on the Fort Irwin Military Reservation, and the site of the camp may or may not be just within the reservation. This will have to be determined locally.
Map Code 15 J-10

San Bernardino County — Just north of Victorville (Interstate 15) is the small town of Oro Grande, which can be seen for miles by the clouds of dust coming from a huge cement plant located here. Oro Grande boomed in the early 1850s when gold was discovered in the Old Silver Mountains and Granite Mountains.

Very little remains to indicate the site of the original camp, which is not believed to be occupied by the present-day Oro Grande. **Map Code 15 K-9**

San Bernardino County — High in the San Bernardino Mountains north of Big Bear Lake is Holcomb Valley, where gold was discovered in 1860, resulting in an inrush of prospectors. Throughout Holcomb Valley will be found scattered and deserted log and frame buildings that once housed miners. The largest community in the district was Belleville, located just to the east of the Holcomb Valley Public Campground. Nothing but piles of rubbish and an old *arrastre* marks the site.
Map Code 15 L-10

San Bernardino County — The site of Ivanpah is on the slope of Clark Mountain, which is north of Mountain Pass and Interstate 15, just west of the Nevada border. It would be better to make local inquiry for directions to reach this site, which contains the remains of two mills, a smelter, and a dozen or so rock and adobe buildings. Silver was discovered here in 1867 and again in 1872. Miners and prospectors swarmed into the area, and the camp produced more than $4,000,000 before it died in 1885. **Map Code 15 J-11**

San Bernardino County — Inquire in Cima or Ivanpah (do not confuse with the site of Ivanpah, above), both stations on the Union Pacific Railroad, for directions to the site of Vanderbilt in the New York Mountains. Gold and silver were discovered here in the 1870s, and the camp reached its peak in the 1890s.

A number of frame buildings remain in this old ghost town, and they have been little disturbed by collectors. **Map Code 15 J-12**

San Bernardino County — The remains of Mescal, an old silver mining town founded in 1887, lies one mile south of Interstate 15 on a dirt road just west of Mountain Pass. **Map Code 15 J-12**

San Bernardino County — Inquire in Barstow (Interstate 40-15) for directions to Coolgardie Camp, located about 18 miles to the north. The first gold discoveries were made here in 1896, and at the peak of Coolgardie's boom, as many as 600 people lived here. Today, the site is marked by little more than acres of tin cans. **Map Code 15 J-10**

San Bernardino County — Inquire in Barstow (Interstate 40-15) or Needles (US 95-66) for directions to Providence, an old mining camp located in the Providence Mountains. Unlike many ghost towns, Providence contains some well preserved buildings of white softstone.

The Bonanza King Mine, discovered in the 1870s and in full production during the 1880s, produced nearly $1,000,000 during one 18-month period. Its ruins are still standing here. To the north about one mile are the ruins of the Silver King Mine. The surrounding mountains are rich in history and archaeology, but be aware that this can be treacherous desert country. Determine road conditions before leaving main highways. **Map Code 15 J-11**

San Bernardino County — On State 127, about 18 miles north of Baker (Interstate 16), are the remains of Silver Lake, a town on the old Tidewater & Tonopah Railroad. About 1910, it flourished as the center for the many mines in the nearby mountains. Only some crumbled adobe walls remain today. **Map Code 15 J-11**

San Bernardino County — From the site of Silver Lake (see above), a dirt road leads northwest 24 miles through Avawatz Pass, which divides the Avawatz Mountains. In the pass, and about 2 miles south of Cave Springs, are the few remains of Crackerjack. This gold mining camp reached its peak in 1907-1908, and was completely deserted by 1918. The site is within the boundaries of Fort Irwin Military Reservation and, therefore, restricted to public travel. **Map Code 15 J-10**

San Bernardino County — About 4 or 5 miles west of Essex (US 66), the remains of neatly laid out roads branching to the right and left will indicate all that is left of the World War II army tent camp once located here. It is said that when the division trained here, it was ordered overseas, and they took only their field equipment with them, burying everything else. **Map Code 15 K-12**

San Bernardino County — Inquire in Essex (US 66) for directions to the remains of the Bonanza King ghost camp in the Providence Mountains north of Mitchell Caverns State Park. There are several old mine sites to explore in this area, and many Indian artifacts have been recovered in the region. There are roads of a sort into the area, but it is best to inquire as to their conditions, and as to the best season to enter the region. **Map Code 15 J-12**

- ## SAN BERNARDINO: 29PALMS, JOSHUA TREE, DALE MINING 1, 2, AND 3!

San Bernardino - 29Palms Joshua Tree Dale Mining 1 2 3

MAP THIS ON A TOPO MAP —
www.1wbta.com/San-Bernardino-29Palms-Joshua-Tree-Dale-Mining-1-2-3

San Bernardino County — The old Dale mining district is east of Twentynine Palms (State 62) and the Joshua Tree National Monument.

- To get there, simply follow the Twentynine Palms Highway (State 62) through Twentynine Palms and on east 14 miles, to the intersection of Gold Crown Road, which turns south. The site of Old Dale is believed to be at this intersection, both to the north and to the south of State 62. No structures are standing, but there are piles of rubble and some old foundations.

  The site of the Virginia Dale mine is located about 5 miles south and a short distance to the east. It can be reached by foot, but watch out for old open mine shafts. A few weathered old buildings still stand here.

  On a hill to the northeast of the mine ruins is the site of part of the living area of the miners. Traces of flooring remain, but vandals have chopped up almost everything available for firewood.

- At Dale the Second, in the same general area, some buildings are still standing, but these are being steadily picked to pieces by desert winds and vandals. Continuing south on Gold Crown Road, and off to the east, is the site of the old Supply Mine, which is the reason for Dale moving the second time. Several old buildings still stand here, but they are rapidly deteriorating.

- The site of New Dale, or Dale the Third, is located on a spur road off of Gold Crown Road. You will know the site when you reach it by the acres of tin cans.

  A few crumbling walls remain at New Dale, but at all three Dales, the rubble has been well raked over by collectors of bottles. Back in the nearby hills are other mine sites, but access to these should be attempted only by 4-wheel drive vehicles.

Map Code 15 L-11

San Diego County — Inquire in Jamul (State 94) for directions to the hamlet of Jamacha. In 1770, there was an Indian village near here, and it is believed that the raiders who destroyed the San Diego Mission in 1775 came from this place. A local legend states that they carried some of the mission's treasures back with them and buried them here. Another legend places the famous Pegleg Smith Lost Mine three miles east of Jamacha. **Map Code 15 N-10**

San Diego County — Inquire in Julian (State 78) for directions to Banner. Now a picnic and campground (admission charged), Banner was an important mining camp during the gold rush in the Julian area. The old buildings in Banner are rapidly being removed, and by this time may be gone entirely. **Map Code 15 M-10**

San Diego County — Big Stone Park, along US 395, about 23 miles north of San Diego, is a picnic ground (admission charged). This was once a favorite Indian campground, and artifacts and Indian paintings are found in a wide area in the vicinity. **Map Code 15 M-9**

San Diego County — Cuyamaca State Park, reached on State 79 south of Julian, is enjoyed annually by half a million people or more, who drive here to picnic, camp, hike, explore the old mining area, and to photograph the wildflowers. The Indians came here to hunt deer and gather acorns. Their ancient campgrounds are still being found in the areas around West Mesa and Green Valley. **Map Code 15 N-10**

San Diego County — Witch Creek Stage Station, in Ballena Valley and adjacent to Witch Creek, was razed in the mid 1900s and only the number was salvaged. Its crumbled walls still stand. The station doubled as a hotel and a saloon, and at one time catered to much of the social register of San Diego. Nomadic Indians once inhabited Ballena Valley and artifacts have been found in abundance in the nearby hills. Witch Creek is on State 78 about halfway between Ramona and Julian. **Map Code 15 M-10**

San Diego County — Oak Grove Stage Station, now serving as a tavern, is a well preserved Butterfield Overland Mail stop, and is located on State 79 just south of the Riverside County line. Of the 10 Butterfield stage stations in southern California, Oak Grove and two others are the only ones still standing. **Map Code 15 M-10**

San Diego County — On State 78 southeast of Escondido is the site of the San Pasqual Battlefield where Brig. Gen. Stephen W. Kearny led an ill-fated charge against the California army under Gen. Andres Pico. It has been said that the Americans buried equipment before going into the battle and never later recovered it. The site is preserved as a State Park and permission to explore here will have to be secured from the proper authorities. Whether or not the equipment supposed to have been buried before the battle is on state property is not known. **Map Code 15 M-10**

San Diego County — Scissors Crossing was so named because State 78 and State S2 cross here in the shape of an open pair of scissors. Before the white man came to this area, many Indian villages were located in the region. Artifacts are still found in this region by those willing to go out and search for them. **Map Code 15 M-10**

San Diego County — The site of the old Carrizo Stage Station is located just off State S2 and almost on the Imperial County line. A few fragments of timber are all that remain of this once important stop on the Butterfield Overland Route.
Map Code 15 N-11

San Diego County — The hamlet of Foster, on State 67 southwest of Ramona, was for many years an active division point for freight and passengers on the San Diego, Cuyamaca & Eastern Railroad. After the disastrous floods of 1916, service was abandoned and Foster virtually died. There are a few abandoned old buildings.
Maps Code 15 M-10

San Diego County — The old adobe Vallecito Stage Station of the Butterfield Overland Route is located on State S2 in the eastern section of San Diego County. It has been restored and is now a County Park. Many stories of ghosts, deeds of violence, and buried treasures are associated with this historic place. **Map Code 15 M-10**

San Joaquin County — Inquire in Lodi (US 50) for directions to Old Oak Grove, now nothing but a scattering of houses and an old cemetery. When the hotel here burned down in 1857, most of the town packed up and moved to modern Elk Grove, one mile away. **Map Code 12 F-5**

San Luis Obispo County — Inquire in San Luis Obispo (US 101) for directions to Santa Margarita Lake. East of the approach to this lake is a byway road to the site of Pozo, born of the gold boom in the La Panza country to the east. There is only a sprinkling of homes here now, and a few deserted old buildings. **Map Code 14 J-6**

San Luis Obispo County — Continuing east past Pozo (see above), the road climbs to Pozo Summit and on to the little town of La Panza, now only a ghost of what it was during the mining boom era. At that time there were several settlements in this area.

- De la Guerra Gulch once had a population of 250, but even the site is lost today.

- There were two camps on Navajo Creek, and their names, as well as their sites, are no longer remembered.

- A place called French Camp was located at the junction of San Juan and Navajo Creeks.

- La Panza itself was located at a different site from 1879 to 1908, and this site is marked by a stone building — the original La Panza post office — now used as a dairy.

♦ Another site once called La Panza, is located on the La Panza Ranch.

Directions to these sites, where known, might be secured at the La Panza Ranger Station, west of the present town of La Panza. Being off the beaten path, these sites should be of real interest to the artifact and relic collector. **Map Code 14 J-6**

San Mateo County — At the mouth of San Pedro Creek, about 2 miles south of Pacifica (State 1), the Portolo Expedition camped by an Indian village from Oct. 31 to Nov. 4, 1769. It is believed that this site has not been searched extensively for relics. **Map Code 12 G-3**

San Mateo County — Near the town of Half Moon Bay (State 1) is the ghost of the once active town of Purisima, on the old Rancho Canada de Verde y Arroyo de la Purisima. Nothing remains except some weathered old buildings rapidly falling into decay. **Map Code 12 G-3**

Santa Barbara County — The little town of Las Cruces, on US 101 above Gaviota Pass, was once a gathering place for early cattlemen who drove their cattle through the pass and down to the old Gaviota landing for shipment. In still earlier times, the region was a battleground during the wars between the coastal Indians and the Tulare from San Joaquin Valley. Artifacts are still found in the area. **Map Code 14 L-6**

Santa Barbara County — The little town of Las Cruces, on US 101 above the little town of Surf, at the ocean end of State 46. Here, Juan de Bautista de Anza, Spanish explorer, camped in 1775. On the north bank of the Santa Ynez River, at a site not included in the campgrounds, de Anza camped on his return trip to the area. **Map Code 14 K-5**

Santa Barbara County — Canada del Refugio runs off of US 101 at a point about 19 miles west of Goleta. This is the approximate site of the old Ortega Wharf, built by Don Jose Francisco de Ortega, one of California's early land barons. Only traces of the foundations remain of Ortega's second home, three miles up the canyon from US 101. His first home was destroyed by the pirate Hippolyte de Bouchard. **Map Code 14 H-6**

Santa Barbara County — Near the little village of Sisquoc (State 176) is the Fremont-Foxen Monument, and near the monument is the site of the home of William Benjamin Foxen. When General Fremont arrived in the area with 700 men on their way to seize Santa Barbara, he was warned that an ambush waited him if he took the planned route. Foxen, married to a Spanish woman, reluctantly agreed to guide Fremont's army through little-used San Marcos Pass, and Santa Barbara was taken without any difficulty. The grounds around the old Foxen home might produce some valuable relics. **Map Code 14 K-6**

Santa Clara County — Inquire in San Jose for directions to New Almaden, about 14 miles south. Although this is not quite a ghost town, it is the oldest mining town in California. The cinnabar deposits here were known to the earliest Indians, and to the Spanish as early as 1824. Although the town has a population of about 150, there are many reminders of its early days, badly vandalized. **Map Code 14 H-4**

Santa Clara County — Inquire in Milpitas (Interstate 680) for directions to Warm Springs, on Foothill Blvd. about 5 miles distant. Here the Spanish-California women once gathered to do their washings. A resort that opened here in 1850 was a favorite watering place until it was destroyed by an earthquake in 1968. A few traces of it are said to remain. **Map Code 12 G-4**

Santa Clara County — On the southeastern outskirts of the Stanford University Campus in Palo Alto (US 101), is an abandoned tunnel, a brick tower, and an arched bridge, all that remains of the Matador Ranch established here in 1874 by "The Frenchman," Peter Coutts. It had a racetrack, orchards, cottages, vineyards, and stables. Coutts disappeared one day in 1880, and it was some time before it was learned that he had returned to France to resume a career as a banker and publisher. Attention is called to the fact that this interesting old site is on Stanford University property. **Map Code 14 G-4**

Santa Cruz County — In the village of Aptos (State 1) is the deserted Ocean View Hotel. Local inquiry would have to reveal whether or not the grounds of this property are available for search. **Map Code 14 H-4**

Santa Cruz County — Along State 1, three miles south of Watsonville, is the site of Casa Materna, the so-called House of Glass, no sign of which remains. Built about 1824 by Don Ignacio Vicente Ferrer Vallejo, the two-story mansion was once the envy of the countryside because of its many glass windows. **Map Code 14 H-4**

Shasta County — Along the road just outside Ingor (State 299), on terraces above Seaman's Gulch, are the ruins of the deserted mine and smelter of the Afterthought Mining Company, built about 1922. It was a million dollar investment, but all that remains of it now are rusted roofs and crumbling brick and stone foundations. **Map Code 12 B-4**

Shasta County — The town of Shasta is on State 299 west of Redding. While it is not exactly a ghost town, it is but a shadow of its former self, when merchants here were sending out $100,000 weekly in gold dust. Its famous rows of brick buildings, once fallen into ruin, are gradually being restored as a State Historical Monument. Very likely you can't do any searching for relics here, but you might try locating one of the nearby placer operations, such as Mad Mule Canyon, Salt Pork Ridge, Gambler's Gulch, Piety Hill, Grizzly Gulch, and Jackass Flat. During the gold excitement, each had its own little camp. **Map Code 12 C-3**

Shasta County — Inquire in Shasta (State 299) for directions to French Gulch, about 3 miles to the north. While French Gulch is certainly not a ghost town (it has a population of several hundred), there are several old ruined buildings in the surrounding area that might bear investigating. **Map Code 12 B-3**

Shasta County — Located on State 299, a few miles west of Shasta, is Whiskeytown, now almost depopulated. Settled by miners on the trail to Oregon, it was so named when a barrel of whiskey fell off a pack mule and rolled into Whiskey Creek. There are a few ruins here. **Map Code 12 C-3**

Shasta County — Under the highest crag in the northwest corner of Battle Rock, most prominent of the spires of the Castle Crags (just south of Dunsmuir, Interstate 5), whites and their allied Shasta Indians fought a battle with the Modocs. Many relics of this battle have been found in the area. **Map Code 12 B-4**

Shasta County — Southwest of Redding (Interstate 5) are the old mining camps of Igo and Ono, both located on State A16. Each town has a sprinkling of population today, whereas they were once booming centers. A few ruins will be found at the outskirts of each. **Map Code 12 C-3**

Shasta County — Inquire in Redding (Interstate 5) for directions to the site of Reading's Bar.

The first gold in Shasta County was found here in 1848.

Once known as One Horse Town, Reading's Bar grew into a town of more than 1,000 population, with stores, hotels, 14 saloons, a newspaper, and a church. After the town was leveled by a fire in 1868, it was never rebuilt. **Map Code 12 C-4**

Shasta County — Inquire in Cottonwood (Interstate 5), itself almost a ghost town, for directions to the Reading adobe. Built in 1846, this crumbling structure was the bunkhouse for Pierson Barton Reading's cowboys. Here, too, once stood a smokehouse, a barn, and Reading's 2-story mansion where the pioneers of northern California frequently gathered. Only ruins remain today. **Map Code 12 C-4**

<u>Shasta County</u> — Just south of Dunsmuir (Interstate 5), and a short distance off the main highway, is the railroad station of Castle Crags.

Inquire here for directions to the site of Lower Soda Springs, located at the mouth of Soda Creek. Lansford Hastings camped here in 1843, and later built Hastings Barracks, an old fort of pine logs. Nothing remains of the fort today. When Modoc Indians swept down on the town of Lower Soda Springs and burned it to the ground, it was never rebuilt. **Map Code 12 B-4**

<u>Sierra County</u> — Sierra City (State 49), founded in 1850 on the North Fork of the Yuba River, has a population of 150 and can hardly be called a ghost town. The original town was wiped out by an avalanche roaring down from the Sierra Buttes that rise sheer above it. Sierra City rebuilt and today is one of the better preserved of the Mother Lode towns. There are many empty and deserted buildings here where metal detectors should respond. **Map Code 12 D-5**

<u>Sierra County</u> — Camptonville, just off State 49 between Downieville and North San Juan, was once a thriving mining center, but is little more than a hamlet today. Repeated fires destroyed most of the old buildings, and little remains here to recall the old boom days. **Map Code 12 D-5**

<u>Sierra County</u> — Inquire in Downieville (State 49) for directions to Forest (also called Forest City), clinging to the walls of a ravine on Oregon Creek. Although not a complete ghost town, there are several ruins here that might bear investigation. In this vicinity are several other old mining camp sites, including Galena, Young's, Railroad, Depot, Hell's Hills, Celestial Valley, Oak Valley, Indian Springs, and Pike City. **Map Code 12 D-5**

<u>Sierra County</u> — Inquire in Downieville (State 49) for directions to the remains of old Goodyear's Bar, a short distance below Downieville where Goodyear Creek joins the North Fork of the Yuba River. Only a few old buildings remain. Located nearby, but their sites now completely lost, were the early camps of Ranse Doodler, Hoodoo, St. Joe's Bar, Nigger Slide, and Kennedy's Ranch. A concentrated search in the brush around here could reveal the site of one or more of these old camps. **Map Code 12 D-5**

Siskiyou County — Hamburg (State 96), now little more than a general store and some tourist cottages, was once a bustling mining camp. In 1863, it all but disappeared when its buildings were washed away by a disastrous flood. A few wrecked and dilapidated buildings remain today. **Map Code 12 A-3**

Siskiyou County — Inquire in Hamburg (State 96) for directions to Scott's Bar, located 3 miles to the southeast in a deep gorge on the Scott River.

The discovery of gold here in 1850 brought an influx of miners. When the placers worked out, the population departed, leaving half the houses empty. Today, Scott's Bar is a ghost town of rapidly decaying buildings. **Map Code 12 A-3**

Siskiyou County — Somes Bar (or Somesbar) is just off State 96 at the confluence of the Klamath and Salmon Rivers. Founded as a mining camp, this is now a favorite fishing and camping site. A few ruined buildings and foundations remain as reminders of gold rush days. **Map Code 12 B-2**

Siskiyou County — Hawkinsville is located just to the north of Yreka (Interstate 5). Only a few old frame houses and some foundations mark the site of this once busy gold mining town. At one time, a string of miners' cabins stretched from here to a point 3 miles down Yreka Creek. Some of these can still be found. **Map Code 12 A-3**

Siskiyou County — Inquire in Yreka (Interstate 5) for directions to Humbug City, once the chief of the mining camps in this area. Some scattered ruins are all that remain of this old camp. **Map Code 12 A-3**

Siskiyou County — Inquire in Orleans (State 96) for directions to Sawyer's Bar, located in the middle of the Salmon Mountains and on the North Fork of the Salmon River. This was once one of the largest of the Salmon River mining camps, but only a few ruins mark the site today.

Both the North Fork and the South Fork of the Salmon River in this area were once dotted with mining camps. Although the names of some of these camps have been forgotten, the site of one is found occasionally. **Map Code 12 B-3**

Siskiyou County — Happy Camp was another sizeable mining town in the 1850s. It is located on State 96 in the northwestern section of the county. There are a few deserted buildings here, and the remains of other forgotten camps are scattered along the Klamath River in this region. **Map Code 12 A-3**

Siskiyou County — Inquire in Yreka (Interstate 5) for directions to the site of Deadwood. Nothing at all remains of this town which once rivaled Yreka as an important mining center. **Map Code 12 A-3**

Siskiyou County — Inquire in Yreka (Interstate 5) for directions to the site of Greenhorn, marked today only by a cluster of old frame structures and ruins. **Map Code 12 A-3**

Sonoma County — Just north of the town of Sonoma (State 12) is the community of El Verano. When the railroad discontinued service here, the town all but died. Today there is a huge empty hotel, stores, and other buildings. **Map Code 12 F-3**

Sonoma County — Inquire in Petaluma (US 101) for directions to Casa Grande, the deserted headquarters mansion of Gen. Mariano Vallejo on his old Rancho Petaluma. The property is overseen by a caretaker. **Map Code 12 F-3**

Sonoma County — Stewart's Point (State 1) has a population of only about 30, and consists of no more than a few frame houses around a general store. On a rocky point at the edge of a cove, and mostly hidden by trees, are the abandoned sheds and trestle from which great quantities of lumber was once shipped. **Map Code 12 E-2**

Stanislaus County — Knight's Ferry, on State 108-120, was once the center of placer mining along the lower Stanislaus River. The ruins of an old sawmill, flour mill, and woolen mill are located just west of the covered bridge, one of the few remaining in California. **Map Code 12 G-5**

Sutter County — Inquire in Tudor, on State 99 south of Yuba City, for directions to the site of Hock Farm, about 3 miles distant. Along the roadside here stands the ruins of an old fort built in 1842. This was John Augustan Sutter's stock farm. After he lost his fortune, he retired here to live in a handsome mansion, no longer standing. **Map Code 12 E-4**

Sutter County — Near the northern end of the bridge across the Sacramento River at Knight's Landing (State 113), is what remains of Cole's Landing, a busy shipping town in early steamboat days. The ruins of the old town have almost disappeared. **Map Code 12 E-4**

Counties T – Z

Meanderings and mysteries. Yes, treasure fans, it's been a wonderful mountain-top experience, just wandering these hills and wondering about these tales. Well, I see we've lost the children and some of the ladies to the mazes of sleep!

So, I will utter the next name very quietly so as to not have tiny folks awaken with a shout for the Hobbit Master! Here's tonight's last mystery…

"A box without hinges, key, or lid, yet golden treasure inside is hid." (J.R.R. Tolkien). Have a last bit of hot chocolate folks… and ponder how we have here no box, no hinges, no key or lid. But within our legends tonight, great golden treasure is hid!

Tehama County — Inquire in Los Molinos (US 99) for directions to the site of Benton City, marked by a concrete monument. A town was laid out here by Peter Lassen in 1847, and settled by Missourians. With the discovery of gold, Benton City was depopulated and abandoned. Hardly anything remains today. **Map Code 12 C-4**

Trinity County — Big Bar (one of several mining camps of this name) is located on State 299 west of Weaverville. Although its population is less than 100 today, it was once an important gold mining camp. The ruins of some old buildings remain. **Map Code 12 B-3**

Trinity County — Del Loma is located on State 299 about 32 miles west of Weaverville. It was once an active mining camp known as Taylor's Flat. Only a few ruins remindful of its early days remain here and they are rapidly disappearing. **Map Code 12 B-3**

Trinity County — Inquire in Weaverville (State 299) for directions to the site of the Bridge Gulch Massacre. Here, in 1852, miners from Weaverville invaded an Indian camp and killed about 100 of them in retaliation for the killing of a single white man.

The women and children huddled beneath a natural bridge were mercilessly knifed to death. **Map Code 12 B-3**

Tuolumne County — Tuttletown, located in Mormon Gulch on State 9 between Melons and Sonora, has slightly more than 100 inhabitants today, several thousand less than when it was a trade center and pack mule stop on the old Slumgullion Road. A few old abandoned buildings remain. **Map Code 12 F-6**

- ## TUOLUMNE COUNTY: RAWHIDE, TABLE MTN. & $6,000,000!

Tuolumne County — Inquire in Jamestown (State 49) for directions to the site of Rawhide. This camp flourished when the Rawhide Mine was producing $6,000,000 from its quartz veins.

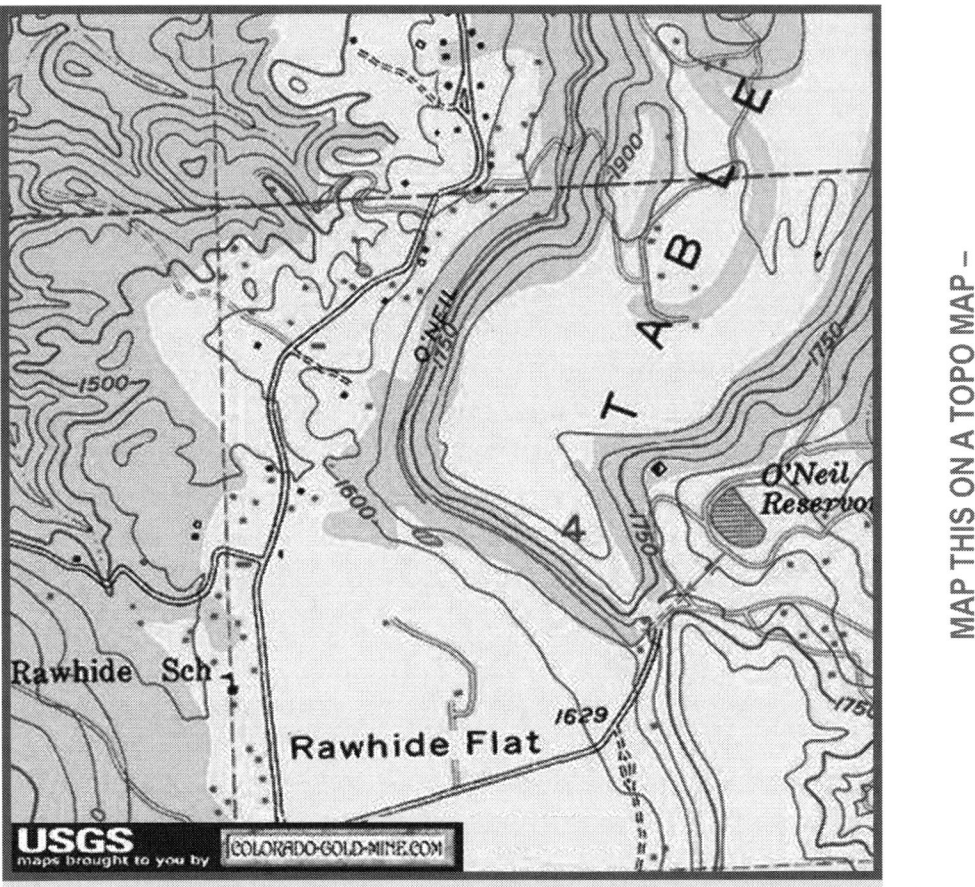

Tuolumne County: Rawhide, Table Mtn. & $6,000,000!

MAP THIS ON A TOPO MAP —
www.1wbta.com/Tuolumne-Rawhide-Table-Mtn-6M-Dollars

From this camp, of which little remains, is a view of Table Mountain. At the base of Table Mountain is a field where about 2,000 Chinese fought a battle with spears, knives, and guns in 1856, the first tong war in California. Artifacts have been picked up at this site. **Map Code 12 G-5**

Tuolumne County — A short distance north of Sonora (State 49) is Shaw's Flat, also located on State 49. Only a few ruined walls remain. The Mississippi House, built in 1850 and still standing, was once a store, saloon, post office, and stage station. The camp sprang up in 1855 when gold was discovered in an ancient river bottom here. **Map Code 12 F-6**

Tuolumne County — Inquire in Columbia (State 49) for directions to the sites of Yankee Hill, Sawmill Flat, and Squabbletown, all located nearby and all important gold camps in their day. Today they are almost non-existent, but their remains might bear investigation. **Map Code 12 F-6**

Tuolumne County — Wood's Crossing, on State 49 between Jamestown and Jacksonville, is marked by a monument of gold-bearing quartz. Nothing remains of this once busy camp that came to life when gold was discovered on Wood's Creek in 1848. **Map Code 12 F-6**

Tuolumne County — Big Oak Flat, on State 120 east of Jacksonville, was founded as Savage Diggings by James Savage, who settled here with his five Indian wives and retinue of Indian servants. Little remains of the original camp. Savage later operated trading posts at three different locations, the sites of which have been completely lost. **Map Code 12 G-6**

Tuolumne County — Groveland was originally called First Garrote, named after an execution method popular here during the gold rush. Reminders of the camp's past are some old ruins, including the iron doors and stone walls of the Wells Fargo Express station. The site is located on State 120 east of Big Oak Flat. **Map Code 12 G-6**

Tuolumne County — On State 120 just to the east of Groveland (see above), is Second Garrote. Little remains of this old camp except the Hangman Tree where criminals of gold rush days were hanged, and the ruins of a few cabins. **Map Code 12 G-6**

Tuolumne County — Priest's Station, or Priest's as it is better known today, is on State 120 a short distance west of Big Oak Flat. It was once a busy supply station for gold miners, but hardly anything remains today. **Map Code 12 G-6**

Tuolumne County — Jacksonville, on State 49 between Sonora and Coulterville, once rivaled much larger towns in importance. It is almost a ghost town today, with all except one or two of its mining days' buildings destroyed by fire. **Map Code 12 F-6**

Tuolumne County — Inquire in Melones (State 49) for directions to Jackass Hill, which once boasted of having a population of 3,000. It was here that men engaged in packing supplies to the miners in the region, camped overnight. Nothing remains today except the restored cabin where Mark Twain stayed for five months in 1864. **Map Code 12 F-5**

Tulare County — Ask in Visalia (State 63-198) for directions to Kaweah, now little more than a name. Founded in 1891 by members of the International Workingmen's Association, it was planned as a socialistic community. When difficulties over land claims arose, it was all but abandoned. **Map Code 14 1-7**

Tulare County — Inquire at the Sequoia National Park Headquarters for directions to Mineral King, a tiny settlement at the base of Sawtooth Mountain, but outside the Park boundaries. Silver was discovered here in 1873, but the deposits were not rich enough for profitable mining. Little remains of the original camp, and the area today is becoming one of summer homes and a starting place for pack trips into the Sierras. Four miles distant is the remains of another old camp, Silver City. **Map Code 14 1-8**

Tulare County — Ask in Delano (State 99) for directions to Fountain Springs. This old Butterfield stage station is now nothing more than a crossroads store and gas station stop. **Map Code 14 J-7**

Yuba County — Camptonville (State 49), a town of about 400 inhabitants today, was once several times this size. Moved twice for hydraulic mining operations, and almost destroyed by fire several times, there are many abandoned shacks and old homes in the area. **Map Code 12 D-5**

Yuba County — Ask in Yuba City (State 99-20) for directions to Sutter Buttes, four jagged rocks jutting up from the valley floor. When the Indians in this area were driven from their homes by horse and cattle thieves, they found hiding places and lived in these buttes. Just prior to the Bear Flag Revolt, Gen. John C. Fremont and his expedition camped at the base of the buttes. Artifacts of various kinds have been found in the area. **Map Code 12 E-4**

Afterword: Treasure For A Modern Day Hunter... Your "Ticket To Ride"

The Accumulative History Of This Great Land

All American War battle sites hold treasure in form of guns, bullets, and personal items of the soldiers, for the modern day hunter. That is why this book has a definite emphasis on the Westward Movement Wars. For instance, the Indian War battles described in the many chapters can be traced on old and current state maps of California. This is also true of many of the events in California history... or the history of any given place.

From the stories of the American Native, to the tales of Westward Movement of the Spanish, the French, and the total variety of our "great melting pot," this land is the summary of all of the personal stories... the accumulative history of this great land.

Doing Your Duty In Researching Everything

Mind your treasure hunting manners and follow the best creeds of our genre, the first of which is... RESEARCH. Without doing your duty in researching everything you can find for an area, your end result will not be what you have expected. Due diligence is a very good thing in most things in life. And treasure hunting success is just another such thing.

We hope the content of this book will set the tone for your search, and that your journey ahead will be a huge success! Welcome to California, a state that holds much promise for you!

Illustrated: Be Careful What You Water Your Dreams With

"Be careful what you water your dreams with. Water them with worry and fear and you will produce weeds that choke the life from your dream. Water them with optimism and solutions and you will cultivate success. Always be on the lookout for ways to turn a problem into an opportunity for success. Always be on the lookout for ways to nurture your dream."
~Lao Tzu

Acknowledgments

I would not even pretend to present this compilation of treasure tales as being solely the result of my personal efforts. Most of these stories have been around for years, told and retold in many places by many different people. I have put into them my own observations and conclusions; there are a few stories new to the total I've picked up over the years; and there are a few additions to the tales others have discovered in recent years. But my greatest effort has been in attempting to fashion sensible stories from a multitude of often-conflicting renditions of the same stories.

I have to thank many people for their efforts to pass along these tales over the years, and in many cases I must beg their forgiveness for ignoring or disagreeing with no few of their conclusions. I would like to mention any number of other people, but should I try to do so, I would surely leave someone out who should not be left out. There is no possible way to credit everyone who did affect this book. Many passed away years ago, but their works certainly affected both myself and my writing. I have tried hard not to stray from the available information. I am sure I have failed to get bits and pieces of information into this work that should be there; there undoubtedly are stories that got left out, but I hope the result is not too disappointing.

> Thank you, all you tellers of California treasure tales who came before me, who sat at other, earlier campfires, spellbinding your listeners. I could never have perched here on my log, telling these tales, without your help!

~H. Glenn Carson

Illustrated: The Valuables Left Behind

"Gold is not all" - Painting by Howard Chandler Christy - c1904, Charles Scribner's Sons
Miner seated with bags of gold outside house, envisioning woman inside window.
Source: http://www.loc.gov/pictures/item/2002711728/
Courtesy LOC.GOV, Library Of Congress, USA

Bibliography

Carson, Glenn. (n.d.). Waybill To Adventure Books – Everything is going to Amazon! In *1WBTA.com – 2012 Is The Year!* Retrieved April 24, 2012, from http://www.1wbta.com.

Carson, Glenn; Penfield, Thomas. (August 31, 2012). Vol. 003: A Guide To Treasure In California, 2nd Edition. In *Vol. 003: A Guide To Treasure In California, 2nd Edition | 1WBTA.com - 2012 Is The Year!* Retrieved August 31, 2012, from http://www.1wbta.com/vol-003-a-guide-to-treasure-in-california-2nd-edition.

DesertUSA.com. (n.d.). Desert Biomes by DesertUSA (Various articles/pages). In *DesertUSA, Explore the deserts of the world.* Retrieved April 24, 2012, from http://www.desertusa.com/index.html.

essortment.com. (n.d.). California Gold Rush Of 1849. In *California Gold Rush Of 1849: essortment, Your Source For Knowledge.* Retrieved August 17, 2012, from http://www.essortment.com/california-gold-rush-1849-44186.html.

Hay, Brenda. (n.d.). California County Map. In *Census Finder: A Directory of Free Census Records.* Retrieved August 17, 2012, from http://www.censusfinder.com/mapca.htm.

Legends of America.com. (n.d.). Welcome to Legends of America!! (Various pages). In *Legends of America - American History, People, Legends, Old West, Travel Destinations, and Lots More. For the Nostalgic and Historic Minded.* Retrieved April 24, 2012, from http://www.legendsofamerica.com/.

MiningArtifacts.org. (n.d.). California Mines (Various public domain images/pages). In *Mining Artifacts & History.* Retrieved April 24, 2012, from http://www.miningartifacts.org/California-Mines.html.

Nevada Outback Gems. (n.d.). Nevada Outback Gems: Natural Nevada Turquoise Jewelry in Silver and Gold, tourmaline, tanzanite. In *DEAD RIVERS OF CALIFORNIA: Tertiary Channels rich in gold nuggets.* Retrieved August 17, 2012, from http://nevada-outback-gems.com/gold_rush_tales/california_gold_rush-tale65.htm.

Niemi, Ryan. (n.d.). TopoQuest - Place Finder (Various maps/pages). In *TopoQuest – Topographic Maps and Satellite Maps Online*. Retrieved April 24, 2012, from http://www.topoquest.com/places.php.

Regents of The University of California, The. (n.d.). University of California: Calisphere, a world of primary sources and more (Various pages/images). In *Calisphere – A World of Digital Resources*. Retrieved April 24, 2012, from http://www.calisphere.universityofcalifornia.edu/.

Rietsch, Pam; livgenmi.com. (n.d.). 1895 Atlas Title Page (Various maps). In *1895 U.S. Atlas*. Retrieved April 24, 2012, from http://www.livgenmi.com/1895/.
☑ Originally printed and copyrighted in 1895 by the Rand McNally Corporation, called: "The New 11 x 14 Atlas of the World."
☑ California 1895 County Maps. http://www.livgenmi.com/1895/CA/County/.
☑ Part 2.7 (p. 26 in this book): "There Are 58 Counties In California." Map used: California 1895 Atlas Map. http://www.livgenmi.com/1895/CA/state.htm.

Schneider, Adam. (n.d.). GPS Visualizer: Do-It-Yourself Mapping. In *GPS Visualizer*. Retrieved August 1, 2012, from http://www.gpsvisualizer.com/.

United States Library of Congress. (n.d.). Prints & Photographs Online Catalog (Various pictures, graphics). In *Prints & Photographs Online Catalog (PPOC)*. Retrieved August 17, 2012, from http://www.loc.gov/pictures/.

United States Library of Congress. (n.d.). Search Results for "bird's eye view california" – 1-20 of 50 from the Library of Congress (Various maps). In *Results for "bird's eye view California"*. Retrieved August 13, 2012, from http://www.loc.gov/maps/?q=bird%27s+eye+view+california.

United States Library of Congress. (n.d.). "Washington, West façade Library of Congress." In *Digital Collections – Washington, West façade Library of Congress*. Retrieved August 12, 2012, from http://www.loc.gov/pictures/resource/ppmsca.18034/.

Wikipedia.org. (n.d.). File:Gold-Gold Providence-Nugget.jpg. In *File:Gold-Gold Providence-Nugget.jpg, Wikipedia, the free encyclopedia*. Retrieved August 18, 2012, from http://en.wikipedia.org/wiki/File:Gold-Gold_Providence-Nugget.jpg.

Wikipedia.org. (n.d.). Library of Congress. In *Library of Congress*. Retrieved August 12, 2012, from http://en.wikipedia.org/wiki/Library_of_Congress.

Wikipedia.org. (n.d.). Seth Kinman (early settler of Humboldt County, California). In *Seth Kinman, Wikipedia, the free encyclopedia*. Retrieved August 29, 2012, from http://en.wikipedia.org/wiki/Seth_Kinman.

Wikipedia.org. (n.d.). Welcome to Wikipedia. In *Wikipedia, the free encyclopedia*. Retrieved March 30, 2012, from http://en.wikipedia.org/wiki/Main_Page.

Ghost Towns

Ghost towns are limited within these pages, except for the Coinshooting Sites pages. It is not because those places where people used to live are not interesting or very much worthwhile to treasure hunters, for they are! The simple problem of not having sufficient space demands the omission of many ghost sites.

Don't ignore those now uninhabited spots. Ghost towns are not just dots on maps; they were where people lived, worked, and at times lost or hid their wealth. For instance, in Colorado there are approximately 4,000 ghost sites. Leanne Boyd and I put together a two-volume set of the *Atlas of Colorado Ghost Towns*. There are two books, more than 350 pages, all sorts of maps and illustrations, and about 4,000 listings of actual sites. If you have any interest in treasure in Colorado, you definitely should have and study these two books.

A listing of our books dealing with Colorado ghost towns is given here for your possible attention and use.

Boyd, Leanne C., and Carson, H. Glenn, *Atlas Of Colorado Ghost Towns, Volume I*, copyright 1984, 134 pages.
www.1wbta.com/073-Atlas-CO-Ghost-Towns-Vol-I

Boyd, Leanne C., and Carson, H. Glenn, *Atlas Of Colorado Ghost Towns, Volume II*, copyright 1985, 192 pages.
www.1wbta.com/074-Atlas-CO-Ghost-Towns-Vol-II

Carson, H. Glenn, *Hunting The Ghost Towns*, copyright 1977, 84 pages.
www.1wbta.com/048-Hunting-The-Ghost-Towns

Save Yer' Eyes! Download Our Catalog!

Trying to marry the print world with the digital is an interesting proposition. Following, you will find the core "catalog" for our new 2012 adventure with Amazon. It also lists sites where you can get original print books, and also for several PDF Ebooks I created in the early- to mid-2000s. To fit this into a 10-page format (snail-mail reasons), I was driven to present it in a smaller font size. This is, BTW (by the way) going into a print version, so that my Dad can send it to his longstanding print book friends and buyers. Font-size: 11px. Yikes.

We are now producing PRINT books at Amazon. But we live in a digital world, still. The PDF Ebook of this catalog will show the 11px font. The beauty of a PDF is that you can zoom and view at a huge size, and STILL have the clickable links. My advice: Download the catalog!!

www.1wbta.com/catalog

And avoid this kind of thing:

Some Other Helpful & Interesting Books For Any State's Treasure Buffs: Our Catalog For Waybill To Adventure's New Millennium Edition Treasure Library

Early-Bird Alerts For New Books – Go REGISTER!!

Register For Email Alerts   :::   http://www.1wbta.com/login?action=register

The NEW Waybill To Adventure Catalog!

- The Waybill To Adventure Catalog – Updated every time a new work is published! You can download a PDF Ebook copy of the catalog, where all these links are clickable!
  Our site: **www.1wbta.com/catalog**

- PLEASE NOTE: In this catalog, you will find mainly TWO links for most of our products. **"Our site"** will take you to that product's page on our Web site, where you will find the most current information including the eventual publication at Amazon. The **"Original book"** link will take you to one of our resources that carry the original book (1st Edition), or the early 2000s PDF Ebooks (2nd Edition), or both.

  Usually these are at *Lost Treasure Magazine Online*, or the *Amazon Marketplace*. Many early books are actually collectibles at this point, so be careful. There are vendors at Amazon, for instance, that place very high prices on these books… $500 or more! But if you look, there are copies available at quite low prices. Somebody listed my brand new *Guide to Treasure in Colorado, 3rd Edition* for a whopping $888.88!

  PLEASE NOTE: The digital Ebooks provided by *Lost Treasure Magazine Online* are THE ORIGINAL VERSIONS of each book. They are NOT the new Editions that my *Waybill To Adventure LLC* and my Dad's *Carson Enterprises* are publishing at Amazon. We have a special partnership with *Lost Treasure* that I initiated several years ago. But the new adventure on Amazon consists of my Dad (finally!) working with me on my now-12-year-old quest for solidly saving his writing legacy!

- NONE of the early versions can measure up to what these volumes are becoming. For instance, the *Guide to Treasure in Colorado, 3rd Edition*, is a 452-page work of art, and you shouldn't miss it! All of our books will be of the same high quality, with massive visual power.

- ✪ A third link will be added once the new book is published at Amazon. The link is named, appropriately: **"NEW @ Amazon."** The bullet point (see to the left) is also different… instead of a spade, it is a STAR. Each new book will add one more of these links into the catalog in that book… which makes the catalog WITHIN the earlier books, outdated. But the catalog will always be up to date on our Web site: **www.1wbta.com/catalog**

Web Site Table Of Contents

- Our Web site has a comprehensive Table Of Contents, where you can see all of the books in one place, and click to your heart's content!
  Our site: **www.1wbta.com/Table-Of-Contents**

Treasure Guide Series

- A Guide To Treasure In Arizona
  Our site: www.1wbta.com/vol-001-a-guide-to-treasure-in-arizona-2nd-edition
  Original book: www.1wbta.com/001-A-Guide-To-Treasure-In-Arizona
- A Guide To Treasure In Arkansas, Louisiana, And Mississippi
  Our site: www.1wbta.com/vol-002-a-guide-to-treasure-in-arkansas-louisiana-and-mississippi-2nd-edition
  Original book: www.1wbta.com/002-A-Guide-To-Treasure-In-AR-LA-MS
- ✪ A Guide To Treasure In California
  Our site: www.1wbta.com/vol-003-a-guide-to-treasure-in-california-2nd-edition
  Original book: www.1wbta.com/003-A-Guide-To-Treasure-In-California
  NEW @ Amazon, info: www.1wbta.com/vol-003-a-guide-to-treasure-in-california-2nd-edition
- ✪ A Guide To Treasure In Colorado
  Our site: www.1wbta.com/vol-004-a-guide-to-treasure-in-colorado-3rd-edition
  Original book: www.1wbta.com/004-A-Guide-To-Treasure-In-Colorado-LTI
  NEW @ Amazon: www.1wbta.com/004-A-Guide-To-Treasure-In-Colorado
- A Guide To Treasure In Idaho
  Our site: www.1wbta.com/vol-005-a-guide-to-treasure-in-idaho-2nd-edition
  Original book: www.1wbta.com/005-A-Guide-To-Treasure-In-Idaho
- A Guide To Treasure In Illinois And Indiana
  Our site: www.1wbta.com/vol-006-a-guide-to-treasure-in-illinois-indiana-2nd-edition
  Original book: www.1wbta.com/006-A-Guide-To-Treasure-In-Illinois-Indiana
- A Guide To Treasure In Kentucky
  Our site: www.1wbta.com/vol-007-a-guide-to-treasure-in-kentucky-2nd-edition
  Original book: www.1wbta.com/007-A-Guide-To-Treasure-In-Kentucky
- A Guide To Treasure In Michigan And Ohio
  Our site: www.1wbta.com/vol-008-a-guide-to-treasure-in-michigan-ohio-2nd-edition
  Original book: www.1wbta.com/008-A-Guide-To-Treasure-In-Michigan-And-Ohio
- A Guide To Treasure In Missouri
  Our site: www.1wbta.com/vol-009-a-guide-to-treasure-in-missouri-2nd-edition
  Original book: www.1wbta.com/009-A-Guide-To-Treasure-In-Missouri
- A Guide To Treasure In Montana And Wyoming
  Our site: www.1wbta.com/vol-010-a-guide-to-treasure-in-montana-wyoming-2nd-edition
  Original book: www.1wbta.com/010-A-Guide-To-Treasure-In-Montana-And-Wyoming
- Treasure Guide To Nebraska, Kansas, North Dakota, And South Dakota
  Our site: www.1wbta.com/vol-011-a-guide-to-treasure-in-nebraska-kansas-north-dakota-south-dakota-2nd-edition
  Original book: www.1wbta.com/011_A-Guide-To-Treasure-In-NE-KS-ND-SD
- A Guide To Treasure In Nevada
  Our site: www.1wbta.com/vol-012-a-guide-to-treasure-in-nevada-2nd-edition
  Original book: www.1wbta.com/012-A-Guide-To-Treasure-In-Nevada
- A Guide To Treasure In New Mexico
  Our site: www.1wbta.com/vol-013-a-guide-to-treasure-in-new-mexico-2nd-edition
  Original book: www.1wbta.com/013-A-Guide-To-Treasure-In-New-Mexico
- A Guide To Treasure In Oklahoma
  Vol. I, Our site: www.1wbta.com/vol-014-a-guide-to-treasure-in-oklahoma-vol-i-2nd-edition

Original book: Vol. I – www.1wbta.com/014-A-Guide-To-Treasure-In-Oklahoma-Vol-I
Vol. II, Our site: www.1wbta.com/vol-015-a-guide-to-treasure-in-oklahoma-vol-ii-2nd-edition
Original book: Vol. II – www.1wbta.com/015-A-Guide-To-Treasure-In-Oklahoma-Vol-II
Vol. III, Our site: www.1wbta.com/vol-016-a-guide-to-treasure-in-oklahoma-vol-iii-2nd-edition
Original book: Vol. III – www.1wbta.com/016-A-Guide-To-Treasure-In-Oklahoma-Vol-III

- A Guide To Treasure In Pennsylvania
  Our site: www.1wbta.com/vol-017-a-guide-to-treasure-in-pennsylvania-2nd-edition
  Original book: www.1wbta.com/017-A-Guide-to-Treasure-in-Pennsylvania
- ✪ A Guide To Treasure In Tennessee
  Our site: www.1wbta.com/vol-018-a-guide-to-treasure-in-tennessee-2nd-edition
  Original book: www.1wbta.com/018-A-Guide-To-Treasure-In-Tennessee-LTI
  NEW @ Amazon: www.1wbta.com/018-A-Guide-To-Treasure-In-Tennessee
- A Guide To Treasure In Texas
  Our site: www.1wbta.com/vol-019-a-guide-to-treasure-in-texas-2nd-edition
  Original book: www.1wbta.com/019-A-Guide-to-Treasure-in-Texas
- A Guide To Treasure In Utah
  Our site: www.1wbta.com/vol-020-a-guide-to-treasure-in-utah-2nd-edition
  Original book: www.1wbta.com/020-A-Guide-to-Treasure-in-Utah
- A Guide To Treasure In Virginia And West Virginia
  Our site: www.1wbta.com/vol-021-a-guide-to-treasure-in-virginia-west-virginia-2nd-edition
  Original book: www.1wbta.com/021-A-Guide-To-Treasure-In-Virginia-West-Virginia

Waybill To Adventure Core Books

- A Guidebook For Better Treasure Hunting
  Our site: www.1wbta.com/045-a-guidebook-for-better-treasure-hunting-2nd-edition
  Original book: www.1wbta.com/045-A-Guidebook-For-Better-Treasure-Hunting
- A New Guide To Treasure Hunting
  Our site: www.1wbta.com/051-a-new-guide-to-treasure-hunting-2nd-edition
  Original book: www.1wbta.com/051-A-New-Guide-To-Treasure-Hunting
- Atlas Of Colorado Ghost Towns
  Vol. I, Our site: www.1wbta.com/073-atlas-of-colorado-ghost-towns-vol-i-2nd-edition
  Original book: Vol. I – www.1wbta.com/073-Atlas-CO-Ghost-Towns-Vol-I
  Vol. II, Our site: www.1wbta.com/074-atlas-of-colorado-ghost-towns-vol-ii-2nd-edition
  Original book: Vol. II – www.1wbta.com/074-Atlas-CO-Ghost-Towns-Vol-II
- Authentic Civil War Battle Sites – Land And Naval Engagements
  Our site: www.1wbta.com/vol-023-authentic-civil-war-battle-sites-land-naval-engagements-2nd-edition
  Original book: www.1wbta.com/023-Authentic-Civil-War-Battle-Sites
- Backroads To Adventure
  Our site: www.1wbta.com/vol-024-backroads-to-adventure-2nd-edition
  Original book: www.1wbta.com/024-Backroads-To-Adventure
- Bonanza Seekers' Handbook
  Our site + 2004 PDF Ebook: www.1wbta.com/vol-026-bonanza-seekers-handbook-2nd-edition
  Original book @Amazon: www.1wbta.com/026-Bonanza-Seekers-Handbook-amaff
  Original book @eBay: www.1wbta.com/026-Bonanza-Seekers-Handbook-eBay
- Cache Hunting
  Vol. I, Our site: www.1wbta.com/vol-027-cache-hunting-vol-i-3rd-edition
  Original book: Vol. I – www.1wbta.com/027-Cache-Hunting-Vol-I

2nd Edition (2006 PDF): www.cache-hunting.hglenncarsonenterprises.com
Vol. II, Our site: www.1wbta.com/vol-028-cache-hunting-vol-ii-3rd-edition
Original book: Vol. II – www.1wbta.com/028-Cache-Hunting-Vol-II
2nd Edition (2007 PDF): www.cache-hunting-ii.hglenncarsonenterprises.com

- Coinshooting
  Vol. I – Coinshooting – How And Where To Do It
  Our site: www.1wbta.com/vol-032-coinshooting-how-and-where-to-do-it-vol-i-2nd-edition
  Original book: www.1wbta.com/032-Coinshooting-Vol-I-How-And-Where-To-Do-It
  Vol. II – Coinshooting – Digging Deeper Coins
  Our site: www.1wbta.com/vol-033-coinshooting-digging-deeper-coins-vol-ii-2nd-edition
  Original book: www.1wbta.com/033-Coinshooting-Vol-II-Digging-Deeper-Coins
  Vol. III – Coinshooting – Metal Detecting At Its Best
  Our site: www.1wbta.com/vol-034-coinshooting-metal-detecting-at-its-best-vol-iii-2nd-edition
  Original book: www.1wbta.com/034-Coinshooting-Vol-III-Metal-Detecting-At-Its-Best

- Colorado Placers And Placering
  Our site: www.1wbta.com/075-colorado-placers-and-placering-2nd-edition
  Original book: www.1wbta.com/075-Colorado-Placers-And-Placering

- Dig Here! Lost Mines & Buried Treasure Of The Southwest
  Our site: www.1wbta.com/vol-036-dig-here-lost-mines-and-buried-treasure-of-the-southwest-3rd-edition
  Original book: www.1wbta.com/036-Dig-Here-Lost-Mines-Buried-Treasure-Southwest
  2nd Edition (2007 PDF): www.dighere.thomaspenfield.treasure-legend.com

- Directory Of Buried Or Sunken Treasures And Lost Mines Of The United States
  Our site: www.1wbta.com/vol-037-directory-of-buried-or-sunken-treasures-and-lost-mines-of-the-united-states-2nd-edition
  Original book: www.1wbta.com/037-Directory-Buried-Sunken-Treasures-Lost-Mines-US

- Get Your Share Of Hidden Riches
  Our site: www.1wbta.com/039-get-your-share-of-hidden-riches-2nd-edition
  Original book: www.1wbta.com/039-Get-Your-Share-Of-Hidden-Riches

- Ghost Sites Of Southwest New Mexico
  Our site: www.1wbta.com/040-ghost-sites-of-southwest-new-mexico-2nd-edition
  Original book: www.1wbta.com/040-Ghost-Sites-Of-Southwest-New-Mexico

- Gold – The ABC's Of Panning
  Our site: www.1wbta.com/044-gold-abcs-of-panning-how-to-find-placer-gold-the-necessary-equipment-and-how-to-use-your-gold-pan-2nd-edition
  Original book: www.1wbta.com/044-Gold-The-ABCs-Of-Panning

- Handbook Of Treasure Signs And Symbols
  Our site: www.1wbta.com/046-handbook-of-treasure-signs-and-symbols-3rd-edition
  Original book & 2nd Edition (PDF): www.1wbta.com/046-Handbook-Of-Treasure-Signs-And-Symbols

- Hedge Yourself Against Disaster
  Our site: www.1wbta.com/047-hedge-yourself-against-disaster-2nd-edition
  Original book: www.1wbta.com/047-Hedge-Yourself-Against-Disaster

- Hunting The Ghost Towns
  Our site: www.1wbta.com/048-hunting-the-ghost-towns-2nd-edition
  Original book: www.1wbta.com/048-Hunting-The-Ghost-Towns

- Lost Ledges Of The West
  Our site: www.1wbta.com/049-lost-ledges-of-the-west-2nd-edition
  Original book: www.1wbta.com/049-Lost-Ledges-Of-The-West

- The Malpais Gold
  Our site: www.1wbta.com/050-the-malpais-gold-2nd-edition
  Original book: www.1wbta.com/050-The-Malpais-Gold
- Pilar La Dura
  Book I – Pilar La Dura – Freedom: A Greater Treasure Than Wealth
  Our site: www.1wbta.com/052-pilar-la-dura-freedom-a-greater-treasure-than-wealth-book-i-2nd-edition
  Original book: www.1wbta.com/052-Pilar-La-Dura-Book-I-Freedom-A-Greater-Treasure-Than-Wealth
  Book II – Pilar La Dura – A Fight For Freedom
  Our site: www.1wbta.com/053-pilar-la-dura-a-fight-for-freedom-book-ii-2nd-edition
  Original book: www.1wbta.com/053-Pilar-La-Dura-Book-II-A-Fight-For-Freedom
- Some Paths To Sudden Wealth
  Our site: www.1wbta.com/067-some-paths-to-sudden-wealth-2nd-edition
  Original book: www.1wbta.com/067-Some-Paths-To-Sudden-Wealth
- The Extraction of Free Gold
  Our site: www.1wbta.com/038-the-extraction-of-free-gold-virgin-placer-gold-2nd-edition
  Original book: www.1wbta.com/038-The-Extraction-Of-Free-Gold
- Treasure! Bonanzas Worth A Billion Bucks
  Our site: www.1wbta.com/068-treasure-bonanzas-worth-a-billion-bucks-2nd-edition
  Original book: www.1wbta.com/068-Treasure-Bonanzas-Worth-A-Billion-Bucks
- Treasure Hunting – A Modern Search For Adventure
  Our site: www.1wbta.com/069-treasure-hunting-a-modern-search-for-adventure-3rd-edition
  Original book: www.1wbta.com/069-Treasure-Hunting-A-Modern-Search-For-Adventure
  2nd Edition (PDF): thing-modern-search.hglenncarsonenterprises.com
- Treasure Hunting Annual
  Treasure Hunting Annual – Vol. 1
  Our site: www.1wbta.com/070-treasure-hunting-annual-vol-1-carson-enterprises-june-1979-2nd-edition
  Original book: www.1wbta.com/070-Treasure-Hunting-Annual-Vol-1-Carson-Enterprises-June-1979
  Treasure Hunting Annual – Vol. 2
  Our site: www.1wbta.com/071-treasure-hunting-annual-vol-2-carson-enterprises-june-1980-2nd-edition
  Original book: www.1wbta.com/071-Treasure-Hunting-Annual-Vol-2-Carson-Enterprises-June-1980

More Selections Of Books & Other Products

Our remaining products – maps, fun stuff, the Principal Gold-Producing Districts, and software – are not carried in other places like Lost Treasure Magazine Online or the Amazon Marketplace. You may find a very occasional item on eBay or even Amazon's Marketplace, but that is very rare. Please, do go and register at the site, as I will be notifying all registered folks via email when new products are ready! Go here to register:

www.1wbta.com/login?action=register

Waybill's Historical Maps Series

- Atlas Of Colorado Ghost Towns
  Vol. I, Our site: www.1wbta.com/073-atlas-of-colorado-ghost-towns-vol-i-2nd-edition
  Original book: Vol. I – www.1wbta.com/073-Atlas-CO-Ghost-Towns-Vol-I
  Vol. II, Our site: www.1wbta.com/074-atlas-of-colorado-ghost-towns-vol-ii-2nd-edition
  Original book: Vol. II – www.1wbta.com/074-Atlas-CO-Ghost-Towns-Vol-II

- California/Nevada Lost Mines Map, 2nd Edition
  Our site: www.1wbta.com/030-california-nevada-lost-mines-map-2nd-edition
- Colorado Gold Placer Map, 2nd Edition
  Our site: www.1wbta.com/035-colorado-gold-placer-map-2nd-edition
- Ghost Town Map Of Colorado – 1923 – 2nd Edition
  Our site: www.1wbta.com/041-ghost-town-map-of-colorado-1923-2nd-edition
- Ghost Town Map Of Oklahoma – 1923 – 2nd Edition
  Our site: www.1wbta.com/042-ghost-town-map-of-oklahoma-1923-2nd-edition
- Ghost Town Map Of Tennessee – 1923 – 2nd Edition
  Our site: www.1wbta.com/043-ghost-town-map-of-tennessee-1923-2nd-edition
- Historical Maps For Many USA States – A Work In Progress, Forever!
  Our site: www.1wbta.com/801-historical-maps-for-many-usa-states
- PLEASE NOTE: As the New Millennium Editions of our books go up on Amazon, you will see that truly, most volumes will have a large number of maps. All of our books are going to be "map books." This will make each volume invaluable to your research. These maps, per book, may include USGS Topographic maps, City-County-State maps, vintage maps for railroads or mines or other specific criteria… and occasionally, there may be a hand-crafted old treasure map!

Waybill's TH'ing & Real-Life Fun Stuff

- Bertha's Tasty Recipes And Cherished Memories – 2nd Edition
  Our site: www.1wbta.com/025-berthas-tasty-recipes-and-cherished-memories-2nd-edition
- Clancy's Treasure Book For Children – 2nd Edition
  Our site: www.1wbta.com/031-clancys-treasure-book-for-children-2nd-edition
- 100 Must-Know Tips And Secrets For Treasure Hunters – 3rd Edition
  Our site: www.1wbta.com/100-100-must-know-tips-secrets-for-treasure-hunters-2nd-edition
- Big Bucks in Treasure Hunting Vol. 101 – 3rd Edition
  Our site: www.1wbta.com/101-big-bucks-in-treasure-hunting-vol-101-3rd-edition
- The School Teacher and the Cowboy: The Story of Maxie & Frank Davies – 2nd Edition
  Our site: www.1wbta.com/102-the-school-teacher-the-cowboy-maxie-davies-2nd-edition
  Original (Lulu Press + iBookstore): www.1wbta.com/102-The-School-Teacher-Maxie-Davies-Lulu-Press

Principal Gold-Producing Districts – New Millennium Versions @Waybill

- Principal Gold-Producing Districts – Alaska – 2nd Edition
  Our site: www.1wbta.com/054-principal-gold-producing-districts-alaska-2nd-edition
- Principal Gold-Producing Districts – Alabama, Georgia, Virginia, North And South Carolina, Tennessee – 2nd Edition
  Our site: www.1wbta.com/055-principal-gold-producing-districts-al-ga-va-nc-sc-tn-2nd-edition
- Principal Gold-Producing Districts – Arizona – 2nd Edition
  Our site: www.1wbta.com/056-principal-gold-producing-districts-arizona-2nd-edition
- Principal Gold-Producing Districts – California – 2nd Edition
  Our site: www.1wbta.com/057-principal-gold-producing-districts-california-2nd-edition
- Principal Gold-Producing Districts – Colorado – 2nd Edition
  Our site: www.1wbta.com/058-principal-gold-producing-districts-colorado-2nd-edition

- Principal Gold-Producing Districts – Idaho – 2nd Edition
  Our site: www.1wbta.com/059-principal-gold-producing-districts-idaho-2nd-edition
- Principal Gold-Producing Districts – Michigan, South Dakota, Wyoming – 2nd Edition
  Our site: www.1wbta.com/060-principal-gold-producing-districts-mi-sd-wy-2nd-edition
- Principal Gold-Producing Districts – Montana – 2nd Edition
  Our site: www.1wbta.com/061-principal-gold-producing-districts-montana-2nd-edition
- Principal Gold-Producing Districts – Nevada – 2nd Edition
  Our site: www.1wbta.com/062-principal-gold-producing-districts-nevada-2nd-edition
- Principal Gold-Producing Districts – New Mexico – 2nd Edition
  Our site: www.1wbta.com/063-principal-gold-producing-districts-new-mexico-2nd-edition
- Principal Gold-Producing Districts – Oregon – 2nd Edition
  Our site: www.1wbta.com/064-principal-gold-producing-districts-oregon-2nd-edition
- Principal Gold-Producing Districts – Utah – 2nd Edition
  Our site: www.1wbta.com/065-principal-gold-producing-districts-utah-2nd-edition
- Principal Gold-Producing Districts – Washington – 2nd Edition
  Our site: www.1wbta.com/066-principal-gold-producing-districts-washington-2nd-edition

Software By Waybill To Adventure

- Version 1.1 – Metal Detector Software – The THer's Virtual Assistant
  Our site: www.1wbta.com/900-Metal-Detector-Software-THers-Virtual-Assistant

www.1wbta.com/catalog

Stop living in denial! Really... download our catalog today! NOTIFY ME IF YOU FIND ERRORS!

Illustrated: Yreka!

Yreka & Mt. Shasta, Siskiyou County, Cal.
Looking South East

Fred A. Walpole - ca. 1884
Yreka (Calif. USA) - Aerial view/Bird's-eye view
Courtesy LOC.GOV, Library Of Congress, USA
View full-size, full-color:
http://www.loc.gov/item/82692061

http://www.loc.gov/item/82692061
The JPEG (1872x1408 px) view is very impressive!

Illustrated: Eureka!

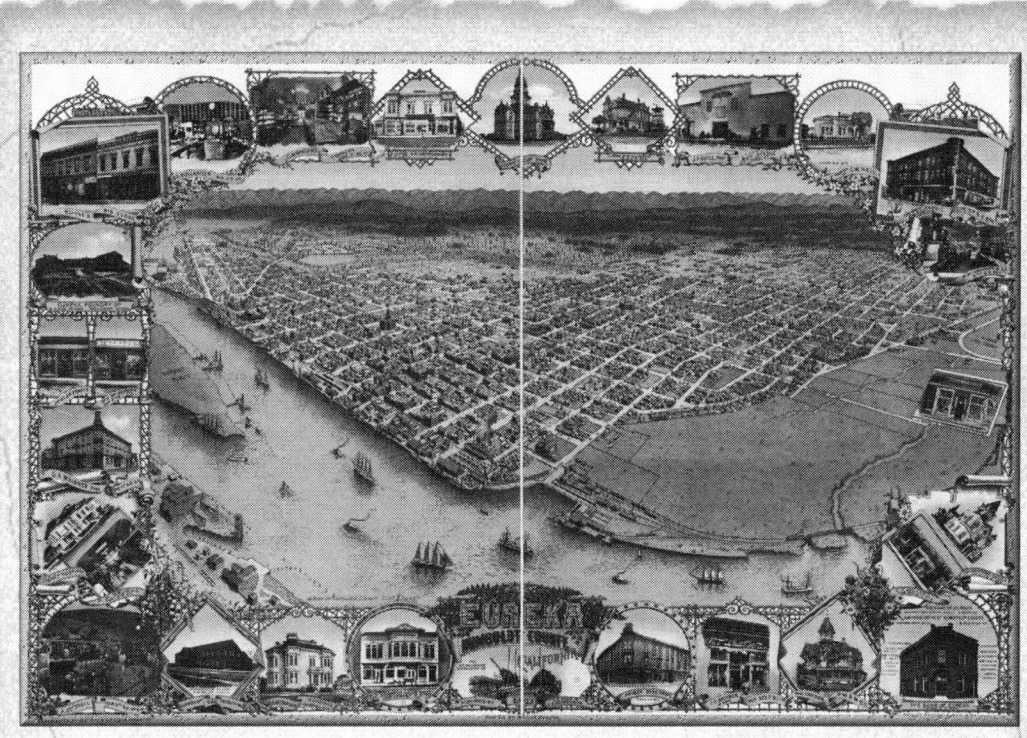

Eureka, Humboldt County, California
Noe (A.C.) & G.R. Georgeson - ca. 1902
Photos by Miller: Eureka
Eureka (Calif. USA) - Aerial view/Bird's-eye view
Courtesy LOC.GOV, Library Of Congress, USA
View full-size, full-color:
http://www.loc.gov/item/75693089

http://www.loc.gov/item/75693089
The JPEG (1542x1062 px) view is very impressive!

Resource: The 1982 Version Of This Book

Original Cover Illustration
by Eugene Shortridge

PRINTED BY CARSON ENTERPRISES
PO Box 716, Dona Ana, NM 88032

(c) 1982 by H. Glenn Carson, or
(c) 2001 by H. Glenn Carson
0-941620-23-9

All rights reserved. This book or any parts thereof, must not be reproduced in any form without permission.

TRUE TREASURE LIBRARY

This book has been in and out of print for several years. The current New Millennium edition at Amazon brings a new look and a lot of new information. However, if you should run into a copy of the original version, as shown above by the book cover and the copyright information, that book is in very limited supply and very few can be found today. A copy hand-signed by Glenn Carson may cost you more, but will eventually be worth more, if it is not already. I find Carson books often, with price tags into the $100s of dollars, which originally sold for under $10.00!

My advice, should you find a copy, would be to purchase it! These copies show up in places such as Amazon Marketplace, eBay, and the out-of-print and hard-to-find booksellers. These would be such online stores as Alibris, Abe Books, Barnes & Noble Out of Print Books, Biblio.com, etc. You can also set up a Google Alert to keep current with availability. Now, *this* is modern-day treasure hunting!

~Leanne Carson Boyd

Resource: Related Items Are Available

There are items for sale on the Web site that will help your research efforts. You will find good discounts for multiple purchases about this State. Go here and be sure to bookmark the page, as I will be adding many products: www.1wbta.com/category/related-items. And make sure to REGISTER on the Web site, so you can be alerted when I publish new books and other products!

Resource: LOC.GOV, The Library Of Congress – We The People Are Grateful

The Legacy
- The legacy was created by those who shaped the journey. Our families, generations back. They didn't realize what a gift they were leaving, but leave it they did.

The Birthright
- Items in the LOC.GOV collections are actually our birthright from our ancestral family(ies). Especially within the current laws of public domain, and pre-1923 works. The collections do not belong to "them," but to us. We, the people.

Keepers Of The Gate
- LOC.GOV must be thanked for housing such an amazing treasure. But they are not the owners, they are the gate keepers.

Usage Herein
- ☑ All LOC.GOV images in this book are pre-1923, as far as can be determined.
- ☑ All images in this book are used for **educational, scholarly purposes and private study.**
- ☑ A credit line should be included with any item used in publications. My credit line is: "Courtesy LOC.GOV, Library Of Congress, USA."
- ☑ "**About Copyright and the Collections** – As a publicly supported institution, the Library generally does not own rights in its collections. Therefore, it does not charge permission fees for use of such material and generally does not grant or deny permission to publish or otherwise distribute material in its collections... It is the researcher's obligation to determine and satisfy copyright or other use restrictions when publishing or otherwise distributing materials found in the Library's collections... Researchers must make their own assessments of rights in light of their intended use."
  Source: http://www.loc.gov/homepage/legal.html
- All other images: 1) Wondrous Wikipedia, 2) other public domain images, and, 3) images by the author(s) of this book.

"Washington. West façade Library of Congress" - ca. 1898
Digital ID: (digital file from original item) ppmsca 18034
http://hdl.loc.gov/loc.pnp/ppmsca.18034
The Library of Congress is the research library of the United States Congress, de facto national library of the United States of America, and the oldest federal cultural institution in the United States.
Courtesy LOC.GOV, Library Of Congress, USA

Parting Words & Sage Advice: Poker Alice

In her later years, Alice claimed to have won more than
$250,000 at the gaming tables and never once cheated.
In fact, one of her favorite sayings was:
"Praise the Lord and place your bets.
I'll take your money with no regrets."

About The Publisher/Authors

WAYBILLTOADVENTURE.COM IS 12 YEARS OLD!
2012! It is onwards & upwards on the electronic highway!

It's been over 40 years of publishing for Glenn and Carson Enterprises! The Grizzly Miner logo is well known in the treasure hunting genre. And the man himself bears quite the resemblance to his logo! Glenn loves his garden and he loves to write! The big news beginning in 2012 is that these works are going on to Amazon.com. Leanne, eldest daughter, is the digital diva to do it!

Mary Carson, my mother, stepped into Glory in December 2004. She is greatly missed. She left quite a writing legacy. You can view these books here:

- Handbook of Treasure Signs & Symbols
  1wbta.com/018hbtss
- A Guide To Treasure In Oklahoma
  Volume 1: 1wbta.com/gdtrok01
  Volume 2: 1wbta.com/gdtrok02
  Volume 3: 1wbta.com/gdtrok03

Treasure Hunting:
A Modern Search
For Adventure
1wbta.com/thamsfa

Cache Hunting
Volume 1

1wbta.com/cache1

Cache Hunting
Volume 2

1wbta.com/cache2

Pilar La Dura,
Volumes 1 & 2
1wbta.com/pilar1
1wbta.com/pilar2

★ LeanneCarsonBoyd on About.Me
about.me/LeanneCarsonBoyd

Made in the USA
San Bernardino, CA
14 March 2019